Anton Oleinik

BUILDING UKRAINE FROM WITHIN

A Sociological, Institutional, and Economic Analysis of a Nation-State in the Making

ibidem-Verlag
Stuttgart

Bibliografische Information der Deutschen Nationalbibliothek
Die Deutsche Nationalbibliothek verzeichnet diese Publikation in der Deutschen Nationalbibliografie; detaillierte bibliografische Daten sind im Internet über http://dnb.d-nb.de abrufbar.

Bibliographic information published by the Deutsche Nationalbibliothek
Die Deutsche Nationalbibliothek lists this publication in the Deutsche Nationalbibliografie; detailed bibliographic data are available in the Internet at http://dnb.d-nb.de.

∞

Gedruckt auf alterungsbeständigem, säurefreien Papier
Printed on acid-free paper

ISSN: 1614-3515

ISBN-13: 978-3-8382-1150-3

Printed in the EU

Soviet and Post-Soviet Politics and Society (SPPS) **Vol. 177**
ISSN 1614-3515

Soviet and Post-Soviet Politics and Society (SPPS)

ISSN 1614-3515

Founded in 2004 and refereed since 2007, SPPS makes available affordable English-, German-, and Russian-language studies on the history of the countries of the former Soviet bloc from the late Tsarist period to today. It publishes between 5 and 20 volumes per year and focuses on issues in transitions to and from democracy such as economic crisis, identity formation, civil society development, and constitutional reform in CEE and the NIS. SPPS also aims to highlight so far understudied themes in East European studies such as right-wing radicalism, religious life, higher education, or human rights protection. The authors and titles of all previously published volumes are listed at the end of this book. For a full description of the series and reviews of its books, see www.ibidem-verlag.de/red/spps.

Editorial correspondence & manuscripts should be sent to: Dr. Andreas Umland, Institute for Euro-Atlantic Cooperation, vul. Volodymyrska 42, off. 21, UA-01030 Kyiv, Ukraine

Business correspondence & review copy requests should be sent to: ***ibidem*** Press, Leuschnerstr. 40, 30457 Hannover, Germany; tel.: +49 511 2622200; fax: +49 511 2622201; spps@ibidem.eu.

Authors, reviewers, referees, and editors for (as well as all other persons sympathetic to) SPPS are invited to join its networks at www.facebook.com/group.php?gid=52638198614 www.linkedin.com/groups?about=&gid=103012 www.xing.com/net/spps-ibidem-verlag/

Recent Volumes

168 *Anna Sanina*
Patriotic Education in Contemporary Russia
Sociological Studies in the Making of the Post-Soviet Citizen
With a foreword by Anna Oldfield
ISBN 978-3-8382-0993-7

169 *Rudolf Wolters*
Spezialist in Sibirien
Faksimile der 1933 erschienenen ersten Ausgabe
Mit einem Vorwort von Dmitrij Chmelnizki
ISBN 978-3-8382-0515-1

170 *Michal Vít, Magdalena M. Baran (eds.)*
Transregional versus National Perspectives on Contemporary Central European History
Studies on the Building of Nation-States and Their Cooperation in the 20th and 21st Century
With a foreword by Petr Vágner
ISBN 978-3-8382-1015-5

171 *Philip Gamaghelyan*
Conflict Resolution Beyond the International Relations Paradigm
Evolving Designs as a Transformative Practice in Nagorno-Karabakh and Syria
With a foreword by Susan Allen
ISBN 978-3-8382-1057-5

172 *Maria Shagina*
Joining a Prestigious Club
Cooperation with Europarties and Its Impact on Party Development in Georgia, Moldova, and Ukraine 2004–2015
With a foreword by Kataryna Wolczuk
ISBN 978-3-8382-1084-1

173 *Alexandra Cotofana, James M. Nyce (eds.)*
Religion and Magic in Socialist and Post-Socialist Contexts II
Baltic, Eastern European, and Post-USSR Case Studies
With a foreword by Anita Stasulane
ISBN 978-3-8382-0990-6

174 *Barbara Kunz*
Kind Words, Cruise Missiles, and Everything in Between
The Use of Power Resources in U.S. Policies towards Poland, Ukraine, and Belarus 1989–2008
With a foreword by William Hill
ISBN 978-3-8382-1065-0

175 *Eduard Klein*
Bildungskorruption in Russland und der Ukraine
Eine komparative Analyse der Performanz staatlicher Antikorruptionsmaßnahmen im Hochschulsektor am Beispiel universitärer Aufnahmeprüfungen
Mit einem Vorwort von Heiko Pleines
ISBN 978-3-8382-0995-1

Table of Contents

List of Figures

List of Tables

List of Images

Acknowledgments

I would like to express my gratitude and appreciation to all those whose assistance and contributions made the preparation and publication of this book possible: the *Soviet and Post-Soviet Politics and Society* series editor, Dr. Andreas Umland (Institute for Euro-Atlantic Cooperation) and the manuscript reviewers, Prof. Peter Solomon (University of Toronto), and Prof. Bohdan Krawchenko, Director General, University of Central Asia at Bishkek and founding Director, Institute of Public Administration, Council of Ministers, Ukraine for their constructive comments and interest in the project; Ms. Olga Strelkova (OMI Russia) for her participation in the data collection for Chapter 3 (she is also a co-author of this chapter); Ms. Oguljemal Yaryyeva (St. Petersburg State University), Ms. Victoria Semenova (University of Mannheim), Mr. Arseny Verkeev (European University at St. Petersburg) and Mr. Gervin Apatinga (Memorial University of Newfoundland and Labrador, MUN) for their involvement in the coding of the data for Chapter 4 and especially Dr. Melanie J. Greene (MUN) for her editing and polishing of the final version of the manuscript. Thanks also go to the Social Sciences and Humanities Council of Canada (SSHRC) for creating powerful incentives to complete this research and writing project in spite of the lack of financial support.

The cover picture, 'Trident' (*Tryzub*), is reproduced by kind permission of Andriy Yermolenko, the Ukrainian artist whose works decorated the tent camp on Maidan from November 2013–February 2014.

Previously published material is reproduced by permission of Taylor & Francis (articles 'The value of freedom: A case study of Ukraine', *Southeast European and Black Sea Studies, 15*(3), pp. 239-259, 'The relocation of a repertoire of collective action: Maidan 2013', *European Journal of Cultural and Political Sociology, 2*(2), pp. 146–171, co-authored with Olga Strelkova and 'Transition impossible? Ukraine between violence and power', *Journal of Political Power, 10*(3), pp. 371–389), Springer (parts of the article 'On content analysis of images of mass protests: A case of data triangulation', *Quality and Quantity*, *49*(5), pp. 2203–2220), Brill (article 'Honor and Human Rights: A Comparative Study of Russia and Ukraine', *Comparative Sociology*, *15*(6), pp. 669–698), the Centre for Baltic and East European Studies at Södertörn University, Stockholm (article 'Price of opulence: On a constellation of interests in the European market for natural gas', *Baltic Worlds*, *8*(3–4), pp. 51–61) and Taras Shevchenko National University of Kyiv (article 'Between the West and the East: Ukrainian economic thought at the crossroads', *Bulletin of Taras Shevchenko National University of Kyiv. Economics*, *9*(174), pp. 56–61).

Introduction
'Looking East, looking West and looking inside'

From an outside to inside focus

This book is written by the author who, prior to 2014, had no strong publication record in Ukrainian studies. He was born in Ukraine and still has family connections in this country. However, he has not considered himself as a specialist in the area—that is, Ukrainian studies. The author started to collect primary data and to study the situation in Ukraine in a systematic matter during the mass protests of November 2013—February 2014 (he visited Kyiv with a research associate collecting visual records and conducting qualitative interviews during the Maidan). He had a feeling that the understanding of these events and subsequent developments, including an undeclared war waged against Ukraine by its neighbour, Russia, represented a theoretical and practical challenge. The challenge has a theoretical dimension since what happened in Ukraine necessitates a rethinking of some foundational concepts for the social sciences in general, namely, freedom, power, violence, human dignity, nation-state, volunteerism—to cite just a few. The challenge has a practical dimension, since the search for solutions to the current crisis in Ukraine remains wide open. Thus, the present book represents an invitation for the reader to follow the author's trajectory and to find a reason for thinking of and studying Ukraine in a systematic manner. The author's experience suggests that a background in Ukrainian studies is not a prerequisite.

Speaking more specifically, the intended audience for this book is mainly social scientists in the West. For most of them, Ukraine represents something alien, little known and problematic. Some even suffer from 'Ukraine fatigue'. Ukrainians do not seem to be particularly receptive to numerous attempts of the West to teach them 'good practices'.

The author does not make the usual assumption that Western scholars and practitioners have any ready-to-implement advices and solutions to problems observed in Ukraine. Instead, an increased awareness of the situation in this country may give one an opportunity for rethinking his or her theoretical and methodological toolbox.

Arguments developed in this book may be of relevance to the Ukrainian audience too. Some of them were initially conveyed in a series of Op-Ed commentaries published in the Ukrainian mass-media from 2014 to 2017: *Ukrains'ka Pravda, Novoe Vremia, Liga.net, Texty.org.ua* (all based in Kyiv) and *Zbruč* (zbruc.eu, based in Lviv). The author's line of arguing diverges from the current mainstream thinking in this country. The prevailing discourse departs from the assumption that solutions to the current Ukrainian crisis are well known and that they could be implemented by re-orienting the country from the East (Russia) to the West (the European Union and NATO).

Such expectations may not be met, however. Since the West may not offer ready-to-implement solutions, Ukrainians have to find them—ideally in collaboration with Western scholars and practitioners. In other words, in both the West and Ukraine, the current crisis calls for re-evaluating some theoretical, methodological and practical assumptions that are normally taken for granted.

This book aims to contribute to the body of scholarly knowledge on Ukraine, as opposed to journalistic accounts, travel diaries or policy briefs. The former does not exclude the latter (e.g., when a study informs a policy), but a scholarly contribution must be assessed against the standards of validity and reliability, in addition to the criteria of newsworthiness, personal and public interest. Despite its sheer size—Ukraine is the largest European country by area and the 8th largest by population, the number of scholarly studies of Ukraine remains rather modest. During the past five years (2012–2016), 4,414 publications discussing this country were indexed in the Web of Science Core Collection, the most comprehensive database of scholarly works. This is significantly less than the corresponding figures for the other European countries in general and Eastern European countries in particular. For instance,

46,973 publications deal with Germany, 37,682—with France, 35,303—with Turkey, 19,926—with Russia, 18,584—with Poland, 11,229—with Romania, 6,545—with Hungary, 5,465—with Serbia, 5,096—with Georgia, 5,065—with Slovakia and 5,039—with Croatia. Only Belarus (N=1,068) and Moldova (N=659) attracted less attention of the Western scholarly community.[1]

Political scientists, economists and specialists in the area studies currently dominate the scholarly writings on Ukraine available in the West. During the same period of time, economists produced 12.4% of all publications discussing Ukraine that are indexed in the Web of Science Core Collection (N=4,414), mostly due to the temporary indexing of two Ukrainian economic journals, Economic Annals-XXI (*Ekonomichnyi Chasopys-XXI*) and Actual Problems of Economics (*Aktual'ni problemy ekonomiki*; see Chapter 8 for a more detailed analysis of articles from the latter periodical); political scientists—9.6%, specialists in international relations—5.4%, specialists in the area studies and specialists in environmental sciences—4.8% each. This distribution suggests that a geopolitical perspective prevails in the Western scholarly discourse on Ukraine: political scientists and specialists in international relations authored 15% of the indexed works.[2] It follows that an outside view prevails over an inside take on Ukraine.

The author of this book attempts to covey a different message. When thinking of Ukraine, it should not be all about geopolitics. The book offers a perspective of a sociologist, institutionalist and economist on the subject-matter. The approaches of these disciplines provide useful insights into the internal organisation and processes of the Ukrainian polity, society and economy. In order to understand the true scope of the current problems that Ukraine faces, one needs to look inside this country, its formal and informal institutions. When geopolitical issues are considered in this book

1 The search with the following parameters—TOPIC: (Ukraine) AND Timespan: 2012-2016—was carried out on February 20, 2017.

2 The distribution of approximately 150 sources cited in this book by discipline is the following: 22% —economic sciences, 22% —history, 18% —political sciences, 15% —area studies, 15% —management, 8% —sociology.

(in Chapter 5 and the Conclusion), they are viewed through the lens of their impact on internal processes.

A sociological and institutional perspective represents a valid option for those who wish to adopt an inside view. The area studies also offer a relevant perspective. However, the area studies place emphasis on uniqueness and specificity. They highlight what is unique in a particular culture, which potentially limits the appeal of this approach to scholars who want to study more universal situations. This book discusses a single country by placing it into the context of more universal concepts and theories. In other words, the reader is invited to navigate between emic and etic categories. Emic research involves understanding a culture from inside. On the other hand, etic research calls for using universal categories (Hofstede & Bond, 1984, p. 421). By learning the limitations of universal concepts and theories in a highly specific situation that emerged in Ukraine after 2013, one becomes motivated to critically reassess them. At the end of the day, the author's ambition is to show how the Ukrainian case may be interesting and instructive not only for specialists in the area studies but also for a larger group of social scientists and observers.

I. A known unknown

As suggested before, Ukraine remains relatively unknown and in any case understudied in the West. In the past, various territories of today's Ukraine were a part of the neighbouring empires: Russian, Polish-Lithuanian, Austro-Hungarian and Ottoman. This situation not only caused significant delays in the process of nation-state building, but also led to the fragmentation of our knowledge about this country and its institutions. All Ukrainians were united in a single political entity for the first time in centuries after WWII only, as a result of the Soviet conquest of Western Ukraine (Subtelny, 2009, p. 480). Studies of this unified Ukraine by Western scholars were primarily guided by geopolitical considerations being a sub-discipline of well-funded Soviet studies. Even after the proclamation of an independent status of Ukraine in 1991—by an

Act of the Supreme Soviet in August that was subsequently validated by a national referendum in December (Harasymiw, 2002, pp. 7–8) — in scientific and everyday discourses Ukraine continued to be often associated, if not confused, with Russia. An excerpt from an interview with a young woman from Ukraine who lived and studied in France for several years illustrates a rather common misperception of Ukrainians as 'sort of' Russians in everyday interactions:

> 'I have always lived with the understanding that I have my own country and reacted rather sharply to attempts to perceive me as someone from Russia'.[3]

As to the scientific discourse, post-Soviet and Russian studies emerged as the key successor to Soviet studies, both organisationally and financially. This dominance of post-Soviet and Russian studies in the area studies offers a first explanation for using Russia as a point of comparison throughout this book and especially in Chapters 4, 5, 6, 7 and 10. Until 2013, the existence of Ukrainian studies in the shadow of post-Soviet and Russian studies was mainly a problem of scholars working in this field. The mass protests of November 2013 — February 2014 and Russia's subsequent military aggression made this situation less tolerable, given a growing interest of policy-makers, scholars and the international community at large in gaining a better understanding of Ukraine and Ukrainian people. The number of articles with the word 'Ukraine' in their headlines published in the leading English-language newspapers skyrocketed in 2014–2015 (Figure 0.1). A similar pattern is observed with regards to Russian-language scholarly publications on this topic: their number had peaked in 2014. The number of English-language scholarly publications devoted to Ukraine also started to rapidly grow in 2014 and kept progressively increasing since then. In other words, there is a demand for studies of Ukraine and this demand remains largely unmet at the time of this writing.

---

3 The interview was conducted in Kyiv in June 2016, more details about the organisation and sampling are provided in Section II of Chapter 10.

Figure 0.1 'Frequencies of references to Ukraine in the titles of scholarly publications and newspaper articles indexed in the Web of Science, LexisNexis and eLibrary correspondingly, 1991–2016'

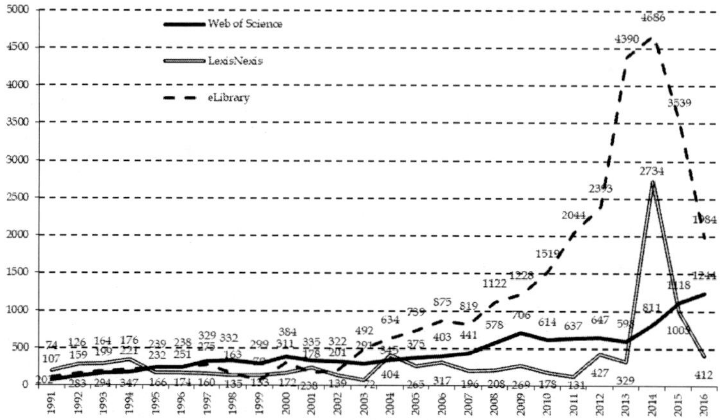

Source: the Web of Science Core Collection, LexisNexis Academic and eLibrary; the search was conducted on February 17, 2017 using TOPIC:(Ukraine), HEADLINE:(Ukraine) and NAME OR KEYWORD:(Ukraina) correspondingly. The search in LexisNexis was restricted to ten major English-language newspapers published in the US, the UK and Canada: *The New York Times, The Washington Post, The Los Angeles Times, USA Today, The Guardian, The Financial Times, The Times* (London), *The Mirror, The Independent,* and *The Globe and Mail.* The search in eLibrary excluded conference proceedings and research reports. eLibrary is the largest online databank of Russian language scholarly publications (http://elibrary.ru/).

Without more systematic studies of Ukraine, our knowledge of this country continues to be fragmented, partial and ad hoc, i.e. driven by particular events, such as the 2013–2014 mass protests. The war between Russia and Ukraine has supposedly contributed to a greater dissociation between the two countries in the minds of Western Europeans and North Americans. If they finally perceive Ukraine as a separate entity, with what might they potentially associate this country and its culture? A comprehensive tourist guide published before the 2012 European men's soccer championship co-hosted by Poland and Ukraine (Ukraine, 2012) provides some clues as to what associations Ukrainians want foreigners to have with their country. A content analysis of visual and textual information on 222 pages of this guide shows that religious symbols (the churches, icons and so on) tend to prevail: there are 131 mentions of them in total. Religious symbols are followed by images of nature (79), military symbols (57), mentions of the arts (47) and references to Cossackdom (32).

The image of Ukraine as a deeply religious country is problematic in several ways. First, even if Ukraine's population places greater trust in the church than the population of some neighbouring countries, Ukrainians' religious devotion is by no way exceptional. The 2011 World Values Survey suggests that the level of confidence in the church in Ukraine can be assessed at 1.96 on a 4-point scale (with 1 meaning 'a great deal of confidence' and 4—'no confidence at all'; N=1,500), which is higher than in Poland (2.31), Russia (2.22), Belarus (2.04), but lower than in Romania (1.90) and 22 other countries out of 60 included in the sample (World Values Survey Association, 2015). Membership in Church and religious organisations is not exceptional either: in 2011, 7.6% of Ukrainians declared themselves inactive members and 4.3%—active members. In Poland, Russia, Belarus and Romania, the corresponding figures are 12%/15.2%, 4.1%/2%, 5.6%/5.1% and 8.6%/10.7%. Second, the Church is a traditional institution, which prompts the question of whether Ukrainian culture has more contemporary correlates.

Cossackdom as a symbol of Ukraine has a more specific and recognisable character. Furthermore, the image of Cossacks as warriors of the steppes would ring a bell for many in North America and Northern Europe since Cossacks have some similar characteristics with American cowboys and the Vikings. 'Today the image of the Cossack is to Ukrainians what the cowboy is to Americans or the Viking to the Scandinavians' (Subtelny, 2009, p. 122; see also Reid, 2015, p. 30). For this reason, references to Cossackdom will be found in several chapters of the book, namely, Chapters 1 and 3. Yet, the question as to whether Ukraine has more recently produced something similarly distinctive remains without a satisfactory answer.

It would be an error to interpret this line of arguing as the author's plea for giving a boost to Ukrainian studies as a way for bridging the gaps in the knowledge of Ukraine accumulated in the West. Ukrainian studies need organisational and financial support indeed.[4] At the same time, their target audience will unlikely be very large since, in order to appreciate their product, the willingness to immerse oneself into Ukrainian culture and to make necessary investments of time and resources is required. In order to identify truly distinctive features of Ukraine and its culture understood here as a web of formal and informal institutions, other measures may be needed too. In addition to developing Ukrainian studies, there is the option of going beyond the relatively narrow boundaries of Ukrainian and post-Soviet studies and of opening the country to more universal investigations. This book shows an example of how this could be achieved with the help of analytical concepts and methods borrowed from sociology, political and cultural, institutional theory and economic sciences (disciplines in which the author is at home).

II. Which case?

A case study of a single country, even with elements of a two-case comparison, likely still does not sound quite appealing to many scholars. Much depends, however, on how carefully the case study is designed and on the justification of its parameters. Case studies deal with a small number of cases and a large number of variables that are brought into explaining the case or cases (Reisinger, 1998, p. 164). The cases at hand are Ukraine, which is the principal object of inquiry, and Russia, a key reference point. The list of variables includes previously mentioned foundational concepts—freedom, power, violence, human dignity, nation-state, volunteerism—and

4 The collection of data for and the writing of this book, for instance, were not sponsored by any specific research grant. Despite obvious limitations that this lack of support caused, there was a resulting advantage too. Namely, no conflict of interest due to the support of an institutional sponsor exists.

several others, such as the national market, economic thought, foreign assistance, shared memory, including myths of origins, myths of war and sacrifice. None of these variables is country-specific per se, which potentially extends the scope of the discussion beyond the area studies. Yet in Ukraine these variables have particular attributes, and interact with the others in a unique manner.

The case study as a research design is often misunderstood and, hence, misused, with negative consequences for its perceived validity. Bent Flyvbjerg (2006, p. 230) differentiates between several criteria for selecting cases for a study: paradigmatic, extreme/deviant, critical and maximum variation cases. Depending on the research question, Ukraine has features of either a paradigmatic case, an extreme/deviant case, or a critical case.[5] The choice of Ukraine for an in-depth case study in this book has precisely such a triple rationale.

II.1 A paradigmatic case

A paradigmatic case helps develop a metaphor or establish a school for the domain that the case concerns. Ukraine may be considered as a paradigmatic case for studying catch-up development. This country is a latecomer in nation-state building. Ukraine's independence in 1991 was preceded neither by the development of a nation nor a state (Chapters 1 and 2). Before 1991, Ukraine existed as an independent state during short periods of time only, for example, between 1917–1920. This short-lived state known under the names of the Central Council (*Tsentral'na Rada*), the Hetmanate (*Hetmanat*) and the Directory (*Dyrektoriia*), did not control the entire territory of today's Ukraine, however (Subtelny, 2009, pp. 350–385). The process of nation-state building started after 1991 only (Harasymiw, 2002), which offers a unique opportunity for studying it in real-time. In most European countries, similar processes took place in

5 If the research design involves a comparison of three or more cases, similar to Ukraine's selection as an extreme case, this country may potentially be considered as one of the maximum variation cases (e.g., when comparing countries with a high, middle and low level of institutional trust, see below).

the previous centuries and, hence, they can only be studied retrospectively using historical approaches and data.

Alexander Gerschenkron (1992) argues that catch-up development is either propelled by the State or externally driven. The other actors—the investment banks, private businesses or civic groups—take the lead in the countries that embarked relatively early on the path of development. For instance, in Russia, the other relative latecomer, 'the State, moved by its military interest, assumed the role of the primary agent propelling the economic progress in the country' in the 18th and 19th centuries (Ibid., p. 120). In contrast to Russia, the State in Ukraine has not been able to assume a similar role until recently. The reason is simple: before 1991, Ukraine had neither a State nor a nation. As for the latter, the population of the Soviet Ukraine was considered to be a part of a larger entity, the 'Soviet people', and the large Russian in-migration took place in the 1960s-1970s (Krawchenko, 1983). Since 1991, the progress toward building a nation-state has been slow. The State formally emerged, but remained weak and ineffective. The existence of multiple identities—Ukrainian and Russian, Ukrainian and Soviet and so forth—suggests that the Ukrainian nation is still in the making (Kuzio, 2015, pp. 3, 13–14). In these circumstances, Ukraine's development has been mostly externally driven and shaped by external forces.

This situation is rather typical in countries going through the process of catch-up development. Their nation-states are often built from the outside in, using blueprints designed by external actors. Nation-state building in these circumstances becomes 'an externally driven, or facilitated, attempt to form or consolidate a stable, and sometimes democratic, government over an internationally recognised national territory against the backdrop of the establishment and consolidation of the UN and the universalisation of a system of sovereign nation-states' (Berger, 2006, p. 6). As a result, Ukraine's emerging nation-state was more dependent on and, consequently, responsive to external actors than to its own people. 'External' nation-state-making process makes the national government's internal legitimacy less important than the alignment and alliances with powerful outside states (Tilly, 1985, p. 186). Ukraine's dependence on external actors also explains its endless oscillation between the East (Russia) and the West (the European Union and NATO) as key vectors of foreign policy. Ukraine's dilemma has been framed in terms of the choice of a closer association, even affiliation, with either Russia or the West. The assumption that the real choice is not between internally and externally driven development, but instead between two vectors of the latter is widely accepted both in Ukraine (Chapter 2) and by international observers. 'Ukraine was repeatedly described as being at the crossroads where it could not make a choice as to whether it would receive a bright future by integrating with Europe or give in to nostalgia by integrating with Russia and Eurasia' (Kuzio, 2015, p. 2).

The situation began to change during the months of November 2013—February 2014 and especially with the start of the undeclared war with Russia in March 2014. In contrast to the 2004 'Orange' revolution, the 2013–2014 mass protests did not occur 'by design' (Chapter 3). External interferences played a marginal role, if they played a role at all. Since they expected accusations of being mobilised from outside the country, 'the first thing that demonstrators did this time was carry signs saying "we are not paid"... To the regime's way of thinking... the Maidan must have been paid for by their opponents—either the West... or the domestic oligarchs outside the "Family"' (Wilson, 2014, pp. 66–67; see also Kuzio, 2015, p. 264). The mass resistance to the military aggression, that took the form of a surge in volunteerism (Chapter 10), has further strengthened the internal actors who are susceptible to potentially assume the lead in the process of catch-up development. In other words, the situation that emerged in Ukraine after 2013 gives a rare chance to study the reorientation from external to internal sources of development. Ukraine has the potential to become a paradigmatic case for a theory of transition from externally to internally driven development.

II.2 An extreme/deviant case

With one of the lowest levels of institutional trust in the world, Ukraine makes a good candidate for an extreme/deviant case. An extreme/deviant case is unusual. In the parlance of quantitatively-minded researchers, an extreme/deviant case can be compared with an outlier whose existence causes troubles but at times suggests useful insights. In 2011, the level of trust in the national government in Ukraine was 3.07 on the 4-point scale going from 1, 'a great deal of confidence', to 4, 'no confidence at all' (World Values Survey Association, 2015; N=2,015). In 2016, the level of trust in the government further decreased to 3.27 (the survey conducted by the Kyiv International Institute of Sociology on a random sample of 2,040 respondents, see Section III of Chapter 6 for more detail). Few countries in the world have a comparable or lower level of institutional trust: in 2011, their list included Slovenia with the score of 3.31, Tunisia—3.22, Romania—3.17, Peru—3.11 and Poland—3.08. In practical terms, the score of 3.27 means that only 1.1% of Ukrainians (excluding those who have no opinion on this issue) have 'a great deal of confidence' in the government, 15.5% have 'quite a lot of confidence', 38.8% have 'not very much confidence' and 44.7% have 'no confidence at all'. The low level of trust in the government represents an obstacle to nation-state building and makes the society particularly vulnerable to external influence or interference. Chapter 1 explores historical roots of anti-statism in Ukraine, whereas Chapter 6 discusses some of its consequences.

II.3 A critical case

Closely related to this line of reasoning is the assumption that the case of Ukraine allows for the study of limits of path dependence. In this quality, Ukraine has features of a critical case. The study of a critical case permits logical deductions of the type 'if this is (not) valid for this case, then it applies to all (no) cases' (Flyvbjerg, 2006, p. 230). With Ukraine's development being externally driven for most of its history, the influence of Russia has been particularly strong since 1654 when the Treaty of Pereyaslav between Ukrainian Cossacks and the Russian tsar was concluded. Russia's influence has created the effect of path dependence in the evolution of institutions in Ukraine, both formal and informal. They have been shaped according to the Russian institutional model or adapted to its particularities. The Russian institutional model—the Russian path—has progressively limited the range of options that individual and collective actors in Ukraine have when solving their everyday and more strategic problems. 'Path dependence is a way to narrow conceptually the choice set and link decision making through time' (North, 1990, p. 98).

The prevalence of the Russian path in Ukraine offers a second reason for using the case of Russia as a point of comparison throughout this book. The case of Ukraine is critical since if the path can be changed in this country, then it can be changed in other countries where the Russian path also prevails. Speaking more broadly, the case of Ukraine aids inquiry into the limits of path dependence in general.

The Russian path is also known under the name of the Russian world. It comes as no surprise that mentions of the latter term in the Russian public and scholarly discourse became particularly common after 2013 (Figure 0.2). The 2013–2014 events in Ukraine were rightly perceived by many in Russia as a challenge to the Russian world. It is worth noting that the sensitivity of the Western public in general, and the scholarly community in the West; in particular, to the underlying concept, is a recent phenomenon. For instance, before 2014 mostly historians and specialists in cultural studies showed interest in taking the Russian world seriously.

Figure 0.2 'Frequencies of references to the "Russian world" in scholarly publications and newspaper articles indexed in the Web of Science, eLibrary and LexisNexis, 2000–2016'

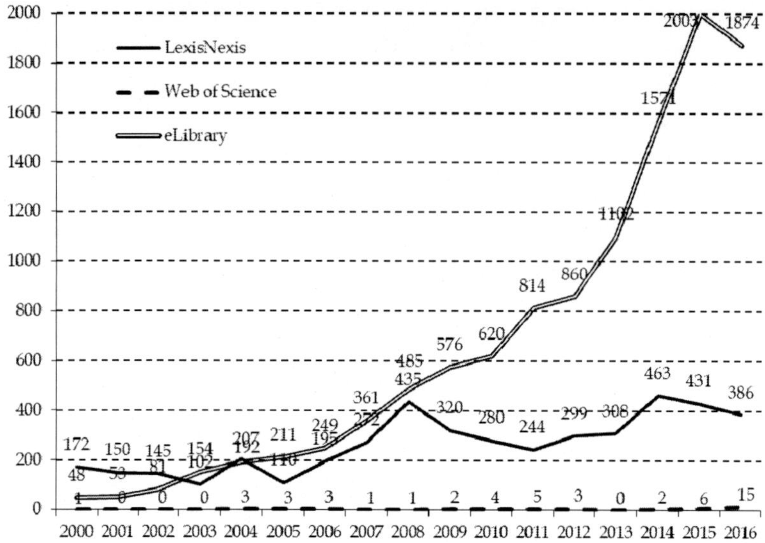

Source: the Web of Science Core Collection, eLibrary and LexisNexis Academic; the search was conducted on February 22, 2017 using TOPIC:('Russian world') in the Web of Science, 'Russkii mir' in eLibrary and 'Russian world' in LexisNexis. The scope of the search was restricted to newspapers in the latter case.

The Russian world as a particular institutional path was initially defined by political technologists (Shchedrovitskii, 2000) and subsequently appropriated by the Russian power elite (Patriarch Kirill, 2011) as a useful justification for Russia's foreign policies in the 2010s. According to the official discourse, the membership in the Russian world is a function of specific values, memories of shared historical past, religious faith, language, and ethnicity. The values system of the Russian world involves the rejection of rationalism and the established rules, especially in the international affairs (Malayarenko, 2016). The assumption of social constructivism is pushed here to its extreme: everything allegedly can be shaped at will and manipulated, which paves the way for the virtualisation of the political, economic and social reality (Wilson, 2005). Chapter 7 discusses some other values that prevail in the Russian world. In the Russian world myths about the historical past highlight the unity of its members and overshadow anything that evokes their histories as separate entities. WWII occupies a central place in the shared memories of the Russian world (Patriarch Kirill, 2011, p. 62). Chapter 1 has the opposite ambition in attempting to identify elements of Ukrainians' shared memories.

The Orthodox Church constitutes the next building block of the Russian world. 'At the foundation of the Russian world lies the Orthodox faith, which we acquired in our common Kievan baptismal font' (Patriarch Kirill, 2011, p. 59; see also Suslov, 2012, p. 584). This quote also explains the importance of Ukraine for the proponents of the Russian world. The Russian world supposedly extends to all places where Russian language is spoken (Patriarch Kirill, 2011, pp. 61–62; Shchedrovitskii, 2000; Suliak, 2012; Suslov, 2012, p. 585). Ethnicity—loosely defined as pan-Slavism—helps justify even a more expansionist version of the Russian world (Senderov, 2015). All Slavs are expected to become its subjects.

To this list, two other attributes of the Russian world could be added: the participation in a common market and the acceptance of a particular model of power relationships: Russian power. The Eurasian Customs Union under aegis of Russia provides an economic foundation for the Russian World. Chapter 9 discusses the issues of building the national market as an exit strategy for Ukraine given this country's heavy economic dependence on the Russian market. Last but not least, the Russian world also relies on Russian power. Russian power lies close to violence (see Chapter 6 for more detail). The discussion of Russian power and its role in ensuring the continuity of the Russian path represents one of the original contributions of this monograph to our knowledge of the Russian world.

III. Is it all geopolitics?

The strategic location of Ukraine at the crossroads between the North (the Nordic countries) and the South (the Ottoman empire), the East (Russia) and the West (Europe) explains why references to geopolitical considerations have prevailed in discussions of the situation in this country since the times of Kievan Rus', i.e. since the 9th-10th century. The first ruling elite of the territories that form what is today Central Ukraine was comprised of the Vikings. Their interest in securing the control of the trade route 'from the Varangians to the Greeks' along the river Dnieper offers a possible explanation (Hedlund, 2005, pp. 28–31). This route carried most of the trade between Northern Europe and Constantinople in the early Middle Ages.

An outside view of Ukraine necessarily had, and continues to have, a geopolitical dimension, in the East as well as in the West, and in the North as well as in the South. An outsider perceives the country as an asset that could potentially strengthen or weaken one's position in the global game. Any change in this country is then seen as a 'move in a zero-sum game between the West and a neoimperial Russia: The more Ukraine integrates with the EU, the less will Kyiv belong to the Russian orbit' and vice versa (Shekhovtsov & Umland, 2014, p. 60). The contents of the 2012 tourist guide mentioned before indirectly confirm the existence of a link between an outside view and geopolitics. This guide contains mentions of the East (Russia), the West (Europe) and the South (the Ottoman Empire, its predecessors and successors) almost in equal proportions: 68, 58 and 32. These figures are comparable with the number of references to internally generated symbols with which Ukrainians wanted foreigners to have with their country: 158 mentions of geopolitical concepts in total against 349 mentions of internal symbols in total.

In addition to these general explanations for the existence of a geopolitical dimension in most discussions of Ukraine, the popularity of a geopolitical take on Ukraine has more specific drivers in the East and in the West. For Russians, especially for Russia's power elite, any attempt by Ukraine to leave the Russian world signals not only a weakened appeal of the underlying institutional model but also a danger of losing one of its central elements. The Russian world without a significant number of Orthodox Christians, Russian speakers and Slavs in its orbit is necessarily defective and doomed to failure. 'Ukraine's desire to preserve its independence and to integrate with the European community has caused much chagrin among Russian pan-Slavists' (Suslov, 2012, p. 582). This feeling has only intensified after the events of 2013–2014 in Ukraine.

In the West, the perception of Ukraine through the lens of geopolitics may become more popular in response to Russia's actions. The return of the advocates and ambassadors of the Russian world to the key premises of geopolitics—an exclusive focus on such factors as geographical location, territorial expansion, interstate competition over finite spaces, balance of military powers between the States and the rejection of international law (Teschke, 2011)—requires an adequate response, perhaps in kind. Chapter 5 also discusses a more subtle and less visible strategy with the help of which Russia's power elite attempt to impose its rules of the game on the international community: by using the energy market as a lever. Finally, some Western scholars and policy-makers find the return to the geopolitical game as justifiable if not desirable. 'The persistent delegitimation of Russia's security concerns, the anti-Russianism of the new NATO members, the failure to overcome the asymmetries in the Cold War settlement, the consolidation of a monological Wider European agenda of EU enlargement and its effective merger with the Atlantic security system, and the dismissal of Russian and other ideas for Greater European unity, have all conspired to create conditions for the confrontation [over Ukraine] in 2014' (Sakwa, 2014, p. 73).

The geopolitical dimension of the public and scholarly discourse on Ukraine has a quantitative expression. Figure 0.1 documents the growing number of publications discussing various aspects of the situation in Ukraine. The relative number of publications mentioning Ukraine in the context of geopolitics is growing even faster since the end of 2013. In 2014–2016 the total number of English-language scholarly publications devoted to Ukraine amounts to 0.37 of the similar figure for the baseline period of 1991–2013 (0.55 for Russian-language scholarly publications on this topic). The corresponding figure for English-language newspaper articles with the word 'Ukraine' in their headlines is 0.79. The frequency of the co-occurrence of the words 'Ukraine' and 'geopolitics' in the topics of scholarly articles has increased by 2.3 times within the same time frame. The frequency of the co-occurrence of the words 'Ukraine' and 'geopolitics' in newspaper articles has increased by 5 times. The geopolitical dimension of Russian-language scholarly publications has also strengthened. The number of publications discussing Ukraine and geopolitics has increased by 3.1 times.[6]

As a result of this return to geopolitics in general, and in the discourse on Ukraine in particular, a binary thinking prevails in today's discussions of the Ukrainian crisis. Ukraine's future is believed to be possible either within the European Union or within the Eurasian Customs Union, as if no alternative—namely, the maintenance of Ukraine's non-affiliated status, existed. Examples of such binary thinking can be found even in the formulations of questions for mass surveys, and, consequently, there is a risk that similarly worded questions might be used in referendums. A survey carried out in October 2016 by 'Rating group Ukraine' included the following question: 'If Ukraine could be a member of one international economic union only, the best option would be (i) the European Union, (ii) the Eurasian Customs Union'.[7] When forced to choose between two alternatives only, the respondents lean toward the first one, the European Union. If the third option, the maintenance of Ukraine's independent status, is offered, a growing number of Ukrainians choose the alternative that does not fit the binary picture. In November 2017, more than a third of them (40%) were

---

6 The search in the Web of Science Core Collection, eLibrary and LexisNexis Academic was conducted on February 17, 2017. The search terms were TOPIC:(Ukraine) AND TOPIC:(geopolit*). Due to a high volume of relevant information indexed in LexisNexis, the search parameters were narrowed down to Ukraine AND w/2 nation* (i.e. Ukraine and nation or its derivatives are found within 2 words of each other).

7 This survey was sponsored by the International Republican Institute (Washington, DC) and the Government of Canada. The report summarizing the results of this survey is available at http://ratinggroup.ua/research/ukraine/obschestvenno-politicheskie_nastroeniya_naseleniya_oktyabr_2016.html, see page 46 in particular.

of the opinion that Ukraine shall maintain its independent status (see Figure 2.1 in Chapter 2 and subsection III.2 of Chapter 10). The maintenance of the country's independent status potentially does not exclude Ukraine's membership in the European Union or other international alliances, but this could better be achieved after strengthening the nation-state. A stronger nation-state will enable Ukrainians to have a louder say in decision making that directly affects them. A historical parallel seems appropriate. When assessing the 1654 Treaty of Pereyaslav between Ukraine and Russia (Ukrainian Cossacks accepted the protectorate of the Russian tsar), Mykhailo Hrushevsky (1996, p. 760) observed that 'should Ukraine concluded a political union with Moscow earlier, when the country was stronger and with more resources, Ukrainians would have been able to better stand their ground and to prevent the transformation of their country into a province of Moscow. The entire history of Eastern Europe would have taken a different direction'.

IV. Towards Ukraine's internally driven development?

The binary thinking of Ukraine produces important omissions and blind spots. In this perspective, the 2013–2014 mass protests are seen as EuroMaidan, i.e. a movement for a closer association of Ukraine with the European Union. All aspects related to the defence of human dignity (the other name of the same event is the Revolution of Dignity) and the protest against violence appear to be relegated to the backstage. As a matter of fact, the issues of human dignity and violence were Ukrainians' key concerns at the height of these protests, whereas the issues of the European integration progressively lost their role as a driver of mobilisation (see Chapters 3, 4, 6 and 7 for more detail).

Moving from an outside to inside focus allows for a move beyond binary thinking. This change in focus leads the impartial observer to see a more nuanced picture of the most recent developments in Ukraine. The 2013–2014 mass protests and especially the undeclared war waged by Russia have created some conditions favourable for the transition from externally to internally driven development in Ukraine. Their success—the then President of Ukraine, Viktor Yanukovych, whose tenure was associated with authoritarian tendencies in state management and the harassment of civil activists, chose to resign and to flee from Ukraine to Russia—can be attributed to the creative use of Ukrainian cultural traditions. Namely, the protesters adapted to the circumstances of their fight for human dignity some elements of the organisation of Cossackdom. 'The Cossack era was further in the past, but a more direct source of inspiration' (Wilson, 2014, p. 70; see also Chapter 3; some other cultural resources that may be used for rebuilding the country from within are discussed in Chapter 7).

Even more importantly, these events marked the birth of the volunteer movement as an element of civil society that is truly independent both from the government and the foreign sponsors (Chapter 10). If the volunteer movement manages to keep momentum actively participating in the building of a nation-state, then an actor susceptible to propel development from inside, the nation-state, will finally emerge in Ukraine. As of the time of this writing, the volunteer movement unites the nation to a greater extent than any other actor, which confirms the plausibility of this scenario.

For these reasons, the sequence of events that started in November 2013 may mark a new period in the evolution of Ukraine's formal and informal institutions. When discussing path dependence, Douglass North (1990, p. 94) observes that 'the consequence of small events and chance circumstances can determine solutions that, once they prevail, lead one to a particular path'. The unique sequence of events in 2013–2016 did not change the country overnight. Important elements of the institutional continuity remain in force and shape the choice sets of actors in Ukraine (see Chapters 6, 7 and 8). At the same time, this sequence of events has the potential to start a new path in Ukraine's institutional evolution. The new path, on one hand, diverges from the Russian world. On the other hand, the movement along the new path may be propelled mostly internally, by the nascent Ukrainian nation-state.

It is more correct to say that as of the time of this writing, in Ukraine there exists a demand for changing the institutional path. Whether this demand will be met depends to a significant extent on actions of the Ukrainian power elite and sub-elite. Not all institutional innovations, especially as far as the nation-state is concerned, can be carried out by members of critical communities (see Chapters 3 and 10 for a discussion of the communitarian model of innovations). The ability of members of the current Ukrainian power elite to meet the demand for changing the institutional path raises serious doubts, however. Individuals and groups, who gained power as a result of the 2013–2014 mass protests (the presidential elections took place in May 2015, the parliamentary elections—in October 2014), do not appear to be up to the task. As reported before, in 2016 the level of confidence in the national government decreased even when compared with the pre-2013 situation.

A closer look at the official political discourse helps produce a more nuanced picture identifying what exactly has changed and what has not. Presidential addresses delivered on a yearly basis by four Presidents of Ukraine, Leonid Kuchma, Viktor Yushchenko, Viktor Yanukovych and Petro Poroshenko during the period from 2000 to 2016, were content analysed using the computer program WordStat version 6.1.24 (15 presidential addresses, 68,563 words in total). In conformity with the comparative approach used throughout this book, the political discourse of three Presidents of the Russian Federation, Boris Yeltsin, Vladimir Putin and Dmitry Medvedev, was used as a point of comparison (23 presidential addresses, 213,145 words in total).

The speeches delivered after November 2013 (3 in Ukraine and 4 in Russia) were compared with the addresses delivered before that date using techniques of quantitative content analysis, namely, two dictionaries based on substitution (Oleinik, 2015d). The first dictionary includes key associations of Ukrainians and Russians with power identified with the help of a mass survey (see Sections III and IV of Chapter 6). The second dictionary includes eight categories that have a close relation to the discussion of catch up development: the West, the East, Non-affiliation, Internally driven, Externally driven, Government, the State and Civil society. These categories operationalise the distinctions between an outside (geopolitical) and inside focus, externally and internally driven development, and potential actors of internal development. For instance, the category 'Civil society' contains the following words and phrases: *gromads'kist**, *gromadians'k** near *suspil** (in Ukrainian), *obshchestvennost**, *grazhdansk** near *obshchestv** (in Russian), *volonter** (in both languages).

The analysis of the relative frequencies of mentions of the key correlates of power shows some signs of Ukraine's departure from the Russian path. The relative number of references to corruption in the Ukrainian political discourse after November 2013 has increased whereas the same indicator changed in the opposite direction in Russia (Figure 0.3).[8] Keeping in mind that the level of perceived corruption remains remarkably similar and high in both countries,[9] this divergence may be indicative of the Ukrainian power elite's greater perceptiveness to the population's concerns. After all, corruption was the second most frequently mentioned association with power in a recent mass survey conducted in this country (Figure 6.1 in Chapter 6). Human rights are mentioned more frequently after November 2013 by the President of Ukraine

8 Accounting for the standard error of the population proportion, not all differences reported in Figure 0.3 are statistically significant. However, the increase in the relative number of mentions of corruption in Ukraine after November 2013 is statistically significant in two senses. On one hand, the post-2013 level showed a statistically significant increase compared to the pre-2013 level in this country. On the other hand, the difference between Ukraine and Russia reached the level of statistical significance after November 2013. The other notable statistically significant change refers to the relative number of mentions of law: it has increased in Ukraine, and decreased in Russia, which in turn statistically changed the difference between the countries into the opposite direction.

9 As per data of the Transparency International, an international non-government organisation (http://www.transparency.org/news/feature/corruption_perceptions_index_2016). For instance, in 2016 the level of perceived corruption in both countries was 29 on a 100 point scale (where 100 refers to the situation of full transparency in the government's operation). In 2013, the level of perceived corruption was 25 in Ukraine and 28 in Russia (in 2014, 26 and 27, in 2015, 27 and 29 correspondingly).

whereas the President of Russia devoted remarkably less attention to this issue. The same situation is observed with several other positive correlates of power as opposed to violence, law and authority. Mentions of honour have increased in Russia but not in Ukraine (see Chapter 7 for an in-depth discussion of human rights and honour as key correlates of human dignity). Nevertheless, references to force have increased in both countries, especially in Ukraine (the same situation with strength), which in the context of the military confrontation should not surprise.

Figure 0.3 'Relative frequencies of mentions of the key correlates of power in the yearly addresses of the Presidents of Ukraine and Russia, 2000–2016, per 100 words'

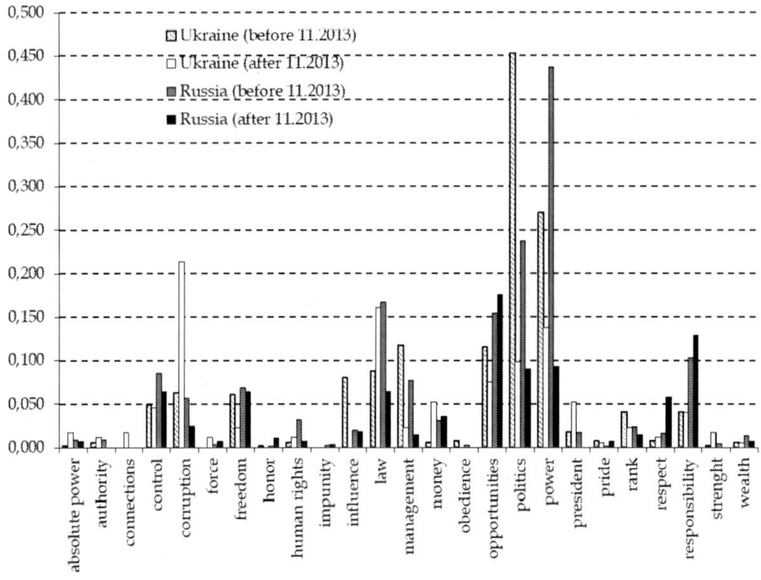

Source: official web-sites of the Ukrainian and Russian presidents; the author's calculations.

At the same time, the Ukrainian power elite still seem to prioritise externally over internally driven development (Figure 0.4).[10] The President of Ukraine now mentions outside centers of influence more frequently than before November 2013 (mentions of Russia expectedly have negative connotations, such as 'Russia's aggression'). The popularity of the idea of the maintenance of Ukraine's non-affiliated status in this country's political discourse has actually decreased after November 2013. The same is true with respect to the reliance on internal sources of development (*vnutrishn** near *resur**, *vnutrishn** near *rezerv**). Given that all three potential actors who could act as an internal driver of Ukraine's development—the nation-state, the government and civil society—are mentioned less frequently after November 2013 than before; the current power elite continue to rely on external sources of development and attempt to find a source of their own legitimacy outside of the country. The relative number of mentions of externally driven development (*mizhnarodn** near *dopomog**) has correspondingly increased. In other words, the events of 2013–2016 were not necessarily a learning lesson for Ukraine's power elite. Without the power elite's readiness to meet the demand for internally driven development, an attempt to escape geopolitics will result in an even deeper immersion into the geopolitical matters.

---

10 When interpreting differences reported in Figure 0.4, the standard error of the population proportion has to be taken into account one more time. For instance, changes in the relative number of mentions of the idea of non-affiliation before and after November 2013 only approach the level of statistical significance. At the same time, references to non-affiliation were more common in Ukraine than in Russia during both periods. References to internally driven development became statistically less frequent in Ukraine after November 2013. If before the Revolution of Dignity this idea was relatively more popular in Ukraine than in Russia, after November 2013 the situation is exactly the opposite, with the differences between the two countries being statistically significant in both cases. The increase in the relative number of mentions of externally driven development in Ukraine reaches the level of statistical significance.

Figure 0.4 'Relative frequencies of mentions of eight categories relevant to the discussion of externally versus externally driven development in the yearly addresses of the Presidents of Ukraine and Russia, 2000–2016, per 100 words'

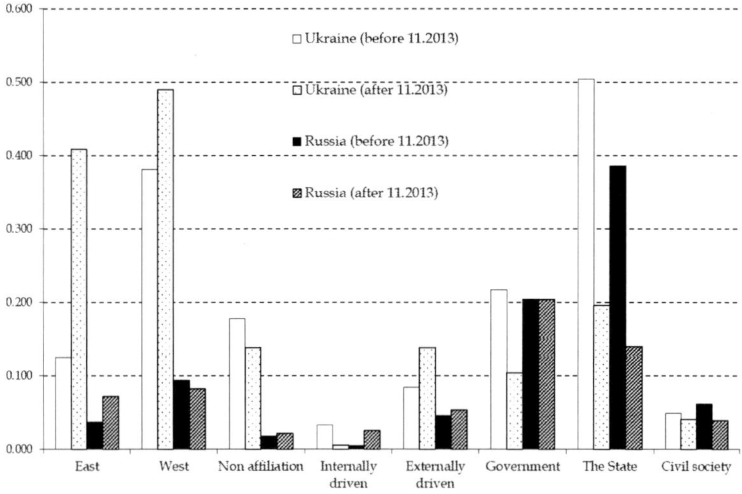

Source: official web-sites of the Ukrainian and Russian presidents; the author's calculations

The fact that the demand for the re-orientation of Ukraine from externally to internally driven development remains essentially unmet by the current power elite calls for searching for other internal actors who could accomplish this transition. Members of Ukraine's sub-elite are one of them: they support the project of nation-state building not only verbally but also by their deeds (Chapters 6 and 10). Namely, they actively participate in the nascent volunteer movement as either contributors of time and efforts or sponsors.

In countries taking the East European route of nation-state formation (see subsection I.2 of Chapter 10 for more detail) exclusively bottom-up and 'horizontal' initiatives might not suffice for succeeding, i.e. for building a sufficiently capable nation-state. There is a need for some 'vertical', 'top-down' approaches involving an organised religion, intelligentsia or sub-elites (Smith, 2004, p. 187). In its present condition, members of Ukraine's sub-elite—people at the intermediate layers of the social, political and economic hierarchies—show promise, but in order to become true drivers of development, they need help and assistance. For instance, their leaning toward nationalism is both a source of their strength and a possible limitation. The task of finding a right combination of nationalism and liberal values (as stated before, the desire to protect human dignity lies at the origin of the 2013–2014 events) has never been easy to complete. This combination can be labelled 'enlightened nationalism'. Nationalism is indeed present in Ukraine, but there have been no efforts to 'enlighten' this movement. Without the input of intellectuals and the existence of active debates, both scholarly and public, and at the national level, prospects of finding a liberal and national formula for Ukraine and streamlining nation-state building toward a liberal nation-state look dim.

Or, it could be that Ukrainian intellectuals do not seem to be prepared to move in this direction. Similar to Ukraine's power elite, they look outside for solutions, not inside. The situation in economic sciences in this country is a case in point (Chapter 8). The country does not have strong traditions of economic thought. Instead of trying to revive economic discussions and debates at the national level, however, Ukrainian economists prefer to simply reorient from the East to the West as a source of theoretical inspirations and solutions to economic problems. Other intellectuals do not see fit to participate in economic debates at the national level either. They apparently did not learn from the mistakes of early leaders of the national movement in the early 1990s who 'derided any early focus on economics and improving the economy as unserious and un-Ukrainian, as reflected in the description of economic policy as *kovbasna polityka* (sausage politics)' (Havrylyshyn, 2014, p. 173). Healthy debates of economic issues at the national level, both in the mass media and national scholarly publications, is a necessary step toward creating the national market as an economic component of Ukraine's nascent nation-state (Chapter 9). It is in this and the related areas that the book may be of interest for the audience in Ukraine, as a contribution to creating and strengthening a space of debates at the national level.

V. What the Ukrainian case can teach the West?

Ukrainians may well expect that their power elite move from an outside to inside focus, becoming more responsive to their needs than to wishes of external actors. Why may Western policy makers and observers be interested in the same change of focus? Some of them may be guided by enlightened self-interest. In his Nobel Lecture former US President Barack H. Obama (2009) elaborated on this point: 'The service and sacrifice of our men and women in uniform has promoted peace and prosperity from Germany to Korea, and enabled democracy to take hold in places like the Balkans. We have borne this burden not because we seek to impose our will. We have done so out of enlightened self-interest—because we seek a better future for our children and grandchildren, and we believe that their lives will be better if others' children and grandchildren can live in freedom and prosperity'.

There are two more compelling reasons for changing the perspective on the situation in Ukraine and the other countries undergoing similar processes: switching from one path of historical development to the other, building a nation-state, and trying to catch up with the level of development. First, when guided by geopolitical considerations, the foreign aid is often wasted at best and appropriated by the corrupt officials at worst (see the Conclusion to this book). A high level of corruption in Ukraine may well be a byproduct of externally driven development. All other conditions being equal, the higher the volume of foreign aid, the higher the level of perceived corruption, as illustrated by the lack of progress towards a greater transparency of the national government in Ukraine after November 2013. In other words, the taxpayers in the countries-donors have a rational interest in urging their governments to move from an outside to inside focus when dealing with the situation in Ukraine.

Second, and even more substantially, the Ukrainian case serves as an invitation for the West to revive democracy in general and truly volunteer initiatives in particular (Chapter 10). It shows the dangers of allowing people vested in power to move too far from power as human ability to act in concert and too close to its opposite, violence (Chapters 2 and especially 6). It demonstrates that it is never too late to say a clear 'No' to the equation of power with violence. The sacrifices that the Ukrainians made during the 2013–2014 protests (more than one hundred protesters—they are called '*nebesna sotnia*', Heavenly Hundred—lost their lives) and when curbing Russia's military aggression (several thousand troops and civilians were killed[11]) could have been avoidable, nevertheless, if civil society in general and the volunteer movement in particular assumed the role of a watchdog of the government much earlier and not limiting themselves to the provision of services. In the West, civil society organisations too often take for granted the government's responsiveness to the citizens' needs. Thus, the Ukrainian case suggests that Western civil society organisations need to exercise more critical control over, and assessment of, the government on a continuous basis as the best guarantee that nations-states in the West operate as a commonwealth (see Section II of Chapter 6)—exactly as they did at the early stages in the development of Western, especially Anglo-Saxon, democracies. In a way, Ukrainian volunteers may be compared with the builders of the first modern democratic nations in the 18th and 19th centuries.

VI. Organisation of the book

Along with this Introduction and the Conclusion, the book includes ten chapters. Their summaries below aim to facilitate the reader's navigation through the text.

Chapter 1 'Lessons of history: at the crossroads between various paths' offers an overview of Ukraine's history through the lens of various paths that this country followed at the different stages of its evolution: the Western (Nordic, Polish and Austrian) paths, the Russian path, and attempts to find an original, Ukrainian path. The

11 As of March 20, 2017, 2,629 Ukrainian military personnel were killed, 9,453 were wounded. These figures do not include volunteer fighters (http://www.pravda.com.ua/news/2017/03/20/7138688/).

Ukrainian path can presently be defined in mostly negative terms, through the references to freedom *from* (externally imposed constraints) and the rebellion against violence. Elements that can define the Ukrainian path positively are also discussed, including key myths that help constitute the Ukrainian identity: Cossackdom, individualism, and democracy. The task of building a Ukrainian nation-state requires that its creators move from the negative definition of their identity to a positive one; for instance, from the rejection of violence to power understood and human ability to act in concert.

Chapter 2 titled 'Value of freedom: the case of the post-Soviet Ukraine'[12] highlights some socio-cultural factors that help contextualise the 2013–2014 protests and especially, subsequent developments. Data that pre-date these protests suggest that binary thinking (the preference for either the Western or Eastern vector of socio-economic development) may be deeply embedded in today's Ukrainian culture, which contrasts with the tradition of prioritising freedom mentioned in Chapter 1. Chapter 2 discusses how freedom was perceived and understood by Ukrainians a few years before the Revolution of Dignity. An instrumental take on freedom (what benefits one derives from maintaining his/her autonomy) seemed to be prioritised over a take on freedom as a terminal value (from this point of view, freedom cannot be traded for any other good). Chapter 2 opens with a philosophical introduction, laying the foundation for the subsequent reasoning. The instrumental and terminal values of freedom are differentiated and considered in the context of its particular forms: freedom *to*, freedom *from* and freedom *together*. It is demonstrated that the contradiction between power and freedom does not hold for all these forms. Namely, freedom *to* has a very similar meaning to power *to* and freedom *together*—to transformative power (or power *with*). This approach sheds new light on the back-and-forth movements between the East (a closer integration with Russia) and the West (a closer integration into the EU)

---

12 Based on the 2015 article 'The value of freedom: a case study of Ukraine', *Southeast European and Black Sea Studies*, *15*(3): 239–259; http://www.tandfonline.com/doi/abs/10.1080/14683857.2015.1015316.

that characterise the post-Soviet period of Ukraine's history. The case study involves using two types of analysis: statistical analysis, namely with the help of a multiple regression model, of the World Values Survey dataset (N=1,000 in Ukraine in 2006) and content analysis of the official programs of ten presidential candidates in 2010.

Chapter 3 'Mass protests in 2013–2014: the revolution of dignity or EuroMaidan?'[13] discusses the case of the successful resistance of Ukrainian protesters to the government's violent attacks in November-December 2013. The ideals of human dignity (they lay at the origin of a first name of these events, the 'Revolution of Dignity', *Revoliutsiia Gidnosti*) appeared to be a stronger mobilising force than the ideas of a closer association with the EU (they explain a second name of these events, EuroMaidan). The chapter argues that the strong capacity they demonstrated for resistance can be attributed to the relocation of modular repertoires of contention (street protests, sit-ins and barricades) onto Ukrainian soil by means of their adaptation to traditional institutions, namely *Veche* (a gathering of community members) and *Sich* (a military camp of Cossacks). The communitarian model of institutional transfers is better suited to the Ukrainian case than the entrepreneurial model: the protests were initiated, organised and sustained by the ordinary people as opposed to the leaders of the opposition parties. Hence, the Revolution of Dignity was an example of leaderless protest, which justifies the need for a more intensive search for sources of socio-economic development within the country—a solution advocated in this book. Three mass surveys conducted during the protests and a series of the qualitative semi-structured interviews (N=31) provide data for the analysis in this chapter.

---

13 Based on the 2015 article 'The relocation of a repertoire of collective action: Maidan 2013', *European Journal of Cultural and Political Sociology*, 2(2), pp. 146–171 co-authored with Olga Strelkova; http://www.tandfonline.com/doi/abs/10.1080/23254823.2015.1110291.

Chapter 4 'Images of the protests: a comparative analysis of the Ukrainian and Russian protesters'[14] continues the discussion of the 2013–2014 events. A content analysis of two banks of images produced during the 2011 protests in Russia (at the time of the 2011 presidential elections, N=382) the 2013–2014 Revolution of Dignity (N=2,344) allows for the comparison of profiles of the protesters in the two countries. It is argued that the mass protests in Ukraine are more solidly connected to the process of nation-state building than in the Russian case, which can explain the opposite outcomes of these two examples of mass mobilisation (the 2011–2012 mass protests in Russia were severely repressed by the government and led to the ongoing period of reaction).

Chapter 5 titled 'Undeclared war: invisible and visible forms of Russia's domination'[15] discusses the response of the EU member-states to Russia's military conflict with Ukraine that started in 2014 and is still ongoing. This war had a chilling effect on supporters of the Eastern vector in Ukraine's development. The number of supporters of Russia in Ukraine has significantly decreased in the context of the war initiated by Russia through the annexing of Crimea and the subsequent arming and staffing of the separatists in Eastern Ukraine. At the same time, the war demonstrated the limits of the country's eventual reliance on the West, namely the European Union. The EU countries turned out to be unwilling to take decisive and prompt measures, mainly economic and political, against the aggressor. The European countries' lack of united response and unwillingness to apply severe sanctions (restrictive measures) on Russia in a timely manner is attributed to a constellation of interests of the European countries and Russia in the European energy market. This constellation was particularly manifest in 2014, when the world prices for oil and gas had reached a historical peak. Max Weber's concept of domination by virtue of a constellation of interests

14 Includes some material previously published in the 2015 article 'On content analysis of images of mass protests: a case of data triangulation', *Quality and Quantity*, *49*(5), pp. 2203–2220.

15 Based on the 2015 article 'Price of opulence: on a constellation of interests in the European market for natural gas', *Baltic Worlds*, *8*(3–4), pp. 51–61; http://balticworlds.com/wp-content/uploads/2015/11/Anton-Oleinik.pdf.

and the related concept of the power triad set the general theoretical framework for the discussion. Statistical data on the energy dependence of the EU member-states on Russia inform it.

Chapter 6 'Transition impossible? Ukraine between violence and power'[16] addresses the issue of the authority culture in Ukraine. 'Russian power', i.e. a particular configuration of power relationship that has been prevailing in the Russian, Soviet and post-Soviet empires is used as a point of reference. Two features of Russian power explain its closeness to violence: mostly negative associations (such as force, money and corruption) and a high power distance. It is argued that a potential for the movement from violence to power understood as human ability to act in concert exists in Ukraine. Members of Ukraine's sub-elites have a chance to become a driving force of this process. Under certain conditions they could take a lead in transitioning to less violent models of power in politics and elsewhere. The data were drawn from three mass surveys conducted in Russia (N=2,939 and N=11,096) and in Ukraine (N=2,040) from July 2016 to January 2017.

Chapter 7 'Human rights and honour: a comparative study of Ukraine and Russia'[17] considers the relative importance attached to honour and human rights in two cultures: Russian and Ukrainian. These cultures have elements of honour cultures, both historically and in the present. Elements of a more universalistic interpretation of human dignity that are expressed through the concept of human rights also exist, especially in the Ukrainian case. However, the movement towards the universalistic understanding of human dignity slows down or can even be reversed in the context of a protracted war. Two sources of data inform the analysis: primary (two surveys conducted on representative samples in Russia, N=1,602, and Ukraine, N=2,020) and secondary (the complete works of two

---

16 Based on the 2017 article 'Transition impossible? Ukraine between violence and power', *Journal of Political Power, 10*(3), pp. 371–389; http://www.tandfonline.com/doi/abs/10.1080/2158379X.2017.1382178.

17 Based on the 2016 article 'Honor and Human Rights: A Comparative Study of Russia and Ukraine', *Comparative Sociology, 15*(6), pp. 669–698; http://booksandjournals.brillonline.com/content/journals/10.1163/15691330-12341406.

poets deemed representative of the two cultures, Alexander Pushkin and Taras Shevchenko as well as documents in the Russian-language and Ukrainian-language segments of the Google online databank). The data were processed using methods of descriptive statistics, binary statistic regression and quantitative content analysis.

Chapter 8 'Ukrainian Economic Thought at the Crossroads'[18] highlights some aspects of Ukrainian intellectual life, namely the state of economic research in this country. Ukrainian economists, similar to Ukrainian society, are in the middle of the process of turning from the East to the West after the 2013–2014 events. However, the visibility of their work remains low both in the East and the West. The analysis of their publication activity for the past 25 years (using data from the Web of Science Core Collection and eLibrary) confirms these assumptions. It is argued that the first step in this eventual re-orientation consists of building the space for economic debates at the national level, within the country. Active and healthy debates at the national level will arguably increase chances of Ukrainian economists to be heard internationally. This solution is in line with the book's central argument: to be successful and respected in the East or/and the West, Ukrainians should first explore and develop intellectual resources within their national borders.

Chapter 9 'The national market in the making' is devoted to the issues of building the national market in Ukraine. Since 1991, Ukraine has had several economic crises (1991–1999, 2009, ongoing since 2014) and a period of economic boom from 2000 to 2008. The current crisis has external (the unfavourable situation in the world commodities markets) and internal (the military conflict with neighbouring Russia) dimensions. The destruction of economic infrastructure and the unpreparedness of Ukrainian producers to compete globally explain its depth and complexity. Radical and non-orthodox measures may be needed to help Ukraine to return

---

18 Based on the 2015 article 'Between the West and the East: Ukrainian Economic Thought at the Crossroads', *Bulletin of Taras Shevchenko National University of Kyiv. Economics*, 9(174), pp. 56–61; http://econpapers.repec.org/article/scnpnoeeq/174a9.htm.

to economic growth. This chapter discusses pros and cons of an asymmetrical solution that involves a combination of protectionism and an outward-oriented strategy during the recovery period. It is argued that it may be more efficient than the country's reliance on foreign loans and aid. The analysis of regional-level data for 2013–2015 lends some support to this argument.

Chapter 10 titled 'Volunteers: actors of internal growth' discusses the volunteer movement in Ukraine. After the 2013–2014 Revolution of Dignity and the subsequent military confrontation with Russia, the volunteer movement became an influential and trusted actor capable of mobilising a large number of supporters and a significant amount of resources. Donations made to volunteer initiatives represent in Ukraine a percentage of the country's GDP similar to that in some Western countries. However, compared with volunteerism in developed countries, volunteer initiatives in Ukraine have several distinct features: a mostly informal character; their reliance on a hard core of committed and active leaders; and connections with the nationalist movement understood here as an actor aiming to attain and maintain the identity of the Ukrainian nation-state in the making. The volunteer movement also has a strong potential for social entrepreneurship that can be used in nation-state building. Data from two sources inform the analysis: a series of in-depth qualitative interviews with leaders of the volunteer movement (N=22) and results of a survey conducted on a representative sample (N=2,040).

The general conclusion to the book 'On the role of foreign donors' addresses the issues of foreign aid and international assistance. The primary reliance on the internal sources of socio-economic development does not exclude the need for external support, especially in a country that still suffers from the protracted military conflict. However, if the reasoning offered in this book is correct, then activities of the foreign donors shall be oriented principally to the support of internal points of growth, social and economic. The task of empowering actors that show promise to propel socio-economic development from within can and should be prioritised. The policies of empowering local actors (as opposed to financing the government and established businesses) take various forms: in addition to more or less conventional grants to NGOs, the foreign donors could more directly support bottom-up initiatives and start-ups that demonstrated their relevance and promise. For instance, in a country with one of the most problematic banking sectors in the world, more could be done to support credit unions (some of them are quite successful at the local and regional level) and other forms of mutual financing.

Chapter 1
'Lessons of history: At the crossroads between various paths'

Introduction: a place between two borderlands

Ukraine literally means borderland (Reid, 2015, p. 1; Subtelny, 2009, p. 3). This association with a borderland leads some to place the definite article before the country's name, *the* Ukraine. This rule applies to countries whose names refer to geographical regions, for instance, the Philippines (the group of islands). Ukrainians object to referring to their country as a simple geographical region and expect that its name be written in English as 'Ukraine' instead of 'the Ukraine' (Taylor, 2013). The use of 'Ukraine', a proper noun, suggests that the country has a character. This issue is not purely linguistic, but prompts a broader inquiry as to what are distinctive features of Ukraine and its culture other than a specific geographical location. This chapter offers a look at the history of Ukraine through such a lens.

If one thinks of Ukraine as a borderland in a figurative sense, the next logical step is to ask: *which* borderland? Ukraine lies at the crossroads between the North and the South, the East and the West (see Section III of the general Introduction to this book). Neighbours both in the East (Russia) and in the West (Poland) can consider Ukraine as their borderland. And they did so indeed in the past. The name *Ukraina* was first used to refer to a clearly defined territory by Poles in the 16th century, when the Ukrainian lands were included in the Polish-Lithuanian Commonwealth (Magosci, 2010, p. 189). The Eastern neighbours, Russians, agree that Ukraine means a borderland, but claim this territory to be their borderland. The conventions of Russian language still require that one says 'on the Ukraine' (*na Ukraine*) instead of 'in Ukraine' (*v Ukraine*). The former means 'on the border'—the Russian border, of course, not the Polish one.[19]

If it is a mistake to perceive Ukraine as a borderland, let alone the Polish or Russian borderland, then where exactly to place Ukraine on the map—an institutional and cultural map foremost, since the exact geographical location of this country has been studied sufficiently well since Stepan Rudnytsky, a 19th-century geographer and cartographer (Stebelsky, 2014)? Mykhailo Hrushevsky, a prominent Ukrainian historian, invites to look for distinctively Ukrainian features in the central part of this country that lies 'in-between' the Russian and Polish borderlands, Eastern and Western Ukraine correspondingly. Culture and institutions in Eastern Ukraine have been heavily influenced by the Russian path of institutional development, also known under the name of the Russian world (see subsection II.3 of the general Introduction to this book). European models and patterns influenced the evolution of culture and institutions of Western Ukraine.

One could argue whether the impact of the Central and Eastern European model (Poland) in Western Ukraine was more significant than that of the Western European model (Austria). But instead of assuming that 'the course of modern Ukrainian history has largely been the tale of two parallel paths, one tread by the West Ukrainians in Austrian Empire and the other by the East Ukrainians in the Russian Empire', as Orest Subtelny does (2009, p. 220), it would be more appropriate to explore the area first identified by Hrushevsky: Central Ukraine. According to him, the area in the middle stream of the river Dnieper (*Dnipro*) 'was the cradle of Ukrainian people' in the 1st-11th centuries (Hrushevsky, 1991, p. 11). Central Ukraine continued to be the heartland of the country

---

19 On more than one occasion the author saw his writings in Russian corrected by the editors of newspapers and journals who substituted '*na Ukraine*' for '*v Ukraine*'. The author went to a Russian-language school and university, so this 'error' can hardly be explained by his ignorance of the relevant rules of Russian grammar.

at the time of Cossackdom from the late 15th to the early 18th centuries. After the fall of the Soviet Union and the declaration of Ukraine's sovereignty, 'some of the biggest transformations in national identity in 1989–2001 [also] took place in Central Ukraine' (Kuzio, 2015, p. 224). Finally, the most recent revival of national consciousness during an undeclared war waged by Russia against Ukraine has been particularly intensive in Central and Central-Eastern Ukraine (see subsection I.2 of Chapter 10). It follows that if one wants to identify a distinctively Ukrainian path of institutional and cultural development, areas that lie in-between the Western and Eastern borderlands perhaps should be explored first.

What may potentially characterise the Ukrainian path of historical evolution? Power is probably the most important explanatory variable that allows explaining the other particularities of the Russian path (Oleinik, 2011a, chapter 4). A specific model of power, Russian power, permeates relationships at the micro- (within a family), meso- (within an organization) and macro- (in politics) levels. This model lies closer to violence than to power understood as human ability to act in concert (see Chapter 6). The European path—in either its Eastern (Poland) or Western (Austria) version—has more dimensions. However, if we follow Michael Mann (1986, p. 1) and see all societies through the prism of 'multiple overlapping and intersecting sociospatial networks of power', then the European path will lie closer to power since it supports democratic structures and processes. For instance, elements of democracy were often driven to the extreme in the history of Poland. The process of deliberations at the regional and national Diets—assemblies of the nobles in the 16th-17th centuries in Poland—could be easily undermined and put in limbo since all the participants had a power of veto. One dissatisfied nobleman could take hostage the fellows regardless of their number. Hrushevsky (1994, p. 326) observes in this respect that the Polish Res Publica—*Rzeczpospolita*—had more in common with anarchy than with a democracy echoing the verdict of Jean-Jacques Rousseau (1844, p. 713): 'Rien na la domine, mais rien de lui obéit'.[20]

In those terms, the Ukrainian path has some unique features indeed. Since the 11th century, Ukraine's historical evolution has been characterised by its population's exemplary resistance to power, especially when violence is substituted for power. The first revolution occurred on Ukrainian soil as early as 1068, when the citizens of Kyiv, dissatisfied with the rule of their Prince (*knyaz'*) Iziaslav, drove him out and installed his nephew Vseslav in his place (Hrushevsky, 1992a, p. 56; Plokhy, 2015, p. 36). It was just the beginning. The other revolution occurred in 1113 when Vladimir Monomakh was proclaimed Prince (Hrushevsky, 1992b, p. 210). The scale and scope of the mass uprising of 1648 had no match elsewhere. 'It is difficult to find a similar revolt of such magnitude, intensity, and impact in the early modern history of all of Europe' (Subtelny, 2009, p. 123). Another large-scale revolt marked the beginning of the 20th century in Ukraine. In 1919, almost the entire Ukrainian countryside revolted against the Bolsheviks' attempt to implement principles of war communism in practice (Ibid., p. 365). The post-Soviet history of Ukraine was not short of revolutions either. The 2004 'Orange' revolution was followed by the 2013–2014 Revolution of Dignity (Chapter 3). In these circumstances, it will not be an exaggeration to say that Ukraine has lived a millennium of rebellions, from the 11th century to the 21th century.

The distinction of being dedicated rebels came at a price, however. It may well be that Ukrainians devoted all of their energies and creativities to protests as opposed to more constructive work. For instance, Ukrainians' 'speciality' in rebellions may have slowed down their progress in nation-state building (Chapter 10). Nikolai

20 'Nothing dominates it, but neither does anything obey it'. Adam Mickiewicz (1917, p. 305) expressed regrets about the time when liberty had not undermined order in the following lines of *Pan Tadeusz*:
'Ah, you young men, do not remember this, how
among our turbulent, self-willed gentry, always under
arms though they were, no police were ever needed:
while the true faith flourished, laws were respected;
there was liberty with order and glory along with plenty'.

Kostomarov (1861, p. 78), a historian of Ukraine, wrote that 'Ukrainians, in the past, appeared unprepared for a statehood'. A century and a half later, Serhii Plokhy reached a similar conclusion: 'Successful rebels, the Ukrainian politicians turned out to be amateurs at building a state and organizing armed forces' (Plokhy, 2015, p. 217).[21] This chapter aims to explore in a systematic manner the hypothesis that if a distinguishable Ukrainian path of historical evolution exists at all, it is the path of rebellion and protest. Particular attention is paid to the myths associated with the perception of Ukrainians as dedicated rebels. It is assumed that these myths occupy the central place in the national consciousness of Ukrainians being at the origin of both their strengths and weaknesses.

I. Longue durée and courte durée

The distribution of noteworthy events in the history of Ukraine is not uniform. The relatively eventful period of Kievan Rus' (the 10th-12th centuries), a first state that existed on the territory of present-day Ukraine, was followed by a several centuries-long pause in the development of Ukrainian institutions. The 17th century marked the other peak in the concentration of significant events. The national-liberation uprising in 1648 led by Bohdan Khmelnytsky resulted in the creation of the Hetmanate, a state not de jure, but de facto. Both the start of the 20th century (an attempt to create an independent Ukrainian Republic in 1917–1919) and its end (the declaration of Ukraine's sovereignty in 1991) show a high concentration of significant events (Figure 1.1).

---

21 Condoleezza Rice, the 66th US Secretary of State, expressed a similar opinion in an interview with a journalist of *Ukrains'ka Pravda* in March 2016: 'Ukraine continues to produce one revolution after the other. Perhaps it is a time to govern the State?' (http://www.eurointegration.com.ua/interview/2016/03/14/7046142/ accessed March 07, 2017).

Figure 1.1 'Distribution of significant events in Ukraine's history mentioned in selected scholarly sources and in the 2012 tourist guide by century, % of the total'

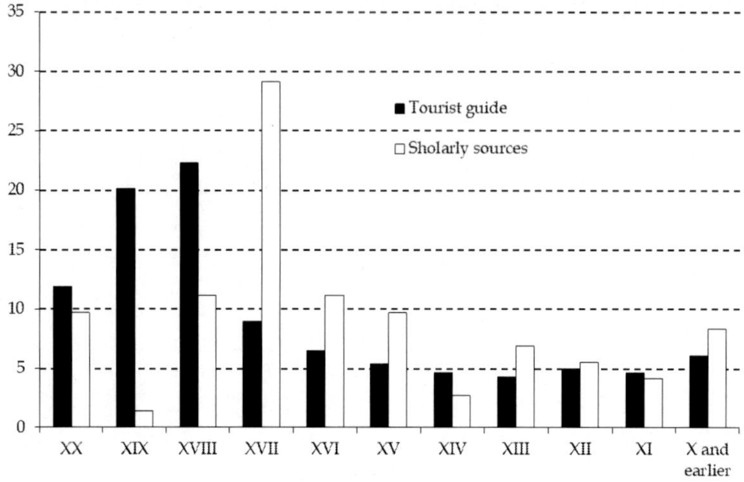

Source: This chart was produced with the help of the content analysis of 40 plus scholarly sources in the field of history of Ukraine cited in this book and of the tourist guide mentioned in the general Introduction (Ukraine, 2012). The judgment as to the significance of an event was made by the coder, i.e. the author, on the basis of the information provided in a particular source.

I.1 Histories of Ukraine

As Figure 1.1 suggests, the noteworthiness of historical events is a highly relative notion. For instance, the publishers of the comprehensive tourist guide (Ukraine, 2012) devoted more attention to the 18th-19th centuries in the history of Ukraine—a period during which Ukraine had been split in two parts. The Russian Empire controlled all territories on the left (East) bank of the Dnieper River along with a significant part of Right-Bank Ukraine, whereas the westernmost region of Ukraine, Galitsia, was included in the Austro-Hungarian Empire. From this point of view, Ukraine's history in the 18th-19th century was more 'imperial' than 'national'.

A rather selective perception of Ukraine's history comes as no surprise. It is quite possible that the publishers of the said tourist guide have gaps in their knowledge of history. However, these omissions may be attributable to their agreement with a particular version of the history of Ukraine offered by the Soviet historiography. The problem is that there is no universally accepted version of Ukraine's history. Instead, several historical schools offer competing versions of Ukraine's past. In function of the assumptions and values shared by their advocates, the competing historical schools highlight various periods and different aspects of this country's history. Paul Magosci (2010, p. 12), namely, identifies four main versions of the history of Ukraine: Ukrainian, Russian, Soviet and Polish. In other words, representatives of all the empires that controlled the territories of present-day Ukraine—with the exception of Austria-Hungary and the Ottoman Empire, developed their own histories of the Ukrainian past.[22]

This chapter does not have an ambition to offer a unified version of Ukraine's history. The author refers to writings of historians who represent three influential versions: Ukrainian (Kostomarov, Hrushevsky, Yavornytsky, Subtelny and Plokhy), Polish (or at least use documents collected and generated by Polish historiography, from Hrushevsky[23] to Gordon) and Russian (Klyuchevsky, or at least use documents collected and generated by Russian historiography, for instance, Tairova-Yakovleva). The exclusive reliance on secondary sources represents a clear limitation of the proposed study. The following discussion offers a reinterpretation of the known facts and myths, in light of the above formulated research

22 One could add a Greek version to this list: after all, Greeks in general and Herodotus in particular were first to write about Ukrainian lands and their peoples (Hrushevsky, 1991, p. 106; Kostomarov, 1861, p. 37; Plokhy, 2015, p. 3). In the 4th-6th centuries Greeks were among colonisers of Crimea and the Black Sea coastal areas in the North. This mission explains their interest in learning more about peoples who lived in regions located further north.

23 Hrushevsky is certainly the most prominent Ukrainian historian and the father of Ukrainian historiography. At the same time, he extensively relied on sources and documents kept in Polish archives. Magosci cites sources produced by Ukrainian, Soviet, Russian and Polish historiographies. Nevertheless, English-language texts prevail among his sources.

question; namely, *is there a distinctive Ukrainian path of historical evolution and, if so, to what extent can it be described in terms of rebellion against violence*? Violence is understood here as the imposition of will by the dominating social agent on the dominated social agent—repeatedly, systematically, and to the detriment of the latter (see Chapter 6).

I.2 A nation-state in its childhood

Whatever the approach chosen, a principal conclusion remains roughly the same. The periods of Ukraine's independent existence are short compared with the periods during which representatives of the other countries kept the Ukrainian lands under their control. In this sense, the periods during which Ukraine was an autonomous entity correspond to *court durée* in this country's history whereas its dependent status can be considered as the essence of *long durée*. Compared with most other European countries, nation-state building in Ukraine started later, in the 17th century. The process has been subsequently interrupted or aborted on multiple occasions. As a result, Ukraine is still in the relatively early stages in building its nation-state.

I.2.a Vikings

Kievan Rus' was the first state to exist on the territory of today's Ukraine. Its heyday falls within the period of the 10th-12th centuries. The history of Kievan Rus' remains a highly disputed topic between Ukrainian and Russian historians. Ukrainian and Russian historiographies perceive Kievan Rus' as a cradle of Ukrainian and Russian states respectively. Russian historians even claim that after the dissolution of Kievan Rus'—as a result of endless disputes and conflicts between the princes of the domains that constituted this state, its population—or at least a significant portion of it—migrated north and northeast, i.e. to the territories of today's Russia. Vasily Klyuchevsky (1956, pp. 284, 286), a Russian historian who worked in the late 19th-the early 20th century, writes: 'people migrated from the areas of the central flow of the Dnieper River in two directions, in two opposite streams. A first stream headed westward… to Galicia and Poland… A second stream of colonisation from the areas of the central flow of the Dnieper River headed northeastward, to the Russian lands lying between the Oka River and the upper flow of the Volga River'. Nikolai Kostomarov (1861, p. 39), a Russian historian sympathetic to Ukrainian people and culture, accepts the hypothesis of the mass migration, but believes that people headed northward to Novgorod, making this place a stronghold of democratic traditions in the Russian lands (in Kyiv, as we will see in subsection II.4 below, city dwellers participated in the decision-making through an institution of direct democracy, *Viche*).

Ukrainian historians strongly oppose this view. Hrushevsky (1992b, pp. 146–147) was probably the first to take on this issue. He disagrees, arguing that, if migration after the dissolution of Kievan Rus' took place at all, it was first and foremost internal migration from the areas lying close to the steppe to the deep forest. Representatives of Ukrainian historiography go even further, arguing that the historical name of Ukraine, Rus', was stolen and improperly appropriated. 'Ukrainian people's historical name—Rus', Rusin, Russian—was appropriated by Russians who profited from their neighbours' political and cultural decline' (Hrushevsky, 1991, p. 1; see also Kostomarov, 1861, p. 41).[24]

The fact that most rulers of Kievan Rus', especially in its early days in the 10th century, were not local nobles but rather came from abroad, remains overshadowed in the debates about the legitimate successors of this state. Kievan Rus' was initially ruled by the Vikings. 'All the rulers of Kyiv up to Sviatoslav had Scandinavian names as did the members of their retinues or *druzhyny*' (Subtelny,

24 The appropriation of cultural symbols produced in Kievan Rus' by its eastern neighbours did not stop here. Some most precious icons were taken from the churches in Kyiv to the newly built churches in the Principality of Vladimir-Suzdal that emerged as a new centre of power after the decline of Kievan Rus'. Namely, the icon of the Mother of God, offered to the first Christians in Kievan Rus' as a gift from Constantinople (now Istanbul), the then capital of Orthodox Christianity, was 'either taken or stolen' by Andrei Bogolyubsky for a church in his new capital city, Vladimir (Hrushevsky, 1992a, p. 277).

2009, p. 15; see also Plokhy, 2015, p. 27). Several Ukrainian and Russian names as a result have Scandinavian roots: Oleh–Helgi, Olha–Helga, Ihor–Ingvar, Sviatoslav–Svienald and so forth. The coming of the Vikings to Kievan Rus' did not result from a military conquest. As a matter of fact, the Vikings were likely invited by the people of Kievan Rus' to govern and to provide military services. A note has to be taken for the subsequent discussion that the first state on the Ukrainian lands can hardly be considered as a predecessor of either Ukrainian nation-state or Russian nation-state for a simple reason: a third party, the Vikings, played a key role in the rise of Kievan Rus'. The question as to what extent and how exactly Scandinavian traditions and institutions mixed up with the local ones remains underexplored. Available sources simply do not shed enough light on this issue.

I.2.b Tatars

Along with internal conflicts, the arrival of the Mongol hordes also contributed to the fall of Kievan Rus'. The next rulers of the Ukrainian lands came not from Northern Europe, but from Asia. The exact timeframe of the Tatars' rule can hardly be determined accurately. In the 13th-14th centuries the Mongols conquered and gained control over most of the Ukrainian lands. With the decline of the Mongols' empire, connections between separate Hordes weakened to the point where some of them started to exist independently. One such Horde settled in Crimea. Crimean Tatars, descendants of this Horde, created a Tatar state in Crimea, the Crimean Khanate, with the capital in Bakhchysarai (Hrushevsky, 1993, p. 295). The Crimean Khanate's influence extended over all northern shores of the Black Sea and the steppe areas that cover a significant part of the territory of today's Ukraine.

Crimean Tatars initially peacefully coexisted with the population of the other Ukrainian lands. The situation changed in 1478 when the Crimean Khanate became a vassal state of the Ottoman Empire. From this year until the 18th century, relationships between Ukrainians and Crimean Tatars were more ambivalent. Hostilities and conflicts, including military, abounded (Yavornitsky,

1990, pp. 237–239). In practical terms, it means that the Tatars' influence on the evolution of institutions in Ukraine, on one hand, lasted at least six centuries. On the other hand, their influence was not uniform at different points in time.

Initially, the Mongols were satisfied with the role of a roving bandit (Olson, 1993) seeking bounty after devastating raids. Since the Ukrainian lands lay at the westernmost edge of the Mongols' vast empire, extending from Pacific Ocean to what is today Western Ukraine, those devastating raids were less frequent and massive than, for instance, in Central Russia. The Mongols chose not to settle in any of these lands, preferring instead to rely on the services of the local princes collecting taxes for them (Kostomarov, 1861, p. 53). In Ukraine, the Galician and Volhynian princes performed this role in exchange for the Mongols' recognition of their other privileges (Hrushevsky, 1992b, p. 187; Plokhy, 2015, 50). Using modern terms, one could call the princes collecting taxes for the invaders 'collaborators'. Such an arrangement allowed the prince not only to secure his power over the subordinates, but even to extend its scope since the Mongols preferred not to intervene in the local affairs so long as their supremacy remained unchallenged and taxes duly flew into the coffers. This also means that the Mongols did not interfere with the cultural and religious life in Ukraine. It is likely for this reason the population of some lands actually sought to enter into direct relationships with the Mongols bypassing their princes. In the 13th century, people from the lands in the vicinity of Kyiv made several attempts to obtain the Mongols' direct rule (Hrushevsky, 1992b, pp. 83, 157–159, 181–182). Those who had managed to rid themselves of the princes were able to revive some elements of democratic decision-making, including the institution of *Viche*.

Relationships with Crimean Tatars in the late 15th-18th centuries were similarly ambivalent, to say the least. On one side, the Crimean Tatars raided the Ukrainian lands, destroying property and enslaving people (the slave trade was one of the specialities of Crimean Tatars: slaves were traded in the capital of their metropole, Constantinople). Cossacks' first function was to protect the Ukrainian lands from those devastating raids. It comes as no surprise that the first mention of Cossacks dates to the end of the 15th century, as we will see in subsection II.1. As a result of the continuous interaction with Crimean Tatars, Cossacks learned from them and creatively adapted to their own needs some military techniques, including the layout of Cossacks' temporary camp, *Tabir* (see Section III of Chapter 3), and elements of the military-administrative organization (Plokhy, 2015, p. 101).

On the other side, Crimean Tatars and their lords, the Ottomans, were important allies of Cossacks and even their protectors at times, especially in the 17th-18th centuries. Crimean Tatars participated in all major battles between the Cossacks and the Poles during the mass uprising of the 17th century led by Bohdan Khmelnitsky. Their contribution was not always unambiguous, since the Crimean Tatars on several occasions changed their minds in the middle of the battle—either withdrawing or stopping to fight, seeing that one side appeared to be a definite victor (they wanted to give a chance neither to the Cossacks nor to their adversaries, the Poles in the circumstances, for getting too strong). However, the Cossacks did not launch major attacks without securing some support of the Crimeans (Hrushevsky, 1956b, p. 167; Hrushevsky, 1956c, p. 178; Hrushevsky, 1996, pp. 288, 697). Cossacks' leaders involved the Crimean Tatars in internal disputes as well. After the death of Khmelnitsky, his successor, Ivan Vigotsky, fought with the Crimean Tatars against those Cossacks who questioned the legitimacy of his election as a supreme leader (Hrushevsky, 1958, p. 218).

In 1651 Cossack Ukraine even had the formal status of a vassal of the Ottoman Empire. The relevant agreement was brokered by the Crimean Tatars, the other vassals of Constantinople, but it did not last for long (Hrushevsky, 1996, p. 54). Nevertheless, it was not the last time the Cossacks accepted the Turkish sultan's lordship. From 1709–1734 Zaporozhian Cossacks sought and received his protection after the battle of Poltava (June 27, 1709) in which they fought on the losing side (the Swedes led by their king, Charles VII). They found refuge from the pursuit of the victors, the Russians led by Peter I, in the areas in the lower flow of the Dnieper River controlled at that time by the Crimean Tatars (Yavornitsky, 1992, pp. 328–, see also subsection II.7 below for more detail).

I.2.c Lithuanians

Following the departure of the Mongols, the Crimean Tatars emerged as a centre of power in Southern Ukraine. Around the same time, in the 14th-15th centuries, Ukraine's northern neighbours, Lithuanians, established control over Central and Northern parts of the country. Relationships between the population of the Ukrainian lands and the Lithuanian rulers were less ambiguous than in the case of the Tatars. The majority of Ukrainian historians agree that among all the foreign masters of the Ukrainian lands, the Lithuanians were probably the most benign and the least intrusive. Hrushevsky (1993, p. 95) writes that 'the Lithuanian lordship did not have an ethnographically foreign character or if it did, its foreignness was minimal'. The Lithuanian princes kept local customs and traditions. Ruthenian (the predecessor of modern Ukrainian and Belorussian languages) became the official language of the government. The Lithuanian princes also allowed the local elites to preserve their political influence and social status without being perceived by the population as tax collectors on behalf of the foreign masters (Subtelny, 2009, pp. 59, 72; see also Reid, 2015, p. 15).

The situation changed when the Grand Duchy of Lithuania and the Kingdom of Poland formed a union in 1569. One of the conditions for the ascension of the Lithuanian Grand Duke Jogaila to the Polish throne via the marriage with Queen Jadwiga of Poland was the Lithuanian elites' conversion to Catholicism and the promotion of this religion in Lithuania, including the Ukrainian lands. The religious question later became an important source of tensions between the Ukrainian population and the Polish elites. Since the time of Kievan Rus', Ukrainians professed Orthodox Christianity.

I.2.d Poles

The 'Polish' period of Ukraine's history also started in the 14th century with the fall of the Mongols' empire. When the Lithuanian princes incorporated Central and Northern Ukraine into their Duchy, Western Ukraine—Galicia and a part of Podolia—was seized by Poland. Subsequently, most Ukrainian lands that had been initially incorporated into the Grand Duchy of Lithuania were annexed to Poland. By the mid-17th century, Poland controlled most of the Ukrainian lands (except in the South, the domain of Crimean Tatars) either indirectly or directly. All regions of Western, Central and Northern Ukraine but one (Berestechko) were incorporated into the Polish crown (Hrushevsky, 1993, p. 3; Hrushevsky, 1994, p. 339). The Poles exercised an indirect control over the Berestechko region in the West since the Grand Duchy of Lithuania was itself an integral part of the Polish-Lithuanian Commonwealth. Poland's control of the Ukrainian lands remained essentially intact until Khmelnitsky's uprising in the second half of the 17th century. Even after this revolution the crown kept control over most of Right-Bank Ukraine until the first partition of Poland in the second half of the 18th century.

The Polish influence on the evolution of Ukraine's institutions is complex and contradictory. Ukraine's contacts with the West initially occurred through the Polish route. Democratic institutions in this country were among the most developed in Europe at that time, even if they did not protect against the potential drift into anarchy as mentioned in the introduction to this chapter. The Polish-Lithuanian union took the form of a commonwealth as opposed to a State, which itself represents a remarkable achievement (see Section II of Chapter 6). The power was divided between the king and the *Sejm*. The *Sejm* reviewed significant initiatives taken by the king approving or rejecting them. The *Sejm* also controlled the budget matters. Even a small nobility had a voice in the Commonwealth affairs. Anna Reid (2015, p. 26) suggests that 'the *szlachta* comprised around 10% of the population, giving a level of representation that would not be bettered elsewhere until the 19th-century British Reform Acts'.

At the same time, the Polish rulers had absolutely no respect for the Ukrainian population, its institutions and language. It would be fair to say that Ukrainians were seen as inferior beings, whose only asset was perceived to be the labour needed to cultivate abundant and fertile arable lands. The perception of the Orthodox Church by the Polish nobility is a case in point. The Catholic Church had a privileged status in the Polish-Lithuanian Commonwealth.

The Orthodox Church was at best tolerated and at worst discriminated against by them (Hrushevsky, 1994, p. 431). In these circumstances, in the 17th century Ukrainians fought for national liberation under the banners of the Orthodox Church. To be a Ukrainian meant for them first and foremost to be an Orthodox believer (Hrushevsky, 1995, p. 295). This point must be kept in mind when considering the frequent references to the issues of religious faith in today's Ukraine (see Section I of the general Introduction to this book).

I.2.e Austrians

As a result of the first partition of Poland in 1772, Western Ukraine (Galicia and Bukovyna) went to the Habsburg Empire, whereas the rest of Ukraine—including the other parts of Right-Bank Ukraine, went to the Russian Empire (Subtelny, 2009, pp. 177, 218–219). Between the end of the 18th century and the start of the 20th century, the West was associated with the Habsburg Empire in the Ukrainians' minds and the major route of Western influences in this country. Since the second half of the 19th century the Habsburg rule had elements of a constitutional monarchy, Western Ukrainians experienced democracy, participating in the parliamentary and local elections. In this institutional context Ukrainians created their first modern political parties (Reid, 2015, p. 72) and participated in a number of bottom-up non-political initiatives; namely, in a cooperative movement.

Western Ukrainians generally had highly positive associations with the Austrian rule, which may potentially explain the popularity of the 'Return to the West' slogan among them (see subsection II.5 below). This positive image must be taken with a grain of salt, however. The Austrian rulers faced multiple challenges trying to impose their control on the Poles who had lost their independent state. Since Galicia was populated by both Poles and Ukrainians, 'the Habsburg governor, Stadion, ... openly favored the Ukrainians throughout 1848 in hopes of using them as a counterweight to the more aggressive Poles' (Subtelny, 2009, p. 247). In other words, the Western Ukrainians' status of a 'best child' of the Habsburg Empire was highly circumstantial and politically motivated. It had less to do with the Austrian rulers' respect to or interest in the Western Ukrainians and their institutions than with geopolitical struggles.

I.2.f Russians

The 17th century national-liberation revolution concluded with the 1654 Treaty of Pereyaslav between the Cossacks and the Russian tsar. An attempt by Ukrainians to escape from the Polish lordship ended up with acceptance of the power of the other lords, the Russians. The Russian rule in Ukraine continued until the end of the 20th century, counting the Soviet period in Ukrainian history, i.e. it covers an entire historical epoch and may still not be completely over.

In contrast to the Western (Central and Eastern European) institutional model imposed in Ukraine by the Austrian and Polish rulers respectively, the Russian institutional model excludes the idea of a limited (constitutional) monarchy or a commonwealth. The Russian idea of the state does not tolerate republican and democratic elements in its organization. In this sense, the Russian state lies close to the German-style State discussed in Section II of Chapter 6 in more detail. Tendencies toward centralization and the authoritarian rule have characterised the Russian state from its origins (Kostomarov, 1861). This state embodies 'Russian power'—omnipresent, highly unequally distributed, self-justifiable, non-instrumental (power being an end in itself for its holders) and violent (Oleinik, 2011a, chapter 3). Cossacks got a chance to see what these features meant in practice very soon after signing the Treaty of Pereyaslav: their attempts to negotiate its terms failed, their efforts to make the Treaty binding led nowhere, and their expectation to have a limited power over them was broken. Moscow lieutenants, *voevodas,* flooded Ukraine soon thereafter. Hrushevsky (1996, p. 765) concludes: 'the Moscow government simply replaced the Warsaw government treating Cossacks in a similar manner'.

Hrushevsky may well have erred here. Both governments were foreign and alien indeed. But in one case the alien government had at least some democratic elements whereas in the other it did not. Cossacks and Ukrainians in general found themselves in a very uncomfortable situation of choosing between two unattractive alternatives: two evils. Not being able to build their own nation-state, Ukrainians were left with no other choice but to accept the rule of either one foreign power or the other. Subtelny attributes this binary thinking to the fact that Ukrainians were caught in the middle of geopolitical conflicts. In the 19th century, it was the fight between two empires, Russian and Austrian. 'Throughout 1848, [Western] Ukrainians found themselves supporting absolutism against Polish and Hungarian insurgents who, by and large, espoused liberal, democratic views' (Subtelny, 2009, p. 251).[25]

The mid-17th century revolution greatly contributed to the perception of Ukraine as a nation different from its Western neighbour, Poland. First attempts to clearly differentiate Ukrainians from their Eastern neighbours, the Russians, date to the 19th century. They were initiated by artists (namely, Taras Shevchenko, see Section II of Chapter 7) and historians (Hrushevsky, Kostomarov). However, this process is still ongoing. Violent acts inflicted by the Russian and Soviet rulers on the Ukrainian population in the past did not suffice to draw a clear boundary between 'Us' and Russians as 'Them' in the minds of Ukrainians, especially in Eastern Ukraine. For instance, Dmitry Yavornitsky (1992, p. 284) seems to excuse or at least to understand the cruelty of the Russian troops in Ukraine after the 1709 battle of Poltava as a confirmation for 'the well-known truth that wars between people of the same religious faith and of the same descent are the most violent and bloody, they can be compared with intra-family hatred'. In a sense, the events studied in this book—the 2013–2014 Revolution of Dignity and the subsequent defensive war with Russia—can be viewed as a decisive attempt to finally put an end to Ukraine's dependency on the Russian rulers.

25 The binary thinking has not disappeared since then. Ukraine's status as a hostage in geopolitical conflicts and the incompleteness of the Ukrainian nation-state contributed to its survival until recently, as discussed in Chapter 2.

I.2.g Independence

Ukraine's existence as an independent entity refers to a series of short moments in this country's history. Ukrainian historians pay particular attention to them nevertheless. They attempt to demonstrate that the 1991 declaration of independence was preceded by several other, equally important attempts to build a Ukrainian national state in the past. The list of candidates for the role of a Ukrainian national state or proto-state includes Kievan Rus', Galicia-Volhynia in the 13th century, the Cossack Hetmanate in the 17th century, and the Ukrainian Republic that existed at the start of the 20th century.

Kievan Rus' does not qualify for this role since, strictly speaking, this entity was not a national state. The Kievan rulers at best were hired expatriate managers. Furthermore, Russians also claim that Kievan Rus' was a predecessor of their national state in the making. Finally, 'there is no genetic link' between Kievan Rus' and Cossacks who also attempted to build a national state five centuries later (Hrushevsky, 1999, p. 58). According to Hrushevsky, successors to Kievan Rus' can be found elsewhere, in Galicia-Volhynia. This principality existed in the 13th century after the decline of Kiean Rus' embodying 'traditions of governance and public life started in Kievan Rus' as well as giving a second life to socio-political institutions and culture that it produced' (Hrushevsky, 1992, p. 1). Galicia-Volhynia was an important centre of power indeed and a real alternative to the nascent Russian institutional model that was materializing in the East, first in the Principality of Vladimir-Suzdal and then in the Grand Principality of Moscow. Two factors prevent a consideration of Galicia-Volhynia as a Ukrainian proto-nation-state. On one hand, its rulers accepted the status of vassals of the Mongols. On the other hand, no genetic link between Galicia-Volhynia and Cossacks existed either.

Cossacks did not have any immediate predecessors. Being a product of interactions with representatives of various cultures (Tatar, Russian, Polish, to cite just a few), Cossack culture and institutions had unique features. Over the course of almost two centuries, Cossackdom managed to produce a system of military organization and administration that could become a foundation of a Ukrainian autonomous state (Hrushevsky, 1996, p. 757; Subtelny, 2009, p. 178). But 'could' does not mean that it 'did'. The Hetmanate—the name of Cossacks' organisation—was an autonomous entity de facto, but not de jure. The Cossack leaders, starting with Khmelnitsky, wanted to find a powerful protector—either the Ottoman Empire, or the Russian Empire or the Kingdom of Sweden, in their fight with the Poles being unprepared to take the full responsibility not only for their country, but even for their fellow Cossacks.

The next notable attempt to achieve Ukraine's autonomous status occurred in 1917–1920, soon after the 1917 revolution in the Russian metropole. On November 22, 1917, the Ukrainian Republic issued the third 'universal' (decree) declaring the country's autonomous status (Subtelny, 2009, p. 350). Thus, the Ukrainian Republic was a first de jure Ukrainian state. Several factors do not allow considering the Ukrainian Republic as the autonomous entity both de jure and de facto. First, this state did not control all the Ukrainian lands. Nestor Makhno and his fellow 'anarchy Cossacks' controlled Ukraine's south (Shkirda, 2004, pp. 1–2). Second, the newly formed Ukrainian power elite—Subtelny (2009, p. 353) calls them 'the young Ukrainian Utopians'—appeared 'incapable of governing'. As a result, the central government failed to establish full control even over Central Ukraine, its formal stronghold. Subtelny (2009, p. 359) further observes that 'in the modern history of Europe no country experienced such complete anarchy, bitter civil strife, and total collapse of authority as did Ukraine at this time'. Third, because of its incapacity to govern, the Ukrainian government sought, similarly to the Cossacks leaders in the 17th century, a power protector. The government of General Pavlo Skoropadsky from an old Cossack family was brought to power by a coup engineered by the Germans. Needless to say, this government was incapable of implementing any independent policies.

In a way, the circumstances under which the 1991 declaration of Ukraine's independence was made were similar to the situation in 1917. The collapse of the metropole—this time it was the Soviet Union, created an opportunity for declaring Ukraine's independent status. This change in the country's status was not brought from within. 'In 1991 there was no revolution: there was a collapse', writes Subtelny (2009, p. 597). The post-Soviet power elite in Ukraine were not any better prepared for developing and implementing policies in an independent manner than their predecessors seventy years earlier. 'This largely modern society lacked… the traditions and institutions of self-government, decision-making, and policy formulation' (Ibid., p. 603). It would be safe to say that in the 1990s-2000s post-Soviet Ukraine, a de jure independent state, initiated a new attempt to build a de jure and de facto nation-state.

As this brief overview suggests, Ukraine had a dependent status and was ruled by the foreign powers most of the time in this country's history. The involvement of multiple and heterogeneous external powers, from the Mongols to the Austrians, and the fact that they controlled different parts of the Ukrainian lands (Southern, Western, Eastern and Central) shall be kept in mind when explaining persistent differences between Ukraine's macro-regions. Compared with the *long durée* of Ukraine's dependent status, this country's independence has been of *court durée*. Ukraine is a latecomer in terms of nation-state building, its nation-state is still in its childhood. According to a survey of foreign and Ukrainian experts conducted in 2012–2013, 100% of them perceived Ukraine as 'a state without a national idea and common identity' (Korostelina, 2014, p. 88). If this discourse was found to prevail among members of the Ukrainian elite twenty plus years after their country had become formally independent, does it follow that Ukraine's independence is nothing more than a myth?

II. Myths of the nation-state in the making

Even if Ukraine's independence was a myth, its persistence in and importance for Ukrainian historiography needs explaining. This question also prompts a broader discussion of the role that myths play in nation-state building, especially at the early stages of this process. Seen from a social constructivist perspective, myths may actually help people to construct the desired social reality. A similar reasoning lies at the origin of the Thomas theorem that stipulates: 'if men define situations as real, they are real in their consequences'

(Merton, 1995, p. 380). It follows that people's beliefs in myths count more than whether those myths have a real foundation or not. Furthermore, the origin of myths has no importance. In their capacity to have real consequences, the myths that originated inside of a community may not differ from the myths that came from other sources; for instance, were borrowed from outside and subsequently adapted to the local needs (Gambetta, 1991).

David Marples' (2007) attempts to argue that some assumptions on which Ukrainian historiography is based have more in common with myths than with historical 'facts' ignore the role of myths in constructing the social reality. If myths fail to have real consequences, this simply means that not enough people believe in them. Or, alternatively, if there is a critical mass of believers, their beliefs may not be strong enough to have real consequences.

Myths play an important role in nation-state building. After all, a nation-state can be thought of as the social reality organised in a particular manner. Anthony Smith (1991, p. 14; emphasis added) defines a nation 'as a named human population sharing an historic territory, *common myths and historical memories*, a mass, public culture, a common economy and common legal rights and duties for all members'. For this reason, every nation constructs myths and Ukrainians are no exception (Smith, 2002, p. 20; Smith, 2004, p. 19). Myths help their members 'define the foundations of their identity and system of values' (Plokhy, 2010, p. xvii; see also Kuzio, 1998, p. 121).

According to Smith, the reliance of East European nations on myth making tends to be heavier than in the case of the other European and North American nations. In contrast to Western Europeans and North Americans, who use a 'civic' model of nationhood, East Europeans and Asians lean toward an 'ethnic' model. The latter involves emphasis on 'genealogy, vernacular cultures (myths, customs, traditions), "ethno-history", [and] popular mobilisation' (Smith, 2002, p. 9). The Ukrainian nation in the making most likely follows the East European path, which explains the relevance of the listed elements to the case at hand. The Ukrainian nation will come into existence when its members accept a critical mass of myths of various kinds—historical (they underpin shared memories of the nation's past), war (they facilitate a clearer differentiation between Us and Them, see subsection I.2 of Chapter 10) and identity (they underpin shared beliefs about the nation's present and future).[26]

Historical myths are a speciality of historians. In addition to their purely academic studies, historians make and disseminate myths. In this respect, historians participate in nation-state building. 'Among Ukrainians, as well as other peoples, it was historians who were in the forefront of the nation-building process' (Subtelny, 2009, p. 226). Since Ukrainian historiography has faced fierce competition from Soviet, Russian and Polish historiographies of Ukraine, instead of a unique set of myths, several sets of myths regarding Ukraine's history co-exist. In these circumstances, changes in the political situation often lead to revising the myths that prevail at a particular moment in time. 'History textbooks… were completely rewritten several times: after the fall of the Soviet Union, the Orange Revolution of 2004, and the election of a new government in February 2010' (Korostelina, 2014, p. 79). Not all of these myths are compatible with the idea of the Ukrainian nation-state, which is our principal interest here.

Among the key myth-makers of historical myths of the Ukrainian nation are Kostomarov, Hrushevsky, Yavornitsky, perhaps Subtelny. The books 'of the Genesis of the Ukrainian people' written in the mid-19th century were likely a first comprehensive attempt to produce a mythology of the Ukrainian nation. Although their author has never been officially revealed, historians assume Kostomarov's authorship (see, for example, Plokhy, 2015, p. 158). These books as well as some subsequent writings of Kostomarov (1861) also show an interesting approach to making Ukrainian

26 Identity myths deserve separate discussion. Andrew Wilson (2002) identified several identity myths in the late 1990s: the myth of the Ukrainian Soviet nation, the myth of the regional identity in Donbas (according to this myth, the region of Donetsk is an urban melting-pot dissolving particularities of ethnicity and origin into a common labour culture), the myth of the southern regional identity (the perception of the region of Odesa as New Russia or European California) and so forth.

myths using Russian myths as a reference point.[27] In other words, they represent an early attempt to differentiate between Us and Them in the case of Ukrainians and Russians. As stated in the general Introduction, the Ukrainian and Russian cases are compared throughout this book.

Yitzhak Brudny and Evgeny Finkel (2011, p. 822) identify three myths that potentially constitute the foundation for shared memories of the Ukrainian nation about their past: the Cossack 'warrior democracy', the Austro-Hungarian legacy of Galicia (the myth of 'the return to the West'), and the short-lived Ukrainian independent state in 1917–1920. This list is not exhaustive since some other myths will also be discussed below. As a matter of fact, the myth of Cossackdom is an umbrella myth: it contains explicit or implicit references to a number of the other constitutive myths; namely, freedom as a core value; individualism, and even the myth of the return to the West mentioned before. The content analysis of the historical sources cited in this chapter confirms that the myth of Cossackdom occupies a central place in the Ukrainian mythology (Figure 1.2). First, Cossackdom was mentioned more often than the other myths (the larger the circle, the more mentions). Second, this myth lies right in the centre of the two-dimensional map of the coding co-occurrences, i.e. it co-occurred with the other myths in the same source relatively more frequently.

Ukrainian historians 'consider that the phenomenon of Cossackdom embodied the best characteristics of Ukrainians, which are supposedly reflected in the Cossack desire for freedom, independence, and a democratic way of life' (Magosci, 2010, p. 188). For instance, the myth of the return to the West may actually have deeper roots than the Habsburg period and go back to the Treaty of Hadiach signed by the successor of Khmelnitsky, Cossacks' Hetman Vigovsky, and the representatives of the Polish-Lithuanian

27 Russian historians and writers also have been making myths that could underpin Russians' shared memories of their past. Sergey Soloviev, Nikolay Karamzin, and Vasily Klyuchevsky are among key myth-makers in the Russian case. An attempt to produce a liberal version of myths about Russia's history was recently made by the writer Boris Akunin in his *History of the Russian State*.

Commonwealth in 1658. This Treaty reflects the Cossacks' disillusionment with the actual implementation of the 1654 Treaty of Pereyaslav with the Russian tsar. The Cossack leaders had a second thought and considered returning to the previously hated Poles, provided that Ukraine was given an autonomous status within the Polish-Lithuanian-Ukrainian Commonwealth. Subtelny's (2009, p. 144) assessment of this historical event suggests that its mythological aspects prevail over factual ones: 'although the Treaty of Hadiach has fascinated historians because of its potential impact on Ukrainian, Polish, and Russian history, its actual influence was minimal because it was never implemented'.

Figure 1.2 'Two-dimensional map of the coding co-occurrences in the historical documents cited in Chapter 1'

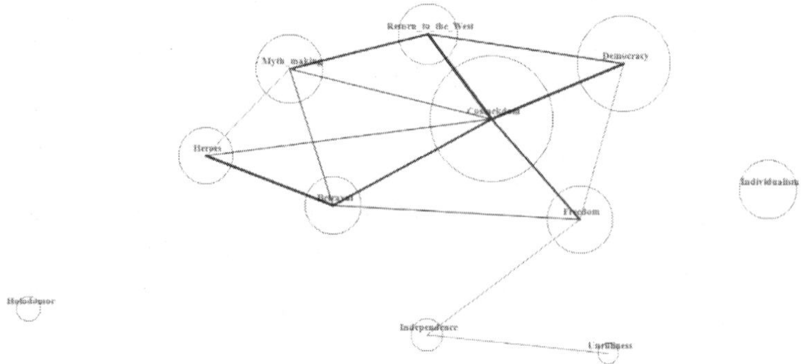

Legend: Stress 0.25, pseudo R^2=0.727. The closer codes lie on the map and the thicker the connecting lines, the more often the corresponding myths are mentioned in the same document.

II.1 Cossackdom

As stated previously, first mentions of Cossacks date to the end of the 15th century, when relationships between the population of the Ukrainian lands and the Crimean Tatars, who became vassals of the Ottoman Empire, deteriorated. The Tatars' raids necessitated a response and the emergence of Cossacks as border guards became one. Cossacks were stationed in towns located across the border between the steppe and the forested area of Ukraine (it started north of today's Cherkasy). Hrushevsky (1993, p. 337) says that Cossacks were first mentioned in 1495, Yavornitsky (1991, p. 337) claims to find a first reference to Cossacks dated 1492.[28] Kostomarov (1861, p. 47) holds even a more radical view, insisting that first mentions of Cossacks can be found as early as in the 12th-13th centuries, but his theory of linking Cossacks to the descendants of one group of the Turks, the 'Black Hats' (*chorni klobuky*), did not find much support among the other historians.

Within the timeframe of one and a half centuries, Cossacks made a remarkable evolution from a loosely organised network of small bands composed of people representing various walks of life (fugitives from the masters or the families, foreigners, including the Tatars, representatives of the nobility, the youth searching for glory and so forth) to a group with its own government, the Hetmanate, and ambitions to establish a state. By the mid-17th century, 'the Cossacks, who had come into existence on the margins of society,... were now thinking about creating a state of their own' (Plokhy, 2015, p. 100; see also Magosci, 2010, p. 251; Subtelny, 2009, p. 116).

The fact that the Cossacks tackled the issue of state-building makes them a perfect candidate for the role of first builders of the Ukrainian nation-state from within. At the same time, the process of state-building also appeared to be highly divisive. Not all Cossacks wanted to be associated with a state, regardless of its nature. Two major categories of Cossacks, Zaporozhian, or 'unregistered', and Ukrainian, or 'registered', held opposite views on the state. The first valued freedom and independence, the second served the government, initially Polish and then Russian, after an unsuccessful effort to create their own state. The adjectives 'registered' and 'unregistered' refer to the Cossack's status either as a state servant receiving a salary or a 'freelancer' selling the service of protection on a

28 The administration of the Museum of Cossackdom in Zaporizhia seems to give more credit to Yavornitsky than to Hrushevsky. At least a calendar devoted to the 500 year anniversary of Cossackdom was printed in 1992.

case by case basis. Institutions and values of the two groups diverged to a significant extent. Unregistered Cossacks leaned toward anarchy, whereas registered Cossacks to some extent accepted statism. The 'hard core' of unregistered Cossacks lived on the island of Khortytsia in Zaporizhia ('below the rapids' on the Dnieper River), which explains their name. The relative size of the two groups varied, but unregistered Cossacks generally outnumbered their registered fellows. For instance, by 1589, there were 3,000 registered Cossacks and 40,000–50,000 unregistered (Subtelny, 2009, p. 111).

II.1.a Zaporozhian Cossacks

Cossacks slowly extended southward the territory under their control. By the mid-16th century they went beyond the rapids and settled on the island of Khortytsia. They were led by the Prince Dmytro (Baida) Vyshnevets'kyi, which further confirms the social heterogeneity of Cossackdom (Yavornitsky, 1990, p. 61). Even though chronologically Zaporozhian Cossacks emerged later than Ukrainian Cossacks, the former quickly became the guardians of original Cossack values, traditions and institutions (Subtelny, 2009, p. 153).

The value of brotherhood had a terminal character for Cossacks. They perceived themselves as knights similar to the knights of Malta: being a Cossack meant for them to be admitted to knighthood. For this reason, all other loyalties—to the family, to the loved one, to the other social groups—were sacrificed in favour of a superior loyalty to the fellow Cossacks. Some taboos that existed among Cossacks can be better understood in this light. Namely, women were not allowed to enter/visit the Cossacks' permanent camp in Khortytsia, *Sich* (Hrushevsky, 1999, p. 230). The Cossacks believed that a married man would place the interests of his wife and family ahead of those of the fellow 'knights'. The status of being married made the Cossack ineligible for any elected post (Yavornitsky, 1990, pp. 131, 138, 181–183). 'The male specialness of the Cossack group was vital to maintaining its intensity as a community, undivided in moments of need by family loyalties' (Gordon, 1983, p. 83).[29]

The military and administrative organisation of Zaporozhian Cossacks also had more authentically Cossack features than that of Ukrainian Cossacks. In short, this organisation can be labelled 'warrior democracy' (see also subsection II.4 below). Basic fraternities—*kureni*—formed a federation rather than a hierarchical organisation. Cossacks from the same Ukrainian land formed a *kuren'*. Its members regularly elected their head, *kurinnyi otaman*. All the *kureni* constituted a *kosh*, the Cossack body living in the *Sich*. The *kosh* leader, *koshovyi otaman*, was also elected on a regular basis.

Cossacks borrowed some names and organisational ideas from the Tatars, the most regular counterparts, creatively adapting them to their needs and local circumstances (Yavornitsky, 1991, p. 43). For instance, when deciding the organisation of the *kosh*, the Cossacks were likely inspired by the practice common among the Tatars who pulled their sheep together entrusting them to the care of the most experienced shepherd among them. The sheep owners held 'shares' of this common enterprise (Yavornitsky, 1990, pp. 58–59). The organisational form initially used exclusively in the context of agriculture, was adapted by Cossacks to their military and administrative needs. In other words, the *kosh* was a union created in the interests of common wealth, and, thus, can be compared with the commonwealth as a form of political and administrative organisation (see Chapter 6 for more detail).

II.1.b Ukrainian Cossacks

Cossacks on the payroll (*reestr*) of the Polish crown, the registered Cossacks, had several privileges compared with unregistered Cossacks. In addition to regularly paid allowances, the government also formally granted full freedom to registered Cossacks within

---

29 Not surprisingly, the cult of masculinity characterised the Cossack culture. Possible parallels between the cowboy figure and the Cossack figure were mentioned in the general Introduction to this book. The parallels do not end at a symbolical level. Both the cowboy culture (Kamir, 2006) and the Cossack culture are highly masculine.

their jurisdictions, whereas unregistered Cossacks were subject to 'the usual jurisdiction of their lords and *starostas*', heads of the local administration reporting to the Crown (Hrushevsky, 1999, p. 378). In practice, this meant that registered Cossacks had their own administration, including judicial. A registered Cossack could be judged by the other registered Cossacks only. Furthermore, the scope of registered Cossacks' administration extended beyond their own ranks. A colonel 'served as both the supreme military and the supreme civil authority in his territory' populated by registered Cossacks with their families and civilians (Magosci, 2010, p. 247). The division between registered and unregistered Cossacks was first formalised by King Stephen Báthory in the early 1580s (Yavornitsky, 1991, p. 14) and maintained by the Polish kings since that time.

The maximum number of registered Cossacks was set by the Crown in consultation with the Diet. A permanent shortage of funds, along with the fear that Cossacks would become too powerful and independent, resulted in a regular mismatch between the number of Cossacks willing to get the official status and the number of places in the register. Those excluded from the register normally went southward and joined the ranks of Zaporozhian Cossacks (Yavornitsky, 1991, p. 43). Their feeling of being excluded by the government has to be taken into account when explaining unregistered Cossacks' drift into anarchism and 'unruliness' (see subsections II.2 and II.6 below). All state-building initiatives within the Hetmanate were carried out by registered Cossacks—more specifically, by their top leaders, *starshina*. Unregistered Cossacks did not participate in those initiatives persistently resisting them (Tairova-Yakovleva, 2011, p. 178). It is likely for this reason that some Ukrainian historians, known for their statist position, starting with Hrushevsky, tended to underestimate the contribution of unregistered Cossacks in the building of the Ukrainian nation (see, for example, his account of the war between the Cossack *starshina* and Zaporozhian Cossacks after the death of Khmelnitsky; Hrushevsky, 1958). The heterogeneous character of Cossackdom allows both proponents of a strong state and anarchists find inspiration in this myth when discussing alternative routes of nation-state building.

II.2 Freedom

Two institutions, the traditional Ukrainian community, *hromada*, and Cossackdom, underpin freedom as a terminal value in Ukrainian culture. Comparing the *hromada* with the traditional Russian community, *obshchina*, Kostomarov (1861, pp. 64, 74) emphasises that members of the former had much greater degrees of freedom than members of the latter. Members of *hromada* had the rights of free entry and free exit. In a similar manner, Zaporozhian Cossacks had the freedom to join or to leave the *Sich* at will (Yavornitsky, 1990, p. 122). When Ukrainian peasants believed that joining a *hromada* benefit their interests, they became members. Even after joining the *hromada*, the peasant kept his property and autonomy. A parallel between a traditional Ukrainian institution, *hromada*, and the institution of commonwealth can be drawn one more time. *Hromada* had some features of a joint-stock company, in contrast to *obshchina* membership, which was ascribed and difficult to change.

In contrast to Zaporozhian *kosh*, *hromada* had more balanced relations between genders. Gender discrimination most likely existed (this issue did not attract enough attention of Ukrainian historiography), but women certainly enjoyed some freedoms that Ukrainian men had. Namely, the degree of sexual freedom of young women in Ukraine was more significant than in Russia, especially before they married. Both young men and young women were expected to have sexual experience before marriage. Women's early sexual experience was not only tolerated but encouraged in a sense (Plokhy, 2015, pp. 20–21; Tairova-Yakovleva, 2011, p. 238). Women enjoyed sexual liberties even at the time of Kievan Rus' (Hrushevsky, 1992b, pp. 385–387), which suggests the presence of a continuous pattern in Ukrainian history.

A deep appreciation of freedom by Cossacks was mentioned previously. The registered Cossack knew no authority over him but the *starshina* (Hrushevsky, 1999, p. 62). The unregistered Cossack acted under fewer restraints, since his superiors did not have many prerogatives of the *starshina* and could be changed easier from below. Traditions of libertarianism and anarchism naturally tended to be stronger among Zaporozhian Cossacks. Even the destruction of the *Sich* in 1775 by the orders of Russian Empress Ekaterina II did not undermine the appeal of these traditions to the now dispersed Cossacks and their descendants. Southern Ukraine in general, and the region of Zaporizhia in particular, remained a stronghold of anarchism until the end of the 20th century. Huliaipole, a town near Zaporizhia, became the capital of Makhno around the 1920s when Makhno and his fellow 'anarchy Cossacks' undertook an attempt to build a society according to anarchist principles (Shkirda, 2004, p. 85) that remains without precedent elsewhere. In an overview of the state of anarchism in the Soviet Union in the 1980s-1990s, references to the events and anarchist groups in the cities of Dnipro (Makhno briefly controlled this large industrial centre) and Zaporizhia are more frequent than mentions of the other places in Ukraine (Dubovik, 2016).

It follows that negative aspects prevail in the definition of Cossacks' freedom over positive ones: the lack of restraints, the absence of all the material and moral oppression by the social hierarchy, the lack of executive power over them (Hrushevsky, 1999, p. 38) and so forth. In these circumstances, the concept of freedom *from* seems to be more appropriate than the concept of freedom *to* (see Section II of Chapter 2). The absence of constraints does not necessarily enable one to get what he or she desires, which is the essence of freedom *to*.

In the final account, one's incapacity to achieve freedom *to* may potentially undermine this subject's freedom *from*. The case of Zaporozhian Cossacks serves as an illustration. Their love for freedom did not exclude their loyalty to the Russian tsar. 'Ordinary Cossacks ideally wanted to keep the freedoms of their ancestors, but under the patronage of the "benevolent and caring" Russian monarch' (Yavornitsky, 1992, p. 250). As a matter of fact, libertarian Zaporozhian Cossacks were more loyal to the Russian tsars than admittedly less freedom loving Ukrainian Cossacks. This example suggests that freedom involves trade-offs and has a price—we will return to this issue in Chapter 2.

II.3 Individualism

The concept of individualism in the cited sources constitutes a separate one-member cluster (Figure 1.2). However, it lies closer to Freedom and Democracy than to the other concepts. A high value attached to freedom in Ukrainian culture goes together with a high degree of individualisation. Hrushevsky (1992b, p. 372) finds first manifestations of the tendency toward individualisation in Kievan Rus'. Discussing various forms of punishment used at that time, he finds a surprisingly infrequent use of corporal punishment. Corporal punishments prevailed over detention and fines in Europe in that epoch (Foucault, 1975). One of the functions of the law in Kievan Rus' (*Russkaia Pravda*) was to protect honour, penalising such acts as detention without legal process, slander and public insults (e.g., a slap in the face) heavier than the infliction of material or physical damages (see Chapter 7 for further discussion of honour and human dignity).

Continuing the comparison of the two forms of traditional communities, historians of Ukraine oppose the individualism of members of the Ukrainian *hromada* to the collectivism of members of the Russian *obshchina*.[30] One's participation in a *hromada* did not exclude the priority of the individual interests over the interests of the *hromada* as a group. Since the *hromada* can be compared to a joint-stock company or a commonwealth, it creates an environment in which individualism prevails over collectivism without excluding the latter as a complement to the former.

At any moment, the Ukrainian peasants could reconsider their involvement in the *hromada* and create an economic and social unit, on the basis of the household, *khutor*, that would be independent and geographically separated from the *hromada*. In the mid-19th century, over 85% of the peasants in Right-Bank Ukraine and almost 70% in Left-Bank Ukraine worked individual homesteads

30 The values of Hofstede's individualism index in Ukraine reportedly remain higher than in Russia up to now (Pilipenko, 2013). This index aims to measure 'the relationship between the individual and the collectivity in human society' (Hofstede, 1980, p. 214) and helps differentiate two types of culture, collectivist and individualist.

(Subtelny, 2009, p. 256). The *khutor* is a family enterprise par excellence (Kostomarov, 1861, p. 79). According to Kostomarov (Ibid., p. 74), the process of individualisation did not stop even there and continued within the Ukrainian family. 'The principle "to each his own" applies within the family: not only do the adults not borrow clothes from one another, even kids have their personal belongings'. By contrast, the *obshchina* as a group 'suppressed the individuality' of its members (Ibid., p. 48).

The geography and particularities of the natural environment may be among factors conducive to the relatively high degree of individualism in Ukrainian culture. Subtelny (2009, p. 5; see also Pipes, 1974, p. 16) hypothesises that 'in the Russian north, the barren, sandy soil, the harsh climate, and the shorter growing season—by at least a month compared to Ukraine—forced Russian peasants to pool their resources and to work the land communally'.

II.4 Democracy

The myth of democracy as an integral part of the Ukrainian national consciousness has two historical roots: the institution of *Viche* that existed in Kievan Rus' and has been revived several times since then, and the institution of *Rada*, a key element of Cossacks' warrior democracy. The modern Ukrainian Parliament, *Verkhovna Rada*, inherited this name.

II.4.a Viche

Two centres of power co-existed in Kievan Rus', a public gathering of the city dwellers, *Viche*, and the Prince, with his court and his army, *druzhina*. In Kievan Rus' all inhabitants of a city could come to the place of a public gathering and participate in a *Viche* regardless of their social origin (Kluchevsky, 1956, p. 192; see also Section III of Chapter 3). The division of powers between the two centres of decision-making was not quite elaborated, but one certainly counter-balanced the other. The *Viche* invited a particular Prince to serve as the ruler, concluded a contract with him, *riad*, and had the power to terminate the Prince's tenure in the case of his unsatisfactory performance (Hrushevsky, 1992b, p. 211). This led to the emergence of a simple yet functioning system of checks and balances.

The Prince's power was not absolute for several reasons. First, the Prince's discretion was limited by certain conditions set by the *Viche* when sending him an invitation to serve or accepting his offer of services. Second, the Prince's power did not have a 'divine' character. The Orthodox Christianity was imported to Kievan Rus' from Byzantium where power of a ruler was believed to be sacred and given by God. However, this belief became neither popular nor widely accepted in Kievan Rus' (Hrushevsky, 1992b, p. 227; Kostomarov, 1861, p. 58). Third, Kievan Rus' was not a centralised state, having more in common with a federation (Hrushevsky, 1992b, p. 207; Kostomarov, 1861, pp. 48, 64). The principalities that formed the 'federation' had a significant degree of autonomy, their own Princes and their own *Viches*.

The traditions of *Viche* did not disappear with the disintegration of Kievan Rus' into a number of loosely connected (if connected at all) principalities and republics. The Novgorod Republic in the 13th-14th centuries kept and further developed the democratic traditions inherited from the time of Kievan Rus' (Kostomarov, 1861, pp. 43, 46). The Novgorod Republic embodied a viable alternative to the model of unlimited power—Russian power, that was emerging and strengthening in the Principality of Vladimir-Suzdal and the Great Principality of Moscow around the same period of time.

The population of the Ukrainian lands subsequently revived the institution of *Viche* on several occasions, when opportunities for democratic decision-making arose. For instance, Western Ukrainians organised several *Viches* both in the cities and the countryside during the 1905–1906 election campaign to elect the members of the 11th Imperial Council of Cisleithania within Austria-Hungary (Subtelny, 2009, p. 328). One of the most recent revivals of the institution of *Viche* occurred in Kyiv and several other Ukrainian cities during the 2013–2014 mass protests (see Chapter 3 for more detail).

However, the strengths of democratic traditions associated with the institution of *Viche* shall not be exaggerated. The *Viche* did not interfere with the day-to-day exercise of power by the Princes. The *Viche* was reluctant even to exercise its core functions of selecting the Princes and enforcing contracts with them. Hrushevsky (1992b, pp. 211–212) calculated that in the 11th-12th centuries the community—*hromada*—participated in the selection of the ruler in 14 cases out of 40 when the Prince changed. The *Viche* proposed its own candidate on 3 to 5 occasions only. He concludes that the Kyivans may have simply wanted to find a Prince that would spare them from the need to participate in politics and governance altogether. 'The alpha and omega of political aspirations of the Kyivan *hromada* was to find a Prince who would take loving care of the entire Russian land. If such a Prince was found, this would be a remedy for all problems that Kyiv faced. The Prince of this kind would be entrusted to carry all business on his own with no input from the community. This was an ideal of the society at that time',—writes Hrushevsky (1992a, p. 295) lamenting that his 'contemporary Ukrainian society tends to have a similar one'. This observation made by Hrushevsky in the early 20th century, when he worked on the second volume of his *History of Ukraine-Rus'*, may well remain valid as of the time of writing this book.

II.4.b Rada: the institution of military democracy

The process of decision-making in Cossackdom also had elements of democracy. All matters of public importance were to be discussed publicly, with the involvement of the interested parties. Cossacks created the institution of *Rada* (council), their general meeting. As a matter of fact, there were *Rady* at each level of the organizational structure of Cossackdom: *kuren'*, the Cossacks' leaders (*starshina*), the Zaporozhian Cossacks' *kosh,* and the registered Cossacks' entire military body. Even pupils in the *Sich* (they learned Cossacks' military art and basics of literacy) had their own *Rada* (Yavornitsky, 1990, p. 147). Participants in these deliberations formed a circle, which aimed to highlight an equal weight given to everyone's opinion. This arrangement explains the other name under which the institution of *Rada* is also known, Cossacks' *kolo,* or circle (Hrushevsky, 1999, p. 222).

Yavornitsky considers the *Rada* as a direct descendant of the *Viche*. He draws an explicit parallel between these two institutions. 'Zaparozhian Cossacks' worldview was based on their community (*hromada*), brotherhood. The Cossacks' community is based on the same principles of people's rule (*narodnopravstvo*) as in Kievan Rus' or in Pskov and Novgorod in the North of Russia. What the ringing of the bell did in the North, was achieved with the help of drums in the South.[31] After hearing the sound of drums, all people, regardless of their rank and social status, headed to the central place to decide the issues of importance for them, in the same manner as free citizens of the Swiss cantons or the American states do today. The *Rada*, the people's *Viche*, was the embodiment of the Cossacks' community' (Yavornitsky, 1990, p. 139). Similar to the *Viche*, the *Rada* limited the discretion of the Cossacks' rulers, their *starshina*. All holders of administrative positions in Cossackdom had to get elected at the *Rada* on a regular basis (Tairova-Yakovleva, 2011, p. 318). Yavornitsky (1990, p. 139) concludes that in Cossackdom 'three factors put limits on the power: regular reporting, time [the limited length of the tenure] and the *Rada*'.

Other Ukrainian historians tend to be more skeptical about the existence of genetic links between the *Rada* and the *Viche*. These two institutions may be similar since they embody principles of archaic, spontaneous democracy. Indeed, both shared the same shortcomings. For instance, 'there was no exact count of votes or identification of a majority—it was assessed by sight. There were no forms of representation' either (Hrushevsky, 1999, p. 222). Linda Gordon, who based her study on the Polish sources, goes even further, arguing that the *Rada* shall be better understood through the lens of Cossacks' individualism. 'The *Rada*... stemmed less from an implicit or embryonic democratic principle than from an individualistic, anti-statist (or historically pre-nation-state) principle' (Gordon, 1983, p. 84). For this reason, she doubts if Cossacks managed to

31 See Picture 3.1 in Chapter 3.

build a democracy however imperfect it might be, preferring to label their system of governance as 'dictatorship tempered by mob intervention' (Ibid., p. 87).[32]

This conceptualisation of Cossacks' system of governance ignores the existence of the three constraints of the power mentioned previously: regular reports, time and the *Rada*. If mob intervention is to be added to this list (see also Kostomarov, 1861, p. 50), then as a fourth constraint in addition to the first three. At the same time, Cossacks' adherence to principles of direct democracy was a serious obstacle to the creation of more complex and stable forms of governance. Direct democracy worked relatively well at the micro- and meso- levels, with the number of parties involved not exceeding several dozen (*kuren'*, *sotnya*—the 'hundred'[33]—Cossacks' basic military unit). At the higher levels of the social and military organisation, direct democracy created more problems than it solved, indeed. Cossacks' inability to move from direct to representative democracy is probably a key explanation for the failure of their entire project, both in military terms and in the terms of nation-state building.

One reason for Cossacks' lack of progress can be found in particularities of their principal occupation—their involvement in low-intensity warfare with the Crimean Tatars and the Ottoman Turks (during their highly successful sea raids to Constantinople and the Black Sea southern shores). Hrushevsky (1999, p. 102) writes that 'harrying the Tatars was their specialty'. The Cossacks' hundred—a military unit composed of up to one hundred Cossacks—was the

---

32 Some elements of 'dictatorship tempered by mob intervention' also existed in the Roman Republic that preceded the Roman Empire. According to Machiavelli, the Roman people's desire not to be dominated by the nobles had weak of any institutional materialization at that time. Nevertheless, the development of an 'antagonistic' political culture and several safeguards against the elite's desire to dominate, such as accusations and plebiscites, produced a version of Republicanism weakly rooted in the institutions of representative democracy (McCormick, 2001). Despite its imperfections, the elites in the Roman Republic were to a significant extent made responsive to or held accountable by the people.

33 The basic unit of the protesters' organisation during the 2013–2014 Revolution of Dignity had the same name.

optimal organisation in those circumstances. The hundred 'suited the best for small encounters with the Tatars' (Yavornitsky, 1990, p. 266). When the Cossacks confronted regular troops, for instance, the Poles, their rate of success was significantly lower. Namely, during the mass uprising of the mid-17th century, the Cossacks, led by Khmelnitsky, scored only one clear victory, near Zhovti Vody in 1648 (Hruschevsky, 1956b, p. 186). In the other campaigns and battles, even when the Cossacks with their then allies—the Crimean Tatars, emerged victorious, they often were unable to capitalise on the success. For instance, the Cossacks formally won the battle of Zboriv in 1649, but appeared unprepared to make the next strategic, as opposed to purely tactical, moves (Hrushevsky, 1956c, pp. 93–101). The lack of managerial skills and, thus, coordination at the macro-level, and the Cossack leaders' incapacity to 'think big' were likely to be blamed. The experience of the small-scale guerilla border war simply left the Cossacks unprepared to face challenges of large-scale coordination.

The Cossacks' successors, the Makhnovists, followed a similar pattern. They were successful in solving coordination problems at the micro- and meso- levels without being able to replicate this success at the macro-level, i.e. in large-scale military operations. In Makhno's army, the basic unit of the size of the Cossacks' hundred was always locally based (Shkirda, 2004, p. 79). Its leader, the 'father' (*bat'ko*) was democratically elected. Makhno's army achieved remarkable victories in the guerilla war against both the Reds, who fought for the communist government, and the Whites, who fought for the *ancien régime*. The Makhnovists' successes in a large-scale war against the Red Army were less than impressive.[34]

---

34 A similar pattern can be observed in the ongoing (as of the time of writing) undeclared war waged against Ukraine by Russia. Ukrainian volunteer fighters (and even the regular Ukrainian troops) established a remarkable reputation in the low-intensity military confrontation of 2015–2016. However, their performance during large-scale military operations, for instance, the 2014 battle of Ilovaisk or the 2015 battle of Debaltseve, was far less impressive. In the latter case, the lack of large-scale coordination played its negative role one more time in Ukraine's history.

The Cossacks and their successors' inability to move from direct military democracy to representative democracy led to the emergence of the gaps between, on one hand, the leadership, and, on the other hand, the rank-and-file.[35] The Cossack leaders simply did not have a strong position in negotiations with the potential allies or actual enemies, being unsure whether they could subsequently be able to 'sell' the deal to the Cossack mass. The 1649 Zboriv Treaty is a case in point. After failing to capitalise on the victory in the battle of Zboriv, Khmelnitsky and the other Cossack *starshina* concluded less than a perfect agreement with the Poles. This agreement would have likely been simply rejected by the Cossacks, which led their leaders not to reveal all its clauses. Khmelnitsky's 'only hope was that changing circumstances may invalidate the obligations he took when signing the Zboriv Treaty' (Hrushevsky, 1956c, p. 227).[36] Hrushevsky's (1999, pp. 435–436) observation that 'agreements with the Cossacks had always been concluded more for the sake of appearances and had never been rigorously implemented' can be better understood in this context. Agreements become binding and enforceable when the signatories have a clear mandate to sign them and can be held responsible for their implementation before their respective constituencies.

---

35 Similar gaps characterise democratic institutions in some Latin American countries, for example, Venezuela. The existing institutions allow and even promote large political participation without creating channels and means for articulating demands and, what is even more important, for reconciling them with the elite's interests. This leads to 'the political system's inability to reconcile intense political action from the grassroots to the conflicting demands of elite politics' (Curato, 2014, p. 114).

36 Difficulties with the implementation of the 2015 Minsk agreement ('Minsk II') between Ukraine, Russia, Germany and France may have a similar origin: its exact terms have not been fully disclosed and the Ukrainian President, Petro Poroshenko, has had a difficult task to 'sell' it to the Ukrainians since the very beginning.

II.5 Return to the West

Western Ukraine was a birthplace of this myth, being at the forefront of the Western influences on Ukraine's institutions. The Western influences spread in Ukraine via two routes: Poland (Hruschevsky, 1992b, p. 501) and Austro-Hungary. Only the latter left unambiguously positive associations in the Ukrainian consciousness, as discussed before. The idea of returning to Europe had supposedly more chances to get good reception if it implied the Austrian connection. 'Nationalists, mostly from ex-Austro-Hungarian Galicia, adopted the "Return to Europe" slogan, as a counterweight to the supposedly Asiatic nature of Tsarist Russia and the USSR' (Brudny & Finkel, 2011, p. 822).

Whatever the implied connection is, there are several obstacles to the reaching of the status of a national myth as opposed to a regional myth by the idea of the 'Return to Europe'. On one hand, attempts to implement Western institutions without first creatively adapting them to the local conditions in the past have been counterproductive: instead of promoting socio-economic development, they suppressed it. On the other hand, the satisfaction of some Western Ukrainians with playing the role of a pupil of the West has some similarities with Little Russianism, the attitude taken by some Eastern Ukrainians vis-à-vis Russia and its culture. The same Western Ukrainians strongly criticised this attitude.

In Ukraine of the 14th-17th centuries, the institutional environment of the urban life in general, and the organisation of crafts and trade in particular, followed the Western European canon. The Polish government and nobles saw fit in importing the German models on Ukrainian soil, hoping to get an additional source of income with their help. Medieval Ukrainian cities lived under Magdeburg Law, supposedly the most progressive at that time. However, outcomes of the implementation of this legal framework were rather disappointing even from a purely fiscal point of view. 'Urban crafts and trade, the urban economic life in general, declined instead of flourishing' (Hrushevsky, 1995, p. 141). Hrushevsky (Ibid., p. 139) attributes this result to the unwillingness or incapacity to adapt the Western institutions to the local conditions; to take into consideration the national and religious particularities of Ukraine.

A similar situation emerged in the late 16th-17th centuries in Ukrainian agriculture. This period was characterised by a rapid growth of demand for agricultural products in the countries of Western and Norther Europe. It seemed that Ukraine as a country rich in natural resources was well positioned to tap into a new source of potential growth. The growing demand for agricultural products did not really benefit the Ukrainian economy, however. Instead of 'creating conditions for a balanced development of agriculture, urban crafts and trade, instead of helping achieve an equilibrium between the production of raw materials and their processing, [this growing demand] led to a forced and unilateral exploitation of Ukraine's resources for export' (Ibid., pp. 168–169; see also Chapter 9).

The expectation that the mere adaptation of institutions of a more developed culture could solve all problems is indicative of Little Russianism or Little Europeanism—depending on which culture serves as a model for institutional importation. Little Russianism is known relatively better. The Little Russian mentality involves the acceptance of 'a "little brother" role in the building of the Tsarist and Soviet empires' (Kuzio, 1998, p. 155). A similar mentality probably exists when one tends to uncritically perceive European culture and its institutions. The Little European adapts a consumerist posture and expects that the adaptation of the European institutional model will suffice for improving his or her quality of life. Subtelny (2009, pp. 218–219) describes the 19th century 'rutenstvo' in similar terms, as an uncritical endorsement of the institutions and practices of the Habsburg Empire. Hrushevsky (1956b, p. 99), who worked in Lviv in the late 19th—the early 20th century, observed some Western Ukrainians' obsession 'to have everything that the Poles have so there is nothing that could indicate the Ukrainians' inferior status vis-à-vis the Poles'.

Neither Little Russianism nor Little Europeanism offers an efficient protection of Ukrainians' national interests. It would be at least unwise to expect that someone will promote and protect these interests if Ukrainians themselves are unable to do so. National interests come first, especially if they conflict the other nation's interests. Expectations that the Europeans would put the other nation's interests first were broken on several occasions in the past. For instance, in the 15th century, the citizens of the Novgorod Republic in vain hoped that Casimir IV, the Grand Duke of Lithuania, with whom they concluded a treaty of mutual cooperation and security, would honour his promise and help them to counter the aggression of Ivan III, the Grand Duke of Moscow. The situation changed and the Lithuanians' best interests were not to get involved in this war (Hrushevsky, 1993, p. 275; see also Chapter 5 discussing a more recent similar case).

II.6 Unruliness

The myth of the 'unruliness' of Ukrainians has roots in Polish historiography. This word is especially common in the Polish sources of the 17th century (Hrushevsky amply cites them in the relevant volumes of his *History of Ukraine-Rus'*). For example, he cited an expression that became common in Poland in the 1630s: in Ukraine '*swawola* rules' (Hrushevsky, 1956a, p. 128). *Swawola* in Polish means unruliness, lawlessness and anarchy (Hrushevsky, 1999, p. 412). The association of Zaporozhian Cossacks with unruliness tended to be particularly strong, whereas registered Cossacks were perceived by the Poles as less 'unruly'. The irony of the situation is that exactly around the same time, Polish society also progressively drifted into 'unruliness'. Participants of the *Sejm* used and abused their right of veto more and more often, thus preventing these assemblies from making any decisions. Between 1652, when the first *Sejm* was dissolved as a result of using the right of veto by a minority, and 1764, 48 *Sejms* were dissolved out of 55 (Hrushevsky, 1994, p. 325).

The idea of unruliness does not necessarily have exclusively negative connotations. It can be used not only as a negative label but also as an element of the positively, as opposed to normatively, constructed Ukrainian national identity.[37] The latter requires studying the context in which Ukrainians developed a distaste for orderliness and subordination—whatever grounds this subordination may have. On one side, Cossacks—these ideal-typical Ukrainians—emerged if not in the no-man's lands but certainly in the no-state's lands. The borderlands, their home, were initially outside of the control of any state—Polish, Russian or Ottoman. Central Ukraine in the 14th-16th centuries was 'a boundless area with no government or control and excepted from the regular system of law enforcement and state administration' (Hrushevsky, 1995, p. 287).

When attempts to establish some rule of law were finally made in the late 16th-18th century, it was the Polish law, i.e. the legal system totally disconnected from the local traditions and institutions. In other words, the state and the law were perceived as alien and imposed since the origins of Cossackdom, which explains 'the Cossacks' permanent opposition to the state order and social regime of Poland' (Hrushevsky, 1999, p. 60). In these circumstances, the Cossack was first and foremost an 'insubordinate man' (Ibid., p. 206).

To summarise, the particularities of the institutional environment in which Cossackdom emerged and was strengthened have to be taken into account when making sense of Cossacks' drift into the unruliness and the rejection of power. Cossacks' *svavillia* (the Ukrainian term for *swawola*) is the exact opposite of *samovlastie* in Russian culture (Oleinik, 2011a, pp. 108–109). *Samovlastie* involves one's unrestricted rule over the others that does not require any justification. One of the meanings attached to *svavillia* refers to the resolution to act disregarding the will and interests of the others. The absolute power in the former case finds its exact opposite, the absolute rejection of any power, in the latter. This tendency to reject

37 Milton Friedman (1966, p. 4) defines a normative approach as a study of 'what ought to be' and a positive approach as a study of 'what is'. In the case at hand, a positive approach to studying the Ukrainian national identity answers the question of 'what this identity is' instead of inquiring what 'this identity ought to be'.

power constitutes an important obstacle to the transition from freedom *from* to freedom *to* in Ukraine, since it involves the rejection of not only violence but also of power as human capacity to act in concert altogether.

II.7 Betrayal

In contrast to the previously discussed myth, the myth of betrayal is embedded in Russian historiography and political discourse. Its origins go back to the 1709 battle of Poltava. The Cossacks switched sides on the eve of the battle, joining the troops of Charles VII instead of fighting against them with Peter I. Peter I can be considered as a creator of this myth or at least he personally contributed to its making (Plokhy, 2015, p. xx). That the Cossacks led by their Hetman Ivan Mazepa switched sides is an established fact, not a myth. However, the Cossacks may well have good reasons for switching sides. One way to understand their decision is to place it in the context of the Cossacks' endless fight for their freedom and autonomy (as suggested even by the position of the code 'Betrayal' in the proximity of the codes 'Cossackdom', 'Freedom', 'Independence' and 'Heroes' on Figure 1.2).

As explained previously, the Cossacks considered the 1654 Treaty of Pereyaslav as a mutually binding agreement. The list of departures of the Russian tsars from their contractual obligations by 1709 grew rather long, from the Cossacks' point of view (Subtelny, 2009, p. 147; Tairova-Yakovleva, 2011, pp. 320–330). The Russian tsars did not honour their promise to respect and protect the Cossack's old liberties, progressively imposing on them the same centralised system of governance as elsewhere in the nascent Russian empire. Peter I refused to send troops to Ukraine to defend its territory against the Poles shortly before the battle of Poltava and so forth.

The deep dissatisfaction with the position of Ukraine within the Russian empire was growing not only in the milieu of the Cossacks' *starshina*, but also among the rank-and-file Cossacks. Speaking more specifically about Mazepa, who was seen by Peter I as a key traitor and his personal enemy, all the favours and awards received by Mazepa from the Russian tsar shall not overshadow the difficult choice the former faced: either he would have been removed from the office by the Cossacks, or he would have lost his power as a result of Peter I's administrative reforms in Ukraine. Mazepa's familiarity with the Jesuits' way of thinking—he studied at the Kyiv-Mohyla Academy that originally replicated the model of the Jesuits' collegiums (Hrushevsky, 1956b, p. 95)—likely facilitated his difficult decision. According to the Jesuits' teaching, an oath or promise made without intention to fulfil it is simply invalid (Hrushevsky, 1956a, p. 172). His promises to Peter I made before the said battle were likely made in such circumstances.

The myth of Mazepa's 'betrayal' brings us back to the discussion of obstacles to nation-state building that exist when the power elite of a state in the making is disconnected from the country's population. Mazepa took his decision without consulting the other Cossacks' leaders not to speak about the rank-and-file (Tairova-Yakovleva, 2011, p. 335). Without securing a solid popular support for the fight for the national independence, the leaders have no other choice but to seek international alliances—with Charles VII, for example. Or, such alliances have a highly circumstantial and unreliable character.

II.8 Holodomor

The Holodomor, a man-made famine in Ukraine in 1932–1933, has several interpretations in Ukraine's historiography. The perception of this event as a mass politically motivated murder of the Ukrainians is embedded in Ukrainian historiography. Marples (2007, p. xii) even argues that 'the interpretation of Famine as genocide was initiated in the North American Diaspora' and only subsequently adapted by Ukrainian historians.

An important nuance must be emphasised in the Ukrainian studies of the Holodomor. The fact that the Holodomor was a mass murder is not disputed by representatives of the other historiographies of Ukraine. The list of its victims in Ukraine includes up to four and a half million people (Appelbaum, 2017, p. 280). The disagreements began when historians attempted to assess to what extent this wholesale killing was purposeful and, if so, what was its exact purpose. Charles Tilly (2002) differentiates between two forms of state-backed exterminations of civilians: genocide (state-directed or state-authorised killing of populations identified by race, ethnicity, and/or religion) and politicide (wholesale killing of populations identified by political affiliation). The Ukrainians constitute the majority of the victims of the Holodomor, but the Russian population of Ukraine did not escape a similar fate either. The Holodomor particularly affected the rural population of the country whose political affiliations and preferences were not always clearly manifested. These considerations raise doubts as to the applicability of the two terms proposed by Tilly to the case of the Holodomor.

Ukrainian historiography actually proposes to perceive the situation through the lens of a mass but discriminate and purposeful killing with the aim of coercing the Ukrainians to be more obedient and accepting of the central Soviet government. 'The Holodomor was not designed to kill an entire ethnic group but rather to kill a large proportion of them in order to bring them to the centralized government' (Korostelina, 2004, p. 78; see also Appelbaum, 2017). This interpretation of the Holodomor fits well the myths discussed previously; namely, the myth of freedom and the myth of unruliness.

II.9 Heroes

No mythology is complete without a list of national heroes. There is little doubt that upon closer inspection no national hero's biography and profile appear to be flawless. Ukrainian national heroes make no exception. However, if one accepts the conceptualisation of myths as self-realising prophecies, then the same reasoning applies to national heroes. They cannot be dismissed as being imperfect. Their strength consists in providing reference points that help better understand the Ukrainian national consciousness.

Both Zaporozhian Cossacks and Ukrainian Cossacks have their own iconic figures. For the former, this role is played by Ivan

Sirko, the *otaman* of the Zaporozhian Cossacks' *kosh* in the second half of the 17th century. As the legend goes, he led the Cossacks in 55 battles and was victorious in all of them but one (Yavornitsky, 1991, p. 200). The historians, who disapprove of the 'unruly' and 'freedom loving' Zaporozhian Cossacks, also refuse to fully appreciate this personality. For instance, Tatiana Tairova-Yakovleva (2011, p. 15) calls him a 'famous political adventurist'. Sirko indeed embodied all the ideal-typical qualities of unregistered Cossacks, along with their strengths and weaknesses mentioned previously.

Bohdan Khmelnitsky, the Hetman of Ukrainian Cossacks and the leader of the mid-17th century Cossacks' uprising, plays a similar role with respect to Ukrainian, or registered Cossacks. His efforts to build a first Ukrainian nation-state cannot be denied indeed. 'Rarely do individuals dominate epochal developments as completely as did Bohdan Khmelnitsky the great Ukrainian uprising of 1648' (Subtelny, 2009, p. 125). Nevertheless, he was probably not up to this task because of his personal qualities and due to the Cossacks' inability to move from direct democracy to representative democracy. On more than just one occasion Hrushevsky unveils motives of personal revenge behind Khmelnitsky's actions during the uprising. Khmelnitsky repeatedly required that the Poles delivered him the small nobleman Chaplinsky, his personal arch-enemy, pretending that the entire Cossacks' army badly wanted the same (Hrushevsky, 1956b, p. 159; Hrushevsky, 1956c, pp. 207, 221; Hrushevsky, 1996, p. 63). Hrushevsky (1997, p. 150) concludes with a note of sadness that 'Khmelnitsky was not a master (*khaziain*), there was no master at all' meaning that the uprising did not produce a true statesman, let alone statesmen.

Ironically, Hrushevsky himself also had a chance to become one two and a half centuries later and also did not quite succeed. Hrushevsky is a Ukrainian national icon in two senses. On one hand, he 'did for Ukrainian history what Shevchenko[38] had done

38 Taras Shevchenko, the national poet, contributed to the national awakening by poetic means. Subtelny (2009, p. 233; see also Section II of Chapter 7 for

for Ukrainian literature' (Reid, 2015, p. 91). He was a leading myth-maker of Ukrainian historiography and, thus, a major contributor to the awakening of the Ukrainian national consciousness. On the other hand, he was also a political figure, the leader—the head of the Central *Rada* (Parliament)—of the short-lived Ukrainian Republic. His credentials in the first quality are undeniable, whereas his track record as the statesman raises controversies. For instance, a middle-age man, who is active in the volunteer movement and participated in the military conflict in the East of Ukraine, gave the following characteristic to Hrushevsky as the leader of the state: 'If he had bones, our history would have been different.—You mean his headship of the state?—Yes, perhaps we would have not a 20–25 year history [as an independent state], but a 100 year history'.[39]

Conclusions

This overview of Ukraine's history and the related myths leads to several conclusions. First, when discussing nation-state building in the Ukrainian case, the history provides relatively few supports. Modern Ukrainian nation-state builders may be better off looking forward and not backward. Moments of Ukraine's independence refer to the *court durée* of this country's history, whereas in the *long durée* of its history Ukraine had a dependent status.

Second, Ukraine's dependent status during most of its history explains the fact that the country's path has an essentially negative definition. Ukrainians are *different from* Poles, as both parties learned from the 17th century to the first half of the 20th century

---

further discussion) writes that 'it is difficult to find another example of an individual whose poetry and personality so completely embodied a national ethos as did Shevchenko for the Ukrainians'.

39 Actually, the interviewee used a stronger argotic expression, 'if he had balls', meaning that if he was more resolute to confront the Russian aggression in the 1917–1919 and able to build a stronger state, the current situation would have been different. The interview was conducted in Kyiv in June 2016, more details about the organisation and sampling are provided in Section II of Chapter 10.

through a series of bloody conflicts in the West of Ukraine, including the Volyn tragedy at the end of WWII[40] (Magosci, 2010, p. 681; Subtelny, 2009, p. 475). Ukrainians are *different from* Russians, as the two parties are currently discovering in the process of the on-going military confrontation in the East of Ukraine. Ukrainians continuously *rebel against* violence.

The question as to whether Ukrainians will be able to define their historical path and, consequently, national consciousness in positive terms—what they are and what they want to be, is still open-ended. Is Ukraine to follow the Western path and to 'return to Europe'? Alternatively, is Ukraine to follow the Russian path and to return to the 'Russian world'? Or can the country define its future on its own terms by choosing a Ukrainian path? One way to positively define the Ukrainian path involves moving from violence to power understood as human ability to act in concert. Without making this move Ukrainians, will likely continue to lag behind the other European countries in nation-state building. Their speciality, rebellion, suffices to reject violence that is externally (by the other countries) or internally (by the State) imposed. Rebellion does not suffice to build a capable nation-state from within. Subtelny (2009, p. 96) observes that 'the problem of a Ukrainian elite, or rather, the lack of one, now emerged as yet another of the central and recurrent themes in Ukrainian history'. The society produced truly decent leaders neither at the time of the Cossacks' uprising in the mid-17th century nor during the 2013–2014 mass protests and subsequent mobilisation against Russia's aggression. One of the qualities of such a leader is exactly to show that the State can be associated not only with violence but also with power, that the State could become a commonwealth. The environment in which the association of the Ukrainian state with power becomes a possibility is composed of

40 The attacks on civilians were designed to eliminate the presence of Poles (some 50,000 were killed) and Ukrainians (some 20,000 were killed) in the areas disputed by both Poles and Ukrainians to the advantage of the future state that would rule these territories after WWII.

institutions of representative democracy built up using the Cossacks' traditions of direct democracy and a national model of public management (Chapter 6).

Chapter 2
'Value of freedom: The case of the post-Soviet Ukraine'

Introduction[41]

Like most fundamental concepts in the social sciences, the notion of freedom has an 'essentially contested' nature: its 'legitimate use cannot be settled by appeal to theoretical criteria alone' (Wartenberg, 1990, p. 12). From a liberal perspective, freedom represents the only basis for agreement among individuals, each with his or her own agenda (Rose, 1995), whereas deterministic approaches question its mere existence.

Even within the liberal camp, there are arguments undermining the unconditioned appeal of freedom. Neoclassical economic theory, for instance, suggests that the task of collecting relevant information for making informed decisions and the responsibility for their consequences makes freedom less attractive. If the associated costs appear relatively high, freedom can be traded for the safety and security associated with a subaltern position (Coase, 1988; Simon, 1951).

The case of post-Soviet Ukraine serves as a good illustration for controversies of freedom. This country enjoyed independent statehood only during very brief periods in the past (e.g., in 1917–1920) and was, for most of the time, a part of more powerful neighbours: the Polish-Lithuanian Commonwealth, the Russian (later—Soviet) Empire and the Austrian Empire, as discussed in subsection I.2.g of Chapter 1. Thus, the Ukraine's Declaration of Independence in August 1991 started an unprecedented period in Ukrainian history.

---

41 An early draft of this chapter was initially presented as the Seventh Memorial Lecture on Freedom (May 2010) regularly organised at the Ukrainian Catholic University in Lviv, Ukraine, in memory of Olelksandr Kryvenko, a prominent Ukrainian journalist and civic activist. The author is especially indebted to one of its organisers, Orest Drul', for his valuable assistance and discussions.

The initial euphoria that resulted from Ukraine's independent status (and revived during the November 2004 mass protests commonly called the 'Orange revolution') has subsequently been replaced by pragmatic considerations of a closer association either with the European Union (EU) or with Russia. A poll carried out on a representative sample (N=1,998) in July 2009 by the Kyiv Gorshenin Institute of Management Issues showed that the absolute majority of Ukrainians saw the economic development of Ukraine conditioned by either eventual membership in the EU (29.1%) or a union with Russia (26.4%). Another representative survey (N=2,009) conducted in December 2009 by the Razumkov Centre for Economic and Political Studies paints a similar picture. When assessing the ideas of Ukraine's eventual membership in the EU and its rapprochement with Russia, respondents support both (44.3% have a positive or rather positive opinion about the former and 65.1%—about the latter; this figure, however, has noticeably decreased after the start of the undeclared war waged by Russia, see Chapters 5 and 10 for a more detailed discussion).

The ratio of supporters of two directions of Ukraine's integration keeps changing, yet the Ukrainian society remains divided in two groups: advocates of the European integration and proponents of the Eurasian integration under the auspices of Russia (Figure 2.1). Conflicts between proponents of the European and pro-Russian orientations took particularly manifest and even violent forms during the crisis that started after the 2013–2014 Revolution of Dignity. This chapter highlights one of the sources of this crisis in Ukraine, without focusing specifically on the most recent developments in this country which will be considered in the rest of the book. Namely, it aims to explore the roots of Ukrainians' ambivalent stance to the status of Ukraine as a formally independent state gained in 1991. While the existing literature acknowledges that this stance tends to be inconsistent (Kuzio, 2012; Kuzio, 2014; Shekhovtsov & Umland, 2014),[42] no satisfactory explanation for the reported contradictions has been offered so far.

Figure 2.1 'Which direction of integration shall be chosen for Ukraine? 2011–2017'

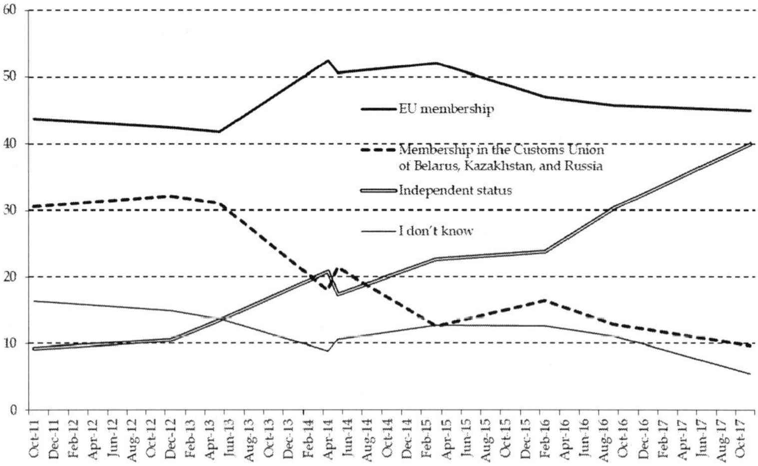

Source: Razumkov Centre, 2013 and 2017 and the Kyiv International Institute of Sociology, 2016.

This chapter discusses the issue of how people value freedom: can it be sacrificed for something more tangible and pecuniary? The underlying assumption is that one's loyalty to the national independence and his or her geopolitical orientations, that arguably represent a manifestation of freedom at the macro-level, can be better understood by studying the valuation of freedom at the micro-level, in day-to-day interactions. The inquiry into the ambiguous status of freedom guides the discussion that follows. The author intends to contribute to the extant literature by indicating that the value of freedom can be assessed with the help of a classification of its various forms (freedom *to*, freedom *from* and freedom *together*). This also serves to link the forms of freedom and those of power.

42 Namely, Anton Shekovtsov and Andreas Umland (2014, pp. 59–60) note that even representatives of Ukraine's nationalists become increasingly open supporters of this country's closer integration into Europe.

The connection between the micro- and macro-levels in the social sciences gives rise to significant theoretical and practical challenges (see, for instance, Coleman, 1990, pp. 21–23); any solution remains partial and contested. The analysis offered in this chapter is based on the following assumption:[43] if one does not value freedom in everyday life, i.e. in interactions at the micro-level, then he/she can hardly be expected to appreciate freedom at the macro level; namely, in national (for instance, to pay attention to the uses of the concept of freedom by political leaders) and international affairs (namely, to value and protect the national independence of his/her country). This assumption resonates with the congruence theory developed by political scientist Harry Eckstein. According to him, a system is stable if authority patterns at the macro-level (in the government operation) are congruent with the authority patterns of other units of society, at the meso- (within organisations) and micro (within families and households) levels (Eckstein, 1998a, p. 4).

Because of the essentially contested character of the concepts discussed so far, the question as to whether people always attach positive value to freedom or this asset transforms into a burden under certain circumstances cannot be answered by applying theoretical criteria only. The empirical study of the case of Ukraine thus complements the theoretical discussion. It is argued that the issue of the terminal and instrumental values of freedom appear particularly important when taking the historical and current political contexts into consideration.

This chapter has four sections. Section I contains a discussion of the relevant concepts. More specifically, it confronts freedom and power as well as their specific forms. The methodological issues for value analysis of freedom are discussed in Section II. Section III specifies two sources of the secondary data used for empirically

---

43 A comprehensive discussion of various strategies for accomplishing it exceeds the scope of the present chapter. The approach chosen here lies close to premises of methodological individualism, namely, 'the interaction among individuals is seen to result in emergent phenomena at the system level' (Coleman, 1990, p. 5).

testing the assumption about terminal versus instrumental value of freedom in the Ukrainian case. They include a mass survey conducted within the framework of the World Values Survey (WVS) project and the official programs of the candidates who ran in the 2010 presidential elections.[44] The results of a multiple regression model and the outcomes of the content-analysis of the official programs are presented in Section IV. Micro-level data described in Section III is thus complemented by some macro-level data analysis in Section IV.

I. Freedom: instrumental and terminal values

There is no stable consensus among representatives of different disciplines in the social sciences with regard to the definition of value. Economists view value as an internal measure of the importance of a good (Pearce, 1992). Marxists gauge this importance by the amount of labour necessary to produce a particular good, whereas neoclassical economists measure it in terms of scarcity and utility. In both cases, value derives from a higher-order concept (labour, utility), which prevents the attribution of value to something, including freedom, for its own sake.

Sociology and social psychology place value at the top of the list of determinants of human behaviour. 'Values can be defined as guiding images of social action which denote some of these as socially desirable and "good", others as "bad"' (Haller, 2002, p. 142). There are two groups of values: terminal and instrumental (Rokeach, 1969). The former refers to desirable ends, the latter—to appropriate means that should be used when dealing with endogenously set objectives. If freedom has a terminal value, it cannot be sacrificed to or 'traded for' anything else.

Analytical philosophers adapt similar approaches to assessing the value of freedom. According to one, the value of our freedom is

---

44 The 2014 presidential elections took place in the conditions of an external intervention and the contents of the candidates' programs were heavily influenced by this fact.

determined by 'the value we attach to the specific things [which we are free] to do' (Carter, 1999 cited in Morriss, 2009, p. 56). Alternatively, freedom has an intrinsic value. This means that people value the mere fact of possessing freedom as opposed to their subaltern status, regardless of the security and other benefits that it can provide.

A comparison with a lottery helps further illustrate differences between the instrumental and terminal values of freedom. On one hand, the individual may be interested in buying a lottery ticket if its price seems reasonable, taking into account the expected value of the lottery. The expected value of the lottery refers to the sum of the payoffs, where each payoff is weighted by the probability that the payoff will occur (Gintis, 2000, pp. 36–37). On the other hand, some individuals, the risk-takers, would buy a lottery ticket even if its price exceeds the expected value of lottery. They find enjoyment and excitement in making the choice in conditions of risk and uncertainty. The question to be asked is whether freedom is valuable in itself or because of a particular ratio of associated benefits and costs?

When discussing capitalism, Karl Marx (1889, chapter 1) starts by considering its core element: commodity. Then he introduces money; capital as a particular organisation of exchanges mediated by money; labour as a very specific type of commodity, and other factors that bring his initially highly abstract analysis closer to reality. The movement from the abstract to the concrete (Oleinik, 2009, pp. 629–632) appears appropriate for making sense of the concept of freedom as well.

Let us consider a solitary individual who lives on a deserted island. Robinson Crusoe's experience would be a rough approximation of such a situation. The only factor limiting the scope of Crusoe's actions is the amount of available resources (wood suitable for construction and ship building, fruits and vegetables, animals, etc.) and his mastery of them (for instance, his abilities as a hunter or a naval architect). Crusoe is free to do anything within this scope of the possible, which gives us a first definition of freedom as one's ability to lead a preferred form of life. John Commons reserves the word 'freedom' only for such contexts and highlights its positive—

because of references to a desired state or outcome—meaning (Commons, 1939, p. 119). Isaiah Berlin (1969) introduces the term 'freedom to' with a similar purpose.

Even in this most abstract case, freedom can hardly be considered separately from another fundamental—and also controversial—concept, namely, power (see Section II of Chapter 6). Power involves the right of control. Without the physical control of relevant resources, Crusoe's freedom would be substantially more restricted: a sand island with a single palm offers far fewer alternative courses of action for its inhabitant compared with the bounty of natural resources that he found on an island near the mouth of the great river Oronoque. Hence, such control represents a necessary condition for freedom *to*.

A web of connections between freedom and power takes more manifest forms if one starts to wonder how Crusoe landed on his island. Peter Morriss (2009, pp. 63–64) argues that it does not matter whether constraints limiting freedom are introduced by another person or by nature. In practical terms, this argument supposes that, while Crusoe was constrained in terms of spatial movements, he did not care whether his containment resulted from a punishment or represented an outcome of a natural disaster. However, Crusoe's plans for ending his containment and his course of action would be completely different in the two cases. An escaped convict considers contacts with other people a source of danger and an eventual constraint on his freedom. A victim of a shipwreck sees everything the other way around.

The arrival of man Friday—a next step in the movement from the abstract to the concrete—provided a good opportunity for exploring the links between freedom and power. With Friday's arrival, what previously was an individual action or decision became social 'insofar as its subjective meaning takes account of the behavior of others and is thereby oriented in its course' (Weber, 1968, p. 4). Man Friday might help Crusoe increase the degree of his freedom *to* or become a source of nuisances and conflicts. In the latter situation, the scope of the individual autonomy of a less powerful actor decreases as a consequence of entering into a relationship (Hiley, 1987, p. 344). In other words, power can restrict freedom.

Freedom in the context of a social relationship acquires new dimensions. If Crusoe managed to control Friday's actions, their interactions take on the form of a power dyad. *A*, Crusoe, gets what he wants at the expense of *B*, Friday. *A*'s power *over B* enhances *A*'s freedom *to* achieve individually unattainable results. 'Power *over* means power over other people, enforcement of one's own intentions over those of others' (Göhler, 2009, p. 28; see also Ledyaev, 1997, p. 98). At the same time, *A*'s power *over B* limits *B*'s freedom *to* taste the fruits of collaborative efforts (and potentially even his freedom *to* do previously—through individual action—possible things). Compared with individual action, social action extends the scope of the possible, but there is absolutely no in-built safeguard that the freedom of all parties involved will necessarily be enhanced, which shall be borne in mind when discussing power as action in concert in Chapter 6.

The eventual structuration of elementary social action in the power dyad lies at the origin of a second form of freedom. Freedom in this new context involves the lack of interference in one's course of action. Commons labels such freedom 'liberty' and defines it 'as mere absence of restraint or compulsion' (Commons, 1939, p. 119). Berlin differentiates this form of freedom with the help of the preposition 'from' (Berlin, 1969). Freedom *from* means that one is not prevented by others from doing what he or she would otherwise do (Dean, 2009, p. 181). Freedom *from* has a negative connotation (it refers to what is absent), whereas freedom *to*—a positive one (Pratchett, 2004, pp. 363–366).

The complex relationship between power and freedom has attracted the attention of many scholars. The writings of Michel Foucault occupy a significant place in these debates. Foucault highlights both the enabling (it enhances freedom *to*) and constraining (it reduces the scope of freedom *from*) effects of power (Allen, 2002). However, in various texts he places greater emphasis either on the latter or on the former. For instance, in *Surveiller et punir* (Foucault, 1975) and the first volume of *Histoire de la sexualité* (Foucault, 1976) Foucault underlines the constraining effects of power. Individuals act even in the most intimate areas, such as sexual relationships, not according to their own needs and wishes but in conformity with priorities set by those who have disciplinary power (Scott, 2001, p. 94).

In his later works, including the last two volumes of *Histoire de la sexualité* (Foucault, 1984a; Foucault, 1984b), Foucault devotes more attention to the enabling effects of power. According to the 'later' Foucault, 'freedom comes from the ability to participate actively and purposefully in power relationships, not from escaping them' (Crane, Knights & Starkey, 2008, p. 304).

Power *to* and freedom *to* have essentially the same meaning: both concepts refer to one's ability to achieve a desired result. Morriss (2009, p. 55) goes so far as to equate them. Nevertheless, this holds true only in the context of individual action. Power *over* undermines *B*'s freedom *to* and explains his desire to gain freedom *from* *A*'s control. Hence, power enhances freedom in the context of individual action; a contradiction between them emerges in the context of social action. Does this contradiction have an inevitable character?

The introduction of a third party into a power relationship, *C* (Oleinik, 2011a, chapters 5–7; see also Section III of Chapter 5), or the delegation of the right of control to *A*'s representatives, 'lieutenants' (Coleman, 1990, pp. 81–82), complicates the picture by making it more nuanced but does not help achieve a finer differentiation of freedom and power in the context of social action. This calls for taking a step further down the road, moving from the abstract to the concrete.

This step requires shifting priorities in exercising power *over* from *A*'s interests to those of *B*. Returning to the parable of Robinson Crusoe, he exercises control over man Friday for the purpose of emancipating and civilising the latter. Crusoe, to use a highly apt English term whose translation into most other languages appears notably difficult, *empowers* Friday. Empowerment can be 'understood as the enhancement of autonomy and solidarity' (Stewart, 2001, p. 1; see also subsection II.3 of the book's general Conclusion). The paradox is only apparent here: Crusoe could gain more in the middle- and long-term by relying on a highly qualified and skillful companion capable of taking initiatives. Crusoe's enlightened self-interest consists in enlightening Friday, to make a play on words (see also Section V of the general Introduction to this book). It follows that the former 'learns certain skills that undercut the power differential between [him] and the dominant agent' (Wartenberg, 1990, p. 184).

Transformative power emerges from such restructuring of the initial dyad. It enhances *A* and *B*'s ability to act in concert and, hence, their freedom *to* do various things together, 'in concert' (Arendt, 1969, p. 44). In order to place greater emphasis on the 'concerted action' of *A* and *B*, it is worth pairing transformative power with a third form of freedom, freedom *together*.[45] It comes as no surprise that the other name for transformative power is power *with* (see Section II of Chapter 6 for further discussion).

The analysis of freedom *together* calls for the introduction of another fundamental concept: trust. Trust is 'the expectation of one person about the actions of others that affects the first person's choice, when an action must be taken before the actions of others are known' (Ostrom, 1998, p. 12). Consequently, trust enables one to achieve outcomes that require substantial adjustments of individual plans or the common efforts of two or more people without relying on power (Adam, 2008, pp. 163–164). By performing this function, trust makes actions 'in concert' possible and, therefore, enhances freedom *together* (see subsection I.2 of the book's general Conclusion). Coordination on the basis of power implies that *B* is guided by the 'visible hand' of *A*. Coordination on the basis of trust means that both *A* and *B* count on the 'invisible hand' of their mutual expectations.

---

45 This rather awkward construction is used for the sake of consistency with the template 'freedom plus a preposition' commonly used in analytical philosophy, the concept 'fraternity' from the democratic discourse would also do the job (Timokhin, 2009; Touraine, 1994, p. 109).

Table 2.1 'Freedom and power: various forms and their interconnections'

Context	Forms of freedom	Forms of power	Link between them
Individual action	Freedom *to* (freedom in the narrow sense)	Power *to*	Similarity
Social action	Freedom *from* (liberty)	Power *over*	Conflict
Social action	Freedom *together* (fraternity)	Transformative power (power *with*)	Complementarity

The dialectics of freedom and power can be summarised with the help of three pairs of concepts (Table 2.1). The three concepts of freedom also differ in function of how its value is assessed, which brings us back to the research question behind this chapter. The instrumental value of freedom can be assessed in a direct manner and without considering other values.[46] Freedom *to* involves evaluating benefits and costs associated with every course of action within the scope of the possible and weighted by their probability. For instance, will Crusoe gain more by acting or by simply waiting for help to come?

Freedom *from* requires that greater emphasis is placed on benefits and costs of actions that would become possible if *B* was not subject to *A*'s control. This can be achieved with the help of counterfactual thinking: 'what would have happened if *A* did not act?' (Lukes, 2005, pp. 43–44; see also Ailon, 2006). Would Friday have been better off if he did not meet Crusoe?

As for freedom *together*, the scope of the possible might not be known in advance, taking into account that *B*'s empowerment pro-

46 It is worthwhile to compare the proposed approach with that of Milton Rokeach. According to the latter, only freedom *from* (freedom defined as independence, free choice) has a terminal value, whereas freedom *to* (independence defined as self-reliance, self-sufficiency) – has only an instrumental value (Rokeach, 1969, p. 554). He also attributes some instrumental value to power *over* (obedience defined as dutifulness, respectfulness). Rokeach (1969, p. 551) argues that values cannot be assessed separately: they form a value system, which implies their relative assessment, i.e. a rank-ordering.

duces effects mostly in the middle- and long-term, which complicates the task of drawing up an exhaustive list of alternative courses of action and evaluating their probabilities. Have Crusoe and Friday increased the scope of the possible for both of them and for any of them as a result of their encounter? In other words, *A* and *B* act under conditions of uncertainty as opposed to risk. 'We speak of *risk* when the objective probabilities (long-term frequencies) associated with all possible outcomes are known to the decision maker. We speak of *uncertainty* if at least some of these objective probabilities are unknown to him (or are not even well defined)' (Harsanyi, 1977, p. 22; emphasis added).

The terminal value of freedom can only be assessed indirectly. If the subjectively assessed value of freedom exceeds the resulting figure in each of these cases, then the difference can be attributed to its intrinsic, or terminal, value. This imperfect proxy nevertheless allows us to grasp the open-ended nature of freedom as something that cannot be reduced to the choice between particular courses of action.

II. Qualitative and quantitative approaches to assessing the value of freedom

The task of assessing the value of freedom necessitates finding quantitative measures, whether absolute or relative (for instance, deriving from a rank-ordering). A number of mass surveys carried out on representative samples in many countries, such as the WVS or the European Social Survey (ESS), specifically focus on values and factors that explain the causes and the nature of their within and between-country variations.

The exclusive reliance on quantitative data can lead to serious pitfalls, however. The issue of freedom appears removed in standardised questions from the particular context of interactions, which complicates the interpretation of answers to such questions. What does the respondent actually mean by freedom or trust (its level is also often measured with the help of standard questions)? The problem grows even more complicated in comparative survey research covering several countries. 'A greater problem involves errors in measurement concerning the comparability of results ascribed to *semantic* (hermeneutic) reasons (how respondents understand and interpret the "proper" meaning of the wording of a given survey question) stemming from *idiosyncratic cultural* and/or *institutional contexts*' (Adam, 2008, p. 177; emphasis added).

A combination of two (or more) sources of data—data triangulation, and research methods—methodological triangulation, helps to address these problems at least in part (Oleinik, 2015c; see also Section I of Chapter 4). Content analysis seems especially promising in this regard: this research method serves to 'quantify' the qualitative data, i.e. texts of public speeches made by Ukrainian political leaders. Content analysis in this particular case is intended to 'decipher' the public discourse using the concepts of freedom, power and trust as a key. Furthermore, the availability of two methodologies and of two sources of data for studying the same phenomenon makes triangulation of their outcomes possible (Jick, 1979). However, a full-fledged version of triangulation requires achieving a high level of compatibility of the concepts used, on one hand, in statistical analysis and, on the other hand, in content analysis. According to the minimalist version of triangulation applied in the present case, the two methodological approaches simply complement each other by highlighting various components of freedom.

The reliance on the secondary data also accounts for a less than perfect fit between, on one hand, the theoretical model outlined in Section I and, on the other hand, the empirical assessment of the model in Section IV. A purposefully designed research instrument, i.e. the questionnaire for a mass survey, would have allowed for much better connections between particular questions and the logic of the movement from the abstract to the concrete in studying the value of freedom.

III. Sources of information

Two sources of the secondary data are used for differentiating the two components of the value of freedom in the case of Ukraine. The first represents outcomes of the WVS that was carried out in several dozen countries, including Ukraine, since the early 1980s (World Values Survey Association, 2009). More specifically, several forms of statistical analysis, including multiple regression, were conducted using the outcomes of its fifth wave (N=82,992 in 55 countries) and their subset, the data produced in Ukraine on a representative sample (N=1,000) in the second half of November 2006.

The fact that the data refer mostly to one country makes cultural and institutional idiosyncrasies in the interpretation of the questions less important. As for the more general problems related to the mass survey data, an attempt to assess their reliability was made by comparing outcomes of two mass surveys carried out in Ukraine around the same period of time, the WVS and the ESS (Round 3, N=2,002 in the second half of December 2006).

The comparison covered the values of several indicators included in both surveys. Its outcomes tend to be convergent, but with one caveat: not all of the questions have identical formulations and the alternatives make the comparison less meaningful. For instance, 7.1% of the respondents declare that they have signed petitions according to the WVS. The ESS shows a similar figure, 5.1%, but it refers only to the last 12 months (the period covered was not specified in the WVS). The question with regard to trust in people in general seems particularly problematic: 17.7% of the respondents lean toward trusting complete strangers according to the WVS (with a 4-point scale, the alternatives 'Trust completely' and 'Trust a little' are combined) and 35.6% — according to the ESS (with a 10-point scale, the four alternatives from 10, 'Most people can be trusted', to 6 are combined).

The instrument was not specifically designed to address the question about the instrumental and intrinsic components of the value of freedom, which limits the range of possible options and excludes a 'first-best' design of the model of measurement. However, it contains several questions that serve as a proxy for various forms of freedom and power, as well as their components. Question

> A173 'Some people feel they have completely free choice and control over their lives, while other people feel that what they do has no real effect on what happens to them. Please use this scale where 1 means "none at all" and 10 means "a great deal" to indicate how much freedom of choice and control you feel you have over the way your life turns out'

serves to measure the overall scope of freedom at the ordinal level. The individual is the unit of analysis (and observation) in this part of the statistical analysis. The scope of individual locus of control serves as a proxy for assessing the value of freedom only in an indirect manner: Rokeach (1969, p. 554) defines freedom as independence and free choice. He includes it in his empirically identified list of terminal values. A better way to make the concept of freedom operational would involve inviting the respondent to rank-order a list of supposedly terminal values and in calculating the rank of freedom.

Particular forms of freedom and power, namely, freedom *from*, freedom *together* and power *over*, are made operational with the help of constructing indexes, i.e. by combining two or more indicators (Jackson, 2003, p. 393). The incompleteness of the available statistical data prevented the operationalisation of the three remaining forms of power and freedom (freedom *to*, power *to* and transformative power). Equal weights were assigned to different components because 'of insufficient knowledge of causal relationships, or ignorance about the correct model to apply' (Hoskins & Mascherini, 2009, p. 474). Reliance on the secondary source once again prevented the inclusion of all relevant questions in the indexes: only those asked in most countries were selected, which paves the way to placing the Ukrainian case in a comparative context. The Freedom From Index (FFI) contains three questions (out of eight relevant questions):

> A173 (recoded by counting values from 6 to 10 only),
> A029 'Here is a list of qualities that children can be encouraged to learn at home. Do you consider *independence* to be especially important?' (nominal

> level, recoded with the help of a dummy variable: '1' if the respondent does) and
> E037 'How would you place your views on this scale? 1 means you agree completely with the statement on the left; 10 means you agree completely with the statement on the right: "People should take more responsibility to provide for themselves" versus "The government should take more responsibility to ensure that everyone is provided for"' (ordinal level, recoded by counting values from 1 to 4 only).

The Freedom Together Index (FTI) refers to various manifestations of actions 'in concert'. It follows the same logic as other similar indexes, namely the index of civil participation adapted for the ESS (Mascherini, Vidoni & Manca, 2011; see also subsection III.1.c of Chapter 10) and the protest index adapted for the WVS (Guérin, Petry & Crête, 2004, pp. 379–381). The former index equals the sum of the variables describing the different degrees of engagement (full membership, donating money, etc.) in various civic organisations (sport, cultural, trade union, etc.). It should be noted, however, that both the FTI and the index of civil participation measure the value of freedom *together* indirectly, by focusing on its outcomes (specific modes of behaviour arguably resulting from a preference for 'acting in concert'). The FTI includes three indicators (out of 47 relevant):

> E025 'Whether you have actually done [signing a petition], whether you might do it or would never, under any circumstances, do it' (recoded as an ordinal-level variable),
> E026 (the same for the alternative 'joining in boycotts') and
> E027 (the same for the alternative 'attending lawful demonstrations').

The average values of the FTI at the country level (i.e., the country becomes the unit of analysis) appear to be correlated with the Freedom House Index in 2006 (r=0.652, p<0.001,[47] N=54), which indicates its criterion valid character. The Freedom House—an international non-governmental organisation—uses two indexes, one for

47 The sample does not have a random character and, hence, only a descriptive meaning shall be attributed to r.

political rights[48] and another one for civil liberties;[49] the average of the two represents a good approximation for the suitability of the institutional environment for acting 'in concert'.

The Power Index (PI) is intended to assess the value attached to power *over*. In contrast to the FTI, it measures the underlying construct in a more direct manner. The PI has four components (four other relevant indicators did not meet the selection criterion):

> E037 (recoded by counting values from 6 to 10 only),
> E042 'Here is a list of qualities that children can be encouraged to learn at home. Do you consider obedience to be especially important?' (nominal level, recoded with the help of a dummy variable),
> E114 'For each [type of political systems], would you say it is a very good, fairly good, fairly bad or very bad way of governing this country? Having a strong leader who does not have to bother with parliament and elections' (ordinal level, recoded by counting values 1 and 2 only) and
> E118 'Which [view] do you think is better? A. A party leader should stand firm for what he or she believes, even if others disagree. B. A party leader should be prepared to cooperate with other groups, even if it means compromising some important beliefs' (nominal level, recoded with the help of a dummy variable).

A correlation between the average values of the PI at the country level and the Power Distance Index, PDI, constructed and calculated by Geert Hosftede helps gauge the criterion-validity of the latter (Hofstede, 1980, pp. 403–410; see also Section II of Chapter 6).[50] The value of Pearson's correlation coefficient suggests a moderate relationship (r=0.38, p=0.016, N=40).

---

48 This includes a series of questions as to whether fair electoral laws, equal campaigning opportunities, fair polling, and honest tabulation of ballots exist; there is a significant opposition vote, de facto opposition power, and a realistic possibility for the opposition to increase its support or gain power through elections.

49 This refers to freedom of expression and beliefs, associational, organisational and individual rights, the rule of law.

50 The values of the PDI can be found at http://www.geert-hofstede.com/hofstede_dimensions.php. For Ukraine, its value was roughly approximated using outcomes of the above mentioned July 2009 poll by the Kyiv Gorshenin Institute of Management Issues. A more direct assessment of the PDI value for Ukraine is offered in Section IV of Chapter 6.

To estimate the construct validity using the individual as a unit of analysis it was decided to explore the associations between the three indexes and the indicator of trust in people in general (question A165 measures it at the nominal level; the respondent is invited to endorse one of two principles: 'Most people can be trusted' or 'One needs to be very careful in dealing with people'). This test of the construct validity is intended to check whether the theoretically predicted associations do, in fact, exist (Bryman, 2004, p. 73).

The outcomes of independent sample t-tests for the equality of means (using question A165 as a grouping variable) appear consistent with the theoretical predictions, even if the relationships tend to be rather weak. For instance, the mean value of the FFI in the group of the respondents who trust people in general (*M*=0.852, *SD*=0.755) exceeds that in the group of the respondents who prefer to be careful in dealing with people (*M*=0.72, *SD*=0.645). The difference between the means reaches the level of statistical significance.[51] The mean value of the FTI in the former group (*M*=0.654, *SD*=0.791) also exceeds that in the latter (*M*=0.58, *SD*=0.777), but this difference does not reach the level of statistical significance. Trustful people have the larger scope of individual locus of control as measured by question A173. The mean value of the overall scope of freedom in the group of trustful people (*M*=6.46, *SD*=2.181) exceeds that in the group of distrustful people (*M*=5.92, *SD*=2.358) at a statistically significant level.[52]

The second source of the data includes the texts of the official programs of the ten highest ranked candidates who ran for the Ukrainian presidency in January 2010 (according to the outcomes of the first round of the elections). The following assumption makes

51 The assumption of homogeneity of variance was assessed by the Levene test, F=3.679, p=0.055, which does not indicate significant violation of the equal variance assumption. Therefore, the pooled variances t-test was run. The mean scores differed significantly, $t(874)$=3.149, p=0.002, 2-tailed.

52 The assumption of homogeneity of variance was assessed by the Levene test, F=6.988, p=0.008, which indicates significant violation of the equal variance assumption. Therefore, the separate variances t-test was run. The mean scores differed significantly, $t(394)$=2.413, p=0.016, 2-tailed.

this dataset eventually compatible with the first one: 'political candidates running for public office have differing value systems and... their appeal to the voter will depend on the degree of congruence between candidate and voter value system' (Rokeach, 1969, p. 558).[53]

All of the texts were content analyzed using the program QDA Miner version 2.0.8 with the statistical module WordStat 5.1.12. More specifically, WordStat offers an option of building dictionaries based on substitution and, hence, running quantitative versions of content analysis. The custom-built dictionary based on substitution has 20 entries corresponding to the topics found in most programs. They were identified after several readings of their texts. However, emphasis was primarily placed on such entries as 'Freedom' (subdivided into 'Freedom *from*' and 'Freedom *together*') and 'Power'. The entry 'Freedom *from*' contains four words: *viln** (liberty and its derivatives; * refers to a 'wild' character, i.e. any letter or a combination of letters), *svobod** (freedom), *deregul** (deregulation) and *detsentral** (decentralisation). The entry 'Freedom *together*' includes co-occurrences of *my* (we) and *razom* (together), *gromad** (civil) and *susp** (society) in the same sentence, words *spil'n** (in concert) and *ob'edn** (unite). The entry 'Power *over*' has two words, *vlad** (power) and *svavil** (discretionary behaviour; see subsection II.6 of Chapter 1).

IV. Unexplained components of freedom

IV.1 Statistical tests

The design of statistical analysis includes several components. At the first stage, methods of bi-variate statistics (correlations and independent samples t-tests for the equality of means) were used to draw up a list of the potential independent variables associated with the overall scope of freedom as measured by question A173.

53 For an empirical test of a similar assumption regarding Leader-Member exchange within an organisation see Ashkanasy & O'Connor, 1997.

This served to identify a 'long' list of the independent variables consisting of Level of income (question X047) measured at the ordinal level (a 10-point scale), Age (question X003) measured at the ratio level, Gender (question X001) measured at the nominal level, the Region where the interview was conducted (question X048) measured at the nominal level, Town size (question X049CS) measured at the ordinal level, Trust in people in general (question G007_34) measured at the ordinal level, and State of health according to subjective assessments (question A009) measured at the ordinal level.

Most of these variables refer to various determinants of the instrumental value of freedom because they influence the scope of the possible for the individual when he or she acts either individually or 'in concert' with others. Some of them appear self-explanatory whereas others require more extensive comments. For instance, Level of income refers to a necessary condition for the instrumental perception of freedom because it determines the range of things that a particular amount of money can buy.

In a sense, State of health has a similar meaning in the present context. The range of things one can do depends on his or her physical condition. Poor health prevents one from being engaged in potentially valuable activities and, hence, represents a physical restriction of freedom. Level of income and State of health predictably appear more correlated with the FFI than with the overall scope of freedom (0.19 versus 0.16 and -0.19 versus -0.22 respectively, N=71,680, all correlation coefficients are significant at $p<0.001$). By assessing the contribution of these two predictors to the variance in the overall scope of freedom one gets a better idea about its instrumental value.

Variable Trust in people in general, on the other part, arguably contributes to freedom *together*. Generalised trust, as opposed to trust in personally known people, makes large-scale actions 'in concert' possible (see also subsection I.2 of the general Conclusion to this book). An empirical study also suggests that trust can be related to state of health by reducing such stress factors as anxiety and fear about the behaviour of others (Jen, Sund, Johnston & Jones, 2010).

Independent sample t-tests with regard to Age recoded at the ordinal level produced a paradoxical—at first glance—outcome. The mean values of the overall scope of freedom vary across six age groups in the Ukrainian case (both in 2006 and 1996) but not in the larger sample of the fifth wave of the WVS. In Ukraine, the older you are, the less free you feel: the mean score on a 10-point scale continuously decreases from 6.79 (5.76 in 1996) among young people 15 to 24 years old down to 5.50 (4.47 in 1996) among the seniors aged 65 years old and older. The difference achieves the level of statistical significance,[54] whereas in the larger sample it does not.

Out of four regions in Ukraine, Western, Eastern, Central and Southern, residents of the first region feel more freedom than the others. For instance, the comparison of mean scores in Western and Eastern Ukraine shows that their difference achieves the level of statistical significance.[55] As for Size of town, inhabitants of medium-sized cities (with a population in the range between 100,000 and 249,000 people) express the strongest feeling of freedom compared with inhabitants of both rural areas and large urban centers.

At the second stage of statistical analysis, the contribution of each of the long-listed variables was evaluated to control for other variables. Before running a multiple regression, the 'Forward: conditional' method, the normality of univariate distributions was screened. Univariate distributions of the ordinal-level variables were reasonably normal. The nominal-level independent variables

---

54 For instance, when comparing mean scores of freedom between two age groups, 25–34 y.o. and 55–64 y.o., the assumption of homogeneity of variance was assessed by the Levene test, $F=13.202$, $p<0.001$, which indicates significant violation of the equal variance assumption. Therefore, the separate variances t-test was run. The mean scores differed significantly, $t(181)=2.443$, $p=0.016$, 2-tailed. The mean score for the younger group ($M=6.40$, $SD=0.134$) exceeds the mean score for the older one ($M=5.74$, $SD=0.237$).

55 When comparing the mean scores of freedom between these two groups, the assumption of homogeneity of variance was assessed by the Levene test, $F=6.667$, $p=0.01$, which suggests some violation of the equal variance assumption. Therefore, the separate variances t-test was run. The mean scores differed significantly, $t(466)=5.316$, $p<0.001$, 2-tailed. The mean score for Western Ukraine ($M=6.83$, $SD=0.147$) exceeds the mean score for Eastern Ukraine ($M=5.77$, $SD=0.136$).

were recoded using dummy variables (e.g., '1' for Western Ukraine, '0' for the three other regions), which allowed their inclusion in the regression.

All seven 'long-listed' variables were included in the multiple regression. The overall regression, including six of the seven candidate predictors, was statistically significant, R=0.425, R^2=0.181, adjusted R^2=0.175, F(6, 860)=31.575, p<0.001 (Table 2.2). It should be noted that the contribution of Age did not exceed the critical value of F set at 3.00 for the Forward method and, as a result, was eliminated at the very beginning. This means that the relationship between freedom and Age can be considered *spurious* after controlling for State of Health. Taking into consideration the poor state of the Ukrainian health system, it comes as no surprise that health rapidly deteriorates with age. In all the remaining cases, the comparison of the zero-order correlations with the partial correlations controlling for other variables shows that the latter appears smaller than the former, has the same sign and is significantly different from 0, i.e. the contributions of the six predictors can be 'partly explained' in terms of one another (Warner, 2008, p. 398).

Table 2.2 'Results of statistical (method = Forward) multiple regression to predict overall scope of freedom (Y) from Level of Income, State of Health, Size of Town, Region, Trust in People in General and Gender'

	Freedom	Health	Income	City	Region	Trust	Gender	B	b	ΔR^2
Health	-0.332**							-0.663***	-0.233	0.109
Income	0.31**	-0.368**						0.224***	0.185	0.037
City	0.119**	-0.011	0.045					0.798**	0.097	0.015
Region	0.163**	-0.186**	0.15**	0.16**				0.563**	0.094	0.009
Trust	-0.136**	0.082*	-0.104**	-0.056	-0.089**			-0.175**	-0.088	0.008
Gender	0.107**	-0.17**	0.076*	-0.024	0.034	-0.075*		0.285*	0.058	0.003
Age (not entered)	-0.216**	0.496**	-0.385**	-0.023	-0.065*	-0.054	-0.29	–	–	–
								8.484***		
Mean	6.09	4.35	2.57	–	–	3.9	–			
SD	2.298	1.894	.814	–	–	1.156	–			
	1–10	1–5	1–10	0, 1	0, 1	1–5	0, 1	R^2=0.181		
	1=none	1=very good	1=1st step	1=100–249,000	1=West	5=not at all	1= Male	R^2_{adj}=0.175		
								R=0.425***		

Legend: * p<0.05, ** p<0.01, *** p<0.001. Criterion: F-to-enter≥3.00.

To assess the statistical significance of the contributions of individual predictors, the *F* ratio for the R^2 increment was examined for each variable in the step when it first entered the analysis. In Step 1, State of Health was entered; it produced an R^2 increment of 0.109, $F(1, 865)=106.129$. In Step 2, Level of Income was entered; it produced an R^2 increment of 0.037, $F(2, 864)=73.94$. In Step 3, Size of Town was entered; it produced an R^2 increment of 0.015, $F(3, 863)=55.199$. In Step 4, Region was entered; it produced an R^2 increment of 0.009, $F(4, 862)=44.054$. In Step 5, Trust was entered; it produced an R^2 increment of 0.008, $F(5, 861)=37.105$. Trust appears negatively related to freedom because of the reverse scale used in the coding. In Step 6, Gender was entered; it produced an R^2 increment of 0.003, $F(6, 860)=31.575$.

Overall, freedom scores could hardly be predicted well using this set of variables, with only approximately 18% of the variance in freedom scores accounted for by the regression. Imperfections in the instrument shall be taken into account when explaining this relatively poor performance. However, this outcome also suggests that the instrumental component of the value of freedom tends to be relatively insignificant. Taken together, health and monetary resources, the two key conditions for freedom *to*, explain only 14.6% of the total variance in freedom scores for Ukraine. The significant residual variance might be attributed to the intrinsic value of freedom and to the imperfections in the instrument.

A further statistical test run on the aggregate dataset of the fifth wave of the WVS confirms that one cannot properly assess the overall value of freedom without taking into account its instrumental value, but the latter fails to explain everything. The mean scores of the FFI, the FTI and the PI were calculated for the 56 countries included in the sample (thus, the unit of analysis is the country at this stage) and then cross-correlated. The FFI appears to be strongly associated with the overall scope of freedom as measured by question A173 ($r=0.682$, $p<0.001$). This means that freedom *from*, taken separately, explains less than half of the variance in the freedom scores ($r^2=0.465$).

Quite predictably, a moderate negative association exists between the PI and the overall scope of freedom ($r=-0.408$, $p=0.002$).

More surprisingly, the relationship between the latter and the FTI tends to be weak (r=0.185 and not statistically significant, were the sample random), but there is a moderate negative association between the FTI and the PI (r=-0.423, p=0.002). It should be noted that freedom *from* arguably negates power *over*, whereas freedom *together* and transformative power have several elements in common. The results reported above confirm that the PI expresses power *over*, not transformative power. Nevertheless, the partial coefficient between the FFI and the PI after controlling for the FTI shows that the FTI partly explains the relationship ($r_{FFI \times PI.FTI}$=-0.568, p<0.001, cf. $r_{FFI \times PI}$=-0.651, p<0.001).

Looking at the dynamics of the Freedom House Index since the start of the 19th century one can observe that the institutional conditions for freedom, namely, democratic institutions and arrangements, steadily spread around the world. On average, there was a net increase of 1.6 new democratic regimes per year during the first half of the century and a net increase of 0.8 new democratic regimes per year during the second (Tilly, 2009, p. 70).

However, a 'bottom-up' look informed by the WVS produces a more mixed and less optimistic picture.[56] The mean feeling of freedom slightly increases over time, but the overall pattern lacks consistency (Figure 2.2). The dynamics of the three indexes constructed in this chapter, the FFI, the FTI and the PI, provides even fewer reasons for optimism. The mean FFI value remains steady, whereas the mean FTI value declines slightly over time. Everyday life provides us with fewer opportunities for feeling free *together*.

56 When comparing the Freedom House data and the WVS data one has to bear in mind the caveat regarding connections between the micro- and macro-levels in the analysis stated in the introduction to this chapter.

Figure 2.2 'Dynamics of the indexes of freedom, 1981–2007'

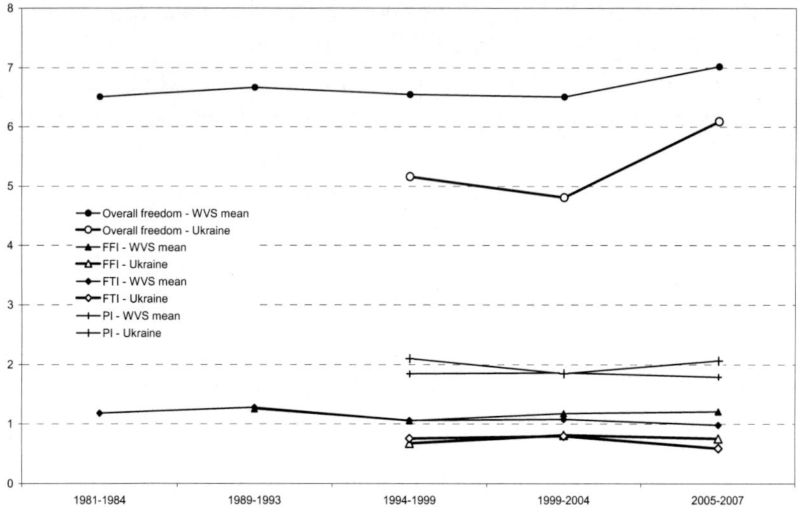

IV.2 Content analysis

Even if the issues of freedom do not dominate the Ukrainian political discourse anymore (in the late 1980s and early 1990s the word *nezalezhnist'*—independence—was one of the most popular), it would be premature to assume their marginalisation. In the custom-built dictionary of today's Ukrainian politics the entry 'Freedom *from*' is ranked fourth out of 20 according to the frequency with which the presidential hopefuls mention it (N=64, found in all 10 texts included in the sample), the entry 'Freedom *together*'—ninth (N=38 in 8 texts). 'Power' has a third rank (N=69 in 10 texts). The entries 'State' (*derzhava*, N=257) and 'Country' (*kraina*, N=212) are at the top of this list.

Taking into consideration the statistical test results discussed above, the prevalence of 'Freedom *from*' compared with 'Freedom *together*' comes as no surprise. The frequency of references to 'Freedom *together*' tends to be higher (χ^2=5.158, p=0.07) in the discourse of the younger generation of Ukrainian politicians (those in their forties or younger) than in the programs of their more senior colleagues.

The analysis of the co-occurrences of the concepts (how often they co-occur in a window of 50 words) visualised with the help of a dendrogram where clusters refer to the co-occurring concepts indicates a somewhat unexpected association of 'Power' with 'Trust' (Figure 2.3).

Figure 2.3 'Dendogram of the co-occurrence of selected concepts in programs of the presidential candidates in Ukraine in 2010'

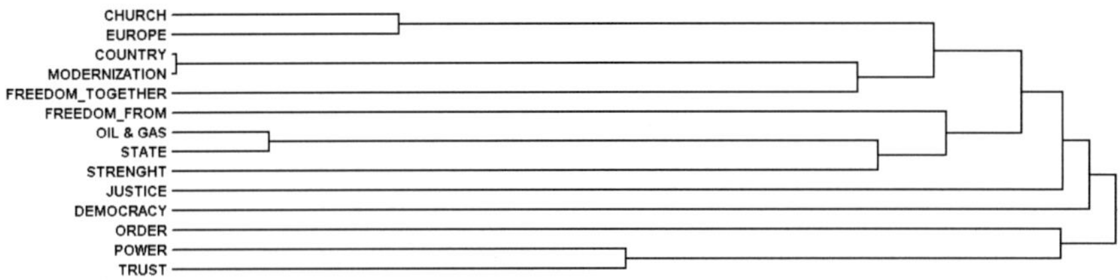

Legend: similarity index: Cosine theta; in a window of 50 words.

A closer look suggests that the association has a negative character: 'I run for the presidency in order to restore lost trust in those who are vested in power' (candidate Sergiy Tyhipko), which does not contradict the previously reported findings. Another association—between 'Freedom *together*' and 'Country'—also deserves mention. The presidential candidates often refer to elements and building blocks of civil society when talking about their country as opposed to the Ukrainian state: 'Public television and broadcasting will be established; access to the internet will be provided to all citizens [of our country]' (candidate Yulia Tymoshenko).

If one restricts the analysis of co-occurrences to the three variables of interest only, 'Freedom *from*', 'Freedom *together*' and 'Power', the first two predictably have a higher degree of similarity. This result holds even after extending the framework of the analysis from a window of 50 words to the entire text of a political program. Eight candidates out of ten include elements of both 'Freedom *from*' and 'Freedom *together*' in their discourse.

In the final account, the discourse analysis complements the statistical tests by helping compare the relative importance of 'Freedom *from*' and 'Freedom *together*' in the Ukrainian context. The former tends to prevail over the latter. Furthermore, it suggests that both forms of freedom occupy a subordinate place to 'Power' in terms of their relative frequencies.

The validity and reliability of such tentative conclusions have to be confirmed on a larger sample of political texts. Nevertheless, one should not completely disregard official political programs: they represent an important source of information for voters. The 2009 survey by the Razumkov Center cited above shows that 75.3% of Ukrainians pay some or significant attention to political programs (only 6.8% of them do not) when deciding how to cast their vote. Even more voters, 84.8%, compare the actual performance and what was declared in the official program with the same purpose.

Conclusion

Taking into consideration the long road to independence, Ukraine represents a relevant case for studying freedom and the value that people attach to it. According to the 2006 data, the overall score of freedom (question A173) has significantly increased, which reversed the previous trend. This pattern might be an outcome of the November 2004 mass protests: they resulted in positive changes in the dynamics of several indicators of social 'health' (Pohorila, 2009), however short-lived these changes turned out to be.

But if one considers the relative standing of Ukraine in the various dimensions of freedom, it appears that this country stands at the bottom of the lists of countries ranked in function of their scores. Ukraine ranked 49 out of 56 according to its overall score of freedom. The value of the FFI places it 54 out of 56, that of the FTI—44 out of 54. The Ukrainians feel that they are less free than the inhabitants of most other countries.

Ukraine has a relatively high rank (11 out of 54) in the realm of power *over*, as measured with the help of the PI. The results of the July 2009 poll by the Gorshenin Institute and of the December 2009 survey by the Razumkov Center confirm a high level of acceptance of power *over* by Ukrainians. The first poll shows that 55.5% of Ukrainians work under the supervision of an authoritarian boss and an almost equal number of them, 55.3%, prefer to have such superior if they had a choice (see also Section IV of Chapter 6 for further data). The support for an authoritarian president tends to be even stronger—59.4%. When asked to choose between freedom and order (a proxy for the acceptance of control) in the second poll, the absolute majority of the Ukrainians, 56.5%, appear ready to sacrifice freedom to order.

The outcomes of the presidential elections in February 2010 seem to confirm this trend as the leaders of the 'Orange revolution' lost those elections. The winner, Viktor Yanukovych, took revenge for his defeat in November 2004 by promoting a conservative agenda (with particular emphasis on reestablishing order) and a stronger economic and political association with Russia. Yanukovych was subsequently ousted from office in February 2014 as a result of a new wave of mass protests that had started in November 2013, which calls for a new wave of studies of the most recent (post-February 2014) trends in the perception of freedom and power by Ukrainians (Chapters 3 and 6).

Further studies are especially needed, taking into consideration two major limitations of the present research. First, it is based on the assumption of a particular connection between the perceptions of freedom at the micro- and macro-levels (see the introduction to this chapter). Second, this research derives from secondary data sources that fit the proposed research design in an imperfect manner. Some loss of data may have eventually occurred as a result of the recoding.

The discussion offered in this chapter should be placed in this context: is it worth attaching a terminal value to freedom in a society in which a significant number of people tend to accept power as a solution to their everyday problems? Today's Ukrainian political culture leaves this question unanswered or leans toward a negative conclusion, especially taking into consideration a rather high level of disappointment with the current instrumental value of the freedom gained in 1991.

The proposed analysis suggests that the question can and should be answered in the affirmative. One cannot rely entirely on power because not all its forms provide us with a key to solving everyday problems. Power *over*, in contrast to power *to* and transformative power, has little instrumental value. However, in the Ukrainian context, power *over* appears to prevail. As in Russia, 'the term "power" is usually used for the description of someone's ability to control (dominate, compel, influence) others, 'power' is imagined as something that is "over" us, that limits our freedom, creates obstacles, etc.' (Ledyaev, 1997, p. 95). Excessive hopes related to such power periodically lead to 'broken expectations' and the search for freedom *from*. In other words, the present conditions produce a drift into the endless back and forth between power *over* and freedom *from*.

In the Ukrainian case, the dialectics of power *over* and freedom *from* shape both internal (relationships between the state and society) and foreign politics. It takes particularly manifest forms when considering interactions with more powerful neighbours, namely Russia and the EU. Prospects of a closer association with both produce high expectations that eventually appear broken, which provokes the desire for freedom *from*. It is worth mentioning that references to Russia and the EU continue to occupy a significant place in the Ukrainian political discourse. All ten official programs studied here mention the EU (with a total frequency of 63) and nine of them mention Russia (N=30).

Compared with freedom *to*, the task of assessing the value of freedom *from* represents a challenge because it requires counterfactual thinking. Thus, it may be more difficult to realise the true value of freedom *from*, which paves the way to its eventual sacrifice to something more 'tangible', for instance, immediate benefits or even a temporary relief of economic or social duress. This voluntary sacrifice does not prevent a search for freedom *from* in the future provided that power *over* continues to prevail.

This line of reasoning does not undermine the desirability of a closer association between Ukraine and the EU. But without placing stronger emphasis—both in political discourse and everyday activities—on freedom *together* the same cycle from hopes to disillusionment may be repeated. In practical terms, such a change in priorities requires systematic attempts to empower actors at the national level: economic, social, political, scientific and cultural, which will be discussed in Section II of the general Conclusion to this book.

Chapter 3
'Mass protests in 2013–2014: The Revolution of Dignity or EuroMaidan?'

Introduction

The mass protests that started in Ukraine on November 22, 2013 were both expected and unexpected. They came as no surprise because the high expectations produced by the so-called 'Orange revolution' of October-December 2004 did not come to fruition. The Ukraine government continues to operate in a non-transparent manner[57] and remains alienated from the ordinary people. On the other hand, the recent protests did not follow a pattern common among those in the post-socialist countries (Serbia in 2000, Georgia in 2003, Ukraine in 2004, Mongolia in 2008, Moldova in 2009, Kyrgyzstan in 2005 and 2010 and Russia in 2011). The 2013 Ukrainian protests did not coincide with elections. They lasted several months without interruption and led to violent clashes with the police. Dozens of people were killed, both among the protesters and the police force.

The long-lasting character of the mass protests deserves special attention. The police made several attempts to dispel the protesters by using force (see Section III of Chapter 4 for the exact timeline)—all of them were successfully countered. Alain Touraine (1992, p. 273) views the capacity of a social movement to resist oppression and to challenge the established order as a key characteristic. The longevity, scope and intensity of the 2013 Ukrainian protests have few, if any, parallels in the history of Ukraine and the other post-socialist countries, making them a success.

---

57 The Ukrainian government is perceived as highly corrupt: the value of the Transparency International Corruption Perception Index was 25 out of 100 in 2013 (2.2 out of 10 in 2004). The lower the value of the index, the higher the level of the perceived corruption.

The Ukrainian protests demonstrate that a corrupt government can be challenged no matter how violent and intimidating the means it uses against the protesters may be. In the words of the people who turned out on the Ukrainian streets, 'we're writing history now with our protests' (male, 25–39 y.o.) and 'we've achieved something even now… Every night, every day here comes at a high price' (male, 40–54 y.o.).[58] This chapter is intended to explore the origins of the strong capacity the Ukrainian protestors demonstrated for resisting the oppressive government.

It is assumed that the exceptional resistance of the Ukrainian protesters can be attributed to the successful adaptation of several universally used strategies of collective action, namely, street protests, sit-ins and barricades, to the local conditions in that country. The question as to whether mass protest strategies have a universal or country-specific character is attracting increasing attention on the part of scholars. The literature on repertoires of collective action does not rule out any of these alternatives. The repertoire of collective action has a country- and time-specific character, as suggested by the works on contentious repertoires in France (Tilly, 1977) and Great Britain (Tilly, 1995).

More recently, however, the concept of modularity has gained popularity. The idea of modularity suggests that successful strategies can be replicated across various countries and periods of time. According to Mark Beissinger (2011), the above-mentioned series of mass protests in the post-socialist countries confirm the hypothesis of modularity.

In this chapter, an attempt is made to confront the concepts of singularity and modularity using the 2013 Ukrainian protests as a 'deviant' case (see subsection II.2 of the general Introduction to this book) that does not fit the common pattern of mass protests in the post-socialist countries (because of the longevity, scope and intensity of the protests and their disconnection from elections). Namely, it is argued that in order to be effective in a particular country at a specific moment, a strategy of collective action shall have some

58 Excerpts from two interviews conducted in Kyiv in December 2013. Parameters of the sample and the interview guide are discussed in Section III below.

'elective affinity' (in Max Weber's terms) with the traditions and values prevailing in this country at that time. In other words, a strategy works if it makes sense to the people who eventually use it. They have no difficulty with connecting the strategy to their everyday experience and with interpreting it in terms of the prevailing culture.

This chapter has four sections, in addition to the introduction and conclusion. Section I discusses the literature on the issue of repertoires of collective action and their transferability from one locale to another. Section II provides some background information about the 2013–2014 mass protests in Ukraine. The sources of the information (a series of semi-structured qualitative interviews and three mass surveys) are outlined in Section III. Section IV shows how outcomes of the content analysis of the interviews can inform the discussion of the transferability of the repertoires. Namely, the content analysis suggests that the strategies of collective action prevalent in the Ukrainian case (street protests, sit-ins and barricades) were adapted to the particularities of the national culture, which explains their relative success.

I. Repertoires of collective action: Between singularity and modularity

Several theoretical approaches prevail in the literature on mass protests: rationalist, structuralist, phenomenological, cultural and relational analyses (for an overview, see McAdam, Tarrow & Tilly, 2001, chapter 1; Tarrow, 2011, chapter 1). For instance, advocates of the relational approach 'treat social interaction, social ties, communication, and conversation not merely as expressions of structure, rationality, consciousness, or culture but as active sites of creation and change' (McAdam et al., 2001, p. 22). This chapter specifically discusses one element of the mass protests agenda, that is, their tactics, and explores the conditions under which the protesters elaborate a strategy of collective action that works, i.e. enhances their capacity to resist. As a result of its focus on the issues of the cultural embeddedness of strategies of collective action, this chapter engages with the concepts and approaches developed within the cultural and relational frameworks.

I.1 Repertoire of collective action

The concept of a repertoire of collective action introduced by Charles Tilly highlights the inherent limitations of alternative options available in a particular locale at a specific moment in time. 'The word *repertoire* identifies a limited set of routines that are learned, shared, and acted out through a relatively deliberate process of choice' (Tilly, 1995, p. 26; see also Alapuro, 2005, p. 378; McAdam et al., 2001, p. 41; Tarrow, 1993, p. 70; Traugott, 1993, p. 310; Wada, 2012, p. 545).

The range of available options, a repertoire, depends on the history of previous interactions between the antagonists. According to institutional theory, the repertoire of collective action tends to be path-dependent (North, 1990). As a result, the repertoire of contention, for instance, in 18th-century France (Tilly, 1977) differs from that in 18th-century Great Britain (Tilly, 1995).

Mark Traugott (1993, p. 309) shows how the actors' 'options are circumscribed both by prior experience and by the material, organisational, and conceptual resources they find readily at hand' using the example of barricades. The strategy of barricade construction was first used in France in the late 16th century. It had its origins in the everyday life of Parisians who chain-locked the secondary streets so their rest was not disturbed by thieves, noisy passers-by and traffic (Traugott, 1993, p. 313). This measure turned out to be effective and Parisians started to construct barricades during mass unrest as a means to protect themselves against the forces of the kings and, in the late 17th and 18th centuries, as a central element of the French revolutions.

I.1.a Street protests

Street protests constitute an integral part of the repertoire in most countries, including Western (Van Aelst & Walgrave, 2001) and Eastern Europe (Guérin, Petry & Crête, 2004). The embeddedness of street protests in urban culture accounts for their popularity in urbanised countries. Namely, Peter Van Aelst and Stefaan Walgrave speak of the 'normalisation' of street protests: protesters increasingly represent various gender, age, income, educational and professional groups. Street performances and carnival elements refer to a special case of collective action in the urban environment. These strategies were used by the protesters in such post-socialist countries as Serbia, Georgia, Russia and Ukraine (Beissinger, 2007, p. 262; Lyytikäinen, 2014; Nikolayenko, 2007, p. 172). A specific form of street marches and meetings, *Viche* and *Maidan*, constitutes a trademark of the 2013–2014 protests in Ukraine.

I.1.b Sit-ins

Sit-ins and the occupation of public spaces and buildings also have their origins in urban culture. Following the 2008 financial crisis, the Occupy movement (Occupy Wall Street and similar actions in major urban centers) had numerous followers in North America and worldwide. The Occupy movement has several predecessors, including the sit-ins at American university campuses in the 1960s (Chabot & Duyvendak, 2002, p. 725). This form of protest also represents an element in the repertoire of contention in some post-socialist countries, for instance in Hungary, Slovakia, Slovenia (Szabó, 1996, p. 1166) and Kyrgyzstan (Temirkulov, 2008, p. 328). In Ukraine, the sit-in took the form of a tent camp (*Sich*) in downtown Kyiv.

I.1.c Strike

Strike as a form of protest prevails in industrial societies. It constitutes an element of the working-class repertoire: peasants, for instance, do not normally strike (Biggs, 2013, p. 409; Givan, Roberts & Soule, 2010, p. 7; Tilly, 1978, p. 159). Strong traditions of workers' self-management make striking a particularly relevant option. For instance, in the early 1990s the prevalent form of protests in Slovenia, a former Yugoslav republic, was the strike (Szabó, 1996, p. 1167). The spread of self-managed enterprises was a distinctive feature of the Yugoslavian model of socialism (Oleinik, 2006). The

Ukrainian protesters also attempted to organise a strike—without much success, however.

I.1.d Violent clashes

Mass protests are not immune to the eventual drift into violence. This drift takes on particularly pronounced forms in societies characterised by a high degree of personification of relationships—traditional and also post-Soviet (Oleinik, 2003, chapter 3). In these circumstances, the protesters have personal targets in mind (a landlord or a political figure), which is also true for repression from authorities (Tarrow, 2011, p. 46). The repertoire of violent forms of contention includes physical clashes of protesters with the police force, the destruction of property, the harassment, intimidation and killing of state representatives and so forth. When discussing violent forms of protest, it should be noted that the protesters' violence is often no more than a mere reaction to the state's violence. 'The uncertain, elastic line between "legitimate" and "illegitimate" violence' of the state (Tilly, 1985, p. 173; see also Coutin, 1995; Kupatadze, 2008) lies at the origin of violent acts committed by the protesters. The excessive use of force by the police allows the protesters to legitimise their resistance and eventual retaliation in-kind. This pattern characterised the interactions between the police and activists of the anti-globalist movement in North America (Thompson, 2007). It can also be seen in several post-socialist countries, for example, Kyrgyzstan (Temirkulov, 2008, p. 328). In the Ukrainian case, physical clashes were an integral part of the protests, especially during the final stage in February 2014.

I.1.e Mass media

The mass media both extends the scope of conventional strategies of mass protests and contributes to the emergence of new elements in the repertoire. As for the former effect, the mass media facilitates the mobilisation of larger groups of protesters and their diversification. When the mass media campaigns play a leading role, as in the case of the White March protests against criminal violence in Belgium in the mid-1990s, the number of protesters exceed the usual figures and they become more diversified (Van Aelst & Walgrave, 2001, p. 478).[59] However, if the mass media are subject to censorship, as in the Ukrainian case, they might eventually constrain the range of options available to the protesters.

I.1.f Internet

The Internet has turned out to be a particularly powerful tool of mobilisation. Some scholars even speak of a new generation of collective action: mass protests mobilised through the Internet (Walgrave, Bennett, Van Laer & Breunig, 2011). Mass protests in the Middle East from 2010–2013—colloquially called the Arab Spring—often started as Facebook groups and Internet forums that eventually gave rise to street protests, sit-ins and other more conventional strategies of collective action (Attia, Aziz, Friedman & Elhusseiny, 2011; Hofheinz, 2011, pp. 1419–1420). The Internet also creates conditions for the rise of new forms of contention, for instance, online petitions and virtual sit-ins (Van Laer & Van Aelst, 2010, p. 1147).

Representatives of the younger generations tend to be particularly active in virtual protests. During the 2013–2014 Ukrainian protests, young people also used the Internet for the purposes of mobilisation (Dickinson, 2014; see also subsection I.1 of Chapter 4). Nevertheless, the question as to whether the mobilisation achieved through the Internet is sustainable or short-lived remains open. The available evidence suggests that virtual communities form more easily than face-to-face communities, but that they can dissolve quickly (Kujawski & Abell, 2011).

I.2 Modularity

Sidney Tarrow (1993, p. 77; see also Tarrow, 2011, pp. 40–41) opposes the 'old' (before 1848) and 'new' (1848 onward) repertoires of collective action. According to him, the strategies forming the old repertoire are local and singular, whereas those that constitute the

---

59 This reasoning also applies to the January 2015 march in France against terrorism. The 4 million strong march was a response to the killing of the *Charlie Hebdo* journalists and resulted from a massive campaign launched by the French media (Contre le terrorisme, 2015).

new repertoire tend to be universal, or modular. Modular strategies can be employed in a variety of settings by a variety of social actors against a variety of opponents. Barricade building is a strategy that was originally singular and then progressively became modular (because of its widespread use during the European revolutions of the 18th century) (Tarrow, 2011, p. 38; Traugott, 1993, p. 317).

Recent scholarship on mass protests places the concept of modularity at the center of the analysis (Beissinger, 2007; Traugott, 1995; Wada, 2012). Namely, it helps explain scale shifts in mass protests, i.e. 'the spread of contention beyond its typically localized origins' (Tarrow & McAdam, 2005, p. 125). The prevailing perspective on scale shift consists in highlighting factors that facilitate the broadening of contention. For instance, how to elaborate and promote strategies of collective action that will eventually be used beyond the borders of a particular locality, community, or country? Less attention is paid to the issues of the adaptation of modular strategies to the new local contexts.

Studies of the Arab Spring and the Coloured Revolutions (a series of mass protests in the post-socialist countries in 2000–2005) are a case in point. They often stem from the assumption that these events have common roots and mechanisms. Namely, the Coloured Revolutions are triggered by electoral fraud, their modular element. This emphasis also suggests that the Coloured Revolutions should be interpreted as a fight for the ideals of representative democracy since elections are a key element. Viewed in this light, elections offer a universal mechanism through 'which conflicts of a nonelectoral nature could be aired' (Tarrow, 1993, p. 84). By framing grievances in terms of electoral fraud, the protesters enhance their social base: 'while authoritarian regimes constantly violate citizens' rights, few incidents personally affect most of the populace at the same time. Stolen elections do' (Kuntz & Thompson, 2009, p. 258; see also Beissinger, 2007, p. 263; Beissinger, 2011, p. 36; Cummings & Ryabkov, 2008, pp. 248–249). Furthermore, the language of electoral fraud can be easily understood almost everywhere—in the West and in the post-socialist and developing countries. The modular protests also tend to take common forms: street protests with carnival elements characterised the Coloured Revolutions

(Beissinger, 2007), whereas online mobilisation was a key feature of the Arab Spring.

The literature identifies several factors that drive the increasing modularity. The emergence of the nation-state is one. 'Modularity… had its main structural counterpart in the penetration, the standardization, and the availability as target and fulcrum of the modern national state' (Tarrow, 1993, p. 83; see also Tarrow, 2011, p. 39). Diverse grievances now have a unique target and there are common mechanisms for voicing them. This finding is particularly important for discussing nation-state building in the case of Ukraine (the general Introduction to this book, Chapters 1 and 10).

Globalisation also contributes to the increasing modularity of the repertoires. Given conditions of globalisation, 'common models of social order become authoritative in many different social settings' (Meyer, 2000, pp. 233–234; see also Appadurai, 1996). Strategies of contention are no exception. They cross geographical and temporal borders, being selected by previously disconnected groups of protesters.

I.3 Relocation

The diffusion model (Biggs, 2013, p. 409; Givan et al., 2010, p. 9; McAdam et al., 2001, p. 26; Tarrow & McAdam, 2005, p. 127; Wada, 2012, pp. 546–548) specifies two principal channels through which a singular strategy may eventually acquire a modular character, brokerage and diffusion. Brokerage involves the linking of two or more previously unconnected social sites by the efforts of collective and individual actors. Pre-existing connections between social sites make diffusion possible. Diffusion has two mechanisms: relational and non-relational.

The relational mechanism involves transferring information along established lines of communication. Protesters from different countries meet face-to-face at common events. They also discuss and exchange information about the strategies that work in the virtual space of the Internet. Networks of activists emerge both in a spontaneous manner and purposefully organised by various sponsors: the international NGOs, the foreign governments promoting the issue of universal human rights etc. For instance, prior to the 2004 Orange revolution, groups of Ukrainian activists participated in a series of summer camps, seminars and workshops dedicated to the discussion of the repertoires of contention that proved their effectiveness in Serbia in 2000 and in Georgia in 2003 (Beissinger, 2007, pp. 262, 270; Nikolayenko, 2007, p. 182; see also subsection II.1.b of the book's general Conclusion). These meetings were sponsored by the Freedom House, the Soros Foundation and the US government.

The second mechanism implies non-relational ways of replication of successful patterns. If protesters develop similar cognitive models and schemes, they tend to use similar strategies of collective action. Common cognitive schemes emerge as a result of people reading the same books, for instance. The Ukrainian protesters, as well as protesters in the other countries affected by the Coloured Revolutions, reportedly found inspiration in Gene Sharp's book (2012) on strategies for a peaceful transition to democracy (Nikolayenko, 2007, p. 182).

Consideration of a cognitive dimension of the diffusion process enables us to obtain a more nuanced understanding of modularity. A strategy of collective action can be either replicated without substantial changes or adapted to the new institutional environment. Sean Chabot and Jan Duyvendak (2002, p. 707) use the terms of dislocation and relocation to differentiate between two forms of modularity: 'Dislocation refers to potential adopters' cognitive and emotional recognition that the foreign innovation may also work outside of its original environment, while relocation involves collective experiments with new protest ideas and practices in the receivers' settings'. Relocation requires more input on the part of the actors involved in the diffusion process. The familiarity with textbook examples does not guarantee the overall success of their undertaking. They must be able to combine the traditional institutions and new norms on which the transplanted strategies are based. In this sense, relocation has more truly innovative elements. It requires the work of adaptation and translation of the modular strategies using local cultural scripts.

The use of a strategy that has proved its effectiveness in a distant cultural environment may appear impossible at first sight. For instance, fasting and other strategies of non-violent resistance popularised by Mahatma Gandhi initially looked completely alien to many activists in the United States (Biggs, 2013, p. 410). Nevertheless, several elements of the Gandhian repertoire were successfully relocated by the American civil rights movement in the 1960s (Chabot & Duyvendak, 2002). The African-American students who initiated the sit-ins explicitly referred to Gandhi's teachings as a source of their inspiration.

Kyrgyzstan offers another illustration of a combination of traditional institutions and transplants. Both the respect for traditions and the use of modular strategies characterised the 2005 Tulip Revolution. Stolen elections played the role of a trigger, but 'the basic methods used to attract supporters to mass mobilisation were pre-existing informal, often traditional, institutions' such as *kurultai* (people's assembly), *aksakals* (the elders) and *palvans* (respected traditional wrestlers) (Temirkulov, 2008, p. 318).

I.4 Actors: entrepreneurs and communities

Who does the cognitive and practical work related to dislocation and relocation? It can be done either by cultural entrepreneurs ('individual brokers') or by community members themselves. Cultural entrepreneurs recombine institutional elements available in a particular culture, making them compatible with transplanted strategies (Tarrow & McAdam, 2005, p. 130). When doing so, cultural entrepreneurs seek either pecuniary or non-pecuniary (status, power) gains (Davis & North, 1970; Oleinik, 2012a).

The communitarian model does not involve dependence on specific individuals. 'The key receiving actors [are] … critical communities and their members' (Chabot & Duyvendak, 2002, p. 727). Community members share the cognitive and practical work necessary for dislocating or relocating a would-be modular strategy. The application of the communitarian model appears to be particularly challenging in the post-socialist countries, as a result of the traditions of authoritarianism at the micro- and macro levels. For instance, several attempts to build a leaderless protest movement in Russia failed (Lyytikäinen, 2014, p. 100).

A consensus is emerging in the literature. Diffusion is far from being an automatic process that can be taken for granted. 'Diffusion… is a creative and strategic process, one that is marked by political learning, adaptation, and innovation; it is not a simple matter of political contagion or imitation' (Givan et al., 2010, p. 3). Since diffusion requires the adaptation of modular strategies to the local conditions, human input is always required. Either cultural entrepreneurs or critical community members become the actors of diffusion. The conditions for successful adaptation remain underexplored, however, which calls for further investigations such as the present one.

I.5 Elective affinity

The concept of elective affinity is well known to cultural and political sociologists, but it is rarely used in the studies of mass protests. Its origins can be traced back to the 1809 novel by Johann Wolfgang von Goethe, *Elective Affinities*[60] (Howe, 1978; Raskov, 2014, p. 121). In Weber's interpretation, elective affinity can be found between seemingly distant and non-related social phenomena: Protestant ethics and capitalist behavioral patterns. Interactions between them through the channels of brokerage (pastors) and diffusion (relational, via Protestant communities, and non-relational, as a result of a common emphasis placed on rationality, in both Protestantism and capitalism) led to the raise of modern capitalism.

In a similar manner, elective affinity can be considered a key condition for the successful transfer of an institution from one institutional environment to another (Oleinik, 2002). For the purposes of this study, elective affinity will be interpreted in a narrower sense, as the eventual compatibility of a modular strategy and tra-

---

60 'Those natures which, when they meet, quickly lay hold on and mutually affect one another we call affined… They … most decidedly seek and embrace one another, modify one another, and together form a new substance' (Goethe, 2005, pp. 53–54).

ditions in the place of its relocation, despite their apparently dissimilar characteristics. It is assumed that a high degree of elective affinity between traditional institutions in a particular country and a would-be modular repertoire facilitates its diffusion in this country. Elective affinity increases the chances for success of the actors of institutional transfers, cultural entrepreneurs or community members. A low degree of elective affinity means that only highly singular strategies can be effective in this particular institutional environment. No actor, however resourceful it may be, will be able to make the modular repertoire work in this culture. The lack of elective affinity normally leads to the opposite outcomes of institutional transfers. Namely, it 'arouses tensions, open gaps, [and] creates frustrations' (Badie, 2000, p. 91).

The existing literature suggests that the effective diffusion of a repertoire of collective action to a given institutional and cultural context requires the work of adaptation on the part of the new users of the repertoire. This chapter contributes to the literature by outlining the exact mechanisms through which this adaptation work happens. Specifically, it highlights the importance of elective affinity between modular strategies and local traditions. It also shows the need for human input in the process of adaptation. This study intends to explore the following research questions. *What conditions are necessary for successfully adopting several modular strategies (street protests, sit-ins and barricades) to the traditional institutions in Ukraine?* These modular strategies have been recently promoted and showcased by such global protests as the Occupy movement. *Who did the work of adaptation in the case of the 2013 Ukrainian protests: cultural entrepreneurs or critical community members?*

II. Case study of Maidan in 2013

The situation in Ukraine at the end of 2013 was chosen for a case study. It may be considered an extreme/deviant case that serves to better understand the issue of modularity and singularity. An extreme case helps 'to obtain information on unusual cases, which can be especially problematic or especially good in a more closely defined sense' (Flyvbjerg, 2006, p. 230; see also subsection II.2 of the general Introduction to this book). First, the 2013 protests do not fit the pattern of the Coloured Revolutions: electoral fraud did not serve as a trigger and the modular strategy of organising street protests according to the scripts of a carnival did not prevail. Second, despite the formally independent status Ukraine gained after the fall of the Soviet Union in August 1991, the building of a nation-state has not been completed yet (Chapters 1 and 2). The country remains heavily dependent on its neighbours, Russia and the European Union (EU), in economic, political and even intellectual terms. The on-going construction of the nation-state in Ukraine places greater emphasis on the local and singular elements of the repertoire, if Tarrow's arguments (1993; 2011) hold. The 'deviant' character of the Ukrainian case serves to shed more light on the tensions between the modular and singular strategies, as well as on the ways for easing them. As a result, the work of adaptation tends to be more challenging in the Ukraine than elsewhere. Thus, if the importance of elective affinity is confirmed for this case, then it also applies to other cases (Flyvbjerg, 2006, p. 230), which makes the Ukrainian protests a good candidate for being a critical case as well.

Large-scale mass protests spread through Ukraine on a regular basis. A first wave culminated in the 2004 Orange revolution. A second wave started in 2010, with protests against the new Tax Code, and culminated in late November-December 2013. The recurrent character of mass protests makes the Ukrainian case especially interesting for study.[61] The existence of multiple events within a single country paves the way for identifying the strategies of mass protests that work in this institutional environment. It will be argued that the effective strategies in the Ukrainian case derive from a successful relocation of modular strategies. The success can be attributed to a high degree of the elective affinity between some modular strategies (street protests, sit-ins and barricades) and the traditional institutions (*Maidan*, *Viche* and *Sich*) coupled with communitarian efforts.

61 In a way, today's Ukraine is similar to France in the late 17th – 18th centuries when France went through multiple revolutions and mass mobilisations.

The protests started in Kyiv, the capital of Ukraine, on November 22, 2013. In contrast to 2004, they were not triggered by stolen elections. President Viktor Yanukovych's refusal to sign an agreement of association with the EU triggered the mass protests. When considering this trigger, one has to bear in mind that no referendum preceded Yanukovych's decision. Furthermore, public opinion in Ukraine was deeply divided on the issue of two alternative directions of association, European and Russian (post-Soviet). A survey conducted on a representative sample of the Ukrainian population in May 2013 by the Razumkov Centre (2013) showed that 41.7% of the respondents supported a closer association with the EU, 31% were in favour of Ukraine's membership in the Customs Union of Russia, Byelorussia and Kazakhstan, and 13.5% wanted to keep their country's independent status (see Figure 2.1 in Chapter 2). In other words, the issue of the economic association with the EU did not play the role of a focal point for the majority of the population.

The protesters—most of them initially represented the younger generations—organised a series of street marches and set up a tent camp in Kyiv's city center. Internet forums and social networks facilitated mobilisation at this stage. The police used force to dispel the protesters on November 30, 2013 and attacked them again on December 11, 2013. The government's attempts to resolve the conflict by applying brute force only strengthened the protesters' desire to resist. Furthermore, their numbers started to grow as members of the older generations joined their ranks. At the height of the protests in December 2013, more than one million Ukrainians participated in some street marches in Kyiv only.

The 2013 repertoire of contention included several strategies: street protests, sit-ins and the occupation of public spaces (the central street, Khreshchatyk, and the central square, Nezalezhnosti) and buildings (the building of the Kyiv City State Administration, the trade union building and the Ukrainian House), barricades, strike, Internet forums and, in January-February 2014, physical clashes with the police and the destruction of property. Even those strategies that were used previously, particularly in 2004, were modified during the 2013 wave of mass protests. These modifications and adaptations will be the focus of this study. They are assumed to be an important factor underlying the participants' exemplary capacity to resist the government's attacks and to sustain their protests during a long period of time. President Yanukovych was ousted from the office by the protesters. This chapter discusses the protesters' success in terms of their exemplary capacity to sustain resistance leaving the assessment of their success or failure to achieve particular long-term goals (such as making the government more responsive to the population) to the subsequent chapters and further studies.

The active phase of the protests lasted three months: from November 22, 2013 to February 22, 2014, when President Yanukovych left office under increasing pressure from the protesters. This study focuses on the period from the end of November through the end of December 2013. During this period, violent strategies for confronting the government were used only sporadically and in a non-systemic manner (in contrast to December-February 2014 when they started to prevail). The rationale for limiting the study to November-December 2013 is two-fold. On one hand, this period marked the height of the protests, judging by the number of participants. On the other hand, the primary data were collected at the end of December and a deeper understanding of the subsequent developments requires collecting additional information.

III. Sources of information

The case study involves using data from various sources, both primary and secondary. The secondary sources used in this case study include three surveys conducted by the Ilko Kucheriv Democratic Initiatives Foundation in December 2013 (twice) and February 2014. The researchers attempted to reach participants in both the street protests in Kyiv (the first survey) and the sit-in on Khreshchatyk (the second and third surveys). The street protests often took the form of a stationary protest (e.g., meetings), as opposed to a moving protest (e.g., marches). They are colloquially called *Viche* and *Maidan*. In the mass media and the research reports, the sit-in is called

Tabir and *Sich* (Ilko Kucheriv Democratic Initiatives Foundation, 2014).

The names chosen are not coincidental. All four refer to strategies of collective action that existed in Ukrainian history (see Chapter 1 and in particular subsection II.4.a). *Viche* refers to a mass gathering in the downtown during which the population (representatives of all social groups without exception) determined the issues of public importance, including the signing of an agreement with a ruler and its cancellation in the case of his unsatisfactory performance (Klyuchevsky, 1956, p. 192; Klyuchevsky, 1957, p. 68). *Viche* existed at the time of Kievan Rus'. The word *Maidan* has a similar meaning. It denotes a public meeting at a central place in a town or village determining the issues of public interest. *Maidan* continued to be operational until the early 20th century.[62] In contrast to *Viche*, an urban phenomenon, *Maidan* is closely associated with the countryside.

A camp of Zaporozhian Cossacks was named *Tabir* (or *Kosh*). It represented a set of tents surrounded by carts that formed a circle (see subsection II.1.a of Chapter 1). This layout served to effectively organise a defense against eventual attacks on the part of an enemy. The word *Sich* denotes a permanent settlement of Zaporozhian Cossacks, their capital (historically located on an island in the Dnieper River in today's Zaporizhia). In other words, *Tabir* refers to a temporary Cossack camp set up during their military expeditions, whereas *Sich* is 'a permanent capital, Cossacks' hard core, the center of Cossacks' domain, their home—broadly speaking' (Yavornytsky, 1990, p. 58).

The primary data include 33 qualitative semi-structured interviews conducted by the author and his research associate both in Russian and Ukrainian during the period from December 27 through December 28, 2013. Two interviews were not recorded and, thus, have been excluded from the analysis below. The interview guide included questions about the respondent's reasons for join-

---

62 A poem by the early Pavlo Tychina, a 20th-century Ukrainian poet, starts: 'On a *maidan* next to the Church, starts the revolution' (1918).

ing the protests, his/her experience of participating in various protest actions, and take on some key concepts such as freedom, trust and power. Twenty out of 31 respondents are *Viche* participants: they did not live in the tent camp in a continuous manner. Nine respondents lived in the tent camp, *Sich*. Two remaining interviews were conducted with the protest leaders with first-hand knowledge of the organisational issues.[63] The median duration of the interviews was 20 minutes.

The interviews were transcribed and content-analysed using the computer program for qualitative and quantitative content analysis, QDA Miner v. 4.1.6. The codebook for the qualitative content analysis contains 23 codes grouped in four categories: Repertoire (various strategies of collective action), Organisation (actors involved in the management of the tent camp and *Viche*), Foundations (understanding of key concepts) and Reasons for protesting (see Appendix for coding frequencies). The use of content analysis can be justified by the existence of a link between instrumental repertoires and discursive repertoires of collective action. 'Like their instrumental counterparts, which create templates for action, discursive repertoires provide contenders with a vocabulary of motives that can be used to legitimate their actions' (Traugott, 1995, p. 5).

The fact that the interviews were conducted in the two languages limited the range of options available for quantitative content analysis and for assessing the reliability of the qualitative coding.[64] The involvement of two coders, the author of the book and

63 The author thanks Orest Drul for his valuable assistance in arranging these two interviews.

64 Namely, the analysis of word co-occurrences (correlational analysis) and the calculation of coefficients of correlations between matrixes of qualitative codes, matrixes of word co-occurrence and matrixes of codes attributed with the help of a dictionary based on substitution (Oleinik, 2011b; Oleinik, Popova, Kirdina & Shatalova, 2014) turned to be unfeasible.

his research associate, was helpful in assessing the reliability of the qualitative coding by calculating Krippendorff's Alpha.[65]

IV. Analysis

The comparison of the data on the protesters from four sources, three surveys and the series of in-depth interviews, suggests the existence of several patterns, namely corroboration (the production of the same results using different research methods) and complementarity (the use of different research methods highlights various aspects of the phenomenon under study) (Brannen, 2005). The pattern of corroboration refers to the gender and age make-up of the group of protesters, as well as to their geographical representativeness. All four sources show that the majority of the protesters came from the Western regions of Ukraine (Lviv, Ivano-Frankivsk, Ternopil', etc.).

They also show that males prevail, especially at the site of the sit-in (in *Tabir* and *Sich*, see Table 3.1). This result resonates with the findings of several other studies of mass protests in the post-socialist countries. For instance, males represented 80–90% of the participants in the mass protests of July 2008 in Ulaanbaatar, Mongolia (Oleinik, 2012a, p. 169; see also Section II of Chapter 4). Males also prevailed among the protesters in 2011 in Russia. For instance, they represented 60–75% of the participants in the largest demonstration on December 24 in Moscow (Figure 4.1 in Chapter 4). These figures

65 Its value is 0.419. Before reaching this level of agreement, the two coders independently coded the interviews 3–5 times. In a project in which 4 researchers coded 37 texts the mean value for all pairs of coders was 0.537 (Oleinik et al., 2014, p. 2716). However, the texts coded in that project took the format of scholarly articles and essays. Transcripts of semi-structured interviews have a looser structure, which complicates reaching an agreement. The existing computer programs do not offer the option of calculating reliability measures for unitising, which deflates all reliability measures for coding texts. Unitising involves identifying contiguous sections (sentences, paragraphs) containing information relevant to specific codes within a transcript. The cut-off value of Alpha proposed by Klaus Krippendorff, 0.667 (2004, p. 241), does not take into account either the format of texts or disagreements regarding unitising (Oleinik et al., 2014).

contrast with a more balanced gender representation in the West (Van Aelst & Walgrave, 2001). One possible explanation refers to the more traditional gender roles in the post-socialist countries, which leads to the prevalence of males in the public sphere.

Table 3.1 'Comparison of the data on the protesters from four sources: three surveys and the series of interviews'

Source of data / **Data on the protesters**		**Street protests (*Viche*)**	**Sit-in (*Tabir*)**	**Sit-in (*Sich*)**	**Qualitative interviews**		
Date		7–8.12.13	20.12.13	3.02.14	27–29.12.13		
N		1,037	515	502	31		
					Total	*Maidan*	*Tabir*
Gender	Males	57.2	85.1	88.1	77.4	68.7	81.8
	Females	42.8	14.9	11.8	22.6	31.3	18.2
Region	West	51.8	42.4	54.8	45.2		
	Center, including Kyiv	30.9	34.4	23	38.7		
	East/South	17.3	23.2	21	16.1		
Age	29 and less	38	34.1	33.2			
	24 and less				19.4		
	30–54	49	52	56			
	25–39				22.6		
	40–54				45.2		
	55 and older	13	13.9	10.8	12.9		
Reasons for joining the protests*	The government's use of physical force against the protesters	69.6	69	61.3	20.5		
	The president's refusal to sign the agreement with the EU	53.5	40	47	18.6		

	Desire to change the power elite; its alienation	49.9	36.2	51.1	14.5
	Perspectives of a closer association with Russia	16.9	14.4	20	13.5
	Dissatisfaction with a low standard of living				11.4
	Personal dislike for President Yanukovych				9.4
	Widespread corruption				8.5
	Fight for Ukraine's true independence				3.6

Legend: * when giving their reasons for joining the protests in the surveys, the respondents could select several alternatives. The list of alternatives in the closed-ended survey question also included some other options. However, they were either not specific (e.g., 'Desire to change life in Ukraine') or received little support among the respondents (e.g., 'The call to action from leaders of the opposition parties').

The pattern of complementarity refers to the reasons for participating in the protests given by the respondents. The surveys and the interviews concur in identifying three most common reasons. The survey questions did not include an exhaustive list of alternatives, however. The interviews allowed discovering a few alternatives that had been omitted from the survey.

The government's use of physical force against the protesters represents the most frequently mentioned reason. The police force used riot batons, rubber bullets, water tanks (at a temperature well below 0°C) and tear gas against them. The police force also arrested a significant number of activists and harassed them in a number of other manners (namely, by employing hooligans, *titushky*, to beat and torture them and damage their cars).

> 'After the beating of the students there was a growing resolution that we'd not allow that again. We don't let them touch our girls, our mothers' (male, 40–54 y.o., organiser, in Russian).

> 'I think the power holders (*vlada*) initially wanted to dispel the protesters by force in order to scare the people. They thought that they would clear up Maidan and that's it. However, this only irritated the people—no one wanted to give up now' (male, 24 y.o. and less, *Viche*, in Ukrainian).

> 'Whoever you talk to, everyone says—does association with the EU really matter now? What is far more important is to protect our children. The people are talking only about this. [They beat] people, children. It's impossible, simply impossible!' (female, 40–54 y.o., *Viche*, in Ukrainian).

The emphasis on saying 'no' to the violence and brutality of the state lies at the origin of the first name of the 2013 Ukrainian mass protests—the 'Revolution of Dignity' (see also Chapters 4, 6 and 7). The protection of human dignity refers to a priority that has recently become modular (Pleyers & Glasius, 2013, p. 69). This goal was prioritised, for instance, by the participants in the Arab Spring. Its adaptation to the Ukrainian context was achieved with the help of frequent mentions of the beating of the students by the police as a turning point in the dynamics of contention. In these circumstances, dignity was understood as the protection of personal and physical integrity.

The president's refusal to sign the agreement of economic association with the EU comes second in all but one case (third in the February 2014 survey). The protest against this refusal lies at the origin of the second, more internationally known, name of the 2013 Ukrainian protests, *EuroMaidan*, i.e. the movement for Ukraine's integration into the EU. It must be noted that this reason was not overwhelming even at the early stages of the mobilisation, contrary to many observers' beliefs.

> 'It's like with a sickness. The individual needs surgery, some medical treatment. It takes time before he recovers. The same is with [the European association]. It does not happen overnight' (female, 40–54 y.o., *Sich*, in Russian).

> 'If one considers the overall timeline, the first issue was about the European association' (male, 40–54 y.o., organiser, in Russian).

> 'Speaking about the people of Ukraine, those who came to Maidan, you see how numerous they are, their aim is to defend the European association' (male, 25–39 y.o., *Viche*, in Ukrainian).

The third most important reason (second in the 2014 February survey) refers to the protesters' desire to change the power elite. The people vested in power are considered selfish and alienated from the ordinary people. The virtual absence of feedback loops in the relationships between the power holders and the ordinary people (except elections whose outcomes can be manipulated) underpins the image of the state and its representatives as a self-sufficient and self-justifiable entity.

> 'We need to change the entire system of [political] power. We've got an overstaffed bureaucracy. They don't work, they are inefficient. They simply sit on the shoulders of the people and do nothing' (male, 24 y.o. and less, *Viche*, in Russian).

> 'The biggest problem, I think, that led people here is their hatred of the power holders (*vlada*). Simply hatred' (male, 40–54 y.o., leader, in Ukrainian).

> 'I came to Maidan to show that the power holders (*vlada*) can be counterbalanced. They [mistakenly] believe that they represent Ukraine' (female, 25–39 y.o., *Viche*, in Ukrainian).

The 2013 protests started after the president had put a halt to an economic association with the EU, but they very quickly went beyond this issue. The protests unveiled a large range of issues that separates and opposes the power elite and the ordinary Ukrainians. The qualitative coding helped identify a number of reasons for joining the protests that were omitted from the survey questions. Their list includes dissatisfaction with a low standard of living, personal dislike for President Yanukovych, wide-spread corruption and the need to secure Ukraine's true independence after more than twenty years as a formally independent state. The last reason emphasises developing internal sources of Ukraine's socio-economic development as opposed to looking eastward or westward for assistance: 'as for me, neither Russia nor Europe matters that much. I want that

Europe existed within Ukraine, so we have a decent life here. We need association with neither of them' (male, 40–54 y.o., *Sich*, in Russian; see the general Introduction and Conclusion of this book and Chapter 10 for further discussion of this idea). Taken together, the four last reasons are mentioned more often than even the government's abuse of physical force! In other words, the 2013 protests did not have a single trigger. Interactions between the violent, self-sufficient and alienated government and the population would have led to an explosion sooner or later.

Now let us turn to the search for explanations for the exceptional capacity the protesters demonstrated for resisting. If the assumption formulated at the end of Section I is correct, then one explanation refers to the embeddedness of the repertoire of contention in Ukrainian traditional institutions. Such strategies as street protests and sit-ins may well have a modular character, but their specific forms developed by the protesters, *Viche* and *Sich*, are deeply rooted in Ukrainian history.

The protesters had a difficult task: to find the traditional institutions that would resonate with the modular strategies. The existence of an elective affinity between the traditional institutional and the modular repertoires requires more than simple similarity. Different, even opposite, natures have elective affinity if their interactions produce a new quality, some added value compared with the initial situation in which they do not enter into contact. In the Ukrainian case, the traditional institutions and the modular strategies form a new substance, namely, the concept of human dignity that held all the elements of the 2013 protests together (Chapter 7). Not all traditional institutions serve to emphasise and protect dignity when they interact with the modular strategies, and vice versa. Only *some* traditional institutions and *some* modular strategies produce this effect, which makes the 2013 Ukrainian events so unique and interesting.

A comparison of the 2013 protests and the 2004 Orange revolution seems particularly enlightening in this respect. The components of the 2004 Orange revolution lacked elective affinity, arguably. Specifically, the traditional institutions were not sufficiently mobilised and they did not resonate with the prevailing (in 2004) modular strategies. In November-December 2004 Maidan was a textbook example of a modular action connected to the electoral process, one of the most universal sources of mobilisation. Carnival elements predominated: rock-concerts, orange strips, and a relaxed atmosphere.

> 'The slogans of the protesters in 2004 didn't make much sense. I assume a reasonable girl of your age does not dream of being raped by a maniac killer. She wouldn't shout "Come and rape me, tell me lies, come to me, I want that you take me [by force]". The protesters shouted stupid things then [in 2004]. But, since we were choosing the lesser of two evils, no one admitted that everything was nonsense' (male, 40–54 y.o., *Maidan*, in Russian).

> 'Can you compare your impressions from the 2004 protests and now?—I vaguely remember that time, but it seemed to me that everything changed virtually overnight. There was a rock concert, many attended and shouted: "Yes! Yushchenko!"[66] Then the people started to sing songs... and put orange strips on their clothes' (male, 24 y.o. and less, *Sich*, in Russian).

People representing the Ukrainian West made up the majority of the protesters in 2013 (see also Table 3.1). They are commonly considered to be the guardians of Ukrainian national traditions susceptible to mobilise and promote them when a moment comes (this pattern started to change more recently, as a result of the undeclared war waged by Russia, see subsection I.2 of Chapter 10). The decisive moment came in late 2013 when a need arose for finding a combination of the traditional institutions and modular strategies that would prioritise the issue of human dignity.

> 'Apathy was prevalent after 2004. I didn't even hope that something similar to what we have now might happen. The people woke up, thank God. I'd add that the Kyivans have been rather passive. Only because the West started to protest, a part of them followed the lead of the people from the Western regions' (male, 55 y.o. and older, *Maidan*, in Russian).

The surveys included a question about the respondent's willingness to participate in various forms of protests (Table 3.2). Their

---

66 The 2004 protests were triggered by the victory of Viktor Yushchenko in the presidential elections that was stolen by Viktor Yanukovych. Both individuals later served as legitimately elected Ukrainian presidents: the first in 2005–2010, the second in 2010–2014.

popularity varies across the different groups of protesters. Authorised meetings and street protests represent the most popular form. The picketing of government bodies comes second (except in the case of the *Viche* participants who place elections second). The inhabitants of the tent camp (*Sich*) expectedly showed a high willingness to take part in sit-ins.

Table 3.2 'In which forms of mass protests are you ready to take part?'

	Street protests (*Viche*)	Sit-in (*Tabir*)	Sit-in (*Sich*)
Elections	51.4	37.8	54.9
Signing of a collective petition, letter of protest	37.2	30	42.4
Authorised meetings and demonstrations	70.7	51.8	56.3
Threat of a strike	28.6	27	39.3
Civil disobedience	35.8	30.9	40.2
Non-authorised meetings and demonstrations	27.8	27.8	45.5
Strike	42.7	31.8	46.6
Hunger strike	10.6	11.4	14.0
Picketing of government bodies	35.4	38.5	56.0
Sit-in at public buildings	13.8	19.5	41.0
Armed units of self-defence	15	21.3	50.4
Other	2.5	6	1.6
None of these	2	2.1	3.4
I do not know	0.5	2.7	3.1

Source: the surveys conducted by the Ilko Kucheriv Democratic Initiatives Foundation (2014).

The popularity of street protests, both authorised and unauthorised (among the *Sich* inhabitants), may be attributed to the progressive adaptation of this modular form to the local conditions and traditions. The form of street protests has been evolving in the direction of greater adaptation to Ukrainian culture.

In 2013, Maidan acquired more traditional elements, while becoming more militant at the same time. The term *Viche* suits the spirit of the 2013 Maidan far better than that of the 2004 Maidan.

One of the links connecting the modular form of street protests to traditional institutions was religion. Priests (Ukrainian Orthodox, Catholic, Muslim and Judaic) and religious symbols were highly visible on the site of the 2013 protests. *Viche* usually started with a common prayer.

> 'Many of them can be seen at the stage. I'm not a specialist, I don't differentiate the churches they represent: Ukrainian Orthodox, Catholic... —You're not a strong believer?—I'm baptised, in the Russian Orthodox Church. However, I don't see much difference between them at the stage. The Church is with the people' (male, 40–54 y.o., *Sich*, in Russian).

Another traditional element can be seen in the manner in which *Viche* functioned as a place for exchanging information. The official mass media were closely controlled and censored by the government.[67] A significant number of the protesters, especially members of the older generations, has limited or no access to the Internet. The relative importance of Internet forums as a mobilisation strategy declined as the protests unfolded and their participants became more diversified, representing the younger and older generations, urban dwellers and peasants. *Viche* was definitely not a Facebook revolution. In these circumstances, *Viche* became a place for freely exchanging information. The protesters received information both from the speakers at the stage and by word of mouth, in face-to-face discussions with other protesters.

> 'There is a need for more information... Many people come here [to Maidan] to get more information, to get handouts, to chat a bit when drinking a tea, to look around and to hear what is said from the stage... Information is a key to success. If we get more information, we'll initiate big changes' (female, 40–54 y.o., *Viche*, in Ukrainian).

> 'When you come here, you learn far more than from TV' (male, 24 y.o. and less, *Viche*, in Russian).

Viche symbolises and operates as a site of direct democracy, which marks a further departure from stolen elections as the unique modular trigger. The issue of stolen elections is only meaningful in the

67 In 2013 Ukraine ranked 126 out of 179 in the World Press Index by Reporters Without Borders (2014), ten positions down compared with 2012.

context of representative democracy. In contrast to representative democracy, in which the procedures claim to be universal, practices of direct democracy have more local and culture-specific elements. In other words, the revival of direct democracy requires more going back and forth between modular and singular strategies of collective action. The shift of focus from representative democracy to direct democracy differentiates the 2013 protests from the 2004 Orange Revolution, and also suggests some parallels between the former and the other cases of growing dissatisfaction with Western representative democracy, namely the Occupy movement and the 2011–2012 Indignados movement in Spain (Pleyers & Glasius, 2013, p. 66).

The revival of traditional forms of direct democracy also highlights their inherent limitations. At *Viche*, decisions were made by a majority vote. However, superior vocal strength often replaced the strength of arguments. No exact count of votes in favour or against a particular proposal was possible either. Similarly to *Viche* in Kievan Rus', 'the number of votes was assessed in a very approximate manner, in function of the strength of cries rather than a true majority of votes' (Klyuchevsky, 1957, p. 69; see also subsection II.4.b of Chapter 1). At traditional *Viche* and in 2013, the intensity of the support for a particular proposal was often judged by how loudly the crowd reacted to it.

Links to traditions are even more pronounced in the organisation of the tent camp, *Sich*. The layout of the tent camp in Kyiv's city center reproduced several features of the Cossacks' *Sich*. A central area (most of Khreshchatyk and the Nezalezhnosti square) was surrounded by barricades that played the role of carts in the original version. The barricades were decorated with banners and fortified with the help of sand bags, stones, metallic barriers and barbed wire. The *Sich* barricades represent a creative adaptation of the French barricades as a modular strategy to the local traditions achieved as a result of making them an element of the traditional institution.

The inner organisation of the tent camp also reproduces features of *Sich*. Fires were lit near the tents. The protesters gathered around them and cooked their meals in *kazans* (large traditional cooking pots). Drums were used by guards—often dressed in traditional Cossack costumes—to wake up the other protesters sleeping in the tents in the case of danger. The authors observed the following scene: a guard with a traditional haircut (*oseledets'*) dressed in a Cossack shirt teaches a kid, who came to *Sich* with his parents on a Sunday, how to play the drum, also in a traditional manner (Picture 3.1).

Picture 3.1 'A guard dressed in a traditional Cossack shirt teaches a child how to play drums'

Source: the author's archive.

The tent camp had its own central place, a space around the stage where prayers were held every morning. During *Viche* (usually organised on Sundays) the tent camp and its central place became the focal point of the street protests. Hundreds of thousands of Kyiv's inhabitants and visitors from the other parts of the country then joined the 'permanent' population of the tent camp (around 5,000 people).

> 'It's Cossacks' *Sich* in a pure form.—Didn't you say before that traditions of Zaporizhia are not completely relevant?—Maybe not completely, but everything looks like *Sich* in Zaporizhia indeed. It's a *tabir*. It's Cossacks' *tabir*. Cossacks organised their camp in a similar manner, when they expected an enemy attack. They surrounded themselves with carts, here we use barricades instead. It's a Ukrainian archetype. Today's Maidan is a mixture of *Viche* traditions, they go back to Kievan Rus',... and the military organisation of *Sich* in Zaporizhia' (male, 40–54 y.o., organiser, in Ukrainian).

> 'How would you describe the atmosphere on Maidan?—Much was said in this regard, I can hardly add anything new. It's like *Sich* in Zaporizhia, but in an up-to-dated version' (male, 25–39 y.o., *Viche*, in Russian).

The analysis of coding sequences and coding co-occurrence confirms that traditions were mentioned in discussions of *Viche* and *Sich* more often than when the interlocutor referred to the other strategies from the repertoire of contention. Namely, the codes 'Traditions,' 'Viche,' 'Camp,' and 'Fight' form a cluster that stands apart from the other codes (Figure 3.1). Of all coding sequences with the code 'Traditions' coming first, the probability of having the code 'Camp' next is higher than any other of the remaining 21 codes. The code sequence 'Tradition'—'Camp' occurs significantly more often than solely by pure coincidence (Z value=3.33, p=0.003).[68]

68 Freq('Traditions')=38, Freq('Camp')=78, 'Camp' follows 'Traditions' 11 times (28.9% of times), 'Traditions' appears before 'Camp' also 11 times (14.1%), 20.8% is the percentage of all sequences equal to the current sequence.

Figure 3.1 'Two-dimensional map of the coding co-occurrence, category "Repertoire" and code "Traditions", multidimensional scaling'

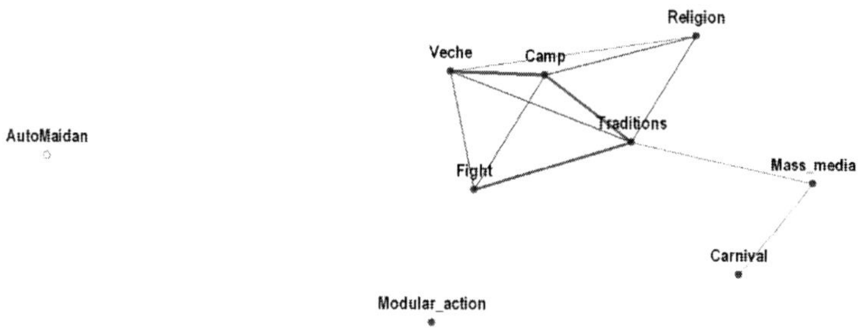

Legend: Stress = 0.2149, pseudo R^2 = 0.8340.[69]

The strategy of strike also represents an interesting case for consideration. Striking is among the four or five most popular strategies among the protesters (Table 3.2). The leaders of the political parties supporting the protests (Vitali Klitschko of Udar, Arseny Yatsenyuk of Bat'kyvshchyna and Oleh Tyahnibok of Svoboda) made several attempts to start a strike as a measure to obtain concessions from the government.[70] These attempts were unsuccessful. An explanation for the repeated failure to organise a strike despite the popularity of this strategy may be a result of a lack of elective affinity with local traditions. The tradition of strikes was revived in the late 1980s—early 1990s when coal miners in Donbas organised several strikes. No specific efforts were made to adapt this strategy to the new circumstances (workers represented 6.7% of the *Viche* participants, 14.4% of the *Tabir* inhabitants and 15.2% of the *Sich* inhabitants). To be workable, the strategy of striking should have been made appealing to office workers, peasants, students and retired people as well.

69 The level of acceptable stress (distortion) in multi-dimensional scaling is conventionally set at 0.15–0.2 or lower (Bernard, 2013, p. 413).

70 For instance, Klitschko intended to start a strike on January 23, 2014 should the talks between the leaders of the three parties and the government fail (Ukrains'ka Pravda, 2014). The talks failed, but the strike did not start.

Non-violent resistance is among the other historical precedents that were not revived during the 2013 protests. Strategies of Gandhian resistance were employed by some Ukrainian political prisoners in Soviet prisons. They explicitly attempted to bring non-violence back into the repertoire of contention before the start of the mass protests in November 2013 (Grytsyak, 2013). Unfortunately, their efforts went virtually unnoticed. The historical repertoire of contention in the Ukrainian case is rather broad. It even contains suicide protest, namely the self-immolation of Oleksa Hirnyk in 1978[71], which could arguably be traced back to Quang Duc's sacrifice (Biggs, 2013, p. 418). However, in order to become workable again, these traditions require significant work to update and adapt to today's modular actions.

The absence of references to Soviet traditions of contention is noteworthy. During the Soviet period, the intellectuals, dissident intelligentsia, positioned themselves as key actors of contention and developed a number of protest strategies, mostly semi-private in nature (discussions 'in the kitchens', the circulation of self-printed manuscripts, *samizdat*). Some Russian protesters reportedly construct their identities with the help of the Soviet past, describing themselves as the heirs of the dissident intelligentsia (Lyytikäinen, 2014, p. 136). The Ukrainian protesters also showed a certain involvement with the Soviet values and practices of contention in 2004 (Fournier, 2010), but in 2013–2014 the tendency to omit everything related to the Soviet past prevailed.[72] The protesters eventually considered traditions of the Soviet dissidence as external, imperial and obsolete. In 2013, their principal attention was devoted to authentically Ukrainian traditions.

What actors did the work of adaptation in the case of *Viche* and *Sich*? If they are political leaders, then the entrepreneurial

71 The Hirnyk case was mentioned in one of the interviews.

72 The protesters even targeted Vladimir Lenin's monuments, which symbolise the Soviet past for them. On December 8, 2014, after several attempts, they finally managed to destroy Lenin's monument in downtown Kyiv, on Taras Shevchenko Boulevard.

model applies. If they are community members, then the communitarian model provides a better fit. Compared with the 2004 protests, the 2013 protests marked a departure from the entrepreneurial model. The leaders of the three above-mentioned opposition parties did not organise the mass protests. They did not run *Sich* on a day-to-day basis either. The leaders were simply unable to assert their control in January-February 2014 when violent clashes between the protesters and the police occurred. On multiple occasions, the interlocutors emphasised that the 2013–2014 protests were people's protests and they refer to the model of leaderless contention. The code 'Self-organisation' has the highest frequency of all 23 codes (Annex).

> 'This Maidan started spontaneously... It doesn't derive from a particular party's initiative. The three parties, Udar, Svoboda and Bat'kyvshchyna, did not call it. This Maidan has a civic character. Up to 90% of the people that we see here came on their own'[73] (male, 40–54 y.o., organiser, in Ukrainian).

> 'I am not a member of any [political] party. I'm a free non-affiliated citizen who wants to defend his rights and the interests of his people' (male, 25–39, *Viche*, in Ukrainian).

> 'One of the achievements of this Maidan is a new organisation.[74] It reminds me of Polish Solidarity. Similarly to Solidarity, the organisation emerged during unrest and I believe it may transform into a solid political force, people's force' (male, 55 y.o. and older, *Viche*, in Russian).

Most institutional innovations during the 2013 protests were carried out in a bottom-up as opposed to top-down manner. There was no architect who invented the new layout of the tent camp. Its inhabitants did so spontaneously. The decision to invite the priests and to start all important events with a prayer was not made by a single individual. The priests visited the protesters' tents regardless

---

73 This statement is confirmed by results of the sociological survey. When answering the question 'Did you come on your own or was your trip arranged by a political party?', from 76.1% (survey 'Tabir') up to 91.9% (survey 'Veche') of the respondents choose the first alternative.

74 The respondent refers to the association 'Maidan' that was established as an organisation not affiliated with the existing political parties. This initiative, however, turned out to be short-lived.

of any centralised decisions. Last but not least, the references to *Sich* and *Viche* also emerged spontaneously.

The cultural entrepreneurs, who were the key figures of the 2004 protests, at best acted at the backstage in 2013. The 2013 protests were not driven from the outside either. The code 'Self-organisation' rarely entered into sequences with the codes 'Russia' (Z value=-1.96, p=0.026) and 'Europe' (Z value=-2.46, p=0.004). More specifically, these sequences occurred significantly less often than solely by pure coincidence. The 2013 protests were driven by 'critical communities'—'networks of excluded citizens who identify new social problems, formulate new modes of thinking and feeling, and develop new political and cultural solutions' (Chabot & Duyvendak, 2002, p. 706). The critical communities used the traditional institutions (*Viche*, *Sich*) as a key resource for their institutional innovations.

Conclusion

Judging by the protesters' exemplary capacity to resist the oppressive and violent government, their institutional innovation—the relocation of the modular repertoire onto Ukrainian soil—can be deemed a success. This study suggests that the elective affinity between the traditional institutions and the relocated strategies made this success possible.

At a theoretical level, the chapter shows the importance of elective affinity for adapting modular strategies to the local institutional and cultural environment. Elective affinity represents a missing element in the diffusion model. The repertoire of the 2013 protests in Ukraine is neither simply dislocated nor created from scratch. It results from an open-ended search for modular strategies that have some elective affinity with the traditional institutions and from their adaptation by means of the efforts of the critical communities.

At a practical level, this chapter provides some insight as to why similar modular strategies work in some cases but not in others. The comparison of the Russian and Ukrainian cases seems to be particularly revealing and deserving of further studies. Recently, there have been multiple attempts at mass mobilisation using modular repertoires in Russia, for example, the 'Oborona' movement (Lyytikäinen, 2014). They culminated in the November-December 2011 mass protests in Moscow and a number of other urban areas. The leaders—the Russian case derives from the entrepreneurial model—used such modular strategies as street protests with carnival elements and sit-ins (the Occupy Abai event in Moscow). Nevertheless, these modular strategies were not really relocated onto Russian soil. 'Oborona' dissolved in late 2011, precisely at the time of a surge of contention. Links that would connect them to traditional institutions (particularly strong *Viches* existed in Novgorod Republic and the Principality of Pskov, see also subsection I.2.a of Chapter 1) were not found.

As a result, the social base of the mass protests was rather limited. It mostly consisted of members of the urban creative class. Russians living in small cities, towns and villages did not understand the format of the mass protests, which undermined their effectiveness and overall strength. The relocation of modular repertoires by the way of their adaptation to the traditional institutions during the 2013 Ukrainian protests, on the other hand, served to involve a larger number of participants with a more diverse social and educational background. Both urban dwellers, including representatives of the creative class, and peasants joined their ranks.

Appendix

Table 'Codebook and coding frequency'

Category	Code	Description	Count	% Codes	Cases	% Cases
Foundations	Freedom	How freedom is defined. What does mean to be free? Not to be confused with perception of a particular political party, Svoboda [Freedom].	16	1.7	13	41.9
	Power	How power is defined and its importance—assessed.	28	2.9	20	64.5
	Traditions	References to the Ukrainian traditions, including traditional holidays (Christmas) in the context of discussing the mass protests. Traditions as a source of ideas and inspiration when protesting. Traditions of the 2004 Maidan when they inspire the 2013 Maidan. Defense of the Ukrainian language as a justification of mass mobilisation.	38	4.0	16	51.6
	Trust	How trust is defined and its importance—assessed.	26	2.7	21	67.7
Organisation_of_Maidan	Local_management	The role of local managers (*sotnyky, desyatnyky, starshi po palatkam, veduchi* on the stage) in the everyday operation of Maidan. The issues of division of labour on Maidan are coded using the 'Camp' code.	21	2.2	12	38.7
	Political_parties	The role of political leaders on Maidan (the 'big three': Arseny Yatsenyuk, Vitali Klitschko, Oleh Tyahnibok), including the role of political parties in general. How is their contribution perceived?	66	6.9	25	80.6

	Self-organisation	Emphasis that people came there without being paid (some personal sacrifice has to be mentioned) and without being members of political parties. References to 'it was my (our) decision'. Self-organisation in everyday life on Maidan—when people do something without being told/receiving instructions, references to volunteerism.	109	11.5	28	90.3
Reasons_for_protesting	Alienation	The general feeling of alienation from the people vested in power. The people vested in power are considered as Them (Us/Them); they do not care about the ordinary people and do not listen to their needs.	60	6.3	23	74.2
	Corruption	Corruption of the government representatives as a reason for participating in the protests. Bribery, administrative barriers etc.	35	3.7	18	58.1
	Economic	Economic reasons for protesting: dissatisfaction with the living standard, the level of salaries, pensions etc. The desire to increase the standard of living.	47	4.9	22	71.0
	Europe	The desire of Ukraine's closer association with the EU as a reason for participating in the protests. The example of Poland as a successfully integrated country. References to President's decision to stop the process of integration as a trigger.	77	8.1	27	87.1
	Independence	The idea of true independence: Ukraine, according this line of reasoning has not enjoyed yet the benefits of its independence. References to building the 'European' (i.e. civilized) order without sacrificing its independence. Ukraine being more or less autonomous and independent both from the EU and Russia.	15	1.6	7	22.6
	President	The feeling (i.e., something emotional or quasi-emotional) of disgust toward President Yanukovych as a reason for joining	39	4.1	19	61.3

		the protest. This code involves a personal perception and personal antipathy (as opposed to the statement that the power elite is corrupted or violent).				
	Russia	The desire to move away from Russia's sphere of influence and not to be under an authoritarian rule. Only negative associations with Russia are coded by this code. The issues of Russian versus Ukrainian language (protection of the latter) are coded by 'Traditions'.	56	5.9	22	71.0
	Violence	The application of physical force and weapons by the police against the protesters as a reason for participating in the protests. References to racketeering, threats, destruction of property (activists' cars).	85	8.9	24	77.4
Repertoire	AutoMaidan	References to the use of cars in protests, to the movement of AutoMaidan (protesters on cars going to Yanukovych's residence in Mezhyhirya, protesting on the Kyiv streets and so forth).	2	0.2	2	6.5
	Camp	Sit-ins and various forms of Occupy (public spaces, administrative buildings). Tent camp (*Sich*, *Tabir*) as an example: observations about the efficiency of the occupation of the downtown. Living in a tent as a form of protest. The division of labour on Maidan: various services (defense, kitchen...) and how order is maintained.	78	8.2	21	67.7
	Carnival	Discussion of carnival (masks, a particular atmosphere, music, shows) as a strategy of mass protests.	9	0.9	5	16.1
	Fight	The idea that a force can be counter-balanced by another force, i.e. the use of force and quasi-military organisation as a strategy for achieving the protesters' goals.	31	3.3	13	41.9

	Mass_media	The role of the mass media in mass mobilisation. Mobilisation with the help of social networks (Facebook etc.) and the Internet. Any references to a 'virtual' dimension of the protests.	10	1.1	6	19.4
	Modular_ action	References to strategies that worked in the other countries and the desire to replicate these strategies in Ukraine (e.g., references to successful protests in Thailand). The idea of this code is the replication of strategies as opposed to their invention.	3	0.3	3	9.7
	Religion	References to religious beliefs and religion in the context of mass mobilisation. Praying as a form of protest.	22	2.3	14	45.2
	Viche	Peaceful street marches and mass gatherings (the ones that occurred in Kyiv during the weekends).	77	8.1	27	87.1

Chapter 4
'Images of the protests: A comparative analysis of the Ukrainian and Russian protesters'

Introduction

A recent wave of mass protests in the Middle East (Iran, 2009; Tunisia, Egypt, Libya, Yemen, Syria, Algeria, Bahrain, 2011, Turkey, 2013) and the countries of the former Soviet Union (Georgia, 2003; Ukraine, 2004 and 2013–2014; Kyrgyzstan, 2005 and 2010; Mongolia, 2008; Moldova, 2009; Russia, 2011) caught most scholars and practitioners (political leaders and their advisors) by surprise. Even when mass protests were largely anticipated and carefully prepared, their dynamics, scope and outcomes often exceeded the boldest expectations (or failed to meet the lowest ones). No one in Mongolia or among scholars of Central Asian studies predicted the mass unrest of July 1, 2008 in Ulaanbaatar (Oleinik, 2012a). Mass protests of November 2004 in Ukraine, colloquially referred to as the 'Orange Revolution', resulted from the implementation of a plan, yet 'to the surprise of the organizers themselves, Kyivans [inhabitants of the capital city] turned out in unexpectedly large numbers' (Bessinger, 2011, p. 25). Meanwhile, mass protests in this country from November 2013-February 2014 did not result from the implementation of a master plan at all, being an example of spontaneous and bottom-up mobilisation (Chapter 3).

The challenges presented by the mass protests of the past decade have both a theoretical and methodological nature. On one hand, the list of factors facilitating mass-scale mobilisation remains wide open. The active participation of both genders, most age groups and socio-economic groups with otherwise conflicting interests (such as students and businesspeople) makes the usual predictors such as ideology or the economic situation less relevant. On the other hand, a number of methodological problems complicate the search for more adequate explanations for the recent wave of mass protests. Primary data collected on site from the protesters is rarely available. The unexpected dynamics and scope of mass protests complicate the task of planning and carrying out data collection in a systematic manner. The researchers may simply not be prepared to appear in the right place at the right time. Field work requires securing ethics approval, which takes time. Western scholars of mass protests also have a limited ability to speak the native language of the protesters, whereas the specialists in area studies often lack the skills required for collecting the primary data on a large scale.

This chapter is intended to address the issue of collecting data on mass protests in general and in the areas without long traditions of empirical studies of mass mobilisation in particular. It explores the significant, and still undervalued, potential of visual records made during mass protests by participants and journalists. Unlike researchers, journalists have more opportunities to be in the right place at the right time. The easy availability of compact cameras and cell phones with built-in cameras transforms any participant into a reporter, as acknowledged by the mainstream mass-media (the 'iReport' program on *CNN* serves as an illustration). The language barrier represents a less serious obstacle for international researchers working with images. It is argued that the content analysis of images of mass protests serves to draw a social portrait of the protester complementing the other sources of the relevant data, namely mass surveys. It also helps to obtain some preliminary insights into which factors facilitate mobilisation.

The present chapter has a predominantly methodological and empirical character. It discusses methodological issues related to the use of visual records. Namely, the chapter explores a new source of the information about mass protests and discusses its validity and reliability. The assessment of the reliability and validity of the data that images of mass protests contain involves comparing outcomes of the statistical analysis and the results of the content analysis of visual records. This chapter contributes to the development of techniques for triangulating the data that were obtained from various sources and have different formats. These techniques may be used not only in studies of mass protests, but in any situation when the information from one source is complemented by data from other sources. The potential of the new methodological approaches is shown through the continued discussion of the 2013–2014 mass protests in Chapter 3.

The choice of triangulation has a pragmatic rationale under the present circumstances. It is argued that the strategy of triangulation allows for dealing with incomplete and eventually biased data. Anthony Onwuegbuzie and Nancy Leech (2005) differentiate between purists, situationalists and pragmatists based on the researcher's take on mixing research methods. Purists argue against triangulation. Situationalists submit that the choice depends on research questions. Pragmatists view triangulation as a tool for solving problems related to data collection and analysis (Fielding, 2010).

Along with the purely methodological value added of including the content analysis of images in the toolbox of studies of mass protests, this chapter discusses its eventual political implications. Assessments of the number of protesters have a political dimension. The power holders—those against whom mass protesters gather—tend to underestimate the size of crowds, whereas protesters and their supporters tend to overestimate them. Karl-Dieter Opp (2011) shows that the real number of participants may differ from both official and unofficial estimates, using as an example the Monday demonstration in Leipzig on October 9, 1989, the first large-scale mass protest against the communist regime in the former German Democratic Republic.

A similar situation has been observed in Russia with respect to the mass protests that took place in Moscow and several other cities across that country between early December 2011 and early May 2012. Representatives of the Russian government systematically underestimated the number of protesters, who in their turn tended to inflate the figures. For instance, the Moscow police estimated the number of protesters on Academician Sakharov Avenue on December 24, 2011 at 25,000–30,000, whereas the organisers of the meeting and the Russian independent press insisted that more than 110,000 people had taken part. Estimates of the number of participants in specific events of the 2013–2014 Maidan diverge as well. The police reported that some 35,000 people joined the march on December 1, 2013, whereas the opposition produced much higher estimates—from 0.5 to one million.

This chapter discusses the outcomes of the content analysis of pictures taken on Academician Sakharov Avenue in Moscow during the afternoon of December 24, 2011, and visual records of Maidan in 2013–2014 in Kyiv. The December 24 event was one of the largest manifestations of protests against the Russian power elite and the alleged involvement of its members in electoral fraud (the parliamentary elections took place on December 4, 2011, followed by the presidential elections on March 4, 2012) since the late 1980s and early 1990s. The December 24 demonstration was preceded by at least two other meetings and followed by several others; in this sense, it may be deemed 'representative' of the entire sequence of mass protests.

Visual records of the mass protests in Moscow are compared with images of Maidan in Kyiv in November-December 2013. Visual records produced in January-February 2014 were excluded from this analysis. The comparison of the Russian and Ukrainian examples of mass mobilisation becomes more meaningful as a result. In both cases, mass protests started unexpectedly in the capital cities. In both cases, protests were initially peaceful and non-violent. In the Ukrainian case, however, the use of violence by the police changed the overall dynamics of the conflict. Its violent dimension took particularly manifest forms in January-February 2014, which explains the exclusion of this period from the comparative analysis in this chapter.

This chapter starts with Section I, which briefly reviews various sources of data about mass protests, including surveys, images produced by the mass media and by private individuals, and social networking sites. Section II presents the key findings of the content analysis of 382 images of the December 24 demonstration and 2,344 images of Maidan in November-December 2013. Particularities of the mass protests in Ukraine are highlighted in Section III. Section

IV discusses several methodological issues in light of these findings.

I. Sources of the data on mass protests: an overview

The list of the principal sources of the primary data on mass protests includes social networking sites, mass surveys, image banks created by the mass media and private individuals, in-depth qualitative interviews, and participant observation. The sources are listed according to their accessibility to researchers who are unable to do fieldwork either during the protests or immediately afterwards, starting with the most accessible ones. General observations about a source of the data are followed by specific comments on using it in the present study (if available).

I.1 Social networking sites

The internet plays an increasing role in social protests. First, it provides participants with an opportunity for finding like-minded people and for getting in touch with them in an expeditious manner at little cost. Virtual communities tend to be unstable and difficult to transform into real ones (Kujawski & Abell, 2011). Nevertheless, they represent a substitute for otherwise absent social links in societies characterised by a low level of generalised trust and weak traditions of civil participation. Probably for that reason, mass protests in the Middle East and the countries of the former Soviet Union often originate with virtual groups established on social networking websites such as Facebook. Mobilisation via Facebook took particularly dramatic forms in Egypt with its 800,000 Facebook users in 2009. Ninety thousand users made online commitments to take part in the key demonstration of January 25, 2011 (Attia, Aziz, Friedman & Elhusseiny, 2011).

Second, social networking sites provide protesters with a readily available infrastructure for coordinating actions after establishing preliminary contacts. Until recently, in countries with long traditions of mass protests (Western Europe, North America), the coordination of protest activities was achieved mainly through organisations: trade unions, political parties, non-government organisations and so forth. The internet offers new opportunities for organizing 'action in concert', to borrow Hannah Arendt's apt expression (1969, p. 44; see also Section II of Chapter 6), without the involvement of organisational hierarchies. 'The locus of control shifts from the organization to the individual' (Walgrave, Bennett, Van Laer & Breunig, 2011, p. 345).

Third, the internet contributes to mobilisation from below at a deeper level as well. It promotes a particular construction of social authority that differs from that embedded in conventional organisations. In fact, the internet allows for interaction without due regard for people vested in power and authority, because anyone can publish on the internet, anyone can establish a new group, and anyone can comment on everyone else's thoughts. The involvement of a figure vested in power—an editor, a bureaucrat, or a professional critic—is not a must anymore. As a result, 'it is *attitude* that changes, the attitude of individual toward authority, a disregard for the long chain of authority, for established hierarchies that used to structure decision making' (Hofheinz, 2011, p. 1425).

The transformation of the internet into a meeting place for protesters and a communication channel between them explains its value as a source of information for scholars of mass protests. It is possible to gather a wealth of relevant information by monitoring groups established on social networking sites and internet forums (Kujawski & Abel, 2011). Facebook is the dominant social network in most countries, but in Russia, its local rival, VKontakte, prevailed as of December 2011 (Economist, 2012, p. 24). Thus, for the purposes of studying the December 24 demonstration, a group established on VKontakte was retained.

As of April 2012, the group *Narod protiv zhulikov i vorov* (People against swindlers and thieves) had 170,315 members, 33,867 of whom were in Moscow. On the eve of each large demonstration, including that of December 24, 2011, the mass media reported the number of members in this group, who had confirmed their participation, as a rough estimate of the scope of the upcoming event. VKontakte allows for the retrieval of information about people committed to taking part in a demonstration, such as their age, gender, education (by using search options one is able to generate lists of account holders of a particular age, gender, etc.) Needless to say, the validity of the social characteristics of would-be protesters or of their stated intentions cannot be guaranteed in this manner.

The 2013–2014 Maidan started after a call was made by Mustafa Nayyem, an opposition journalist of Afghan origin, through his Facebook account. However, the level of internet penetration in Ukraine is significantly lower than in Russia (see subsection III.3 of Chapter 7 for further detail). As a result, mobilisation through the internet did not play a prominent role in the Ukrainian case, especially in the subsequent expansion of the scope of mass protests. Groups created on Facebook helped the activists to reach out to new participants, complementing the other, more conventional strategies of mass mobilisation (see Chapter 3). The internet did not serve as a substitute for the latter nevertheless. In other words, the internet was not a key driver of the 2013–2014 Maidan. At the same time, Facebook played an important role as a tool of the mobilisation of volunteers after the Maidan (see subsection IV.1 of Chapter 10).

I.2 Mass surveys

Mass surveys provide the quantitative data largely used in studies of mass protests. Two types of surveys can be usefully differentiated in this respect. The first type refers to general surveys containing questions about the respondent's eventual participation in mass protests. The results of general surveys may be available on the internet, which explains the attractiveness of this source of data for researchers with a limited knowledge of local culture and restricted opportunities for being eye-witnesses. However, the reliance on general surveys leaves the researcher with no other option than to make far-reaching inferences from what the respondent says. For instance, the respondent's claim about his/her participation in a demonstration automatically leads to his/her inclusion in the group of protesters (as in Bessinger, 2011). The researcher rarely attempts to assess the validity of such claims, despite a high associated risk of social (un)desirability. Only on rare occasions is the researcher not only willing to acknowledge the problematic character of the respondent's claims with respect to his/her involvement in protests, but also has means for assessing their validity (Opp, 2011).

The second type of mass surveys refers to specialised surveys. The administration of custom-designed mass-surveys relieves the researcher's dependency on questionable interferences. They are administered during a mass protest event by means of face-to-face interviews or shortly afterwards by means of mail-in questionnaires initially distributed on-site. The organisation of custom-designed mass surveys requires more resources and time. It also implies the researcher's capacity to anticipate mass protests.

Even if the researcher's predictions are confirmed, he/she faces challenges pertaining to ethics review. Ethics review authorities rarely render their decisions on short notice. Furthermore, in the case of surveys of participants in mass protests, ethics review authorities have particularly strong concerns as to the protection of personal information. In some countries, taking part in mass protests means exposing oneself to substantial risks.

Specialised mass surveys have their own sources of bias. In their pioneering study of bias in protest surveys, Stefaan Walgrave and Joris Verhulst (2011, p. 212) identify three sources of bias: selection, cooperation and response. Selection bias derives from the non-random selection of respondents in a crowd. Stationary protests, as opposed to moving protests, appear particularly vulnerable to selection bias because of the difficulties involved in dividing the stationary crowd into 'imaginary' sectors. Noncooperation bias exists if the protesters, who agree to take a questionnaire, differ from those who refuse. Response bias exists if the protesters, who actually respond to questions included in the questionnaire, differ from those who do not.

In addition to the information on the Russian protesters from the website VKontakte, the present study relies on data gathered through a mass survey. The management of Levada Center, a leading independent survey center in Russia, kindly provided the author with access to the complete dataset of a mass survey administered during the December 24 demonstration through face-to-face standardised interviews. Sixteen professional interviewers and 21 sociology graduate and undergraduate students conducted a total of 791 interviews. There were 215 documented refusals, which corresponds to a 71% response rate.

Technically speaking, the December 24 demonstration had features of a stationary protest: it took place in a closed segment of Academician Sakharov Avenue. However, the interviewers were instructed to recruit every fifth protester passing through security checks at the sole entrance to the meeting place. In other words, the interviewers were instructed to recruit the respondents from a moving crowd on a random basis.

Non-cooperation bias arguably represents the most serious threat to the external validity of the outcomes of this particular survey. Most refusals came from protesters aged 55 and older, which further raises concerns as to external validity. It is a documented fact that 'older people are more prone to collaborate with the researchers' (Walgrave & Verhulst, 2011, p. 219).

The outcomes of the mass survey were analysed using the SPSS v. 19 statistics software from IBM. The output includes descriptive statistics with respect to the protesters' socio-economic profile.

A series of surveys were conducted during the mass protests of 2013–2014 in Kyiv by the Ilko Kucheriv Democratic Initiatives Foundation (2014). The fact that these protests included elements of both a moving (namely, the Sunday marches) and stationary protest (the tent camp on Maidan Nezalezhnosti, the central square) represented an additional problem in the Ukrainian case. The first survey was conducted on 7–8.12.2013 (N=1,037) among participants in a march, i.e. in a moving protest. The second survey was carried out on 20.12.2013 (N=515) among inhabitants of the tent camp. The third survey was also conducted among the same population (N=502) on 3.02.2014, but it fell outside the temporal scope of the discussion in this chapter (see Table 3.1 in Chapter 3).

I.3 Image banks

Images are widely used in the media reports about mass protests, yet their value and potential as a source of information for scientific research remain underestimated. Images included in the mass media reports constitute a first category of visual records. They are readily available in the printed press and on the internet. Images produced by the protesters themselves constitute a second category of visual records suitable for analysis. They can be retrieved from specialised image hosting websites such as Flickr.com. As of December 2010, Flickr had more than 40 million members (Rose, 2012, p. 84), being the world's largest depository of pictures.

Social networking sites also serve as depositories of images produced by protesters. Instead of uploading pictures to specialised image hosting websites, some protesters may prefer to post them on their personal pages or group pages created for the occasion of mass protests. The function of social networking sites as image depositories must be differentiated from their function as a source of personal information about protesters. The latter function is discussed in subsection I.1 (see also Cho & Park, 2003); the former function is discussed in this subsection.

Each category of images has particular features. Images produced by the mass media can be better classified in the category of documentary photography. Documentary photography involves an attempt to send a particular message to the viewer, often serving as a tool 'to pressure for change' or to uphold the status quo (Rose, 2012, p. 23). For this reason, documentary photography is commonly subject to 'framing': the composition, geometrical perspective, and colours of a visual record all help highlight some aspects and overshadow the others. For instance, empirical studies confirm the existence of framing in the coverage of the Iraq war by the British and UK press (Fahmy & Kim, 2008), in the picturing of overweight people by the US news channels (Heuer, McClure & Puhl, 2011), and in the representation of genders in the anti-globalist movement by the alternative media (Kolářová, 2004).

Images produced by protesters have a different rationale. Instead of sending a 'message', their purpose consists in memorising an event in which the individual has taken part. Here 'photography's capacity to provide extra-somatic memory' is engaged (Prosser & Schwartz, 2005, p. 123). Images from the second category can be classified as street photography (Rose, 2012, p. 26). Compared with documentary photography, street photography produces more ideologically neutral visual records. The author of a street photograph has less time and skills to play with geometrical perspective or to think about a picture's composition. He/she is simply a witness, not an artist.

Two sets of visual records constitute a third source of data used in the reported study. For the purposes of this present study, 382 images of the December 2011 manifestation in Moscow of both types were collected. They come from a variety of sources: pictures taken by the author on the spot, pictures taken by the other participants and posted on the internet (at Flickr and VKontakte), and photo reports prepared by professional photojournalists for the Russian major independent mass media (*Forbes*, *Vedomosti*, *Gazeta.Ru*, *Ezhednevnyi Zhurnal*, *RBC Daily* and *Bol'shoi Gorod*). 'Studies of online images represent a relatively recent phenomenon' (Ozel & Park, 2012, p. 1014), and this chapter aims to contribute to their wider use in empirical research. Forty-five percent of the images can be categorised as documentary photos; 55% are street photos. The criteria for including an image in the research sample are purely technical in nature: the image has to be high resolution and there should be more than 15–20 visual records available from the same source.

Images of Maidan in November-December 2013 (N=2,344) mostly come from the Flickr depository and the author's archive (in addition to conducting interviews with inhabitants of the tent camp and participants in the Sunday march, see Section III of Chapter 3, the author and his research associate also took pictures during their field work). In contrast to the Russian case, documentary photos represent a much smaller share in the Ukrainian databank. Maidan is an umbrella term covering a wide range of diverse events that spread over a few months. The mass media produced snapshots of some of them without offering a complete coverage free of omissions. Street photos better reflect the day-to-day life of Maidan. The photos subject to analysis document 38 days in the life of Maidan, from November 22-December 29, 2013.

The visual records were subsequently subject to content analysis using the QDA Miner v. 4.0.4 software by Provalis Research (Montréal, Canada). The techniques of content analysis are better known when applied to texts. The content analysis of texts (letters, Tweets, advertisements, novels, scholarly chapters and so forth) involves 'making replicable and valid inferences' from them (Krippendorff, 2004, p. 18). Complex texts subject to content analysis are divided into fragments. The coder attaches specific meanings (codes) to these fragments. He/she then compares constellations of codes across texts looking for emerging patterns. In order to assess the reliability and validity of the coding, the involvement of several coders may be needed, which serves to calculate the level of intercoder agreement (Oleinik, Popova, Kirdina & Shatalova, 2014).

Picture 4.1 'Content analysis of a picture of the 2011 mass protests in Russia using QDA Miner'

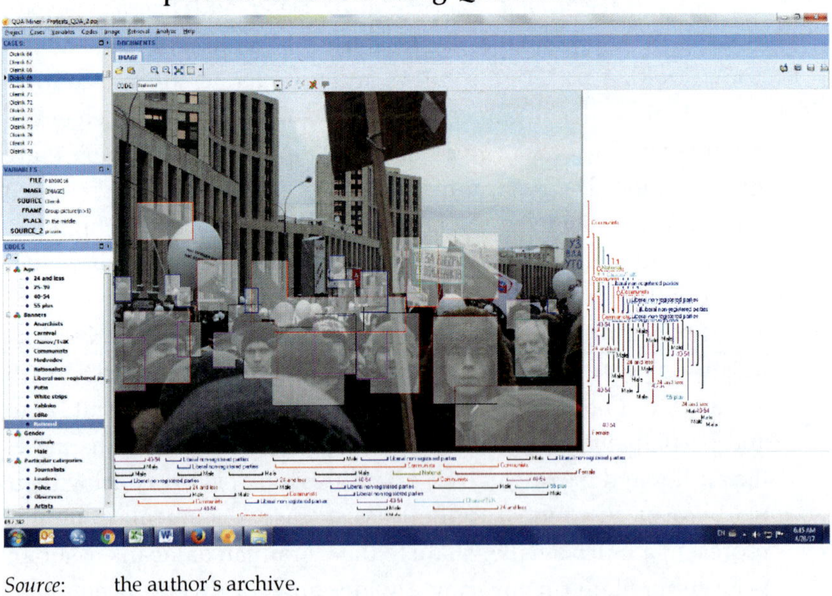

Source: the author's archive.

Content analysis of visual records commonly involves the transformation of images into a matrix with variables (such as date, sources, gender of the characters, etc.) in columns and cases (particular pictures) in rows. This approach allows for the use of standard statistics, yet it involves the loss of a significant amount of data. QDA Miner enables the researcher to attribute codes to specific *fragments* of a picture, similar to the coding of complex texts. Thus, multiple elements on images with a complex composition (common in street photography) can be coded separately without running the risk of losing data (Pictures 4.1 and 4.2). QDA Miner makes it possible to retrieve fragments associated with a particular code at will. Also, the techniques of multidimensional scaling can be easily applied.

Picture 4.2 'Content analysis of a picture of the 2013 mass protests in Ukraine using QDA Miner'

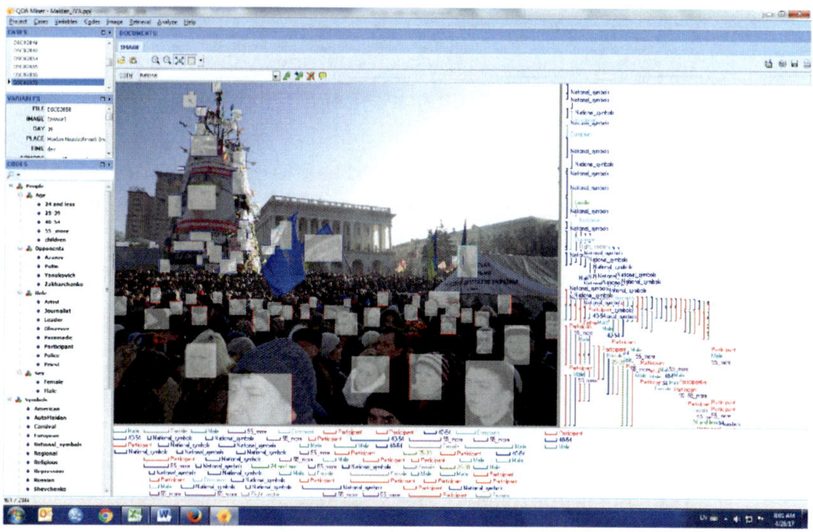

Source: the author's archive.

The collection and analysis of visual records posted on the internet does not require free and informed consent—neither from their authors nor from the people pictured on them. The main issue of research ethics arguably refers in this case to the protection of personal information (O'Connell, 2013, p. 33). The researcher collects the information freely available on the internet. However, the analysis of this information enables the researcher to identify gender, age and some other personal information about the people pictured on visual records.[75] Thus, the researcher must store the visual records in a secure place and eventually publish them in a form that prevents the identification of specific individuals.

The design chosen for the content analysis involves using a photograph as a unit of observation, and its particular element (an individual with an identifiable face, a banner) as a unit of analysis. The codebooks (Tables A and B in Appendix) include the basic socio-demographic characteristics of the protesters (gender, age) and indicators of their political preferences (mentions of the then incumbent president Dmitry Medvedev and the then prime minister Vladimir Putin in Russia or the then president Viktor Yanukovych in Ukraine) and affiliation (anarchists, communists, liberals, nationalists, and centrists).

The primary focus on the socio-demographic characteristics of the protesters and easy-to-identify political symbols (the colours of the parties' banners are known) explains the preference for an objective method of coding, as opposed to the determination of latent content that necessitates a subjective interpretation of symbols. For instance, the three red banners in the left part of Picture 4.1 are symbols of the Communist party of the Russian Federation (the logo can be seen on one of them). A test of validity was, nevertheless, deemed necessary: the event took place in December when the outside temperature dipped below -20°C (December 2013 in Kyiv was also cold). This means that heads were covered and the protesters often wore winter coats that were not gender specific. In the case of mass protests taking place in the summer, it is easier to identify the protester's gender and age even for an outsider (Oleinik, 2012a).

Four coders independently coded a sub-sample of 34 images of the Russian sample (10% of the sample).[76] A similar approach

75 The development of automated face recognition technologies raises concerns as to the protection of the privacy of individuals whose pictures are freely available on the internet (Risen & Poitras, 2014).

76 Dr. Natalia Ryzhova, Dr. Tatiana Zhuravskaya and Ms. Anna Stupnikova (all from the Institute of Economic Research of the Far Eastern Branch of the Russian Academy of Sciences in Khabarovsk) participated in the coding along with the author. Their involvement is highly appreciated.

was adapted in a study of images of political figures in South Korea (Ozel & Park, 2012). They represent different genders and different age groups (two are in their late twenties, one in her late thirties and one in his forties). The initial level of inter-coder agreement as measured by Krippendorff's Alpha and Scott's Pi (Bernard & Ryan, 2010, p. 305; Oleinik et al., 2014; Warner, 2008, p. 834) was moderate,[77] yet the coders tended to disagree with respect to the protesters' age. Thus, a second round of coding was deemed necessary after modifying the age groups.[78] In the final account, the values of Krippendorff's Alpha for all pairs of coders are in the range of 0.61–0.71; that for the four coders is 0.44.

The subsample of 34 images of the Russian protesters was also analysed using the on-line computer program for detecting and recognising faces on visual records, Face.com (presently acquired by Facebook). However, the level of agreement between the four coders and the software when assessing the age and gender of a particular protester turned out to be low (the values of Krippendorff's Alpha for all pairs vary from 0.02 to 0.53, that for the four coders and the software is 0.05). In other words, manual coding allowed to achieve a minimally acceptable level of reliability, whereas the program for detecting faces in an automated regime produced less reliable outcomes.

The author then proceeded with the coding of the entire Russian sample of images without the involvement of the other coders.

Four coders were also involved in the coding of images from the Ukrainian sample.[79] Due to its sheer volume, the process of coding consisted of several stages. At the first stage, three coders—all graduate students with some familiarity with Ukrainian culture but

77 The agreement criterion used is the frequency of codes in case, which complicates the task of reaching an acceptable level of agreement compared with a less stringent—yet more commonly reported one (the presence or absence of codes in case).

78 The codebook had initially contained separate codes corresponding to five age groups: 20 y.o. and younger, 21–30 y.o., 31–40 y.o., 41–50 y.o. and 51 plus y.o.; they were subsequently transformed into four age groups: 24 y.o. and younger, 25–39 y.o., 40–54 y.o., 55 plus y.o.

79 See the Acknowledgments section for their names.

not Ukrainian nationals—independently coded the same subset of 292 images randomly selected from the Ukrainian sample (12.5%). Several rounds of the coding were required before a satisfactory level of inter-coder agreement was reached. The values of Krippendorff's Alpha for each pair of coders exceed 0.7: 0.735, 0.734 and 0.728; for the three coders, the value is 0.66. At the second stage, each research assistant coded 684 images randomly assigned to her or him. The involvement of a fourth coder—a graduate student with absolutely no familiarity with Ukrainian culture, coded a subsample of randomly selected 406 images (17.3%) using the same codebook—was needed for two reasons. On one hand, his input allowed assessing the reliability of the coding at the second stage. The values of Krippendorff's Alpha between the fourth coder's input and that of the other three coders were similar—0.5–0.6, which suggests that the coding continued to be reliable at the second stage. On the other hand, a radically different cultural background of the fourth coder gave an opportunity for seeing to what extent a coder must be familiar with a culture whose visual images he or she analyses. The fact that the values of Krippendorff's Alpha were lower than at the first stage gives some support to this assumption.

I.4 Other sources

Other sources of the data worth mentioning include qualitative in-depth interviews (Clément, Miryasova & Demidov, 2010), participant observation (in addition to administering face-to-face interviews, the professional interviewers of Levada Center were instructed to produce field notes on the relative number of men and women, of representatives of various age groups on Academician Sakharov Avenue), and sociological intervention. The results reported in the field notes are summarised and reported in this chapter under the heading 'Observation.' Sociological intervention refers to a particular method for collecting primary data through group interviews. It was specifically applied for studying the first large-scale protest movement in the former socialist countries, Solidarność in Poland in the early 1980s (Touraine, Dubet, Wievorka & Strzelecki, 1982).

The issues of validity are rarely explicitly discussed with respect to using in-depth interviews and participant observation to study mass protests. It is conventionally assumed that, when properly applied, these methods tend to be weak in terms of external validity and good in terms of internal validity. Sociological intervention provides a particular test for assessing internal validity in an empirical manner. If the participants in group discussions end up accepting an interpretative framework offered by the researchers and using it to explain the experience of their involvement in a protest movement, then the underlying theory is deemed to be valid (Wieviorka & Dubet, 1996).

Each source of the data has its own flaws in terms of validity, accessibility and several other criteria. This observation suggests that several sources of data should be used in parallel. In addition to data triangulation, triangulation also exists in other forms: theory triangulation (Ma & Norwich, 2007), investigation triangulation (the involvement of more than one researcher), and methodological triangulation (the use of multiple research methods). Triangulation serves to increase the validity of the findings, both external and internal (Jick, 1979; Oleinik, 2011b). The term 'triangulation' was borrowed from geodesy where the precise location of a point on a surface requires using several (at least three) points of reference. By way of analogy, triangulation in the social sciences requires using various sources of data and/or methodologies in the study of the same phenomenon.

The 'between methods' triangulation, for instance, involves comparing the outcomes of a survey with the results of a series of in-depth qualitative interviews—provided that both methods address similar research questions. By administering two quantitative methods—face-to-face standardised interviews and mail-in questionnaires, to the same sample of protesters, Walgrave and Verhulst (2011) accomplished 'within method' triangulation.

The assumption of validation by convergence has been recently challenged in the scholarly literature on triangulation, however. On one hand, Julia Brannen (2005) argues that triangulation has four possible outcomes: corroboration (the production of the same results using different research methods), elaboration (the quantitative data analysis exemplifies how quantitative findings apply to particular cases), complementarity (the use of different research methods highlights various aspects of the phenomenon under study) and contradiction (different research methods produce divergent results). None of these outcomes shall be disregarded as valueless.

On the other hand, the belief in validation by convergence has specific epistemological roots. 'A positivist researcher is likely to view the congruent results from multi-method data collection as enhancing the validity... of the study's findings. An interpretivist... might suggest that there is a consensus of social reality between respondents' (Perlesz & Lindsay, 2003, p. 33). The latter position derives from a post-positivist belief that reality does exist but can never be perfectly apprehended. Namely, the available data in the present case tends to be incomplete and eventually biased, whereas methods for analysing it have their own flaws (e.g., a less than perfect level of inter-coder agreement). Under these circumstances, triangulation is expected either to validate the content analysis of visual records by the convergence of its outcomes with the descriptive statistics, or to suggest a complementary character of the existing sources of data.

This study is intended to compare the outcomes of the assessment of the protesters' socio-demographic profile and political preferences using four sources of data in the Russian case: (i) the VKontakte social networking site; (ii) the survey carried out by Levada Center; (iii) the participant observations made by the Levada Center interviewers (the researcher as a full observer) and (iv) the image bank comprising pictures produced by the mass media and by the protesters themselves. Specifically, the outcomes of a descriptive statistical analysis of (i), (ii) and (iii) are compared with those of the content analysis of (iv), relying on the logic of the 'between methods' triangulation. In other words, this chapter compares the descriptions of participants in the December 2011 mass protests produced with the help of data triangulation (the use of data from the four sources) and methodological triangulation (the statistical analysis and the content analysis). In the Ukrainian case, two sources of data—the mass surveys and the image bank, are compared.

This chapter addresses three research questions. Two are methodological in nature and a third one is empirical. First, *do the outcomes of the statistical analysis and the results of the content analysis of images of mass protests converge with respect to some key socio-demographic and political affinities of the protesters?* If this were the case, scholars studying mass protests would find a new source of the readily available data in the visual databases that can complement the other sources.

Second, *does the media coverage of mass protests differ from images produced by the participants*? Does the aggregate picture obtained with the help of documentary photography tend to be more valid than that deriving from street photography? Third and most relevant to the book, *what common and divergent patterns do the images of the mass protests in Russia and Ukraine contain?*

II. Sociological profile of protesters in Moscow and Kyiv

II.1 December 2011 Moscow protests

As mentioned before, there is no agreed upon figure as to the total number of protesters who gathered on Academician Sakharov Avenue on the December 24, 2011. The assessments available range from 25,000 (the police's estimate) up to 110,000 plus (the organisers' estimate).

The content analysis of images taken at the height of the demonstration (around 3:00 pm)—those providing a panoramic view of various segments of the crowd—suggests that the density of protesters varied from 4 per square meter near the stage on which leaders delivered their speeches to 2.5 in the middle of the crowd, 3 before the security checks and 0.5 in the area located after the security checks. Knowing the surface of each of these four 'imaginary' sectors (RIA Novosti, 2011), one can calculate the approximate total number of protesters. A similar approach was used for assessing the number of participants in the Leipzig Monday demonstration on October 9, 1989 (Opp, 2011, p. 604). The resulting figure—85,000–90,000—lies closer to the upper estimate. However, this does not account for the people who either arrived late (some people remained at the scene of the protest until late evening) or departed before the meeting ended.

In purely quantitative terms, the December 24 meeting in Moscow drew more people than the mass unrest of July 1, 2008 in Ulaanbaatar (10,000–20,000; Oleinik, 2012a) yet fewer than the Leipzig Monday demonstration (130,000 plus; Opp, 2011, p. 604) and especially the November 2004 protests in Kyiv (200,000 plus, up to 1 million at the height of the demonstration; Bessinger, 2011, p. 25). If one takes into account the differences in the total population of these cities (0.5 million in Leipzig, 1.2 million in Ulaanbaatar, 2.7 million in Kyiv, 11.5 million in Moscow), the level of mobilisation in the case of the Moscow demonstration was relatively weak.

The number of participants in events of the 2013–2014 Maidan was significantly higher than in any of those cases. The first truly mass Sunday march—*Viche*—occurred on December 1, 2013 after the police's attempt to dismantle the protesters' tent camp by force; severely beating its inhabitants. After that moment, the tent camp started to acquire more and more features of *Tabir* and *Sich*, two Ukrainian traditional institutions (see subsection II.1.a of Chapter 1 and Section III of Chapter 3). With the help of a technique similar to that described above, the number of participants in this event can be assessed at 300,000–550,000.[80] The subsequent Sunday marches-*Viches*, including the march of the Millions of December 8, reportedly attracted a comparable number of participants—around 0.5–1 million.

All four sources suggest the existence of a gender gap among protesters in Moscow (Figure 4.1). However, the gap appears more

---

80 See, for instance, two examples of the calculation at https://ain.ua/2013/12/03/kievlyanin-s-pomoshhyu-matematiki-i-google-earth-pro-podschital-kolichestvo-lyudej-na-yevromajdane and http://d-i-a-s.livejournal.com/457244.html. The average figure—350,000—was reported by Walker, Shaun (2013, December 8). Decisive day in Ukraine as new protests loom. *The Observer*, p.27.

significant when assessed with the help of the content analysis of visual records. As a point of comparison, the gender gap in the case of the July 1, 2008 mass unrest in Ulaanbaatar estimated in a similar manner was even wider: 89% of protesters were men and 11% were women (Oleinik, 2012a). A plausible explanation could be the more traditional character of Mongolian society. Males outnumbered females on Maidan too. However, the gender gap was slightly narrower in Kyiv (see Table 4.2 below). Results of the survey conducted by the Ilko Kucheriv Democratic Initiatives Foundation also confirm this finding.

Figure 4.1 'Distribution of the protesters in Moscow by gender, four sources of information compared, %'

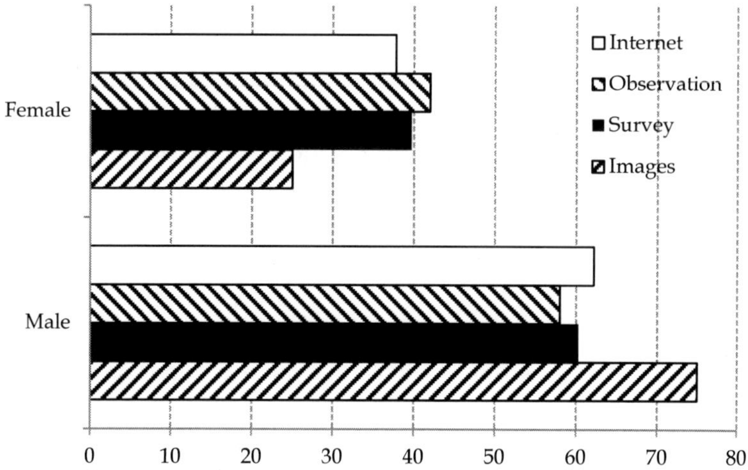

A closer look at the Russian protesters' age profile outlined with the help of the information from the four sources shows a divergent pattern in the case of the social networking site (Figure 4.2). Young people tend to be overrepresented among protesters based on the VKontakte information.

Figure 4.2 'Distribution of the protesters in Moscow by age, four sources of information compared, %'

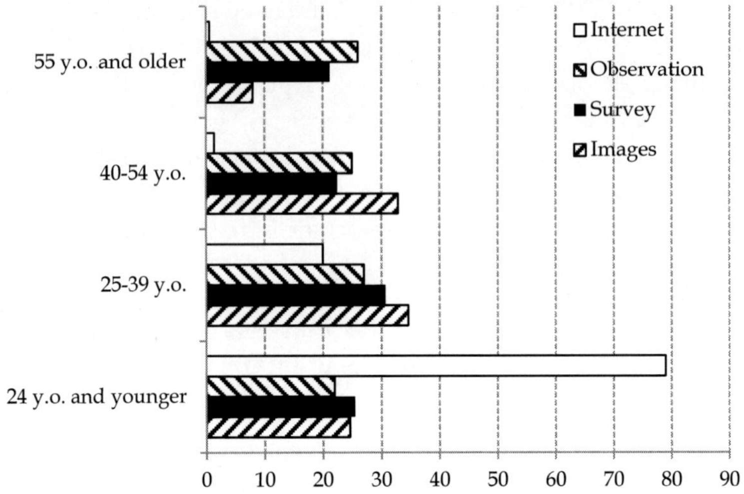

Compared to the clearly 'deviant' case of the social networking site as a source of data on the protesters' age,[81] there is probably no single ground for preferring one of the remaining sources of information over the others. For instance, if one accounts for the above mentioned highest refusal rate among the older demonstrators, their number significantly exceeds that of the protesters in the group of those aged 40–54 years old (the latter group has the lowest reported refusal rate). If in Russia, similar to Western Europe, 'older demonstrators display more protest' (Walgrave et al., 2011, p. 340), then why, at the same time, do they demonstrate the least cooperation with the researchers, contrary to what is reported in Western Europe (Walgrave & Verhulst, 2011, p. 219)?

Visual records are further differentiated according to their source: private collections, including image banks available on the internet, and mass media coverage. There is no difference in the

81 A possible explanation may refer to the unwillingness to disclose personal information, including demographic data online that characterises collectivistic cultures (Cho & Park 2003, pp. 2325–2326). Russian culture has several collectivistic features. The other explanation refers to a low level of the validity of personal information posted on-line in general.

coverage of males and females in the two categories of visual records: the differences in the frequencies with which males and females are pictured (as measured with the help of F-ratio) do not reach the level of statistical significance in the Russian case. There are no statistically significant differences in the picturing of older protesters either (those from the age groups of 40–54 years old and of 55+ years old). Young protesters are more often seen in images from the private collections: $F(1, 528)=17.011$, $p<.001$ for the age group of those 24 years old and younger, $F(1, 742)=26.735$, $p<.001$ for those aged 25–39 years old.

Nevertheless, the most notable difference in the coverage of the same event by the mass media and by private individuals concerns the protesters' ideological affinities (assessed by counting banners and other ideologically charged symbols). The independent mass media—most of them have a liberal orientation—tend to pay relatively less attention to their 'ideological foes,' communists and anarchists, in their photo reports (Table 4.1).

The survey sample may have another bias: nationalists tend to be underrepresented among Levada Center respondents. Both documentary and street photography suggest that nationalists formed the third largest group at the scene of the protest; whereas only a tiny minority of the respondents acknowledged an ideological affinity with a nationalist ideology.[82] This discrepancy between the survey outcomes and the content analysis of images may arguably derive either from a selection (the nationalists turned out to be less approachable or the interviewers made less effort to contact them) or noncooperation (the protesters supporting nationalistic ideas do not easily admit their ideological affinities because of the risk of social undesirability) bias.[83]

---

82 The respondent could select several options when answering a survey question about his/her ideological affinities, hence the total count in the 'Survey' column exceeds 100%.

83 A binary logistic regression analysis shows that the supporters of nationalist ideas tend to be relatively younger and less educated than the other protesters. The outcome variable is a stated affinity with nationalist ideas (0 = No stated affinity, 1 = Stated affinity). Six predictor variables were included in the model. The first refers to the respondent's gender (0 for females, 1 for males).

Table 4.1 'Distribution of the Russian protesters by ideological affinities, various sources of information compared, %'

	Survey	Images, total	Images by two types of sources			
			Private collections	Media coverage	F ratio	P value
Anarchists	2.8	5	6.2	2.7	3.699	0.055
Communists	25.7	28.6	33.7	20.7	5.416	0.02
Nationalists	6.1	22.2	22.6	21.9	0.649	0.421
Liberal non-registered parties	69	40.7	33.5	52.1	0.433	0.511
Yabloko (a liberal registered party)		3.5	4	2.5	1.991	0.159

The second refers to the respondent's age at the scale level of measurement. The third refers to the respondent's education (0 for people with no university education, 1 for those with some university education). The fourth is a response to the survey question about whether or not the respondent learned about the December 24 demonstration from the internet (0 for those who did not and 1 for those who did). The fifth refers to the respondent's relative well-being (0 for people who cannot afford to buy a car, 1 for those who can). The sixth refers to the respondent's liberal values (0 for people who do not identify themselves as liberals, 1 for those who do). The binary regression logistic regression procedure in SPSS was used to perform the analysis. The method for entering predictors was 'Forward Stepwise' (Likelihood Ratio). In Step 1, Age was entered. It produced a Cox and Snell's R^2 increment of 0.02 and a Nagelkerke's R^2 increment of 0.055. In Step 2, Education was entered. It produced a Cox and Snell's R^2 increment of 0.01 and a Nagelkerke's R^2 increment of 0.025. A test of the full model with the two predictor variables, Age and Education, compared with a constant-only or null model was statistically significant, $\chi^2(2)=24.105$, $p<0.001$. The strength of the association between, on the one hand, the affinity with nationalist ideas and, on the other hand, Age and Education, was not strong with Cox and Snell's $R^2=0.03$ and Nagelkerke's $R^2=0.082$. The sign of B for Age is negative, that for Education is positive. In other words, the relative prevalence of older protesters suggested by the survey could have resulted from the relative underrepresentation of young protesters with nationalist ideas in its sample.

II.2 Maidan in November-December 2013

Unfortunately, gaps in the coverage of Maidan by the mass media prevent a meaningful comparison of documentary and street photography in the Ukrainian context. At the same time, the survey data produced by the Ilko Kucheriv Democratic Initiatives Foundation (see Table 3.1 in Chapter 3) paves the way for the other type of triangulation, between methods. The collected visual data cover the period between the first two of three surveys carried out in Kyiv during Maidan, as well as events that preceded the first survey. As indicated previously, while still a minority on the site of mass protests in Kyiv, females showed up in relatively greater numbers than in Moscow. The content analysis of images of Maidan suggests the ratio of 26 to 74, whereas the survey data (the average for the three surveys) indicate the ratio of 28 to 72 (Table 4.2). It follows that both Russian and Ukrainian societies are highly gendered, but gender inequality tends to be relatively higher in the former case.

Table 4.2 'Distribution of the protesters in Ukraine and Russia by age, gender, ideological affinities and role, visual records, %'

Category: Code	Russia, December 2011, % of the category	Ukraine, November-December 2013, % of the category
Age: 24 and less	24.8	15.9
Age: 25–39	34.9	32.7
Age: 40–54	32.6	32.2
Age: 55 plus	7.7	20.6
Total (Age)	*100.0*	*100.0*
Gender: Female	24.0	26.0
Gender: Male	76.0	74.0
Total (Gender)	*100.0*	*100.0*
Ideology: Anarchists	4.8	n.a.
Ideology: Communists	28.7	n.a.
Ideology: Nationalists	22.4	56.5
Ideology: Liberals	44.1	n.a.
Ideology: Centrist	n.a.	43.5
Total (Ideology)	*100.0*	*100.0*
Role: Journalists	2.8	1.0
Role: Leaders	2.4	1.6

Role: Police	4.5	4.0
Role: Artists	0	0.4
Role: Participants	90.2	88.5
Role: Observers	0.1	3.9
Role: Paramedics	0	0.2
Role: Priests	0	0.4
Total (Role)	*100.0*	*100.0*
Enemy: Putin	63.9	8.0
Enemy: Yanukovych	n.a.	80.3
Symbols: National (% of Grand total)	0.7	27.9
Symbols: Carnival (% of Grand total)	0.29	0.07

Source: the author's content analysis of images (N=382 in Russia and N=2,344 in Ukraine).

The age groups in the survey data are not the same as in the visual data. Despite this discrepancy, both sources show that the majority of Ukrainian protesters are middle aged, that is, in their 30s and 40s. According to the two surveys conducted among participants in the march and the stationary protest—the tent camp, a third of the protesters (35.8%), were in their 20s or younger; half (51.5%), were between 30–54 years old; and a tenth (10.8%), were 55 years old and older. Estimates of the relative numbers of the youth and senior people, obtained with the help of the survey data and the visual data, diverge nevertheless. The survey data suggest that the youth outnumbered the seniors, whereas the visual records show the inverse pattern. The timing of the measurement may be a factor. The content analysis of visual records leads one to believe that the two age categories—24 years old and younger, and 25–39 years old, can be found relatively more often on photographs taken in the evening and at night than during the daytime (17.9% and 41.8% against 13.6% and 30.5% respectively). People 55 years old and older, in contrast, are seen more often during the daytime (10.2% against 22.1%). If the surveys were conducted in the evening, then the most senior protesters may have been relatively less reachable.

The survey conducted among participants in Maidan does not reveal their ideological affinities. The reason is simple: the absolute majority of the respondents, 81.1%, declared that they do not have membership in a political party, civil organisation or civil movement. The content analysis of visual records shows the prevalence of the centrists (Udar and Bat'kyvshchyna parties[84]) and nationalists (Svoboda party and Pravyi Sektor [Right Sector]). To the very limited extent that political parties influenced the internal dynamics of Maidan, they convey center-right ideologies, which sharply contrasts with a strange mixture of liberal, communist and nationalist ideologies in the Russian case. On an imaginable political continuum going from the right to the center, Pravyi Sektor has the rightmost position, then Svoboda, then Udar and Bat'kyvshchyna. In contrast to the three last parties, Pravyi Sektor did not have an official status at the time of Maidan. Banners of Pravyi Sektor greatly outnumbered banners of the three official parties on pictures of the protests taken in the evening and at night (39.2% of all banners against 22.9% of banners attributed to Svoboda, 21.2% – to Udar and 16.7% – to Bat'kyvshchyna). In the daytime, banners of the official parties were relatively more visible. Regardless of their status and place on the political spectrum, the four political forces formed an opposition to the then president Yanukovych and the government formed by its party, Partiia Regionov (Party of the Regions[85]). Mykola Azarov was the head of this government.

III. Internal dynamics of the Ukrainian protests

Visual images shed an additional light on the discussion of Maidan in Chapter 3. The content analysis of visual records complements the previous analysis in the sense that it shows when and how exactly EuroMaidan started its transformation into the Revolution of Dignity. The surveys (Table 3.1 in Chapter 3) show that the government's use of physical force against the protesters became a key

84 At the Parliamentary Assembly of the Council of Europe (PACE) they have an observer status in the European People's Party group that has a centrist orientation.

85 This party can be better described by a particular model of power that its representatives endorse (see Section IV of Chapter 6) than by its ideology.

trigger for mobilisation as early as in the first week of December 2013. In other words, the surveys did not capture the initial Euro-euphoria that characterised EuroMaidan. The visuals allow doing so.

The transition from EuroMaidan to the Revolution of Dignity started in early December, after the government attempted to silence the protesters by force during the night from November 29 to November 30, 2013. Before that moment, the protesters included mostly students who were mobilised by the idea of Ukraine's closer integration with the European Union. Students—people aged 24 or under—formed a sizeable group of protesters on pictures taken between November 22 and November 29 (Figure 4.3). During the same period, European symbols—for instance, flags of the EU—clearly prevailed on the site of pass protests (Figure 4.4). Symbols of Bat'kyvshchyna, the registered political party situated more closely to the center of ideological spectrum than the other political forces present on Maidan, outnumbered these forces' symbols on images of the first stage of Maidan (Figure 4.5).

The second stage in the evolution of Maidan includes events that occurred between the police's first attack on the tent camp and the second attempt of the government to rely on violence. The police launched a new attack on the tent camp during the night from December 11 to December 12. The second stage was characterised by two truly mass Sunday marches on December 1 and December 8. The European symbols became much less visible than before: their relative share in the total number of all symbolical objects fell two-fold, from 25.7% to 11.2%. Simultaneously, the share of the older age groups started to grow at the expense of that of the youth. Protesters between the ages of 25 and 39 years old formed a majority at this stage. Nationalist political forces gained a foothold with symbols of Svoboda becoming most common and overshadowing those of Bat'kyvshchyna. If the protests at the first stage were oriented against the government's U-turn on the road to European integration, at the second stage, the protesters were essentially angered by the use of force against the peaceful and unarmed students.

The third stage was marked by the government's increased reliance on violence. The relative share of European symbols further decreased, down to 9.5%. On the visual level, nationalist ideas continued to prevail with one notable change. Now Pravyi Sektor became a symbolic leader of the protests relegating Svoboda to the second place. The shift of emphasis from the ideas of European integration to the protection of human dignity led to a new change in the social profile of the protesters. Now representatives of the two older age groups—people in their 40s and older—formed the majority of the protesters. Maidan that started as an initiative of the youth one month later was driven by the older and more mature citizens.

Along with changing patterns in the 2013–2014 mass protests, there was also a constant. During all the three periods under consideration, national symbols prevailed on Maidan. Depending on the stage of the protests, they represented from 72 to 84% of all symbolic objects; 80.8% on average. The prevalence of national symbols, first and foremost, Ukrainian flags, constitutes the most visible particularity of Maidan compared with the December 2011 demonstration in Moscow. In the latter case, despite a sizable presence of nationalists, Russian flags remained at the backstage. They represented less than 1% of all symbolic objects (see Table 4.2). In Kyiv, Ukrainian flags represented almost a third of coded elements, 27.9%,—more than any other code, let alone symbolic objects. It seems that the Russian nationalists who joined the December 2011 demonstration were disconnected from the Russian nation-state (or even its idea), whereas the Ukrainian nationalists on Maidan protested and fought under the national banners. Maidan was the expression of the awakening of national consciousness since its very beginning.

The absolute prevalence of the national symbols on Maidan is further confirmed by the analysis of coding co-occurrences. Figure 4.6 shows that national symbols occur far more frequently than the other codes. Among the codes with which national symbols co-occur are regional symbols, symbols of the EU, and banners of Pravyi Sektor. Figure 4.6 also offers an additional illustration of the previously reported finding that males prevailed among the protesters in Kyiv (codes 'Role: participant' and 'Gender: male' form a cluster). The cluster of codes 'Age: 25–39' and 'Age: 40–54' indicates that the core of the protesters in Kyiv was composed of people in their middle age, which differentiates the Ukrainian case from the Russian one, as argued before. The closeness of codes 'Weapons: masks' and 'Age: 24 and less' suggests that masks and balaclavas were worn mainly by the youth.

It is also worth noting that the American symbols were not seen in any significant numbers, neither in Moscow nor in Kyiv, which provides a solid counter-argument against the allegation—made by the Russian government officials and popularised by the mainstream mass media in this country—that both protests were engineered and financed by the US.

Figure 4.3 'Distribution of the protesters in Ukraine by age and period of Maidan, visual records, %'

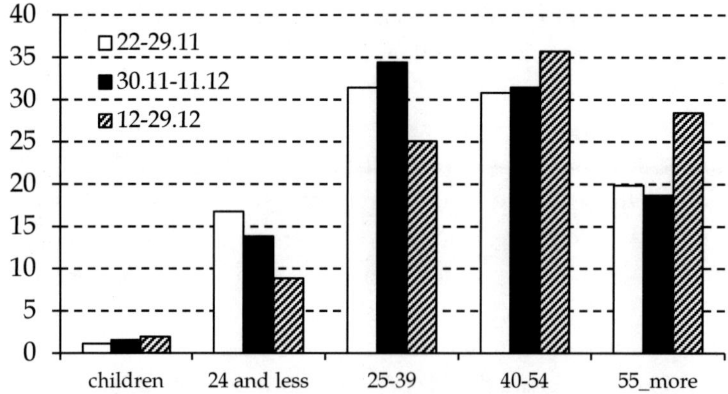

Figure 4.4 **'Distribution of symbolic objects by period of Maidan, visual records, %'**

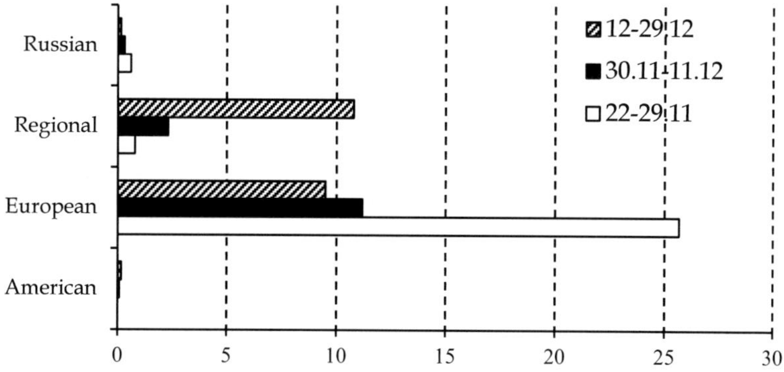

Legend: relative frequencies of national and some other symbols are not shown.

Figure 4.5 **'Distribution of political parties' banners and other symbols by period of Maidan, visual records, %'**

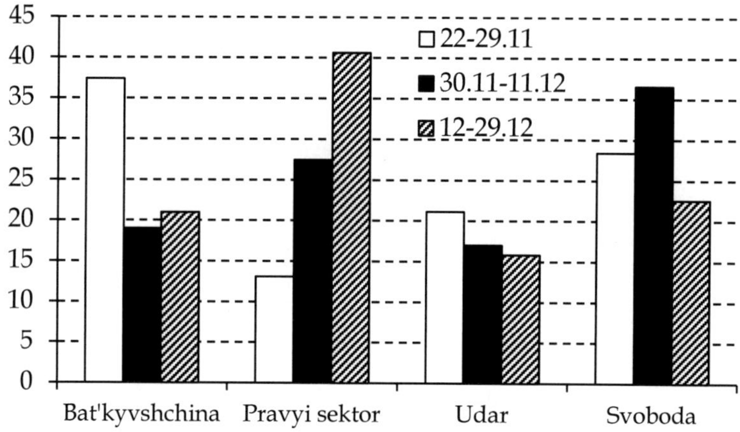

Figure 4.6 'Two-dimensional map of the coding co-occurrences in Ukraine'

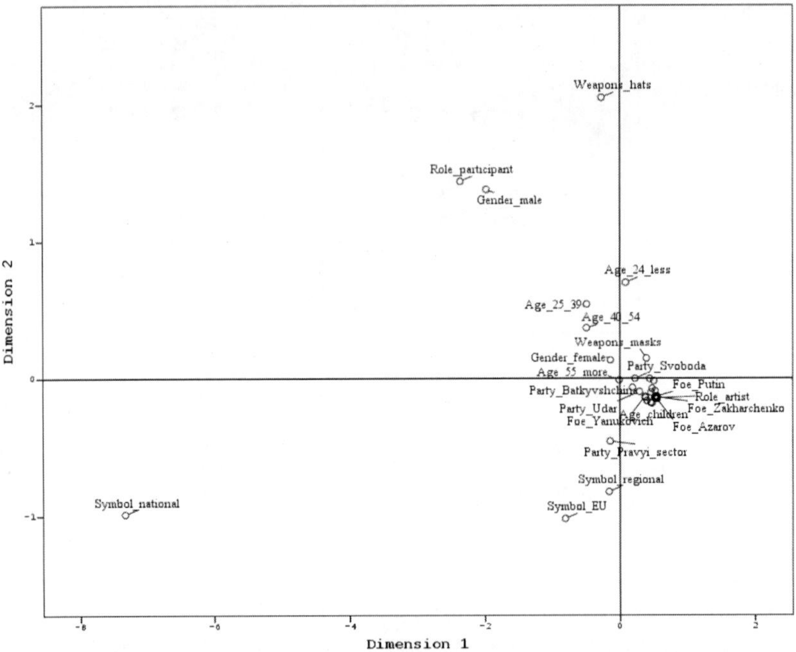

Legend: Stress = 0.0859, pseudo R^2 = 0.995. This figure was produced using the multidimensional scaling (ALSCAL) module of SPSS. The input matrix contains relative frequencies of the forty-two codes, with all pictures taken on a particular day of the protests being the unit of analysis. Euclidian distance was used as a proximity measure (derived stimulus configuration).

IV. Visual records compared with the other sources of data on mass protests

The reported outcomes of the statistical analysis and of the content analysis of visual records show both divergent and convergent patterns. For instance, in the Russian case, they converge with respect to the assessment of the prevalence of liberal ideas among the protesters and the popularity of a critical stance toward two key representatives of the Russian power elite, Putin and Medvedev. Our knowledge of these particular aspects of reality is thus validated by the convergent outcomes of the triangulation.

However, divergences regarding the gender and age of the protesters (the content analysis of images suggests a more significant over-representation of males and under-representation of older people), and the affinities of protesters with nationalistic ideas (an under-representation of nationalists in the survey) indicate that no single source can be considered as absolutely valid. These divergent triangulation outcomes suggest a complementary character of the alternative sources and research methods. When possible, the survey outcomes shall be complemented by the data from other sources, namely, from visual databanks. The content analysis of visual records appears particularly helpful in studies of such sensitive topics as the protesters' ideological affinities.

Visual records refer to a still underexplored and undervalued source of data on mass protests. The content analysis of visual records produces outcomes that usefully complement findings made with the help of mass surveys. The range of hypotheses that can be tested with the help of this research methodology is rather limited. However, it certainly includes the hypothesis of the normalisation of both protest and the protester. As for the data retrieved from the social networking sites, the validity of such data remains limited. Social networking sites are popular mainly among youth. The value of such sites for studying this particular category of protesters remains to be explored, probably with the help of methods of triangulation.

Visual records do not form a homogeneous category. Documentary photography takes the form of mass media photo reports. Such images are often subject to framing and editing. Street photography refers to private collections and internet depositories of pictures. Street photography produces images that are arguably closer to the situation of 'one-to-one correspondence to what they are recording' (Rose, 2012, p. 5).

This study confirms that the media coverage of mass protests does indeed differ from images produced by the participants in such protests. The photo reports available on the websites of the major Russian independent mass media tend to devote less attention to representatives of particular segments of the ideological spectrum, namely, the left part (communists and anarchists). In this sense, street photography deserves particular attention on the part of scholars studying mass protests.

The photo reports also feature the protestor leaders more often than the rank-and-file protesters: $F(1, 96)=30.753$, $p<.001$. As a matter of fact, the private collections included in the sample for content analysis do not contain a single picture of the leaders. In other words, documentary photography, despite its potential flaws, should not be completely excluded from the content analysis of images of mass protests. Some research questions cannot be properly addressed solely with the help of street photography. Journalists have access to some areas of the protest scene that remain outside the reach of the rank-and-file protesters. The Russian journalists produced relatively more pictures of the front stage (30.4% of pictures from the media reports compared to only 2.8% of pictures from private collections). They also produced most of the panoramic pictures (5.8% of pictures from the media reports compared to 1.4% of the pictures from private collections).

Conclusion

This chapter offered a discussion of the advantages and eventual pitfalls associated with using a relatively new source of data on mass protests. This source refers to image banks containing visual records produced by both professional journalists and ordinary people who take part in mass protests. The latter category of visual records has much in common with street photography. Compared with documentary photography of professional journalists, street photography has more one-to-one correspondence to what it is recording. In more technical terms, the internal validity of street photography tends to be higher than that of documentary photography.

Modern technologies make the production of visual records easier than ever. Compact cameras and cell phones with built-in cameras are with us almost everywhere, which explains their value as tools in providing extra-somatic 'memory'. The internet facilitates the task of storing and sharing images made by hundreds and thousands of people who participate in the same protest event. As of April 2012, a search using the Google Images engine listed about 11,900 visual records in response to a request worded 'December 24, 2011 meeting' (*miting 24 dekabrya 2011*). Flickr.com had more than 26,000 images with the 'Tahrir' tag (the name of the scene of the 2011 protests in Egypt). This data is readily available to be properly incorporated into research on mass protests. The eventual development of computer programs for retrieving data from websites in an automated regime ('scrapers') serves to reduce the time and costs associated with this operation (Cho & Park, 2012).

The content analysis of visual records includes the standard variables of age, gender, and occasionally political affinities (operationalised through banners and slogans). The identification of the protester's gender rarely poses a problem (if one leaves aside the issue of trans-gendered people, which constitutes a limitation of the present study). The correct identification of his/her age is more challenging. The involvement of a group of coders representing different age groups serves to increase the internal validity of codes associated with the 'Age' variable. The use of methods of triangulation has similar effects; its applicability is not limited to the coding of age only. The external validity of this kind of content analysis can be improved by applying procedures of random sampling. The existence of large stratified image banks such as Flickr provides numerous opportunities in this respect.

The content analysis of images also facilitates comparative studies of mass protests. Further studies in this direction will address concerns as to the generalisability of the proposed approach beyond the chosen event and national context. The content analysis of images potentially has fewer restrictions than the content analysis of texts when applied to comparative studies. For instance, it is not absolutely necessary for the coders to know the languages of countries in which pictures have been taken. The application of the same codebook to sets of images produced during mass protests either in different countries or at different points in time in the same country serves to collect cross-sectional and/or time-series data.

Does the normalisation of protests affect only specific countries? Does the scope of the protest increase or decrease over time?

With respect to the third research question, the comparative content analysis of images of the mass protests in Moscow and Kyiv offers several insights that complement the discussion of Maidan in Chapter 3. Compared with the December 2011 protests in Moscow, events of Maidan attracted a larger number of participants. Initially, the mobilisation in Ukraine resulted from the desire of the youth for Ukraine's integration into the EU. The name of EuroMaidan correctly depicts the situation during the first stage in the evolution of Maidan. However, EuroMaidan began its transformation into the Revolution of Dignity in early December 2013. The ideas of European integration lost their relative importance since then. The change in Maidan's main objective had an immediate effect on the social profile of its participants. The youth played a leading role in EuroMaidan. Representatives of the older generations assumed this role at the subsequent stages in the evolution of Maidan, which refers to the other important distinction between the Ukrainian and Russian mass protests. National symbols greatly outnumbered the other symbols and, as a matter of fact, the other codes, during the entire period analysed in this chapter. It means that Maidan was closely linked to a nation-state building project since its very beginning (see also Chapter 10 for further discussion). The nationalists were also visible on the site of the mass protests in Moscow, but they preferred waiving the flags of the Russian empire to waiving the Russian national flags. A relatively marginal place of the Russian national flags on Academician Sakharov Avenue on December 24, 2011 suggests that in contrast to Maidan, the Russian mass protests were disconnected from the process of nation-state building.

Appendix

Table A 'Codebook for the content analysis of visual records of the December 24, 2011 demonstration'

Category	Code	Description	Count	% Codes	Cases	% Cases
Age	20 and less	People aged 20 and less	33	0.4%	20	5.2%
Age	21–30	People 21 to 30 y.o.	693	7.9%	222	58.1%
Age	31–40	People 31 to 40 y.o.	540	6.2%	223	58.4%
Age	41–50	People 41 to 50 y.o.	499	5.7%	212	55.5%
Age	51 and more	People 51 y.o. and older	355	4.1%	166	43.5%
Banners	Anarchists	Flags, banners with anarchist symbols	83	0.9%	30	7.9%
Banners	Carnival	Elements of carnival (masks, carnival dress etc.)	25	0.3%	22	5.8%
Banners	Churov/TsIK	Images of Vladimir Churov (chairman of the Central Electoral Commission), references to his name	28	0.3%	28	7.3%
Banners	Communists	Flags, banners with the CPRF symbols	494	5.6%	100	26.2%
Banners	Medvedev	Images of Dmitry Medvedev, references to his name	24	0.3%	24	6.3%
Banners	Nationalists	Flags, banners with nationalist symbols and slogans	385	4.4%	82	21.5%
Banners	Liberal non-registered parties	Flags, banners of the other non-registered parties (Partiia truda, Solidarnost', Parnas, etc.)	701	8.0%	130	34.0%
Banners	Putin	Images of Vladimir Putin, references to his name	124	1.4%	105	27.5%
Banners	White strips	White strips as a symbol of protests	238	2.7%	120	31.4%

Banners	Yabloko	Flags, banners with symbols of the Yabloko political party	59	0.7%	32	8.4%
Banners	EdRo	References to the United Russia	17	0.2%	15	3.9%
Banners	Russian	Russian national tricolour (white-blue-red) flags	65	0.7%	44	11.5%
Gender	Female	Females	960	11.0%	280	73.3%
Gender	Male	Males	3046	34.8%	360	94.2%
Particular categories	Journalists	Journalists on duty (cf. journalists as participants)	112	1.3%	37	9.7%
Particular categories	Leaders	Political leaders, organisers	95	1.1%	42	11.0%
Particular categories	Police	People in uniform on duty	183	2.1%	33	8.6%
Particular categories	Artists	Performing artists				
Particular categories	Observers	People observing the protests without participating in them (usually they stay on the margins)	5	0.1%	2	0.5%
Particular categories	Priests	People dressed as priests				
Particular categories	Paramedics	People with clearly identifiable Red Cross				
		Total	8764	100	382	100

Table B 'Codebook for the content analysis of visual records of Maidan in November-December 2013'

Category	Code	Description	Count	% Codes	Cases	% Cases
People\Age	children	Age of the actor pictured on the image: school age and younger	107	0.2	524	22.4%
People\Age	24 and less	Age of the actor pictured on the image: 24 and less	1051	2.4	1049	44.8%
People\Age	25–39	Age of the actor pictured on the image: between 25 and 39	2377	5.4	972	41.5%
People\Age	40–54	Age of the actor pictured on the image: between 40 and 54	2346	5.3	645	27.5%
People\Age	55_more	Age of the actor pictured on the image: 55 and older	1501	3.4	101	4.3%
People\Opponents	Azarov	Portraits of the former prime minister of Ukraine, any mentions of or references to him	41	0.1	35	1.5%
People\Opponents	Putin	Portraits of the current president and former prime minister of Russia, any mentions or references to him	30	0.1	30	1.3%
People\Opponents	Yanukovych	Portraits of the former president of Ukraine, any mentions of or references to him, including Vityok, Vitya	298	0.7	215	9.2%
People\Opponents	Zakharchenko	Portraits of the former Minister of the Inferior of Ukraine, any mentions of or references to him	3	0.0	3	0.1%
People\Role	Artist	The actor playing a musical instrument, singing on the stage	27	0.1	22	0.9%
People\Role	Journalist	The actor who is conducting an interview, holds a camera, tape recorder, conduct live reportage, sits in a car with a logo of a TV station such as Gromads'ke, Espresso etc.	75	0.2	64	2.7%
People\Role	Leader	Leaders of the political parties or civic organisations: Vitali Klitschko, Oleh Tyahnibok, Arseny Yatsenyuk, Ruslana, Petro Poroshenko, Oleksandr Turchynov, Yulia Tymoshenko	116	0.3	102	4.4%

People\Role	Observer	Someone who is observing; he/she is present on the site of protests without being involved in any kind of action; usually observers are seen on the 'margins' of the site of protests. The application of the 'Observer' code necessitates that an image contains two type of characters (i) those actively acting (e.g., Participants) and (ii) those passively observing the actively acting. Please look at Flickr_343 or Flickr_256 to see an example	292	0.7	140	6.0%
People\Role	Paramedic	The actor with Red Cross (or the other identifiable medical symbol) on his/her dress and/or a box with Red Cross	18	0.0	10	0.4%
People\Role	Participant	Someone who is involved in marching, chanting, yelling, throwing stones or Molotov cocktails, waving flags, holding symbols or mottos, physical confrontation, food cooking and distribution, cleaning the camp site etc.; someone who is in the center of protests	6612	14.9	1536	65.5%
People\Role	Police	The member of the police force or military on duty dressed in a uniform	301	0.7	114	4.9%
People\Role	Priest	The actor dressed as a priest	28	0.1	16	0.7%
People\Sex	Female	Sex of the actor pictured on the image: female	5463	12.3	847	36.1%
People\Sex	Male	Sex of the actor pictured on the image: male (in the case of toddlers, the colour of the dress may be suggestive: blue v. pink)	1916	4.3	1513	64.5%
Symbols	American	Flags, any mentions of or references to the US	13	0.0	13	0.6%
Symbols	Auto-Maidan	Cars decorated with symbols of protests, any mentions of or references to AutoMaidan	26	0.1	18	0.8%

Symbols	Carnival	Carnival masks, guitars (when not on the stage), piano (when not on the stage), other musical instruments (when not on the stage), mock dress, e.g. prisoner's dress	32	0.1	24	1.0%
Symbols	European	Flags, any mentions of or references to the EU and member-countries	1972	4.4	915	39.0%
Symbols	National_symbols	Blue and yellow flags and ribbons, trident, traditional dress, e.g., baggy pants or shorts with *vyshivanka*, traditional hair dress, e.g., *oseledets'*, the 'Glory to Ukraine' expression; however, words written in blue and yellow are not necessarily coded as national symbols, e.g., Maidan written in such a way	12354	27.9	1707	72.8%
Symbols	Regional	References to the names of regions : Volyn, Lviv, Trenopil, Galichina, Cherkassy, Dnipropetrovsk, including on the bricks	698	1.6	191	8.1%
Symbols	Religious	Icons, crosses, Bible and other religious symbols except a priest's dress	59	0.1	42	1.8%
Symbols	Repression	Any mentions of or references to Berkut—special police forces; pictures of the wounded used by the protesters	61	0.1	49	2.1%
Symbols	Russian	Flags, any mentions of or references to Russia (including '*Moskali*') and the Customs' Union. Images of Vladimir Putin are coded separately	46	0.1	41	1.7%
Symbols	Shevchenko	Any mentions of or references to Taras Shevchenko: portraits, monument, quotes, e.g. '*Boritesya – poborete*' (Fight and you shall overcome)	20	0.0	19	0.8%
Symbols\Party_symbols	Fatherland	Party Bat'kyvshchyna (Fatherland): white & red	954	2.2	317	13.5%

Symbols\Party_symbols	Right_sector	Right sector: red & black; UNA-UNSO: black cross on red background	950	2.1	472	20.1%
Symbols\Party_symbols	Strike	Party Udar (Strike): red	683	1.5	249	10.6%
Symbols\Party_symbols	Svoboda	Party Svoboda: blue & yellow	1180	2.7	344	14.7%
Weapons	Barricades	Fortifications built by the protesters; to be normally coded as a single element unless one clearly sees several barricades on the same image	146	0.3	146	6.2%
Weapons	Batons	Riot batons used by the police force	139	0.3	51	2.2%
Weapons	Firearms	Rifles, machine guns, hand guns etc.	1	0.0	1	0.0%
Weapons	Hats	Hard hats when used by the protesters: military, construction & moto/bicycle and by the police force; if they are decorated - attach in addition the code 'Carnival' or a code referring to Symbol. Note: hard hats are coded when worn by both the protesters and the police force	1659	3.7	263	11.2%
Weapons	Masks	Balaclavas, masks, gas masks when used by both the protesters and the police force	441	1.0	144	6.1%
Weapons	Molotov	Molotov cocktails: bottles with inflammatory essence thrown by the protesters		0.0		
Weapons	Other	Other weapons used by the protesters: sticks, ancient stone throwing machines etc.	11	0.0	4	0.2%
Weapons	Shields	Shields when used by the protesters: self-made, taken from the police or by the police; if they are decorated - attach in addition the code 'Carnival' or a code referring to Symbol.	276	0.6	39	1.7%

		Note: shields are coded when carried by both the protesters and the police force				
Weapons	Tires	Burning tires used by the protesters	1	0.0	1	0.0%
Weapons	Water	Water cannons used by the police force, including mounted on armored cars		0.0		
Weapons	Wounds	Real wounds, including the dead, as opposed to images of the wounded, of both the protesters and the police force	11	0.0	11	0.5%
		Total	44336	100.0	2344	100

Chapter 5
'Undeclared war: Invisible and visible forms of Russia's domination'

Introduction

The question as to whether the preferences and behaviour of power elites in the EU member-states are influenced by the Russian power elite—by means of the implementation of a particular energy policy, has not yet received a satisfactory answer. Journalistic accounts of this matter outnumber careful scholarly analyses. Specifically, a publication in *The Telegraph* blog section on European power elites' responses to the 2014 Russian military confrontation with Ukraine[86] set a stage for a lively public discussion (Persson, 2014) without yet leading to more systematic studies.

The country will be considered as a unit of analysis in this chapter. Country is understood here as its power elite—a group of individuals 'in positions to make decisions having major consequences' (Mills, 1957, p. 4). A conventional definition of power says that the party in a position to impose its will on the other party, despite the latter's eventual resistance—has power (Weber, 1968, p. 53; see Chapter 6 for a more detailed discussion). The power holder changes the behaviour of the other parties so they start to further the former's interests. If Russia manages to change the preferences and policies of European countries in a manner beneficial to Russia then this country has power—de facto. In particular, if

86 As of the publication date of this book, the military conflict is far from being over. Despite several efforts to 'freeze' it (they resulted in two Minsk agreements brokered by Germany and France in September 2014 and February 2015), the fighting with the use of heavy weapons continues. For instance, the seizure of the town of Debalt'eve in Eastern Ukraine by the Russian troops and separatists happened after reaching the second Minsk agreement. A fragile balance of forces might be broken again at any moment. However, since the confrontation started in 2014 and the data used in this chapter do not reflect the most recent developments, the term '2014 military conflict' will be used.

Russia manages to produce some desirable reactions of the EU member-states to Russia's role in the 2014 military conflict with Ukraine, then Russia has power in relationships with the EU member-states. The EU member-states' unwillingness to impose severe sanctions on Russia serves the interests of the latter.

The purpose of this chapter is to explain Russia's upper hand in relationships with EU member-states through the existence of a constellation of interests of Russia and the EU member-states in the European market for natural gas. The unveiling of Russia's power requires a re-examination of conventional perceptions of the market as a constraint on a power holder's discretion, namely, in international relationships. In particular circumstances that are arguably present in the European energy market (and in the national and regional markets in Russia, as shown previously in Oleinik, 2011a; Oleinik, 2015a) the market becomes a pillar of domination instead of being a liberating force. Domination refers to the situation when power is exercised 'repeatedly, systematically, and to the detriment of the dominated agent' (Wartenberg, 1990, p. 117).

I. Techniques of power: from force to domination by virtue of a constellation of interests

What techniques of power does Russia use to secure a desirable outcome? Are the European countries forced into a certain course by Russia? Force as a technique of power involves 'the creation of physical obstacles restricting the freedom of another' (Wrong, 1980, p. 24). In international politics, the use of force amounts to a direct military invasion. Russia used its military force against Georgia (in 2008) and Ukraine, while staying clear of relying on this technique of power in its relationships with the EU member-states.

Are the European countries coerced into adapting a softer position with regards to Russia's use of force against Ukraine? Coercion makes the use of force or the other negative sanctions optional. The coerced actor has a choice, however restricted this choice may be: either he or she obeys or the coercing actor applies negative sanctions (Coleman, 1990, p. 71). Russia's willingness to cut natural gas supplies was demonstrated in January 2009 during unresolved payment disputes with Ukraine. Russia, nevertheless, values its reputation as a reliable natural gas supplier to the European Union and continues to emphasise that it has never cut natural gas deliveries to its Western customers at will.

Maybe Russia manipulates the EU member-states? The technique of manipulation works through the limitation or selective determination of 'the [manipulated] subject's information supply, e.g. by withholding pertinent information not easily available to the subject from other sources' (Ledyaev, 1997, p. 191). The Russian power elite has managed to impose tight control over the mass media, a key vehicle for disseminating information. This control was initially asserted at the national level (Wilson, 2005) and, more recently, at the international level too—with the emergence of *Russia Today*, a global TV network heavily subsidised by the Russian government. Russia's capacity to withhold pertinent information at the international level remains limited, however. *Russia Today* faces competition from several other, more established global TV networks.

Does Russia use corruption to silence the critics of its internal and foreign politics? In this context, corruption as a particular technique of power involves attempts to cause a decision maker to breach ethical and/or legal rules, which he or she is otherwise expected to follow, in the power holder's interests (Hodgson & Jiang, 2007, p. 1053). In the case of corruption, obedience pays: the corrupt decision maker receives a pecuniary compensation for deviating from the prescribed course of action. In contrast to force, coercion and manipulation, the dominated agent (the decision maker) has positive incentives for aligning his or her interests with those of the power holder (the agent offering the bribe). The use of corruption by members of the Russian power elite to promote their interests cannot be excluded (Osipian, 2010). There are precedents when the Russian power elite hired former high-ranking European officials offering them lucrative jobs, probably in recognition of their contribution to the promotion of Russia's interests.[87] Nevertheless, the use of corruption can hardly explain the persistent and widespread refusal of the European countries to take a more critical and tougher stance on Russia's actions. The mean 2013 Transparency International Corruption perception score for the EU member-states is 63.6 out of 100 (Russia has the score of 28; the lower the score, the higher the perceived level of corruption), which suggests a relatively low level of corruption in the operation of government.[88]

This chapter aims to explore whether an often-overlooked technique of power, namely, domination by virtue of a constellation of interests in the market, sheds new light on the European response to Russia's internal and foreign policy, especially in its 'near abroad' (Russia's policy toward Ukraine is considered to be a case in point). Max Weber sets domination by virtue of authority, a well-researched topic in political sociology and political science, against domination by virtue of a constellation of interests without providing much detail. He simply notes that 'because of the very absence of rules, domination which originates in the market… may be felt to be much more oppressive than an authority in which the duties of obedience are set out clearly and expressly' (Weber, 1968, p. 946). The following discussion will focus more specifically on a possible constellation of interests of Russia and the EU member-states in the natural gas market.

The use of this technique of power involves reliance on the market but requires that the power holder creates structural imbalances that undermine the principles of free competition. The interests of the parties transacting in the non-clearing market form a constellation, which does not exclude the possibility of one party having the upper hand and imposing its will on the others. If a rational

87 For instance, Gerhard Schröder, a former Chancellor of the Federal Republic of Germany, is the Chairman of the Shareholder Committee of 'Nord Stream' AG, the operator of a natural gas pipeline directly connecting Russia to its largest European consumer, Germany, through the Baltic Sea (http://www.nord-stream.com/about-us/our-management/ accessed November 19, 2017).

88 Transparency International (2013). Corruption Perception Index 2013. Retrieved from https://www.transparency.org/cpi2013/results.

agent acts under market constraints designed and imposed by the power holder, then the former has an interest in accepting the latter's upper hand. The dominated agent's gain is positive. Its other alternatives prove to be poorer in the circumstances. A similar observation applies to an agent that does not deal with the power holder in a direct manner, but transacts with the first dominated agent. The second agent is dominated by the power holder as well, but also receives a positive gain. At the end of the day all the parties involved have an interest in maintaining the status quo, i.e. the domination of one of them. The dominated parties are better off in not criticising the power holder than in challenging the latter and the system that it created.

A working hypothesis is the following: *the stance of an EU member-state on the issue of the imposition of sanctions (restrictive measures) on Russia in the context of this country's military conflict with Ukraine in 2014 will depend on the scope of the EU member-state's reliance on natural gas supplies from Russia and the EU member-state's position in intra-European trade.* Natural gas supplies from Russia serve as a proxy for *direct* contacts between the power holder and the dominated agent. The indirect contacts are operationalised with the help of intra-European trade statistics. A country that does not buy natural gas directly from Russia may nevertheless benefit from having access to goods and services produced by the key customers of Russian natural gas. In other words, the interests of Russia as the key supplier of natural gas, its European customers, and customers of products made with the help of Russian energy supplies, are expected to form a constellation. This hypothesis will be formally tested using statistical data after the concept of domination by virtue of a constellation of interests is confronted with the prevailing accounts of the European energy market at a theoretical level in the two next sections.

II. Markets versus empires

There are two popular approaches to theorising the situation in the European energy market. 'The "Markets and Institutions" approach is derived from economic liberalism; it emphasises the importance of energy markets and multilateral cooperation in international energy relations. The "Regions and Empires" approach is, in contrast, based on economic nationalist principles. It depicts international energy relations as a competition between blocks of states over the control of energy resources and energy markets' (Schmidt-Felzmann, 2011, p. 575; see also Correljé & Van der Linde, 2006; Finon & Locatelli, 2008). The first approach places emphasis on the invisible hand of the market and its role in resource allocation. The second approach highlights the visible hand of the people in control of governments, i.e. the power elites.

The scholarly discourse on energy policies in general—and European energy policies in particular, is currently framed in 'either-or' terms. Either the invisible hand of the market guides energy supplies, or the visible hand of government or large corporations' shareholders[89] takes precedence over the market play. The two hands operate independently from each other. As a matter of fact, the invisible hand of the market is believed to make the visible hand of government unnecessary and redundant and vice versa.

Predictions as to the situation in the European energy market made on the basis of the 'Market and Institutions' approach sound overly optimistic. Even if the market falls short of the perfectly competitive ideal, it still has the capacity for self-corrections. The existence of a monopoly or oligopoly (because the European market for natural gas has three key suppliers, Russian Gazprom, Norwegian Statoil and Algerian Sonatrach; see Jansen, Van Lier, Van Witteloostuijn & von Ochssée, 2012) does not necessarily mean that a monopolist or an oligopolist is able to impose his or her will on the other market participants.

---

89 In the case of Gazprom, the Russian government holds more than half, 50.23%, of this corporation's shares (http://www.gazprom.com/investors/stock/ accessed July 16, 2014). It means that Gazprom is guided by the visible hand of the Russian government. For the sake of simplicity, the issue of relationships between shareholders and managers will be left aside, namely the question whether the latter group has a significant degree of autonomy from the former group.

First, all market participants win something: they receive a positive utility. Advocates of the 'Market and Institutions' approach consider irrelevant the fact that a rent generated by a transaction might be unequally distributed.

Second, agents acting in an imperfectly competitive market develop a significant degree of mutual dependence. The European customers might depend on Gazprom, but Gazprom also depends on them. 'Russia... find[s] [herself] substantially financially dependent on Europe, on the revenues generated by [her] export of oil and natural gas. Gazprom receives about 65 percent of its revenues from Europe, and directly generated 8 percent of Russian GDP in 2005' (Ericson, 2009, p. 35). Mutual dependence causes a strategic convergence of interests of Russia and the European countries that even major geopolitical conflicts do not undermine. The European countries continued to supply Russia (in the shape of its predecessor, the Soviet Union) pipes, binding tapes, drills and bits even during the economic embargo following the Afghanistan invasion, and credit terms remained favourable (Maddock, 1980, pp. 28–29; see also Hashim, 2010 for a similar argument regarding the current situation). Advocates of the 'Market and Institutions' approach see it as a proof of the prevalence of 'win-win' transactions in the market, however imperfect the competition might be.

Third, in the conditions of restricted supply, customers may also decide to form a countervailing monopsony. Proposals to move in this direction are being actively debated in the European countries (Ericson, 2009, p. 40) without yet leading to practical changes, however. The existence of a bilateral monopoly limits structural preconditions for capturing the rent generated by a transaction and increases the importance of the strategies used by the parties involved. A party's bargaining power refers to its ability to select the strategy of negotiation to maximise the share of the rent captured by the party.

Keith Dowding differentiates between luck and power in this respect (Dowding, 1996, chapter 3). Luck derives from structural factors that enable one party to impose its will on the others. Narrowly defined power refers to a strategic component. The strategic component of power involves selecting a strategy, a technique for imposing one's will on the others.

Are Russia's positions of power in the European energy market due to luck alone? It can be argued that the structural imbalances that currently characterise this market have to be made endogenous to our models. In addition to exploiting its position of power to its advantage, Russia also invests heavily in infrastructural projects that will further enhance structural components of its power (namely, the 'Blue Stream', 'Nord Stream' and 'South Stream' pipelines[90]). And European countries seem to be willing to accept Russia's continuous expansion in the European energy market.

The recent developments in the New Institutional Economics, the NIE, help better differentiate the market for natural gas from the other segments of the European energy market. The NIE add a third element to the dichotomy of the market and the organisation (government being one of them): hybrid forms or relational contracting. 'The parties to [hybrid modes of contracting] maintain autonomy, but the contract is mediated by an elastic contracting mechanism' (Williamson, 1991, p. 271). Claude Ménard describes the contracting mechanism in terms of authority, 'that is, the conscious and deliberate delegation of the capacity to make a subset of decisions to a body in charge of coordinating' (Ménard, 2005a, p. 96). The important role that authority plays, as a particular case of power in the operation of hybrids, deserves mentioning. The visible hand of authority complements the invisible hand of the market.

Transactions between the key oil and gas companies in the European Union and Russia take the form of long-term contracts with built-in mechanisms of adjustments ('authority') to external shocks. Attempts to increase the share of transactions on the spot market (these transactions involve no long-term commitment of any party) have been unsuccessful so far, especially in the natural gas market. Gazprom clearly prefers signing long-term contracts and strategic

90 The 'South Stream' project is now put on hold. Russia considers developing an alternative project with similar parameters, 'Turkish Stream', however.

bilateral agreements with its European customers (Finon & Locatelli, 2008, p. 430; Correljé & Van der Linde, 2006, p. 540).

The preference for relational contracting has an economic rationale. The New Institutional economists explain the choice between alternative forms, the market, the firm and relational contracting, in the terms of asset specificity (Williamson, 1991). Specific assets cannot be redeployed without a loss of value. They produce the most when being employed only in a particular transaction. The specificity of assets has several components: site specificity (bilateral dependency results from location constraints), physical specificity (assets that use specific inputs such as customised computer programs), dedicated assets (large investments made for satisfying the needs of a particular customer), human assets (firm-specific knowledge and skills), brand name capital and temporal specificity (lock-in among parties involved in a technological process) (Ménard, 2005b, pp. 55–56).

The three first components are present in the case of the natural gas market (the degree of asset specificity in the market for oil is also high, but tends to be lower than in the natural gas market). Major natural gas fields in Europe are located on Russian territory, which makes its delivery to non-European markets more expensive ('site specificity'). The cheapest way to transport natural gas over long distances is in compressed form through a large diameter pipeline ('physical specificity'). Its construction requires substantial investments ('dedicated assets') (Ericson, 2009, p. 29). The development of the market for liquefied natural gas (LNG) also requires investment in specific assets (cargo ships and terminals).

Hybrid forms incorporate power only in a weak form: they involve delegating a 'subset' of decisions, whereas the rest of their activities are still coordinated by the conventional visible hand, i.e. the Russian government in the case of Gazprom. Parties maintain their autonomy and avoid relationships of subordination. So, in the end, the concept of hybrids is of little assistance in explaining the eventual transformation of the market into a tool for enhancing power. We observe just the opposite: how authority as a particular type of power relationships helps to maximise the output of specific assets in the market environment.

In contrast to the optimism of the 'Market and Institutions' approach, the 'Regions and Empires' approach leads to mostly pessimistic conclusions. Specifically, the latter approach predicts that power play will take the place of market play. In market play, all parties involved win. In power play, there is only one winner. The winning party achieves this outcome at the expense of the other parties.[91]

When applied to the European energy market, the 'Regions and Empires' framework suggests that Russia will use energy supplies as a lever for securing unilateral gains, pecuniary or geopolitical. 'From the perspective of "Regions and Empires", the EU's energy relations with Russia (and other third states) are understood as a geopolitical power struggle' (Schmidt-Felzmann, 2011, p. 575; see also Finon & Locatelli, 2008, p. 425; Correljé & Van der Linde, 2006, p. 536). Advocates of this approach produce numerous examples that, they believe, confirm its validity. The Soviet Union entered into the European energy market in the 1960s. Initially supplies of oil had an irregular character. For instance, the Soviet Union sold crude oil in exchange for various products that the Soviet economy failed to produce in sufficient quantities. In order to enter the market, the Soviet Union set asking prices sometimes two times lower than the market price at that time (Gaidar, 2006, p. 109). In other words, the European countries had power over the Soviet Union as a new entrant to the European energy market. The situation later changed. The Soviet Union learned how to increase its power and to be less dependent on the market. Egor Gaidar claims that the Soviet leadership in the 1970s actively participated in manipulating the European crude oil market by contributing to the prolongation of the 'oil war' of Arab countries against the Western countries. Relevant operations of its ally, the People's Liberation Front of Palestine, were instrumental in this regard (Ibid., p. 191).

---

91 The 'Market and Institutions' approach can be described in the terms of 'pure collaboration' games, whereas the 'Regions and Empires' approach refers to zero-sum games. In the 'pure collaboration' game the players win or lose together, having identical preferences regarding the income. The zero-sum game represents their opposite (Schelling, 1960, p. 84).

The Soviet Union was also an exclusive supplier of oil and natural gas to the East European market (now a part of the European market). This country was able to impose additional—mostly geopolitical and political—conditions for receiving its oil and gas. For example, 'in exchange for a guarantee on energy exports the Soviet Union may demand that Eastern Europe as a whole follows a cautious line on economic reform, more in tune with its own conservative program' or limits contacts with the West European countries (Maddock, 1980, p. 34). At that time, however, the energy weapon played a secondary role in Russia's repertoire of techniques of power, supplementing, rather than substituting, for force (military presence and control).

Russia, which succeeded the Soviet Union's role as a key supplier of oil and natural gas to the European market, strengthened its position of power even further. Now this country imposes conditions for receiving its oil and gas not only on East European countries, but on West European countries as well. An analysis of voting patterns of a Parliamentary Assembly of the Council of Europe (PACE) resolution and a PACE recommendation criticising Russia's military conflict with Georgia August 2008 show that Russia succeeded in demanding that customers of its energy products take a more neutral stance (Moraski & Giucanu, 2013).[92] The course of action chosen by Russia less than one year later, in January 2009, further confirms arguments of advocates of the 'Regions and Empires' approach. Russia used cuts in gas supplies to Ukraine to strengthen its bargaining position in a dispute with this country.

The representation of the two prevailing approaches in the opposite terms certainly facilitates the understanding of the underlying rationale: the market and power relationships are the alternative foundations of the European energy policy. At the same time, this black and white take on the issue does not allow a more nuanced picture: namely, can the two hands, the invisible hand of the

92 As of 2014, the PACE includes 28 national delegations of the EU member-states and 18 national delegations from the European countries that are not members of the EU. In other words, the EU member-states form a majority at the PACE.

market and the visible hand of government, operate in concert instead of one excluding the other? Speaking more practically, can the power elite of a large energy supplier transform the market into a tool for enhancing its power without renouncing the centrality of the market? If the answer to this research and practical question is affirmative, then a combination of the 'Regions and Empires' approach and the 'Market and Institutions' approach may provide a better fit for the observed patterns in European energy policies.

III. Market-based empires

The concept of the power triad paves the way for considering both structural and strategic components of power within a single theoretical framework (this concept is discussed in detail in Oleinik, 2011a; Oleinik, 2015b). This analytical tool aims to highlight the eventual transformation of strategic components of power into its structural components and vice versa. Russia's efforts to embed the European natural gas market into an infrastructure that facilitates the further strengthening of its positions of power result from conscious choices made by the Russian power elite. The European countries' power elites also make conscious choices when accepting Russia's expansion: in 2011 Russia provided 21.23% of total energy supplies (natural gas, crude oil and solid fuels combined) to the EU member-states, 3.44% more than in 2004 (Table 5.1). The awareness that a high degree of dependence on energy supplies from Russia can be—and actually has been, used by this country as a tool for promoting its geopolitical objectives is outweighed by some other considerations, apparently. The concept of the power triad helps unveil these additional considerations.

The power triad includes three agents: a gate-keeper (*C*), an agent enjoying a structural advantage (*A*), for instance, facing limited competition, and an agent transacting with *A*, who has no structural advantage (*B*). *C* plays a key role within the power triad. *C* erects barriers—technical, institutional, geographical or financial—to market entry. With their help *C* controls entry to the market. To get access to the market, *A* must accept *C*'s conditions: either to pay the price of the entry ticket or to further *C*'s interests in some other manner. In the exchange, *A* gets the privilege of acting with fewer competitors: only few of them manage to enter the market. Many (*A'*-type agents) saw their access to the market denied, as a result of restrictions imposed by *C*. *B* enters the market without restrictions, but has to buy goods or services from *A*, who either charges a higher price in conditions of imperfect competition or demands from *B* other favours that further *A*'s interests. It should be noted, however, that *B* has an interest in buying goods or services from *A* since the available alternatives are poorer in the terms of the associated utility.

C benefits most from the existence of the power triad. *C* decides the number of *A*-type agents to be admitted to the market, maximising the rent that he or she captures. The barriers represent a structural component of *C*'s power. *C*'s decisions with respect to the ratios of the number of *A*-type agents to the number of *B*-type agents and to the number of *A'*-type agents refer to a strategic component of *C*'s power. *A* also captures a rent as a result of acting in the conditions of limited competition (a part of *A*'s profits is subsequently transferred to *C* in compensation for the latter's gate-keeping). *B* buys goods and services that he or she would not otherwise be able to buy at a better price or to buy at all. *C*, *A* and *B* maintain their formal autonomy. Neither *A* nor *B* enters into relationship of formal subordination to *C*. *C* imposes his or her will on *A* and *B* 'from behind the scenes'. *C*'s activities remain mostly invisible for *A* and especially for *B* (*B* does not enter in direct contact with *C*). As a result of this lack of formalisation, *A*'s and *B*'s duties of obedience are not set out clearly and expressly, as observed by Weber.

C, *A* and *B* all gain from participating in the power triad, however unequal their gains may be. *C*'s, *A*'s and *B*'s interests form a constellation in the market with restricted access, which lays the foundation for *C*'s and *A*'s domination by virtue of a constellation of interests. This constellation contributes to the strengthening of *C*'s and, to a lesser extent, *A*'s power. *C*'s power within the power triad is embodied in two hands: the visible hand of the gate-keeper and the invisible hand of the market with structural imbalances created by the gate-keeper. *A* needs one hand, invisible, to impose his or her will on *B*. In other words, to make sense of how the power triad works, one needs to combine assumptions of both the 'Markets and Institutions' approach and the 'Regions and Empires' approach.

Compared with more conventional models of power relationships, the power triad may seem to some to be an excessively complicated construct. For instance, Dowding (2014, pp. 566–567) insists that by focusing on 'a simple bilateral bargain between state actors and business' we could gain as much insight. According to him, the introduction of a third party into the model is simply unnecessary. Do we really need to take into account all three actors, *C*, *A* and *B*, when discussing power reproduced and enhanced through the market?

If one considers 'a simple bilateral bargain', then the set of options available to its parties remains an exogenous factor to the transaction. Dowding (1996, p. 24) agrees that 'changing the choice situation of people is… an important way of altering their individual and collective power' without showing how the choice situation can be subject to a bilateral bargain. To say that we have the available options 'by virtue of the circumstances', as Dowding suggests, is to acknowledge their exogenous character. The concept of the power triad aims to show how the choice situation can be changed and by whom. *C*, the gate-keeper, determines the choice situations of *A* and *B*. This concept also explains the acceptance of *C*'s and *A*'s power despite the unequal distribution of gains from the transaction. Even *B*, whose gain turns out to be the smallest, does not object to the existence of the power triad.

IV. The 2014 Ukrainian crisis through the lens of the power triad

A study of the reaction of the European countries to the 2014 Russian military confrontation with Ukraine further illustrates the usefulness of the concept of the power triad. The crisis started after Ukrainian protesters in Kyiv ousted Viktor Yanukovych, a pro-Russian president, from office in February 2014. Profiting from the weakness of the Ukrainian state at these turbulent times, Russia first seized Crimea and then started to support pro-Russian separatists in Eastern Ukraine (in the regions of Donetsk and Luhansk) supplying them with arms, including heavy, financial and human resources (Russia sent 'volunteers' and military personnel to fight on the separatists' side).

Details of the Ukrainian crisis and its internal dynamics are of no concern here (see Chapters 3, 4 and 10). The discussion will focus instead on the reaction of the European countries to Russia's role in the crisis. One could have expected an immediate and strong condemnation of the violation of Ukraine's territorial integrity by Russia. First, Ukraine is geographically a part of Europe and has land borders with the four EU member-states (Poland, the Slovak Republic, Hungary and Romania). Second, one of the reasons behind the 2013–2014 Ukrainian protests refers to the desire for greater integration with the European Union. A series of surveys conducted among protesters in Kyiv in December 2013—February 2014 show that the second most popular reason for joining the ranks of the protesters refers to Yanukovych's refusal to sign an agreement of association with the European Union (Ilko Kucheriv Democratic Initiatives Foundation, 2014; see Table 3.1 in Chapter 3). Third, the Russian involvement undermined a principle that has historically underpinned the European geopolitical constructions, namely, the balance of Europe. 'The balance of Europe primarily meant the impossibility of the strongest state laying down the law to any other state' (Foucault, 2007, p. 299).[93] Fourth, Russia's role in the crisis

---

93 The applicability of the balance of Europe principle in today's circumstances is contested. Some experts and political advisers both in the West and Russia mention this principle, claiming that its non-respect caused the escalation of the Ukrainian conflict, however. For instance, a Russian expert and political adviser, Alexandr Dugin, considers the balance of forces as a key element of *realpolitik* at the international level (Dugin, 2008). John Mearsheimer, an American expert in international relationships, agrees: 'the West had been moving into Russia's backyard and threatening its core strategic interests... Elites in the United States and Europe... tend to [erroneously] believe that the logic of realism holds little relevance in the twenty-first century' (Mearsheimer, 2014, pp. 77–78). Russian President Vladimir Putin echoes this line of reasoning stating on July 1, 2014 that the arrival of NATO troops in Crimea 'would have dramatically changed the balance of forces in the Black Sea region' (cited in

highlighted the need for enforcing (as opposed to merely declaring) norms that restrict the use of force in international relationships (namely, Chapter VII 'Action with respect to threats to the peace, breaches of the peace, and acts of aggression' of the Charter of the United Nations).[94]

The European countries responded by imposing individual sanctions (restrictive measures) on several mid-level Russian officials and leaders of the separatists.[95] So called 'sectorial' sanctions, i.e. sanctions affecting Russian banking system and industries, were considered at a very advanced stage in the military conflict. The 'sectorial' sanctions were not consistently and fully applied, however.

The issue of sanctions was a source of controversies and debates among the European power elites. Instead of producing a

---

an official communique, http://itar-tass.com/politika/1291203 accessed June 30, 2017). The Russian and European power elites undoubtedly disagree as to who first attempted to change the balance of Europe, but they both tend to acknowledge its importance in an either explicit or implicit manner.

94 On March 27, 2014 Ukraine secured a resolution of the United Nations General Assembly titled 'Territorial integrity of Ukraine' (100 votes in favour to 11 against, with 58 abstentions) that calls on member-States to 'desist and refrain' from actions aimed at disrupting Ukraine's national unity and territorial integrity, including by modifying its borders through the threat or use of force.

95 The Council of the European Union took a series of decisions with respect to the restrictive measures 'directed against certain persons, entities and bodies in view of the situation in Ukraine': Decision 2014/199/CFSP of March 5, 2014 (it concerns 18 persons, including Viktor Yanukovych), Decision 2014/145/CFSP of March 17, 2014 (21 persons), Decision 2014/151/CSFP of March 21, 2014 (12 persons), Decision 2014/216/CFSP of April 14, 2014 (7 persons), Decision 2014/238/CSFP of April 28, 2104 (15 persons), Decision 2014/265/CFSP of May 12, 2104 (13 persons and 2 entities), Decision 2014/308/CFSP of May 28, 2014 (17 persons and 2 entities) and Decision 2014/455/CFSP of July 11, 2014 (11 persons). As of July 17, 2014, the restrictive measures apply to 114 persons and 4 entities (none of which in the energy sector). Full texts of these decisions are available from the EUR-Lex web-site (http://eur-lex.europa.eu/search.html?instInvStatus=ALL&text=%22restrictive%20measures%22%20ukraine&qid=1404774373429&DTS_DOM=PUBLISHED_IN_OJ&textScope=ti-te&type=advanced&lang=en&SUBDOM_INIT=PUBLISHED_IN_OJ&DTS_SUBDOM=PUBLISHED_IN_OJ accessed July 17, 2014).

united and univocal response to Russia's seizure of Crimea and her destabilising role in Eastern Ukraine, the European Union turned out to be divided among a group of countries favouring a 'soft' response and a group of countries supporting tougher measures against Russia. Experts of 'Open Europe', a European think-thank, labelled the former groups as 'Doves' and the latter group as 'Hawks' producing an ordinal-level assessment of the intensity of support for tougher sanctions on Russia (Open Europe, 2014; see Table 5.1). Can the variation in the level of support for tougher sanctions on Russia be explained in the terms of the European countries' dependency on energy supplies from this country? Does the concept of the power triad shed additional light on this issue?

Table 5.1 'Energy dependence of the EU member-states on Russia and their stance on sanctions on Russia in the first half of 2014'

	Coefficients of total energy dependence on total energy supplies (crude oil, natural gas and coal) from Russia, member-countries of the EU*			Average share of natural gas supplies from Russia in total net supplies	Average total trade turnover with Russia as a % of GDP	Open Europe's Dove/Hawk scale (5 refers to a strong support, -5—to a strong opposition)
	2011**	2006***	2004***	2010–2012****	2010–2012******	2014*****
Austria	23.433	22.312	21.351	60.00	1.7	-1
Belgium	20.081	18.295	16.75	0.30	3.1	4
Bulgaria	62.585	38.705	37.504	88.85	13.8	-5
Cyprus	0.05	n.a.	n.a.	0	12.4	-4
Czech Rep.	45.088	26.124	24.653	57.50	7.3	1
Denmark	6.613	5.635	5.67	0	1.7	3.5
Estonia	11.640	15.55****	13	100.00	26.2	4
Finland	44.081	36.896	40.882	100.00	10.2	-0.5
France	13.604	10.614	8.025	16.00	1.3	0.5
Germany	24.679	23.024	21.525	37.30	2.9	-1
Greece	25.968	23.634	23.678	55.60	3.0	-4
Hungary	44.759	51.089	48.699	79.90	10.8	-2
Ireland	0	0	0	0	1.0	3
Italy	17.647	17.145	22.336	28.85	3.1	-3
Latvia	23.396	37.28****	67.701	100.00	47.9	4
Lithuania	136.073	64.191	47.168	166.40*******	22.0	5
Luxemburg	3.958	n.a.	n.a.	24.10	0.4	-4

Malta	0	n.a.	n.a.	0	34.4	0
Nether-lands	30.287	13.971	11.3	5.20	14.1	-0.5
Poland	26.318	30.361	27	58.60	7.7	5
Portugal	2.250	0.054	3.791	0	0.6	0
Romania	3.792	19.611	22.28	24.30	3.1	4
Slovakia	77.875	52.56	53.702	83.50	14.7	-1
Slovenia	8.039	6.475****	7.288	60.20	4.6	-3
Spain	10.174	10.968	9.235	0	1.0	-3.5
Sweden	22.858	11.269	8.288	0	2.6	3.5
United Kingdom	6.254	6.343	2.7	0	1.3	4
EU-27	21.23	18.72	17.19	23.43	9.37	0.33

Legend: * the coefficient of dependence equals the sum of products of the share of a particular source of energy in total energy consumption, the share of import in its consumption and the share of supplies from Russia in its total imports; **** Data on crude oil are missing; ******* including re-export.

Sources: ** European Commission, 2013, pp. 165–219; the Eurostat data (http://epp.eurostat.ec.europa.eu/portal/page/portal/eurostat/home, accessed July 9, 2014) and the author's calculations; *** Oleinik, 2011a, p. 9; **** Eurogas, 2013, p. 6; Eurogas, 2012, p. 6; Eurogas, 2011, p. 8; ***** Open Europe, 2014; ****** Federal'naia Sluzhba Gosudarstvennoi Statistiki, 2013, Table 14.7 at p. 248; Federal'naia Sluzhba Gosudarstvennoi Statistiki, 2011, Table 14.7 and the author's calculations.

A power triad exists in the European natural gas market. Within this power triad, Russia, *C*, controls access to its pipelines delivering gas to the European customers represented by national energy companies. As a condition of access to a reliable source of relatively cheap energy (compared to the other sources), *C* expects that *A* will further *C*'s interests, pecuniary or non-pecuniary, including geopolitical. The European energy companies with privileged access to the pipeline, *A*, have a structural advantage over the national companies with no direct access to the pipeline, *A′*. As a result, the national economies of the European countries with direct access to the pipeline get a competitive advantage over the other European national economies. *A* produces goods and services at relatively lower costs (the price of gas is directly or indirectly—via the price of electricity—included in cost calculations for most goods and services), which makes them more competitive in the European market. Consumers of these goods and services, *B*, benefit too: they buy products for a better price (compared with domestically produced goods and services[96]), all other things being equal.

C, *A* and *B* all receive a positive gain. Their interests form a constellation in the European natural gas market embedded in the network of pipelines either inherited from the Soviet era or built recently. In these circumstances, *C*'s power has both components, structural and strategic (the latter refers to Russia's efforts to set prices in a selective manner in relation to how a particular customer furthers Russia's interests and to promote new infrastructural projects that will further enhance its gate-keeping ability).

If the European natural gas market operates as the power triad so described, then several predictions can be formulated and empirically tested. Namely, the bigger the share of natural gas supplied from Russia in a country's total net supplies, the lower the level of support for tougher sanctions on Russia (in other words, *A*'s and *C*'s interests tend to be positively associated). Also, the bigger the share of natural gas supplied from Russia in a country's total net supplies, the more positive the country's trade balance (*C*'s,

96 Which does not exclude that *B* overpays for goods and services compared to the situation when *A* produces them in conditions of perfect competition.

A's and *B*'s interests tend to be associated). *B* buys *A*'s goods and services, thus a negative trade balance serves as a proxy for playing *B*'s role.

To test these predictions, several OLS regressions of a EU member-state's level of support for tougher sanctions on Russia were run on the coefficient of its dependence on total energy supplies from Russia, the share of natural gas supplies from Russia in net total supplies, the total trade turnover (export and import combined) with Russia as a percentage of GDP, GDP per capita, the intra-European Union trade balance without raw materials as a percentage of GDP[97] and several dummy variables specifying the European country's geographical location.[98] 3-year average values of the ratio-level variables (2010–2012) were used to eliminate possible fluctuations and the impact of the inauguration of 'Nord Stream's' first line in November 2011.[99]

The European country's stance on the sanctions is used as a proxy for Russia's interests as C within the power triad. Only a non-pecuniary, geopolitical dimension of these interests is taken into account in this model. The degree of the European country's dependence on energy supplies from Russia is operationalised through two variables: the aggregate coefficient of total energy dependence, and the share of natural gas supplies from Russia. The higher their values, the more chances that a particular European country plays *A*'s role within the power triad. The European country's trade turnover as a percentage of its GDP represents the other dimension of its economic dependence on Russia. It should be noted that of these three indicators of the European country's economic dependence

97 The distribution of these variables was visually inspected prior to regression analysis. This 'eyeballing' suggested that the normality of distribution condition was not significantly violated.

98 Outcomes of Levene's Test of Equality of Variances show that the assumption of homogeneity of the variance in the dependent variable, the European country's stance on sanctions on Russia, is met for all the dummy variables.

99 Croatia joined the European Union in 2013, which explains its exclusion from the present analysis.

on Russia, the share of natural gas supplies refers to the most specific assets (pipelines, storage facilities and the other transport infrastructure) whereas the trade turnover relates to the least specific.

The intra-EU trade balance serves to operationalise *A*'s and *B*'s interests: *A*'s interests if the particular country's balance is positive and *B*'s interests in the opposite case. *A*'s and *B*'s interests have a pecuniary dimension in this model. *A* and *B*'s motivation is pecuniary and their choices rational in the circumstances. A control variable—GDP per capita—is also entered to test the assumption of *A*'s pecuniary interests.

Table 5.2 summarises results of the regression analysis. Models 1 and 2 show that, taken separately, neither the coefficient of total energy dependence nor the share of natural gas supplies from Russia explains the variation in the level of support for tougher sanctions on Russia. The addition of the trade turnover with Russia in Model 3 does not change the situation. Outcomes of the regression become statistically significant with the addition of several dummy variables specifying the European country's geographical location in Model 4: namely, the North European countries and the countries sharing land borders with Ukraine support tougher sanctions to a much greater extent than the other countries. The entry of GDP per capita significantly improves the quality of the model (Model 5) and makes the impact of the share of natural gas supplies from Russia significant. The control variable, GDP per capita, 'is discovered to be the mediating factor through which an independent variable [the share of natural gas supplies] has its effect on a dependent variable [the stance on sanctions on Russia]' (Babbie & Benaquisto, 2002, p. 436). This finding turns out to be relevant to the previously discussed argument about *A*'s *pragmatic* interest in accepting *C*'s power.

Table 5.2 **'Results of Statistical (Method = Enter) Multiple Regression to predict stance on sanctions against Russia in the first half of 2014 (Y) from Coefficient of total energy dependence on total energy supplies (crude oil, natural gas and coal) from Russia (Lg10), average share of natural gas supplies from Russia in total net supplies (SQRT), average total trade turnover with Russia as a % of GDP (Lg10), average GDP per capita in current USD (SQRT), average intra-EU27 trade balance (without raw materials) as a % of GDP and geographical location (dummies for common borders with Russia and Ukraine, for countries of Northern, Southern, Western and Eastern Europe), standardised (Beta) coefficients, 2010–2012'**

Model	**1**	**2**	**3**	**4**	**5**	**6**	**7**
2011 coefficient of total energy dependence on total energy supplies (crude oil, natural gas and coal) from Russia (Lg10)[(a)]	0.031 (0.155)						
Average share of natural gas supplies from Russia in total net supplies (SQRT)[(a)]		-0.038 (-0.19)	-0.151 (-0.64)	-0.249 (-1.23)	**-0.455 (-2.56)***	**-0.533 (-2.22)***	**-0.419 (-1.96)***
Average total trade turnover with Russia as a % of GDP (Lg10)[(a)]			0.213 (0.9)	0.193 (1.)	0.098 (0.54)	-0.103 (-0.44)	-0.130 (-0.55)
Common border with Ukraine (dummy)				**0.441 (2.32)***	**0.276 (1.7)^**	0.042 (0.22)	

Common border with Russia (dummy)				-0.09 (-0.41)	-0.025 (-0.14)	0.255 (1.24)	
Western Europe (dummy)				0.252 (1.02)	**0.516 (2.37)***	0.185 (0.62)	0.211 (0.74)
Southern Europe (dummy)				-0.099 (-0.4)	-0.294 (-1.39)	**-0.673 (-2.74)***	**-0.799 (-3.34)****
Northern Europe (dummy)				**0.805 (2.79)***(c)	**0.875 (3.7)****(c)	0.297 (1.03)(d)	0.384 (1.42)(d)
Average GDP per capita in current USD (SQRT)(b)					**-0.761 (-3.25)****	**-0.824 (-2.49)***	**-0.858 (-2.87)****
Average intra-EU27 trade balance (without raw materials) as a % of GDP(e)							**-0.274 (-1.57)^**
C (unstandardised coefficient)	0.127 (0.09)	0.485 (0.48)	0.104 (0.09)	-1.791 (-0.91)	**7.808 (2.32)***	**11.464 (2.78)****	**11.577 (3.3)****
R^2	0.001	0.001	0.034	0.588	0.740	0.568	0.585
R^2_{adj}	-0.039	-0.038	-0.046	0.436	0.625	0.376	0.431
F-statistic	0.24	0.36	0.425	**3.876****	**6.414*****	**2.956***	**3.818****
Observations	27	27	27	27	27	27	27

Legend: ^ significant at *a*=0.1, * significant at *a*=0.05, ** significant at *a*=0.01, *** significant at *a*=0.001. Statistically significant coefficients are given in bold. *t* values are bracketed. (c) with the Baltic states, (d) without the Baltic States (they are included in Eastern Europe).

Sources: (a) see Sources of Table 5.1; (b) World Bank, 2017; (e) the Eurostat data (Table ext_lt_intratrd, available from http://appsso.eurostat.ec.europa.eu/nui/show.do?dataset=ext_lt_intratrd&lang=en).

There is uncertainty as to where to place the Baltic States (Lithuania, Latvia and Estonia)—some sources include them in Northern Europe, whereas the other consider them to be a part of Eastern Europe—regressions were run using two versions of the dummy variables for Northern and Eastern Europe. Model 6 is identical to Model 5 except in relation to the Baltic States (now included in Eastern Europe). The negative impact of the share of natural gas supplies becomes even stronger. At the same time, the positive impact of sharing land borders with Ukraine almost disappears: the original relationship is 'shown to be false through the introduction of a test variable' (Babbie & Benaquisto, 2002, p. 434), GDP per capita. In these circumstances, it was decided not to enter the two dummy variables for countries with common borders with either Ukraine or Russia in Model 7. Instead, the intra-EU27 trade balance was entered. This variable has a negative—and marginally statistically significant (p=0.13)—impact on the dependent variable. In other words, the European countries with a positive intra-EU27 trade balance tend to adapt a softer position on sanctions on Russia. *A* converts its privileged access to Russian gas pipelines into competitive advantages in the intra-European trade. *B*, a customer of *A*'s products, has a negative trade balance. *B* buys more products from *A*, but receive relatively fewer benefits from the existence of the power triad than *C* and *A*. *B*-type countries tend to concentrate in Southern Europe: Italy, Spain, Portugal and Greece all have negative intra-EU27 trade balances. Model 7 explains slightly more than 43% of the variation in the European countries' stance on sanctions on Russia.

Conclusions: The price of comfort and opulence

In the final account, the hypothesis about the existence of the power triad in the European natural gas market turns out to be tentatively confirmed (it would be necessary to run more comprehensive tests using a longer list of indicators, especially with respect to *B*'s interests, before making any definitive claims). Russia, *C*, provides European countries with relatively cheap natural gas. Compared with the other sources of energy (namely crude oil and coal), the market for natural gas can be manipulated relatively more easily since its infrastructure includes highly specific assets (pipelines and storage facilities) that may possibly be transformed into a structural component of power.[100] Russia's power elite seized this opportunity by developing a second component of power: strategic. The strategic component of Russia's power consists in getting the key European markets 'wired' to Russian pipelines and in using the strategy of gate-keeping, i.e. providing privileged access to the pipelines only to those customers who willingly further the Russian power elite's interests.

The reaction of the EU member-states to Russia's military confrontation with Ukraine in 2014 is a case in point. The Russian power elite got what its members wanted, i.e. the refusal of the European power elites to impose tougher sanctions on Russia. The concept of the power triad shows that fears that Russia will arbitrarily cut gas supplies to European customers or, even worse, use military force against them have little basis. *C* has an interest in building and maintaining the reputation of a reliable supplier provided that *A* and *B* accept *C*'s rules of the game. *C* has power by virtue of a constellation of *A*'s and *B*'s interests with *C*'s interests. *C* does not 'buy' or corrupt *A* in a conventional sense of this word. *C* simply changes *A*'s and *B*'s choice situation in such a manner that they pragmatically decide to support *C*'s endeavors.

The concept of the power triad also suggests that it would be a mistake to explain the European response to the Ukrainian crisis in the terms of bilateral relationships only. The interests of European countries, including those outside the reach of Russian pipelines (at least so far), form a constellation. Focusing on bilateral relationships overshadows the fact that *B*-type agents, customers of

---

100 The entry of the coefficient of total energy dependency into the regression models instead of the share of natural gas supplies from Russia shows that the latter variable has a weaker predictive power: the models' quality decreases.

goods and services produced by the countries with privileged access to Russian pipelines, lose in relative, but not in absolute terms.

Neither *A* nor *B* has an interest in changing the status quo, i.e. in taking serious steps undermining the power triad in the European energy market. In these circumstances the considerations of 'mutual solidarity' (Schmidt-Felzmann, 2011) and even duty (the United Kingdom accepted the role of guarantor of Ukraine's unity and territorial integrity in 1994[101]) become irrelevant. *A*'s and *B*'s pragmatic interests turn to be more powerful drivers of their behaviour. It means that the power triad will likely continue to exist in the European energy market.

101 As per Budapest Memorandum on Security Assurances of December 5, 1994 (see also the introduction to Chapter 10). Two other guarantors were the United States and the Russian Federation.

Chapter 6
'Transition impossible? Ukraine between violence and power'

Introduction

Power constitutes one of the foundations of human relations. Power is explicitly or implicitly at play in various domains, from family and school to government and international affairs. However, a consensual definition of power exists neither in the scholarly literature nor in everyday discourse. Max Weber's conceptualisation of power can be found in many textbooks. According to him (Weber, 1968, p. 53), '"power" is the probability that one actor within a social relationship will be in a position to carry out his own will despite resistance, regardless of the basis on which this probability rests'. This definition offers a useful starting point in discussions of power rather than representing their end point, i.e. an assumption that anyone could take for granted.

Along with freedom (Chapter 2), human dignity (Oleinik, 2016a; Rodriguez, 2015) and many other core concepts in the social sciences, power remains 'essentially contested' (Wartenberg, 1990, p. 12). Philosophers, political scientists and sociologists continue to strongly disagree on how power operates and on its effects. Disputes typically revolve around the question of whether all parties involved in a power relationship gain or there are always winners and losers (Haugaard, 2014). On one hand, power can be compared with a non-zero-sum or even a pure collaboration game that has positive effects. In a pure collaboration game, the parties win or lose together. In a non-zero-sum game, the parties win and lose together, yet to an unequal extent (Schelling, 1960, pp. 84–87; see also Footnote 91 on p. 232). On the other hand, power can be perceived as a zero-sum game in which one party gains at the expense of the other. In the latter, zero-sum perception, power then has negative associations for everyone except the winning party.

These debates are not abstract and purely theoretical. Instead, they are deeply embedded in everyday experiences that can be conducive to either positive or negative associations with power. In some cultures, negative perceptions of power prevail. In others, people attach more positive subjective meanings to power. Among the cultures indexed in the Human Relations Area Files (HRAF), there are examples of both.[102] In Central Thai culture, 'among modern people the old perception of power as an amoral or immoral force is strengthened by the experience of disorder and insecurity' (Mulder, 1996, p. 59). The following words of a member of an African American community illustrate a more positive take on power: 'We have the perception of power, not real power. We have to organize people—do like the Koreans and Jews. Collectively we have the money to do things' (Gregory, 1998, p. 165).[103] Power is understood here as a possible outcome of joining efforts 'to do things' outside the reach of any Afro-American taken separately.

This chapter discusses problems associated with the transition from a negative perception of power to a more positive one focusing on the case of Ukraine. Negative associations with power prevail in Ukraine culture. The observation made with respect to Central Thai culture likely applies to the Ukrainian case too. Since March 2014, Ukraine has found itself in the face of military aggression from Russia (Chapter 5). In order to protect the territorial integrity of their country, Ukrainians might need to find internal sources of social and economic development. In other words, they need to join efforts as a means to extend the scope of the possible in the present circumstances.

This requires, however, that Ukrainians are able to move from power as a zero-sum game to power as a non-zero-sum game, if not a pure collaboration game. Without such transformation of power,

---

102 The search in the eHRAF databank was carried out on January 30, 2017.

103 Hanna Arendt's understanding of her Jewishness helps make this line of arguing even more subtle. For her, being a Jew has less to do with a particular ethnic origin than with the capacity to resist oppression through collective action (Allen, 1999, pp. 109–122; see also subsection I.1 of the general Conclusion of this book).

perspectives of building a sustainable nation-state in Ukraine remain dim (see Introduction and Conclusion to this book). However heroic and selfless individual and group actions of Ukraine's volunteers may be (this issue is discussed in detail in Chapter 10), their efforts simply do not suffice to 'do things' for common cause and common wealth. What follows is a discussion of factors that could either facilitate the potential change in the perception of power in Ukraine or make it impossible.

II. Conflicting discourses on power

Two terms help differentiate a negative perception of power relationships from a positive one in the scholarly discourse on power. Power in the narrow sense implies the latter, whereas violence—the former. Hannah Arendt proposes the relevant distinction in her essay 'On Violence'. In her thinking, power designates people's ability to join their efforts for the purpose of achieving objectives that are out of reach of individual effort. 'Power corresponds to the human ability not just to act but to act in concert' (Arendt, 1969, p. 44). Since power extends the scope of the possible for individuals through group action, it produces positive effects. The coach, who compels the swimmer to do specific exercises as a condition for a successful swim across the English Channel, has power.[104] His or her actions make possible a result that would otherwise be unthinkable for both. By contrast, violence has purely negative connotations. The powerholder imposes his or her will on the subordinate without considering the latter's interests. The powerholder wins, the subordinate loses. The coach, who encourages or simply tolerates hazing in a team for the sake of maintaining control over its members, acts violently. Seen from this perspective, 'power and violence are opposites; where the one rules absolutely, the other is absent' (Arendt, 1969, p. 56).

104 This example is inspired by conversations with Pavel Kuznetsov, the first Russian national to swim across the English Channel.

To avoid possible confusion of power as a generic concept and power as the human ability to act in concert, some authors add adjectives to this noun or use a different term altogether. Amy Allen (1999, p. 113) proposes the use of the term 'solidarity' for differentiating 'the collective power that grows out of action in concert'. Thomas Wartenberg (1990, chapter 9) uses the concept of 'transformative power'. Mark Haugaard (2015; 2014) develops the idea of 'concerted power'. Transformative power benefits both the powerholder and the subordinate. A novel nuance is also added: the powerholder, among the other things, aims to empower the subordinate, to make him or her more capable of autonomous actions in the future. The concept of concerted power highlights the embeddedness of power in institutions, processes and, speaking more generally, in culture. Some institutional and cultural environments facilitate actions in concert, whereas in the others joint efforts appear unlikely. 'Power is created by social systems and confers capacity for action upon actors' (Haugaard, 2014, p. 5; see also Allen, 2002).

The other particular forms of power, namely, power *over*, power *to* and power *together* (or power *with*, as some scholars also label it), discussed in Chapter 2, can be derived from any of these two, higher-order concepts of power (transformative power, concerted power) and violence. Power *over* can, for example, be associated either with violence, as in the case of the slave owner's power over the slave, or with power, as in the case of the bureaucrat's power over the citizen exercised within the limits of the laws and for common good (Haugaard, 2015, pp. 154–155).

In the context of governance, the institutional form of commonwealth has beneficial effects on power being at the same time an outcome of actions in concert. On the other hand, the institutional form of the State has no immunity against the transformation of power into violence. Thorstein Veblen's observations of Germany in the wake of WWI are illuminating in this respect. He opposes two forms of community, the English-style commonwealth and the German-style State. The first involves government by consent and has some common features with a joint-stock company

(Veblen, 1939, p. 170). Similar to stockholders, members of a commonwealth make sacrifices (i.e., they give up some autonomy and freedom) in exchange for increased chances of prosperity. In the pursuit of prosperity, citizens join resources and efforts in a way similar to what they did in establishing the East India Company.

The German-style State has a different rationale. 'In some potent sense, the State is a personal entity, with rights and duties superior and anterior to those of the subjects, whether these latter be separately or collectively, in detail or in the aggregate or average. The citizen is a subject of the State' (Ibid., p. 161). Since the interest of the State is 'superior and anterior to' that of its subjects, a drift into violence exists. The movement toward violence does not disappear even if state officials, who interpret the State's interest, act within the limits of their mandate. The citizen simply has no say in the interpretation of the State's interest. Bureaucratic corruption only strengthens the association of the State with violence. 'Bureaucratic corruption takes place when those in authority use what should be concerted power for purposes other than those intended' (Haugaard, 2015, p. 155).

All modern states had at their origin violence, as shown by Charles Tilly (1985) in his analysis of the parallels and interdependence between state-making and war-making. Agents of early European States were busy eliminating or neutralising their rivals both inside the territories under their direct control (Tilly calls this process 'state making') and outside these territories ('war making'). 'State making' and 'war making' implied attempts of agents of early States to carry out their will at the expense of the rivals and the populations in general. Violence left no place for power in these conditions.

Population changes, the accumulation of knowledge, and technological changes – including in the military domain, led to the redistribution of violence potential within and between the states (North, 1981, pp. 205–210). This redistribution in turn created opportunities for people to join efforts independently of State coercion and to transform – on this basis, a State into a commonwealth. Even in Europe, however, similar processes had divergent effects. A commonwealth emerged in England and its colonies, whereas

Spain and its colonies continued to embody a statist model. 'The evolution of North America and of Latin America differed radically right from the beginning, reflecting the imposition of the institutional patterns from the mother country upon the colonies and the radically divergent ideological constructs that shape the perceptions of the actors' (North, 1990, p. 102). Douglass North (Ibid., p. 94; see also Section IV of the book's general Introduction) also uses the concept of path dependence to further theorise subsequent institutional evolution. Radical changes in the path are not only unlikely. Attempts to change the path by external intervention often have an opposite effect. For example, the exportation of Anglo-Saxon political models to Africa and Asia on several occasions aroused tensions with local institutions. Instead of leading to the emergence of commonwealth as a universal model, the institutional exportation and importation brought frustrations and conflicts (Badie, 2000).

The model of power relationships that prevails in Russia and its former colonies, the countries of the Soviet Union, lies much closer to violence than to power. Some scholars even consider this particular model—Russian power—as the practical embodiment of violence. Yuri Pivovarov (2006, p. 22; see also Makarenko, 1998) claims, for instance, that Russian power materialises itself in violence. Violence constitutes its essence in contrast to violence as a means, a technique of the power that is otherwise not necessarily violent. In addition to its closeness to violence, some other features are attributed to Russian power: power has a self-justifiable character and does not find its justification in an external source (the law, tradition or divine grace); power is an end-in-itself as opposed to power as a means to attend other ends;[105] violent techniques for imposing will such as force, coercion or manipulation (Ledyaev, 2008);

105 There are opposing views as to whether violence is associated with power as an end-in-itself. Arendt (1969, pp. 4 and 51) argues that power is an end-in-itself whereas 'the very substance of violent action is ruled by the means-end category'. Mark Haugaard (2015, p. 150) shares this opinion. In the case of violence, the powerholder perceives power as a terminal value. Violence can be converted in any other valuable resource (money, academic credentials etc.),

an extreme asymmetry in the distribution of rights and obligations between the powerholder and the subordinate, and the absence of feedback loops in their relations (Oleinik, 2011a, chapter 3). All these characteristics help operationalise connections between Russian power and violence.

Russian power, similar to the other configurations of power relationships, involves path-dependence. The Russian 'path' significantly diverges from the path associated with the transformation of the State into a commonwealth (Hedlund, 2005; Pipes, 1999). The gulf between these paths is reportedly deepening, even though no specific quantitative assessments have been made at different points in time.

Congruence theory offers a possible theoretical explanation for the stability of Russian power over time. This theory predicts that in a stable system, 'general orientations toward governance and direction, superordination and subordination' at the micro- (within a family, a micro-group), meso- (within an organisation) and the macro (in politics) levels tend to be congruent (Eckstein, 1998a). Harry Eckstein (1998b, p. 360) calls these general orientations 'authority culture'. An authority culture with elements of violence at all the levels of social organisation makes violence self-sustainable. Conversely, an authority culture with elements of commonwealth permeating various institutions and organisations makes power self-sustainable. This potentially appealing assumption finds theoretical support in the studies of the authoritarian personality. They demonstrated 'close correspondence in the type of approach and outlook a subject is likely to have in a great variety of areas, ranging from the most intimate features of family and sex through relationships to other people in general, to religion and to social and political philosophy' (Adorno, Frenkel-Brunswik, Levinson & Sanford, 1950, p. 971). The empirical evidence produced in support of these claims is either scarce, as in the case of congruence theory, especially in the post-Soviet context (Reisinger, 1998), or is

whereas the opposite conversion is not always possible. As a result, the powerholder wants to stay in power for as long as possible, which does not make much sense if means-end considerations prevailed.

subject to methodological criticism, as in the case of the work on the authoritarian personality (see Samelson, 1993 for an overview). This calls for empirical studies of power and violence, especially in comparative perspective.

Cross-cultural empirical studies of power relationships remain rare, however. For example, the HRAF does not list 'power' as a separate subject, with 'judicial authority' being the closest match. The concept of power distance proves to be an exception. Comparative empirical studies that involve measuring power distance abound (Beugelsdijk, Maseland & Van Hoorn, 2015; House, Javidan, Hanges & Dorfman, 2002; Maleki & de Jong, 2014; Rinne, Steel & Fairweather, 2012). The concept of power distance was first proposed in the framework of a comparative study of managerial cultures carried out by Geert Hosftede (1980, p. 99) in the late 1970s. Power distance is understood as 'the extent to which the less powerful members of institutions and organizations within a country expects and accept that power is distributed unequally' (Hofstede, 1991, p. 28). This concept allows operationalising a dimension of authority cultures and measuring it quantitatively on the scale from 1 (low power distance) to 135 (high). 'High Power Distance cultures perceive inequality as the basis for societal order... In low Power Distance cultures, hierarchical positions are merely functional, so that higher and lower ranked people remain essentially equals' (Beugelsdijk et al., 2015, p. 230).

The power distance index (PDI) has several versions, from the original one (Hofstede, 1980, pp. 403–410) up to the most recent (Hofstede & Minkov, 2013). The 1980 instrument captures the difference between power and violence particularly well. First, it includes three questions. Two of them help measure the degree of inequality in the distribution of rights between the powerholder and the subordinate (questions on the actual and the desired boss). The third component of the PDI deals with feed-back loops in their relations or the lack thereof (the question on whether the subordinates are afraid to express their disagreements). Second, only the 1980 instrument was designed with the specific purpose of measuring power distance in mind. The subsequent versions include indirect measures identified on the basis of ecological correlations using the World Values Survey data. The indirect measures may simply refer to aspects of power relations other than those encapsulated by the concept of power distance.[106] Third, more abstractly formulated questions about value orientations from the latest versions of the PDI have weaker connections with the respondent's everyday experience. 'Asking someone to describe the actual situation may in fact be a more effective way for detecting her or his implicit ideology than asking for agreement with ideological statements' (Hofstede, 2006, p. 886).

The calculations of the PDI involve the distinction between the social or professional group as a unit of analysis and the individual as a unit of observation. In other words, the PDI is suitable for studying various groups at the national and sub-national levels, but not individual attitudes and orientations (Hofstede & McCrae, 2004).[107] The measurement of the perception of power at the individual level requires developing other instruments (Cavazotte, Hartman & Bahiense, 2014; Conduit, 2001; Erez & Early, 1987; Fine, 2013; Lam, Schaubroeck & Aryee, 2002).[108] The F-scale and related instruments, including Altemeyer's RWA scale, aim to study the authoritarian personality and, for this reason, their design explicitly focuses on the individual as a unit of analysis (Adorno et al., 1950, pp. 226–227). The RWA scale was translated into Russian (McFarland, Ageyev & Abalkina, 1993). Data gathered with its help allowed Yuri

106 A 2017 survey using an on-line panel in Russia (the next section provides more details about parameters of this survey) included both versions of the instrument. The calculation of values of the PDI for various social and professional groups produced rather divergent results. For instance, high power distance Russian macro-regions according to the 1980 version turned out to be among the group of low power distance macro-regions if the 2013 instrument is used. No explanation for such discrepancies was offered by the authors of the 2013 instrument.

107 Hofstede nevertheless claimed that his culture dimensions, power distance being one of them, can be validated by the data using the individual as the unit of analysis, for instance, the Rokeach Value Survey (Hofstede & Bond, 1984).

108 The 2017 survey included an instrument for measuring power distance at the individual level (Erez & Early, 1987). However, the value of Cronbach's Alpha did not exceed 0.5, which prevented further uses of this instrument in the analysis. This outcome is consistent with results reported in Conduit (2001).

Levada (1993, p. 40) and his associates to describe what they called 'hierarchical egalitarianism'—the tendency of the Soviet people to accept a highly unequal distribution of rights and obligations between the powerholder and the subordinate, so long as these inequalities derive from established hierarchies.

Available cross-cultural data on power distance lend support to the assumption of path-dependence. The relative positions of and differences between countries remain remarkably stable even if the mean PDI scores somewhat decrease (Beugelsdijk et al., 2015, p. 237). This means that, overall, societies may become less tolerant to inequalities in the distribution of power, as suggested by the decreasing mean PDI scores, and this trend affects most countries included in the World Values Survey sample, as indicated by the stability of the countries' relative positions. The previously stated caveat must be kept in mind nevertheless: the latest versions of the PDI may not capture the distinction between power and violence as well as the 1980 version did. Unfortunately, no comprehensive comparative data have been produced using the 1980 instrument since the late 1970s.

III. Ukraine as a case in point

Studies focusing on one or two countries may appear, at first sight, to be of limited interest for scholars of power and violence or specialists in cross-cultural studies. In order to identify universal and country-specific features of a phenomenon, one needs to make cross-cultural comparisons using bigger samples. There is neither a valid (i.e. using the 1980 instrument) and recent estimate of power distance across a large number of countries, nor a quantitative estimate of the other dimensions of authority cultures.

There are several reasons to believe that an in-depth study of Ukraine and its comparison with neighbouring Russia will provide insights of relevance not only for specialists in the area studies but also for scholars of power, violence and authority cultures. Both countries have authority cultures placing great emphasis on violence. Russian power is even seen by some as the embodiment of violence. Ukrainians made several attempts to move from a culture of violence to a culture of power; most recently—during the 2013-2014 mass protests. Thus, the comparison of the perception of power in general, and values of the PDI in these countries in particular, sheds light on particularities of violence as opposed to power and simultaneously helps assess limits of the path-dependence on a specific model of power relationships. The research question addressed in this chapter can be narrowed down accordingly: *what are opportunities for and obstacles to the path change that involves moving from violence to power in the post-Maidan Ukraine*?

In Ukraine, the culture of violence has a long-standing tradition. On one hand, Ukraine literally means a borderland, a place 'on the edge' (Chapter 1). Ukraine lies between Europe and Asia, between the lands populated by settlers and the lands populated by nomads (until the 16th-17th centuries). Areas 'on the edge' remain outside of the state's control longer than more central regions. Today's Southern Italy, namely, Sicily, serves as an illustration. In the 17–18th centuries Sicily was a part of Spain, but a very peripheral part. After being incorporated into Italy, Sicily remained 'on the edge', which also implies the absence of a credible central authority (Gambetta, 1993, p. 78). The state was associated with violence in the eyes of Sicilians. The Mafia that emerged as a substitute for the absentee state contributed to the strengthening of this association instead of breaking it. Taras Kuzio (2012, p. 430) draws an explicit parallel between the two cases: 'Ukraine resembles a "Post-Soviet Italy" where citizens are alienated from, and indifferent to, the state, which provides them with few services, a state that is widely disrespected and to which you should try your best not to deal with and to pay few taxes'.

On the other hand, after the incorporation of Ukraine into the Russian empire (Left-Bank Ukraine[109] was incorporated in the 17th century, Right-Bank Ukraine in its entirety—between WWI and WWII), the authority culture in Ukraine has been significantly in-

109 Left-Bank Ukraine is a name for a part of today's Ukraine on the left (east) bank of the Dnieper River, Right-Bank Ukraine is correspondingly located on the right (west) bank.

fluenced by Russian power. The subjection to Russian power became a second factor that underlies the culture of violence in Ukraine. During some periods, violence generated by Russian power took extreme forms transforming into terror. Terror is… 'the form of government that comes into being when violence, having destroyed all power, does not abdicate but, on the contrary, remains in full control' (Arendt, 1969, p. 55). The rule of Stalin had multiple features of terror in general, and in the Ukrainian context in particular. Specifically, the 1932–1932 famine occurred to a significant extent 'by design'. In the words of Orest Subtelny (2009, p. 416; see also subsection II.8 of Chapter 1), 'Stalin… consciously allowed the famine to wipe out resistance in a particularly troublesome region of his empire'. In 1937 Stalin also ordered to liquidate the entire leadership of the Ukrainian Soviet government and the Communist Party of Ukraine (Ibid., p. 420).

In Ukraine, Russian power has never managed to completely prevail. The authority culture of this country contains several rather heterogeneous elements, Russian power being one of them. The other important element is the rejection of violence. Ukrainians at times go so far as to reject any power relationships, violent and non-violent altogether. Anarchism and anti-statism have always been present in Ukraine (Gaidai, 2007a; Gaidai, 2007b; Kuzio, 1998, p. 7). In some moments they even prevailed, as in the 1920s, the time of Nestor Makhno's libertarian experiment in Huliaipole (today's region of Zaporizhia; see subsection II.2 of Chapter 1). On more than just one occasion, Ukrainians reacted to the violence that took particularly manifest forms by rejecting it. Bohdan Harasymiw (2002, pp. 7–8) rightly observes that Ukrainians started to endorse the idea of independence from the Soviet Union only after the August 1991 coup.

The oscillation between violence and its rejection in the name of anti-statism continued during the post-Soviet period in Ukraine's history. Even if now Ukrainians had their own state, the national government would continue to reproduce previous authority patterns. As the theory of path-dependence predicts, the path cannot be changed overnight. In Ukraine, it has not radically changed over a period of more than 20 years. The first post-Soviet governments were staffed by the Soviet-era cadres (Shulga & Boyko, 1999). However, even when a generation change in the power elite happened, the new generation still embodied violence, not power. The powerholders in now independent Ukraine perceived power as a terminal value, i.e. as an end-in-itself (Nastych, 2003, pp. 318–319). Accordingly, they attempted to stay in the office as long as possible. Former President Yanukovych was among the group of people who stayed in power in the 2000s longer than the others (Kostiuchenko, 2012). The other distinctive feature of Russian power, an extremely asymmetric distribution of power, has also continued to determine the political landscape in post-Soviet Ukraine. Similar to post-Soviet Russia, power is heavily concentrated in the executive branch of government and, more specifically, in the institution of Ukraine's strong presidency. Paul D'Anieri (2015, p. 12) argues in this regard that 'the fundamental imbalance in raw political power has been the underlying source of the more immediate problems in Ukrainian government, such as weak parties, selective law enforcement, and a fragmented parliament'. It comes as no surprise then, that democracy, one of the forms of power, is dissociated in Ukrainians' minds from the idea of the state. Since the 1990s, in contrast to Poland, 'in Ukraine people supporting democracy were less likely to support incumbent authorities' (Johnson, 2005, p. 79).

The 2013–2014 Maidan was, first and foremost, a protest against violence. The ideas of the integration with the European Union payed only a secondary role, especially as the protests unfolded (Chapters 3 and 4). The use of violence by the police against the protesters was a trigger that changed the overall dynamics of the protest and significantly extended its scope. The 2013–2014 Maidan also showed inherent limitations of the Ukrainian way of rejecting violence. Ukrainians manage to reject violence from time to time—without, however, being able to find a viable alternative, i.e. to move toward concerted power. The data presented in the next section suggest that a positive program for changing the nature of power relationships is still absent.

This study involves a two-case comparison; the authority culture in Ukraine is compared with that in Russia. This research design is not exceptional in cross-cultural studies (see, for instance, Cavazotte et al., 2014 for a Brazil-US comparison). Because of its closeness to the ideal type of violence, the Russian case is paradigmatic for the negative view of power (Flyvbjerg, 2006). In its turn, the Ukrainian authority culture has features of a critical case (subsection II.3 of the book's general Introduction). If the transition from violence to power appears possible in Ukraine, then it will also be possible in the other post-Soviet countries and elsewhere. Conversely, if the path cannot be changed in Ukraine, then chances for a successful change in the other post-Soviet countries are also dim.

There were several previous attempts to conduct small-scale comparative studies of power relationships in Ukraine (Brice & Jones, 2008; Brice & Richardson, 2009; Ivanickova, Mihalcova & Pruzinsky, 2015; Pilipenko, 2013). All of them, however, involved relatively small purposeful samples, which limits the external validity of the reported results. Outcomes of three mass surveys inform the present study. Two internet surveys using one of the largest on-line panels in Russia were conducted in July 2016 (N=2,939) and in January 2017 (N=11,096). In 2015, Russia had 73.4 Internet users per 100 people (World Bank, 2017). The first survey included an open-ended question on associations with the word 'power' (*vlast'* in Russian). The respondents could indicate as many alternatives as they wished. To enhance the representativeness, its results were weighted by age and gender using the Federal State Statistics Service (FSSS) of the Russian Federation data. The second survey included a battery of questions from the Power Distance Indexes, versions 1980 and 2013, as well as a few other related questions and controls. For the sake of consistency with the publicly available PDI data, only a subsample of respondents in the active labour force (N=7,825) was used for the purpose of calculating the PDI in the two versions. To enhance the external validity, results of the second survey were also weighted by sex and age of the active labour force in Russia using the FSSS data.

In Ukraine, a face-to-face survey using a random nationwide[110] sample (N=2,040) was conducted by the Kyiv International Institute of Sociology in September 2016. The questionnaire included questions necessary for calculating the PDI (the 1980 version), a semi-closed ended, multiple choice question on associations with the word 'power' (*vlada* in Ukrainian) and a series of related questions and controls. The questionnaire had two versions, Russian and Ukrainian. The list of alternatives for the semi-closed ended question contained most frequent associations with power found in the Russian on-line survey. The frequencies of the associations were calculated using the entire sample. As in the Russian case, only responses of those in the active labour force (N=821) were used in the calculation of the PDI values at the national and group levels. Since the ratio of Internet users is lower in Ukraine (49.3 in 2015) than in Russia, an on-line survey would have produced less valid and reliable results in this country. In any case, the survey design in Ukraine ensures higher external validity and reliability of its outcomes than the survey design in Russia, which constitutes one of the limitations of this study.

IV. Path-dependence and changes in the perception of power

In both Russian and Ukrainian cultures, power has predominantly negative connotations (Figure 6.1)[111]. Force is by far the most frequent association with power spontaneously mentioned by the respondents in Russia (17.4% of all counted associations), which provides some support for the assumption that Russian power lies close to violence. In Ukraine, money is the most frequent association with power (8.3%

110 The sample does not cover some districts in the regions of Donetsk and Luhansk in the East that Ukraine's government did not control at that time. The data for Crimea, the Ukrainian territory annexed by Russia in March 2014, was collected via the on-line survey described previously.

111 Taking into consideration the large total number of associations indicated by the respondents, 12,684 in Ukraine and 3,019 in Russia, standard errors of the population proportions tend to be small. It means that even small differences reported in Figure 6.1 are statistically significant, with no exception.

of all associations) closely followed by corruption (7.6%). In the other study of associations with power in Ukraine (Pilipenko, 2013, p. 123) money and corruption also topped their list. The other frequent associations with power are also negative in the two cases. For instance, the popularity of 'opportunities' could likely be explained by opportunities that positions in power provide to their holders. It is not excluded either that 'respect' in this context means something other than the powerholder's respectful attitude to the subordinate. A Google search using a combination of two keywords, 'respect' and 'power' in the Russian segment of the internet produced 'respect to power' as the closest match.[112]

Figure 6.1 'Associations with the word "power", % of all associations'

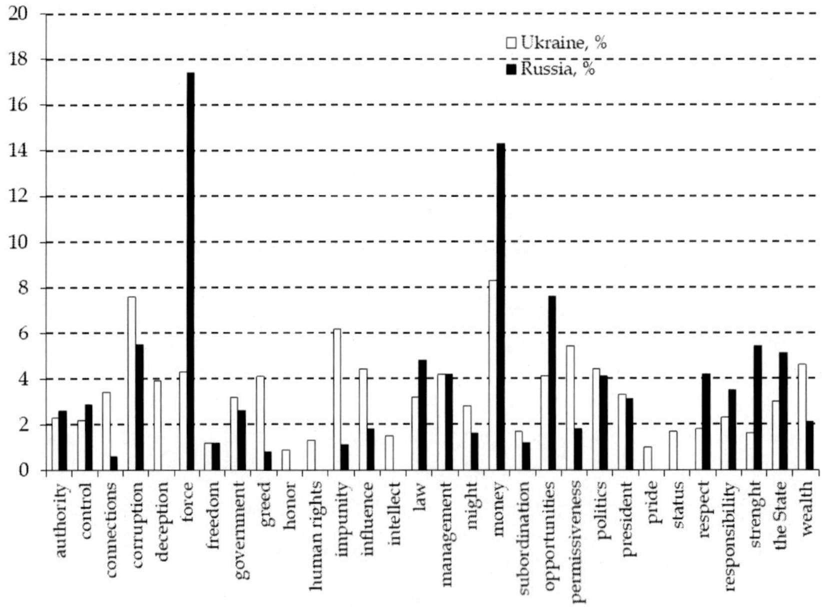

Source: responses to an open-ended question in Russia (N=2,939) and to a semi-closed ended multiple choice question in Ukraine (N=2,040).

112 The search was conducted on February 4, 2017 using Google.ru as a search engine and a combination of keywords *vlast'* and *uvazhenie*. 5 out of 10 top matches included 'respect to power'.

Positive associations are far less prevalent. For instance, mentions of the law represent 4.8% of all associations in Russia and 3.2% in Ukraine. References to authority as legitimate power (the imposition of will on legitimate grounds) represent 2.6% associations in Russia and 2.3% in Ukraine. Freedom is mentioned in 1.2% of associations in both cases. Only a tiny minority of Russians and Ukrainians believe that power may potentially extend the scope of the possible. These findings are in line with the observation that 'in Russian [...] "power" is imagined as something that is "over" us, *that limits our freedom, creates obstacles*' (Ledyaev, 1997, p. 95; emphasis added).

Figure 6.2 shows how often particular associations with power co-occur in responses in Ukraine. Negative associations with power—deception, greed, permissiveness, impunity and corruption—form a loose cluster. Money, the most frequent association with power in Ukraine, is relatively rarely mentioned together with the other associations and for this reason stands alone. However infrequent, positive associations of power with authority, respect, law and responsibility form a noteworthy cluster. This cluster further includes the state. It means that in the mind of a relative small group of respondents, power has positive associations and is connected to the state as a potential 'conductor' of 'actions in concert'. The discussion below contains some clues as to who might be a part of this group.

Figure 6.2 'Two-dimensional map of the co-occurrence of associations with power in Ukraine'

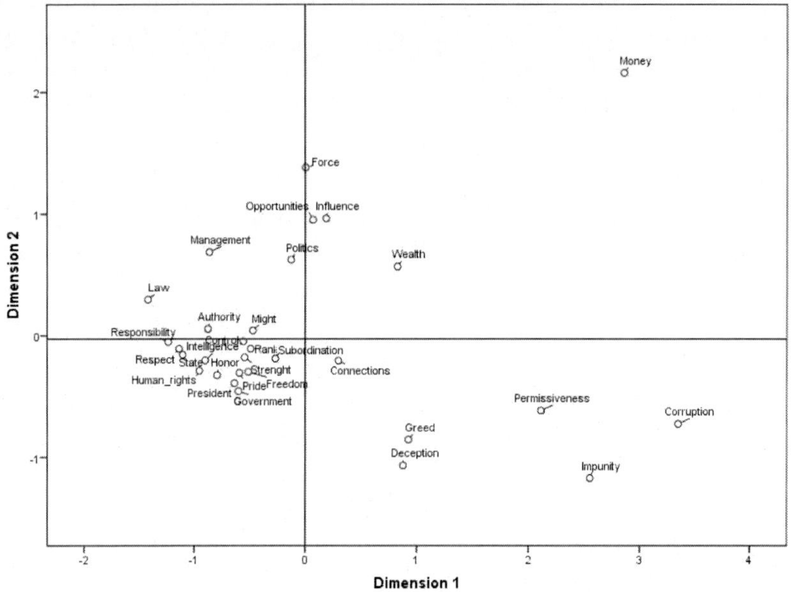

Source: responses to a semi-closed ended multiple choice question (N=2,040). This figure was produced using the multidimensional scaling (ALSCAL) module of SPSS with Euclidian distances as a proximity measure and tied observations untied.

Legend: Stress = 0.12549, pseudo R^2 = 0.95798.

The other indication of the closeness of the authority cultures in both countries to violence can be found in high PDI values. The PDI value is 110.7 in Russia and 100.9 in Ukraine. Even if the PDI value in Ukraine is significantly (9%) lower than in Russia, both countries would probably be included in a group of authority cultures, allowing for the most unequal distribution of power in the world, as Hofstede's (1980, p. 79) original data suggest. The same supposedly applies to the other post-Soviet countries too, since their authority cultures were also heavily influenced by Russian power. Namely, the PDI calculated for a group of state servants in Kazakhstan falls in this range too (106.1; Oleinik, Yermekov & Kuatbekov, 2015).

A closer look, however, reveals that, along with similar patterns, notable distinctions also characterise the authority cultures in Russia and Ukraine. Hofstede (1980, pp. 80–81) originally found that PDI values tend to be higher for women than for men. Women in Russia indeed seem to accept a more unequal distribution of power than men (115.4 against 106), whereas in Ukraine the differences between the genders appear to be insignificant (100.9 against 101). The study of the impact of education on power distance allows identifying the other particularity of the authority culture in Ukraine (Figure 6.3). The group of people with complete higher education (with a university degree) has the second lowest value of the PDI in this country. In Russia, education does not necessarily mean a lower tolerance for inequality in the distribution of power. The impact of income shows similar patterns. In Russia, members of middle- and high-income groups actually accept a more unequal distribution of power (the PDI values are 116.9 among those who can buy anything they want except real estate and 120.1 among those who can afford buying even real estate). In Ukraine, members of the middle-income group (they can buy some expensive items like home appliances but not a car) have the lowest PDI value. It should be kept in mind that GDP per capita is four times plus higher in Russia than in Ukraine (9,092.6 USD in 2015 against 2,115 USD; World Bank, 2017). Thus, the relative share of high-middle and high income groups in the total population in Russia far exceeds that in Ukraine.

Figure 6.3 'PDI values in various social groups, Ukraine and Russia'

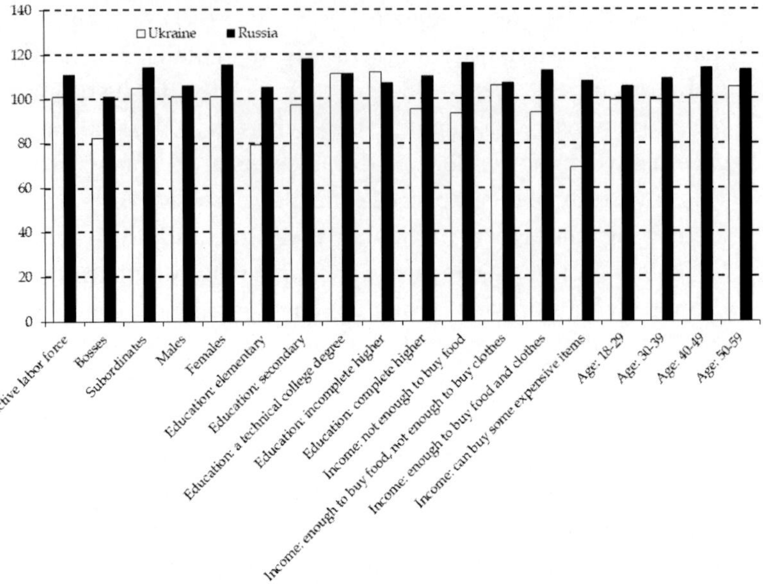

Source: the survey data (N=821 in Ukraine and N=7,825 in Russia) produced using the 1980 instrument for measuring the PDI.

Values of the PDI practically do not vary across age groups in Ukraine (except for the group of people in their 50s). By contrast, Russians in the most active age group (40–49 y.o.) are also the most tolerant of inequality in the distribution of power. As a result, this particular age group also shows the greatest difference between the two countries, 101 in Ukraine against 113.7 in Russia, in spite of the fact that its members started adult life in similar circumstances, i.e. after the fall of the Soviet Union. These findings suggest that the paths of Russian and Ukrainian authority cultures may have started to diverge only recently, within the past 20 years.

A difference that would likely be the most relevant to the discussion of a possible path change lies elsewhere. Bosses, i.e. respondents who have at least one subordinate, are far less prepared to accept an unequal distribution of power in Ukraine (82.5) than in Russia (101). The group of bosses has a lower PDI value in both countries, nevertheless. Bosses identified in the surveys represent sub-elites. Wright Charles Mills (1957, pp. 3–4) defines the power elite as a group 'of men whose positions enable them to transcend the ordinary environments of ordinary men and women; they are in positions to make decisions having major consequences'. Accordingly, 'the position of sub-elites may be that of representing elites before the rank and file, or vice versa' (Etzioni-Halevy, 1993, p. 96). If the perception of power among members of sub-elites shows a promise of moving from violence to power, then the prospects of a path change are not so dim, after all. Such reasoning calls for a more detailed look into the authority subculture of Ukrainian bosses.

The ratio of the number of bosses to that of subordinates in Ukraine and Russia (0.2 and 0.28 correspondingly) and the mean number of subordinates per one boss (15.5 and 13) are comparable. Despite these structural similarities, Ukrainian bosses went further from violence to power than their Russian counterparts.

A binary logistic regression analysis, method 'Forward: conditional' (with the probability of F to enter a new variable set at $\leq$ 0.05 and the probability of F to remove a variable—at $\leq$ 0.1.), helps identify variables that have an impact on odds (chances) of having at least one subordinate for a member of the active labour force in Ukraine. The long list of the predictor variables included various associations with power (separate dummies for those who indicate a specific association), questions on the actual and desired type of boss from the PDI instrument, a question on the desired type of a political leader (separate dummies for those who select a specific type of boss and political leader), as well as socio-economic and political indicators available in the dataset, namely, the respondent's age (separate dummies for members of six age groups), gender (dummy for females), level of education (separate dummies for secondary, for vocational, for incomplete higher, for complete higher education and for holders of a technical college degree), occupation (separate dummies for workers, for office workers, for self-employed individuals and for business owners), self-reported wealth (separate dummies for the upper-middle, middle/lower-middle and low income groups), place of residence (separate dummies for the cities of various size), region (separate dummies for the macro-regions), language (dummies for Ukrainian and *surzhik*, a mixture of Russian and Ukrainian), voting intentions (separate dummies for those who intend to vote for particular parties and presidential candidates in the next parliamentary and presidential elections), geopolitical (separate dummies for supporters of Ukraine's association with the EU, the Customs Union and for those who want to maintain its independent status) and political (dummy for those who agree with specific statements regarding the annexation of Crimea by Russia, the military aggression in the regions of Donetsk and Luhansk etc.) attitudes.

Table 6.1 contains the results of the binary static regression. Reported changes in the odds, Exp(B), are relevant to the comparison of the odds of the membership in sub-elites across various groups or conditions (e.g., males versus females). The analysis was set up so that the coefficients in the binary logistic regression can be interpreted as information about the comparative odds of having subordinates for people who do *not* have a particular characteristic (e.g., complete higher education), compared to people who *do* have it. This means that when Exp(B) exceeds 1.00, people with this characteristic are *less* likely to have subordinates. If the odds are less than 1.00, those who have this characteristic are *more* likely to have subordinates.

Table 6.1 'Results of a binary statistic regression to predict the odds of having subordinates in Ukraine'

	B	S.E.	Wald	Exp(B)
Voter of UKROP	-2.399	0.674	12.681***	0.091
Will not take part in the next parliamentary elections	-0.800	0.396	4.083*	0.449
Voter of Dmytro Yarosh	-1.582	0.672	5.543*	0.205
Voter against all at the next presidential elections	-1.678	0.400	17.616***	0.187
Will not take part in the next presidential elections	1.481	0.499	8.796**	4.397
Voter for the association with the Customs Union	-1.482	0.344	18.579***	0.227
Voter for NATO	-1.248	0.312	15.947***	0.287
Influence is associated with power	0.730	0.305	5.723*	2.076
Might (*mogutnist'*) is associated with power	0.912	0.372	6.017*	2.488
Freedom is associated with power	-1.039	0.522	3.959*	0.354
Authority is associated with power	-1.481	0.404	13.409***	0.227

Intelligence is associated with power	2.147	0.607	12.516***	8.563
Pride is associated with power	-1.186	0.537	4.869*	0.306
Actual boss usually consults with the subordinates before reaching a decision. He/she then expects all to work loyally to implement it, whether or not it is in accordance with the advice they gave	-1.797	0.377	22.679***	0.166
Desired boss is of the same type as above [the 3rd type in Hofstede's classification]	1.349	0.376	12.875***	3.854
Member of parents' associations at schools, kindergartens	-1.934	0.662	8.545**	0.145
Did not participate in any volunteer initiatives	0.613	0.288	4.522*	1.845
Education: complete secondary	-1.468	0.466	9.904**	0.230
Education: complete higher	-0.878	0.311	7.946**	0.416
Lives in a village	1.285	0.402	10.238**	3.615
Age: 30–39	-1.153	0.314	13.472***	0.316
Age: 40–49	-0.730	0.344	4.498*	0.482
Occupation: peasant	1.061	0.385	7.603**	2.889
Occupation: farmer, entrepreneur	-2.024	0.476	18.044***	0.132
Wealth: Not enough even for buying food	2.841	0.962	8.720**	17.130
Wealth: Can afford some expensive items	-1.458	0.464	9.882**	0.233
Constant	8.627	2.090	17.039***	5582.927
Nagelkerke's R^2	0.534			

Legend: results significant at a 0.05 level are marked by *, at a 0.01 level—by **, and at a 0.001 level—by ***. Reference categories are: Do not know/Difficult to say (for the voting intentions, the geopolitical orientation and the involvement into volunteerism), elementary education (for Education), 60 plus y.o. (for Age), 'No answer' (for Wealth), Other (for Occupation), Town (for the place of residence), the Eastern macro-region (for Region), Boss who usually makes his/her decisions promptly and communicates them to his/her subordinates clearly and firmly, expects them to carry out the decisions without raising difficulties (the 1st type of boss in Hofstede's classification; for Actual and Desired type of boss).

Members of sub-elites in Ukraine are relatively overrepresented in the most productive age group (30–49 years). Gender does not have a significant impact on one's chances to become a boss. Members of sub-elites either support political forces that make the building of Ukrainian nation-state their priority (Dmytro Yarosh as a potential presidential candidate, the political party 'UKROP'—the union of Ukraine's patriots) or have not yet found a political force to be associated with. Their intention to support Ukraine's membership in NATO at first sight contradicts their willingness to see Ukraine as a member of the Customs' Union operating under auspices of Russia. However, the latter likely has a pragmatic character in the conditions of the deep current economic crisis (Chapter 9)[113] since members of sub-elites do not see Ukraine's membership in the Custom's Union as a long-term priority, as suggested by an insignificant impact of the relevant control variable. Compared with subordinates, members of sub-elites more often have positive associations with power, such as freedom and authority. They prefer to work under the leadership of unquestionably non-authoritarian bosses (a manager of the 3rd type in Hofstede's classification).

Members of sub-elites have a track record of participating in volunteer initiatives. The existence of a link between volunteerism, including its most recent forms, i.e. volunteer initiatives related to the defense against Russia's military aggression and the help to forced internal migrants (Chapter 10), is further confirmed by the data on the average number of associational memberships. On average, subordinates participate in 0.41 associations included in the list of 18 alternatives. The corresponding figure for bosses is 1.14 (results of a t-test show that the difference between the means is statistically significant at $p<0.001$, $t=-5.175$, $df=170.340$, equal variances not assumed). Bosses are more actively involved in volunteer initiatives related to the defense against Russia's military aggression and the help to forced internal migrants. They, on average, participate in 0.41 volunteer initiatives, whereas subordinates—only in 0.15 (results of a t-test show that the difference between the means is statistically significant at $p<0.001$, $t=-4.573$, $df=172.227$, equal variances not assumed). The mean amount of bosses' contributions to volunteer initiatives during the past 12 months was 2,119.8 UAH (83.63 USD[114]), the corresponding figure for subordinates was 226 UAH (8.92 USD; results of a t-test show that the difference between the means is statistically significant at $p<0.001$, $t=-3.718$, $df=126.113$,

113 In 2014, the country's GDP contracted by 6.6% to the previous year, in 2015—by 9.8%, as per data of the State Statistics Service of Ukraine available at http://www.ukrstat.gov.ua/.

114 Using the mean exchange rate for 2016 as of October 31, 2016 (25.3482 UAH per 1 USD); data from http://www.exchangerates.org.uk/USD-UAH-exchange-rate-history.html, accessed October 31, 2016.

equal variances not assumed). Bosses also spent more time on volunteer initiatives than subordinates (15.6h per month against 1.9h; this difference between the means, however, does not reach the level of statistical significance if a conservative separate variance t-test is used). In addition to being valuable in and of itself, the experience of volunteerism is associated with a lower tolerance of inequality in the distribution of power. The PDI mean for a group of respondents who at least once worked as a volunteer during the past 12 months (N=103) is 86.6, whereas the PDI for a group of respondents without such experience (N=719) is 102.8.

This sociological portrait shows that members of Ukraine's sub-elites have good chances to become a driving force in the movement from violence to power. In order to succeed, however, Ukraine's sub-elites need to pay attention to particularities of national managerial culture. The relatively high PDI value in Ukraine means that neither managerial practices imported from Russia nor those borrowed from the Western countries may work effectively in this country. Russian managerial practices involve a remarkably higher level of tolerance to inequality in the distribution of power. In a sense, the events of 2013–2014 were a reaction to attempts to introduce Russian managerial practices at all levels of public and corporate management in Ukraine. Promoters of these practices (they are associated with former President Yanukovych and the group of 'Donetskie' at large named so after the region of Donetsk) positioned themselves as 'effective managers' attaching a very particular meaning to this expression: someone being able to carry out his (in these circumstances, gender matters) will by all available means, including violent. Western managerial practices, on the other hand, require a much higher level of intolerance to inequality in the distribution of power than currently observed in Ukraine. For instance, the PDI values for the UK, Germany, the Netherlands and Canada fall within the range from 35 to 40 (Hofstede, 1980, p. 79).

The collected data offer some support for the assumption of congruence theory on the existence of links between the perceptions of power at the various levels of the social organisation. Specifically, the type of a political leader under whose leadership different groups of respondents would like to live is associated with the PDI value for these particular groups. When choosing between six political leaders known either for their authoritarian or libertarian orientations, the group of Stalin's supporters expectedly had the highest PDI value (120.2), whereas the group of Makhno's supporters – the lowest (43.45). The group whose members would prefer to have someone like Augusto Pinochet, the other dictator, as a political leader had the PDI value of 115.2. The group of supporters of Václav Havel, the last president of Czechoslovakia and the first president of the Czech Republic known for his democratic credentials, as a role model for a political leader had the PDI value of 90.7 and so forth.

Conclusions

The analysis offered in this chapter contributes to the theory of path dependence, providing additional evidence that changes in authority cultures have an incremental character, if they happen at all. Despite revolutions, however radical they may look at first sight, changes in the perception of power never happen overnight. Power as a zero-sum game involves the existence of one winner and leads for this reason to the spread of violence. The dissatisfaction of the losing parties as a result of this outcome does not suffice for changing the rules of the game and for moving from violence to power as human ability to act in concert. The 2013–2014 mass protests in Ukraine are a case in point. These protests challenged the prevalent association of power with violence in this country. Two years after the end of the latest Maidan, however, power continues to be associated with violence in Ukrainians' minds and the PDI value in this country also remains very high.

Are Ukrainians doomed to continue the path of violence as the ultimate manifestation of power relationships? This study shows that some grounds for hope indeed exist in Ukraine. The national sub-elites may become the driving force for the movement from violence to power in Ukraine. They have the necessary potential: members of sub-elites are socially active, they have more positive associations with power than Ukrainians in general, and they may support efforts to re-build (or, rather, to build from scratch) the

Ukrainian nation-state. The link between sub-elites and volunteerism seems particularly promising in this respect (see also Chapter 10 and the general Conclusion to this book).

Chances to succeed in the movement from violence to power will depend on the capacity of sub-elites and members of a new power elite recruited from their ranks to solve the following dilemma. On one hand, the ultimate goal of reforming the system of governance in Ukraine is to associate this country's nation-state with power, not violence. On the other hand, the prevailing authority culture still contains several elements of violence, including the high PDI value. The model of liberal authoritarianism may potentially offer a solution. In the case of liberal authoritarianism, a high level of inequality in the distribution of power becomes a means to push through radical changes instead of being an end-in-itself. In Ukraine's past, including most recently, the situation has been the opposite: 'absolute power is a goal in itself rather than a means to push through radical changes, one reason being Ukraine's leaders across the political spectrum lack vision and implementable programs' (Kuzio, 2012, p. 431). Will absolute power be used for the purpose of building a commonwealth in the place of Ukraine's State? As of today, this question remains wide-open. The analysis in this chapter suggests that a window of opportunity for moving in this direction exists. However, such a move is not inevitable and much will depend on the capacity of sub-elites to become conscious of the existence of this chance and to properly seize it. As suggested by a substantial number of undecided voters among members of sub-elites (see above), the demand for an actor able to articulate and implement the relevant political and managerial agenda is still unmet as of the time of writing this text.

Chapter 7
'Honour and human rights: A comparative study of Ukraine and Russia'

Introduction

The principal objective of this chapter is to highlight how meanings attributed to human dignity vary from one cultural context to the other. It can be assumed that the perception of human dignity tends to be culturally embedded.[115] This assumption further implies that culture-specific interpretations of human dignity have different degrees of universality and malleability. Some of these interpretations prevail in multiple cultural settings, whereas the others are unique to a particular culture. Some interpretations change and adapt to new circumstances more easily than others.

This chapter more specifically attempts to assess the validity of the above formulated assumptions in the case of Ukraine and Russia. The two countries have a common geographical location (Eastern Europe—they share a common land and water border) and history (before the 1991 declaration of national independence, Ukraine had been a part of the Russian and Soviet empires for more than three centuries, see Section I of Chapter 1). The countries have different official languages, Ukrainian and Russian,[116] although the latter is often used in everyday communications in some regions of Ukraine, namely the eastern and southern regions. Russia and Russian culture are relatively better researched and known in the West

---

115 The concept of cultural embeddedness is also actively used by economic sociology. Economic sociologists show, with its help, how a particular cultural environment shapes transactions on the market (Swedberg, 2003, p. 247).

116 A common misunderstanding even among specialists in Russian (formerly Soviet or Communist) studies is that the Ukrainian language is nothing but a Russian dialect. It should be recalled in this respect that 'the [Russian imperial] academic community recognised Ukrainian as a language in its own right' so early as in 1905 (Plokhy, 2015, p. 193).

because of the central place that they occupied in the Russian and Soviet empires. Ukraine is now attracting increased attention of scholars and policy-makers abroad (Section I of the book's general Introduction), especially after the two waves of large scale mass protests in 2004 (the so-called 'Orange Revolution') and 2013–2014 (the events known under the names of 'Revolution of Dignity' and EuroMaidan).

The high degree of proximity between the Russian and Ukrainian cultures makes these two countries good candidates for a critical case study (subsection II.3 of the Introduction). Critical cases permit logical deductions that if something is true in one case, then it is equally true in others. Under the present circumstances, if the assumption that meanings attributed to human dignity are culturally embedded is validated for the case of similar cultures, such as Russian and Ukrainian, then this assumption arguably applies to all other cases. The major changes initiated by the 2013–2014 mass protests, namely, the reorientation of Ukraine's foreign, economic and cultural policies from the East (Russia) to the West (the European Union) and the ongoing military confrontation between the two countries, also offer a rare opportunity for assessing the assumption of the malleability of culturally embedded perceptions of human dignity. Is an interpretation of human dignity specific to a particular culture susceptible to change, or is it path dependent? The concept of path dependence purportedly applies to cultural evolution.

Two research questions guide the following discussion. The first research question is *what meanings are attributed to the notion of human dignity in today's Ukraine and Russia*? Particular attention will be devoted to two possible correlates of human dignity: human rights and honour. The list of correlates is typically much longer (Oleinik, 2016a). It contains such concepts as autonomy, respect, and self-respect, among several others. The reason for focusing on the relative importance of human rights and honour in order to make sense of human dignity in today's Russia and Ukraine is twofold.

On one hand, human rights and honour refer to two models of social organisation: horizontal and hierarchical respectively. Human rights are closely associated with the idea of equality. Individuals are endowed with some fundamental natural rights 'by virtue of their humanity as opposed to their being conferred upon them by the State or the law' (Green, 2007, p. 152). One's position in social hierarchy has no bearing on the entitlement to human rights. On the other hand, honour is restricted to the selected few (Brennan & Lo, 2007, p. 46). The amount of honour depends on one's position in the social hierarchy. Since Russia is close to the ideal type of a society founded on power and hierarchy (Oleinik, 2011a, chapter 3), a study involving this country requires consideration of the two modes of social organisation: horizontal and hierarchical.

On the other hand, human rights and honour occupy an important place in the discourse on post-Soviet transformations. Human rights are a key element of 'a critique of prevailing local cultures' (Kabasakal Arat, 2006, p. 425), especially with respect to local cultures that appreciate power and hierarchy, as in Russia. Internal and external critics of the authoritarian tendencies observed in post-Soviet Russia commonly mention the issue of human rights. Honour is evoked in responses to these critiques by members of the Russian power elite.[117] In keeping with this logic, even aggressive acts undertaken by Russia, such as the annexation of Crimea in 2014 and the military intervention—both manifest and covert, in the Luhansk and Donetsk regions of Ukraine (also started in 2014), may eventually be presented as a 'natural' reaction to a failure to respect 'Russia's distinctiveness and internal sense of honor' (Tsygankov, 2012, p. 5).

The second research question deals with the persistence and change in the perception of human dignity by Russians and Ukrainians. *Does the relative importance of human rights and honour change over time in the Russian and Ukrainian cultures?* The second research

117 The Russian power elite's rejection of references to human rights may eventually go so far as to the closure of the UN Human Rights Office in this country (this happened in March 2016).

question requires a retrospective look at the issues under consideration. For instance, what meaning was attributed to human rights (or similar concepts) and honour in classic Russian and Ukrainian literatures? Both emerged in the 19th century.

This chapter is organised into three sections, not counting the introduction and conclusion. The first section offers an overview of scholarly publications on human rights and honour in the context of human dignity. It concludes by outlining some types of culture, depending on whether human rights or considerations of honour are given priority. The second section presents the sources of the data used in this study. Both primary (results of representative surveys in Russia and Ukraine) and secondary (the works of two 19th-century authors who laid the foundation for modern Russian and Ukrainian literature and the Internet) provide data for the discussion. The third section compares the current meanings attributed to human dignity in the two countries with those that prevailed in the past. Particular attention is paid to identifying the socio-economic predictors of one's preference for either human rights or honour as a correlate of human dignity. This analysis helps assess the potential of various socio-economic groups for eventually revolutionising the prevalent cultures.

I. Human rights and honour in the context of dignity

The extant literature includes a significant number of sources on human rights and honour. Attempts to place them in the context of discussions of human dignity are less common, however. Social scientists refer to honour in their works, but rarely as a potential correlate of human dignity.

I.1 Dignity perceived through the lens of human rights

The connection between human dignity and human rights is established in the 1948 Universal Declaration of Human Rights. 'All human beings are born free and equal in dignity and rights', reads

Article 1 of this document that constitutes a starting point in any discussion of human rights.[118] Human dignity and human rights are mentioned together in several other articles of this foundational document; for instance, when discussing the need to protect one's privacy (Article 12), the importance of the social security system (Article 22) and the protection against unemployment and discrimination in the workplace (Article 23).

The interpretation of human dignity in terms of human rights involves using the individual as a unique point of reference. Neither society nor the state is supposed to direct the individual as to how to use basic human rights, let alone limit their scope. 'Rights are under the control of the rightholder, who in large measure manages the use of the right and thereby the consequences of having that right' (Donnelly, 1982, p. 305). To be more precise, society is expected to provide individuals with the means needed to fully realise their rights (legal, such as the rule of law, and economic, such as the creation of conditions for full employment), but not to interfere with the free exercise of the basic human rights by these individuals (Drydyk, 2011, p. 43).

If human dignity is expressed through the language of rights, jurists and legal scholars dominate the relevant discourse. It comes as no surprise that legal scholars produced most publications on human rights indexed in the Web of Science Core Collection: 4,293 out of 23,171 (18.3%). Sociologists came a distant seventh with 1,078 publications (4.7%).[119] One possible explanation can be found in differences in the assumptions: except advocates of rational choice theory, few sociologists endorse an individualistic, rationalised take on human being.

Legal sociology and anthropology (Benda-Beckmann, 2002; Wilson, 1997) make attempts to go beyond the perception of the law exclusively through the lens of legal texts and institutions (courts of law, law enforcement mechanisms and so on). Legal sociologists

118 The United Nations (1948). The Universal Declaration of Human Rights. Retrieved from http://www.un.org/en/universal-declaration-human-rights/.

119 Search was carried out on March 7, 2016 using TOPIC:('human rights') as a search term.

and anthropologists produce several insights relevant to the inquiry into the eventual connections between human dignity and human rights in Russia and Ukraine. First, they argue that human rights present one path to the realisation of human dignity among several others. 'All societies have conceptions of human dignity, but the concept of human rights emerged… in response to the rise of modern states and modern markets' (Freeman, 2004, p. 382). Legal sociologists and anthropologists make a plea for defining law without a compulsory connection to the state, for being sensitive to the existence of plural laws—state, customary, and religious (Benda-Beckmann, 2002, p. 49; Benda-Beckmann & Benda-Beckmann, 2006, pp. 3–14). Customary or religious law does not involve operationalising human dignity through human rights. Sociological knowledge and know-how appears indispensable for studying correlates of human dignity other than human rights and for using them to protect human dignity in practice.

Second, the realisation of human dignity via the concept of human rights tends to be culturally embedded. This concept originated and initially prevailed in Western discourse on human dignity. 'The human rights doctrine is an offspring of four major Western intellectual movements—humanism, natural law, natural rights and liberalism' (Menachem, 2006, p. 626; see also Cobbah, 1987, p. 311; Donnelly, 1982, p. 303; Said, 1979, p. 77; Shultziner, 2007, p. 82). Some authors add Christianity to the list of Western sources of human rights (Lee, 2011).

The fact that various actors—both state and non-state, in a global context, now also acknowledge the importance of human rights does not undermine the assumption of their cultural embeddedness. On one hand, the spread of elements of individualism and rationalism in non-Western cultural contexts increases the chances for accepting human rights as a key correlate of human dignity. On the other hand, human rights can eventually be translated and adapted ('vernacularised') to the non-Western discourses on human dignity even without having modernisation-Western style, as a precondition.

One of the authors of this idea, Sally Merry (1997, p. 29; see also Merry, 2006, chapter 1), draws a parallel with various dialects of English—African American, Nigerian, Pakistani and so forth. Accent, local terms and expressions make the originally alien language more adapted to the local conditions and, hence, more useful for expressing particularities of social action in a particular place and time. In a similar manner, if people learn how to translate their local grievances into the non-local language of human rights, they both reach out to a larger audience—that of speakers of the non-local language—and start to perceive local practices in a different light. 'They thereby reframe, say, a man's "disciplining" of his wife as spousal "abuse"' (Benjamin, 2008, p. 470). This translation is neither automatic nor easy, however. It requires conscious efforts from cultural entrepreneurs and/or community members (see, for instance, a discussion in Chapter 10). It also necessitates the existence of favourable external conditions.

I.2 Dignity perceived through the lens of honour

Compared with human rights, the concept of honour has a longer history. Human rights entered into the discourse on human dignity after WWII, becoming particularly popular after the 1960s, together with a growing disillusionment with the 'really existing socialism' (Stevenson, 2014, p. 182). The importance of honour as an expression of human dignity was acknowledged as early as the time of Ancient Rome (Lewis, 2007, p. 93; Rilye, 2010, p. 118). Citizens who occupied high public offices, such as the various magistracies, were called *dignitates*. The understanding of human dignity in an elitist manner, as something that only the select few can claim, lies at the origin of references to honour in traditional societies (Brennan & Lo, 2007, p. 46). Seen from this perspective, honour simply cannot be inherent in all human beings, which marks a further departure from the concept of human rights. Honour symbolises distinction and one's aristocratic origin.

A key component of relationships based on honour refers to the need for external assessments of one's worth. In the case of human rights, the individual constitutes the unique point of reference, whereas considerations of honour involve references to other people and their opinion about the individual. 'The honourable person is one whose self-esteem and social standing is intimately dependent on the esteem or the envy he or she actually elicits in others' (Miller, 1993, p. 84 cited in Kamir, 2006, p. 197; see also Shultziner, 2007, p. 84).[120] The source of human rights lies inside the human being; the source of honour lies in one's social environment.

The assumption that considerations of honour played a central role in the past probably explains why, compared with the other social scientists, historians appear to be the keenest on studying honour. Of 16,225 texts devoted to issues of honour, 1,718 (11%) were produced by historians. Once again, sociologists lag far behind. They authored 290 texts (1.8%), standing at the 17th rank in the list of all contributors to this area of knowledge.[121]

It would be a mistake, however, to assert that 'honor is incompatible with the spirit of our age' (Bowman, 2002, p. 8). Considerations of honour continue to be present in today's societies. A group of social psychologists attempted to empirically differentiate traditional and modern perceptions of honour (Helkama, Verkasalo, Myyry, Silfver, Niit et al., 2012, pp. 282–283). For instance, a modern perception of honour may eventually be related to achieving or, rather, failing to achieve ('dishonour') certain goals that individuals or groups consider important. Cultural sociology could be instrumental in identifying and studying specific contexts in which a high value is still attached to honour.

Cultures valuing honour have been discovered in various parts of the world, both Western and non-Western. Scholars of Islam mention its sensitivity to the issues of honour. According to Islamic doctrine, the imperative of respecting the subjects' honour and reputation represents one of the limits placed on powerholders

---

120 A parallel can be drawn here with Georg Simmel's theory of value. According to him, value can be assessed only through its relation to another value. He calls this process 'reciprocal verification' (Simmel, 1978, p. 115).

121 Search was carried out on March 7, 2016 using TOPIC: (honour NOT 'in honour of') AND TOPIC: (honor NOT 'in honor of') as a search term. The search term was narrowed down to exclude publications prepared in honour of a particular scholar, particularly common in economic sciences. Was the search term not narrowed down, economists would have come first in this list.

by their faith (Waardenburg, 2002, p. 172). The limits of the power-holders' absolute discretion are not expressed in terms of human rights, however. They take the form of the rulers' obligations towards their subjects (Said, 1979, pp. 73, 77).

Several examples of cultures based on values of honour were found in societies undergoing the process of modernisation understood here as the growing separation of functional subsystems, including the market, politics, the government and so forth (see Boltanski & Thévenot, 1991; Walzer, 1983). Pierre Bourdieu describes Algeria of the early 1960s as a society attaching a great deal of importance on honour, individual and group. He emphasises the opposition between the necessary particularism of honour to the universalism of human rights: 'The ethos of honour is opposed, in its very principle, to a universal, formal code affirming the equal dignity of all men and therefore the identity of their rights and duties' (Bourdieu, 1979, p. 129). Pino Arlacchi (1986) discusses a similar obsession with honour in Southern Italy, home to the traditional Mafia. It should be noted that the birth of the Mafia coincided with the start of the process to modernise that traditional society, namely, the emergence of regional and national markets. Cultures (or subcultures) valuing honour can be found even in the US, namely in the military, on the streets of some urban areas (Bowman, 2009), or in the Western states at the time of settlement (Kamir, 2006).

Regardless of the particular temporal period of their existence—traditional or modern, honour cultures include the process of invidious comparison as their key element. Since honour always has a relative character, its assessment requires endless comparisons of who has more and who has less honour. Any change in the circumstances calls for re-evaluating the relative standing of the individuals and groups. If a challenge is left without a proper response, one's honour appears to be undermined (Bourdieu, 1979, pp. 100–112; Kamir, 2006, p. 203). Thorstein Veblen (1934, pp. 31–32) captured the dynamics of the invidious comparison well: 'the invidious comparison can never become so favourable to the individual making it that he would not gladly rate himself still higher relatively to his competitors in the struggle for pecuniary reputability'. In the final account, if human dignity is associated with honour, then one's dignity can be asserted through invidious comparison only.

The vicious circle of invidious comparison takes particularly manifest forms in the context of protracted conflicts. As a matter of fact, the need to save one's face (the other name for one's honour) constantly drives an individual or a group to fight back. If one chooses to turn the other cheek after being slapped on the face in a culture valuing honour, the individual or group is subsequently marginalised. The problem is that the logic of 'responding adequately' produces a similar response from the opposite party. Who started a conflict becomes irrelevant as time passes. The Newtonian proposition that for every action there is an equal and opposite reaction may well apply to relationships based on the continuous reassessment of relative forces, as observed by Herbert Simon (1953, p. 503).

I.3 Types of culture depending on the relative importance of honour and human rights

The discussion of human rights and honour allows differentiating between several types of cultures, depending on the relative importance attached to the former or latter correlate of human dignity. Honour cultures and dignity cultures are of particular relevance for this study (Helkama et al., 2011, pp. 281–282; Kamir, 2006, pp. 197–203). In honour cultures, human dignity is understood in terms of honour rather than human rights. In dignity cultures, a more universalist interpretation of dignity, namely, through its association with human rights, prevails. A hierarchical social organisation prevails in honour cultures. The more honourable an individual or a group, the higher are their relative ranks, and vice versa. Since the source of honour – invidious comparison – lies outside the individual or a group, they are less self-sufficient and more dependent on the others, especially those with a capacity to change one's rank, i.e. the powerholders. Honour cultures imply a clear differentiation between Us (a reference group, people of the same rank) and Them (people and groups of higher or lower ranks). Conflicts in honour cultures tend to be protracted and difficult to put an end to.

Russian and Ukrainian cultures are good candidates for an inquiry into honour and dignity cultures. Russian culture has features of an honour culture. A comparative study of the young people's values showed that in the group of Russian high school students (15–17 y.o., N=299) honour had the highest rank (10th out of 67) of all 13 groups in five Western and Eastern European countries (Helkama et al. 2012, p. 284). Honour has traditionally been valued in Russia. Precisely, the popularity of duelling in the first half of the 19th century suggests that honour was considered an important correlate of human dignity not only in the context of post-Soviet transformations (when Helkama and co-authors carried out their comparative study), but also in Russia's past (Reyfman, 1995).

Despite having common historical roots with Russian culture, Ukrainian culture might be less honour-centered. An analysis of the synonyms of dignity in 17th-century Ukrainian dictionaries suggests that, on one hand, honour does not appear to be a key correlate of dignity and, on the other hand, the Ukrainian and Russian lists of synonyms diverge over time (Drul, 2014). Weaker traditions of national nobility in Ukraine (because of its dependent status in the past) provide a possible explanation. Values of honour, as mentioned previously, were particularly appreciated in aristocratic milieus.

Attempts to make the transition from an honour culture to a culture based on the more broadly defined value of human dignity took particularly manifest forms in Ukraine during the 2013–2014 Revolution of Dignity. During this revolution, the idea of human dignity appeared to be a more powerful driver of mass mobilisation than the ideas of closer integration with the European Union that underpin the second name given to those events, EuroMaidan (Chapters 3 and 4). It is possible, however, that the subsequent and ongoing military conflict with Russia may become a breeding ground for prioritising honour. One can expect that, the longer this conflict remains without resolution, the higher the chances are for prioritising honour in the culture of today's Ukraine, which would undermine the ideals and values promoted by the Revolution of Dignity.

This study is exploratory in nature. There have been few empirically oriented inquiries into human dignity, especially using primary data, in the context of these two cultures. For instance, Helkama et al. (2012) used a small non-representative sample in their inquiry into the role of honour in Russia. A specifically designed larger-scale study helps to confirm or reject the assumption that Russian culture is an honour culture. The comparison of the Russian and Ukrainian cases also serves to develop an empirically informed opinion on the issue of (in)compatibility between human rights and honour as correlates of human dignity.

II. Research design and sources of data

A multiple case-study design (Bryman & Bell, 2016, p. 44) was used for collecting and analysing data. Namely, two cases, Russian and Ukrainian, were contrasted using the relative prevalence of various correlates of human dignity as a criterion for comparison. This study focused on two correlates of human dignity: human rights and honour.

The case study format does not place restrictions on using data from various sources. The primary data were collected with the help of an online survey carried out in December 2015 in Russia (N=5,068) and Ukraine (N=954) using the panels of an on-line pollster. The online survey included a single open-ended question 'What words come to mind when you think of human dignity?'[122] The 20 most frequently mentioned correlates of human dignity were: politeness, loyalty, pride, goodness, love, courage, male dignity (maleness), responsibility, understanding, decency, human

122 Formulated in this way, the question elicits information about a particular cultural domain, namely, human dignity as a cultural domain. Cultural sociologists and anthropologists define a cultural domain as a 'list of things that people in a society think somehow "go together"' (Bernard, 2013, p. 261). The emphasis is placed on what the respondent believes to be associated with human dignity as opposed to the respondent's *personal* preferences in this context.

rights, self-respect, willpower, conscience, justice, status, respect, intelligence, honour, and honesty. In other words, honour and human rights were among the respondents' top choices in their answers to the open-ended question.

The online survey was followed by face-to-face surveys on representative samples administered in January 2016 by the Levada-Center (Moscow) in Russia (N=1,602) and in February 2016 by the Kyiv International Institute of Sociology in Ukraine (N=2,020[123]). The face-to-face survey contained the semi-closed-ended question 'What words come to mind when you think of human dignity?' with the 20 alternatives listed above plus the alternative 'Other (please specify)' and a series of the controls (the respondent's age, gender, marital status, etc.). Two versions of the questionnaire were used in Ukraine, Ukrainian and Russian; they were produced after a series of consultations with Ukrainian native speakers (Newman, 2006, pp. 444–445).[124]

The secondary data also come from two sources. The Google online databank represents the first. Google provides search services in both Russia (Google.ru) and Ukraine (Google.com.ua). A contextual search using all twenty correlates listed above was carried out on February 3 and March 23, 2016. It served to identify the number of documents in which these correlates co-occur with the word 'dignity'.[125] Since the number of documents in the Russian-language and Ukrainian-language segments of the Internet are unequal, relative frequencies were used—the number of the co-occurrences divided by the total number of documents containing the reference term, i.e. dignity.

---

123 The annexed Crimea was not covered in any of the surveys. The Ukrainian survey, however, covered parts of the regions of Luhansk and Donetsk that the Ukrainian government did not control at the time this chapter was written.

124 The author is particularly grateful to Orest Drul, Lviv, and Evgen Ilyenko of the Kyiv International Institute of Sociology. The Ukrainian version was chosen by 44.8% of the respondents, the Russian version by 43.4%, and the rest (11.8%) used both languages in their responses.

125 For instance, the number of documents in which both 'love' and 'dignity' are found and so forth.

The second source included the complete works of Alexander Pushkin[126] and Taras Shevchenko,[127] two 19th-century poets who are commonly considered to be the founding fathers and most representative figures of the modern Russian and Ukrainian literatures, respectively. Comparisons of Pushkin and Shevchenko are not uncommon both in the scholarly literature in the national languages (Muravieva, 2013; Nikolenko, 2011; Tzjaven, 2015) and in the English-language specialised publications (Manning, 1944).[128] Most comparisons have been made by linguists, however, with a focus on the issues in linguistics and language studies. For instance, both Pushkin and Shevchenko found inspiration in romanticism in general and in the works of Lord Byron in particular (Muravieva, 2013; Nikolenko, 2011). Both poets fought for the promotion of the national language, Russian (since French was popular among the Russian nobility) and Ukrainian (since this language was considered as a dialect in the Russian empire) respectively (Tzjaven, 2015, p. 233). The status of Pushkin as a figure representative of modern Russian literature and Shevchenko's similar status in modern Ukrainian literature (Aleksandrova, 2015; Levada, 1993, pp. 222-227[129]) justifies the choice of their works as a snapshot of the 19th-century Russian and Ukrainian cultures.

---

126 A set of 10 volumes published in 1977–1979 by the Leningrad branch of Nauka Publishers (Leningrad, currently St. Petersburg). Retrieved from http://www.feb-web.ru/feb/pushkin/default.asp?/feb/pushkin/texts/push10/d00.html.

127 A set of 6 volumes published in 2001–2003 by Naukova Dumka (Kyiv). Retrieved from http://litopys.org.ua/shevchenko/shev.htm.

128 Pushkin and Shevchenko attract comparable attention in the West. Google Books Ingram Viewer search using their names (https://books.google.com/ngrams/graph?content=A.+Pushkin%2CT.+Shevchenko&year_start=1800&year_end=2010&corpus=15&smoothing=3&share=&direct_url=t1%3B%2CA.%20Pushkin%3B%2Cc0%3B.t1%3B%2CT.%20Shevchenko%3B%2Cc0) shows that in some periods the number of publications mentioning Pushkin's name exceeded the number of publications citing Shevchenko (the 1940s-1950s), whereas in the other periods the situation was inverse (the first half of the 1960s, the late 1970s—the mid-1980s).

129 A first mass survey carried out on a representative sample in the Soviet Union in 1989–1991 under auspices of Yuri Levada, the founder of Levada-Center,

There were at least two reasons for using several sources of data (the online surveys, the face-to-face surveys, the online databanks and the complete works of the two poets), under the circumstances. The first reason involves the benefits of data triangulation conventionally defined as the use of a variety of data sources (Oleinik, 2015c; Perlesz & Lindsay, 2003). Datasets rarely cover all relevant aspects of the topic under discussion. Thus, gaps and omissions in one dataset may eventually be bridged with the help of information from other sources. For example, searches in the Google online databank provide the most up-to-date information that changes from day to day. However, these 'big data' (Berman, 2013) only partially cover the relevant aspects of cultures.

Second, the list of the correlates of human dignity cannot be compiled in an a priori manner. In addition to human rights and honour, the extant literature discusses several other correlates of human dignity, such as autonomy (Brennan & Lo, 2007, pp. 47–50; Chalmers & Ryuichi, 2007, p. 160), respect (Stevenson, 2014, p. 186), intellect (Menachem, 2008, pp. 636–637), rank (Drul, 2014; Luban, 2005, p. 840) and others. However, there is no guarantee that a theoretically informed list of the correlates will be a good fit in any particular cultural setting. People may simply use different concepts and words to think and speak of human dignity in day-to-day interactions. The open-ended question on the correlates of human dignity helped identify key elements of the culture-specific discourse on human dignity. This custom-built list of correlates was subsequently used for analysing both the primary and secondary data.

The face-to-face survey data were processed with the help of SPSS software version 23, using descriptive statistics operations and running binary statistic regressions to predict the choice of a particular correlate of human dignity. The online survey data and

---

showed that Shevchenko was named as the symbolic figure in Ukraine's history. The other proof of a highly symbolic status of Shevchenko in Ukrainian culture can be found in the fact that his portraits and quotes from his poems (the most popular being 'fight and you shall overcome' from the 'Caucasus' poem) were common at the sites of the 2013–2014 mass protests.

the works of Pushkin and Shevchenko were content analysed using the specialised computer programs QDA Miner version 4.1.22 and WordStat version 6.1.24. A unique feature of these programs is the combination of both qualitative and quantitative methods of content analysis. Specifically, a dictionary based on substitution (Oleinik, 2011b) was created with the same entries outlined before (politeness, loyalty, pride, and so forth). Two versions of the dictionary were used, one containing the 20 correlates of human dignity and the other, an extended dictionary, containing synonyms of the 20 correlates.[130] All sources were analysed in the language of the original. The volume of the works of the two poets subjected to the content analysis was comparable: 755 texts containing 306,473 words for Pushkin and 237 documents containing 319,012 words for Shevchenko. By comparing outcomes of the content analysis with results of the surveys, one is able to ascertain whether the relative importance of honour and the other correlates of human dignity in Russia and Ukraine has changed over time.

III. Discussion: between honour and human rights

The data collected indicate both similarities and divergent patterns in the perception of human dignity in the Russian and Ukrainian cultures. The data also suggest that some elements of the culture-specific interpretation of human dignity, namely, the importance placed on honour, has a malleable character. It can change, even on a relatively short-term basis.

130 For the Russian version of the dictionary based on substitution, the dictionary of synonyms by Abramov was used (http://www.gramota.ru/slovari/info/abr/, http://словарь-синонимов.рф/), for the Ukrainian version, the dictionary of synonyms by Karavanskii (http://hohlopedia.org.ua/slovnyk_synonimiv_karavanskogo/) was used.

III.1 What meanings are attributed to the notion of human dignity in today's Ukraine and Russia?

A preliminary inspection of the patterns in the responses to the semi-closed-ended question shows that the respondents in Ukraine tended to select more alternatives at a time (6 on average) than the respondents in Russia (5.3 on average). In order to enhance the compatibility of the data from the two countries, the battery of 20 Yes/No questions (whether a particular alternative is selected) could have been converted into a multiple response question. The reported frequencies would have been 'normalised', then, by the total number of selected alternatives.

Upon closer inspection, however, it was decided to report the data in the original format, i.e. as frequencies of selecting particular correlates of human dignity taken separately. In Ukraine, the social impact of the ongoing (as of when this book was written) military conflict between the two countries may be felt more intensively. Furthermore, it appeared that the respondents from the Ukrainian regions of Donetsk and Luhansk (N=104) chose even more alternatives (8.2 on average). Taking into consideration the fact that these regions are in the centre of the military confrontation, the relative number of selected alternatives in answers to the question on human dignity may be deemed indicative of the perceived importance of this topic. The more alternatives one selects, the more importance is placed on the topic under the circumstances. This finding is also arguably relevant to the discussion of the malleability of the perceptions of human dignity.

Table 7.1 'What words comes to mind when you think of human dignity?, % of respondents in Russia and Ukraine who selected a particular alternative and its relative rank [in square brackets]'

	Russia, N=1,602	Standard error of the population	Ukraine, N=2,020	SE of the population
Decency	50.6 [1]	1.25	55.9 [1]	1.10
Honesty	39.3 [2]	1.22	49.3 [2]	1.11
Conscience	36.7 [3]	1.20	43.6 [4]	1.10
Self-respect	36.2 [4]	1.20	31.5 [7]	1.03
Responsibility	35.7 [5]	1.20	40 [5]	1.09
Justice	35.6 [6]	1.20	45.9 [3]	1.11
Respect	29.2 [7]	1.14	29.5 [9]	1.01
Honour	28.9 [8]	1.13	30.3 [8]	1.02
Courage	28.3 [9]	1.13	26 [11]	0.98
Loyalty	25.5 [10]	1.09	23.8 [13]	0.95
Goodness	24.4 [11]	1.07	32.6 [6]	1.04
Pride	23.3 [12]	1.06	20.6 [17]	0.90
Intelligence	23 [13]	1.05	22.6 [14]	0.93
Human rights	22.5 [14]	1.04	25.6 [12]	0.97
Willpower	19.4 [15]	0.99	18.9 [19]	0.87
Politeness	19 [16]	0.98	27.5 [10]	0.99
Love	16.8 [17]	0.93	22.3 [16]	0.93
Male dignity	15.8 [18]	0.91	22.4 [15]	0.93
Understanding	13.6 [19]	0.86	19.5 [18]	0.88
Rank	10.1 [20]	0.75	6.7 [20]	0.56
Other	0.6	0.19	0.4	0.14
Don't know / No answer	4.5	0.52	1.7	0.29

The relative frequencies with which Russians and Ukrainians select particular correlates of human dignity show that decency and honesty are top correlates of human dignity (Table 7.1) in both countries. There is no clear 'outlier', i.e. an alternative selected far more frequently than the others. The analysis of the extent to which people agree on the contents of human dignity as a particular cultural domain (cultural consensus analysis, see Bernard, 2013, pp. 432–447) suggests that consensus is reached with respect to none of the 20 correlates.[131] Conscience comes third in Russia, whereas justice ranks third in Ukraine. Honour is found among the top 10 correlates placing eighth in both countries. Human rights come to the respondents' mind less frequently: this correlate ranks 12th in Ukraine and 14th in Russia.

Accounting for the standard error of the population, 11 correlates appear to be specific to Ukrainian culture compared with Russian culture: decency, honesty, conscience, justice, responsibility, goodness, politeness, human rights, male dignity, love and understanding. The list of the correlates specific to Russian culture compared with Ukrainian culture includes self-respect, courage, pride, rank and the option 'Do not know/No answer'. Finally, differences in the relative frequencies of honour, respect, loyalty, intelligence, willpower and the option 'Other (please specify)' do not attain a level of statistical significance.

These findings serve to substantiate references to dignity during the 2013–2014 revolution in Ukraine. By using the word 'dignity' when referring to their protests, the Ukrainians most likely wanted to assert the value of decency, honesty, justice, responsibility and conscience. These characteristics appear among the top five correlates of human dignity in Ukraine. Furthermore, they were selected more frequently in Ukraine than in Russia.

---

131 Cultural domain analysis, namely, the calculation of chance-adjusted probabilities of selecting a particular correlate of human dignity, was performed using Anthropac version 4.98 (http://www.analytictech.com/anthropac/apacdesc.htm) on random sub-samples (N=180) constructed with the help of SPSS from the Russian and Ukrainian representative samples because of the Anthropac limited capacity to process large volumes of data.

Figure 7.1 'Two-dimensional map of the co-occurrence of the 20 correlates of human dignity in Russia'

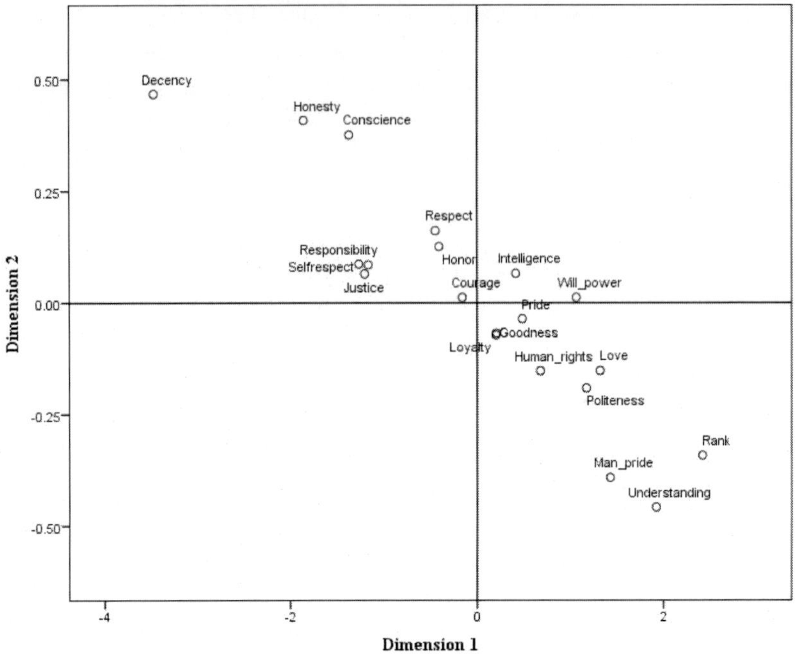

Legend: Stress = 0.00791, pseudo R^2 = 0.99981. Figures 7.1 & 7.2 were produced using the multidimensional scaling (ALSCAL) module of SPSS. In order to minimise the level of stress (it should ideally not exceed 0.015, see Bernard, 2013, p. 413), size difference was used as a proximity measure, and tied observations were united. Size difference was calculated using the following formula: $Size_{(x,y)} = \frac{(b-c)^2}{(a+b+c+d)^2}$, where a is the number of cases (responses) with both correlates (e.g., honour and human rights) present; d refers to the number of cases with both correlates absent; c and b are the numbers of cases with only one correlate present.

Techniques of correspondence analysis, including multidimensional scaling, shed additional light on the comparative patterns that characterise the Russian and Ukrainian datasets. Correspondence analysis serves to measure the degree of dependence between variables (Beh & Lombardo, 2014). It can be adapted to the circumstances of the comparative case study as a method for studying how often particular correlates of human dignity tend to co-occur in the respondents' choices, i.e. how dependent the choice of one correlate is on the choice of the others. The most and least frequently selected correlates can be found in the upper left and lower right areas of a two-dimensional map demonstrating the co-occurrence of the correlates of human dignity in Russia (Figure 7.1). They co-occur with the other correlates relatively less frequently. In contrast, the Russian respondents selected courage, loyalty, goodness, intelligence, pride and honour (in this order) together with the other correlates more often. Being a necessary part of the relevant synonymous lists, these correlates can be viewed as indicative of the interpretation of human dignity in Russian culture.

Figure 7.2 'Two-dimensional map of the co-occurrence of the 20 correlates of human dignity in Ukraine'

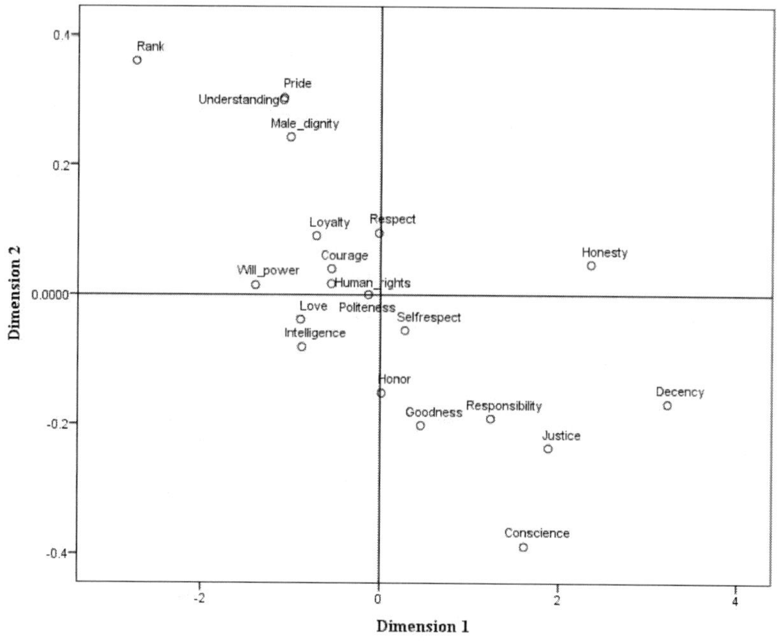

Legend: Stress = 0.01092, R^2 = 0.99967.

The picture for Ukrainian culture has some particularities (Figure 7.2). In its center, we find human rights, self-respect, courage, and respect (in this order). The central location of human rights in the

Ukrainian discourse on human dignity deserves special mention. It suggests the existence of a more significant potential for moving toward a more universal understanding of human dignity in the Ukrainian case than in the Russian case. Honesty refers to the other interesting situation. Both in Ukraine and Russia, honesty is the second most frequent correlate of human dignity. But in Ukraine, honesty is selected together with the other correlates more often than in Russia (as indicated by its position further away from the diagonal and closer to the second axis).

To summarise, the analysis of the meanings attached to human dignity in the two cultures show both similarities and divergent patterns. Judging by the average number of alternatives chosen by the Ukrainian respondents (6 compared to 5.3), they perceive human dignity as an issue of relatively greater significance. Human rights play a relatively more important and central role (this alternative is selected both more frequently and more often together with the other correlates) in Ukraine. Honour occupies a similar—and prominent—place in the two cultures. If these countries have elements of an honour culture, is this finding characteristic of the current situation or have considerations of honour played a significant role in the past as well?

III.2 Has the relative importance of human rights and honour changed over time in Russian and Ukrainian cultures?

There is no historical data in a comparable format. For instance, it would be instructive to compare the figures reported above with those that refer to the situations that existed at the time of the 2013–2014 revolution, before the 2014 aggression of Russia, and before Ukraine's 1991 Declaration of Independence. The decision to compare the current understanding of human dignity with the relative frequencies of the same correlates of human dignity in the works of the two 19th century poets results from practical considerations of feasibility. The content analysis of the works of Pushkin and Shevchenko provides an opportunity to compare today's interpretations of human dignity with interpretations that can be deemed representative of the 19th century Ukrainian and Russian cultures.[132]

Table 7.2 'Relative frequencies and ranks [in square brackets] of the 20 correlates of human dignity in the works of Alexander Pushkin and Taras Shevchenko'

	Shevchenko (short)	Pushkin (short)	Shevchenko (extended)	Pushkin (extended)
Decency	21.94 [4]	3.59 [12]	56.72 [4]	21.21 [11]
Honesty	17.55 [5]	16.31 [9]	23.82 [7]	23.49 [10]
Conscience	5.02 [12]	18.60 [7]	5.01 [15]	18.60 [12]
Self-respect	0.00 [18–20]	0.00 [18–20]	1.57 [18]	9.79 [15]
Responsibility	0.00 [18–20]	0.98 [14–15]	4.07 [16]	10.77 [14]
Justice	3.13 [13]	7.83 [11]	122.84 [1]	50.90 [7]
Respect	6.27 [11]	11.42 [10]	19.12 [8]	45.03 [8]
Honour	7.52 [8–9]	37.20 [5]	36.04 [5–6]	71.78 [6]
Courage	0.63 [15]	1.63 [13]	10.34 [13]	75.70 [5]
Loyalty	6.58 [10]	26.10 [6]	8.77 [14]	31.00 [9]
Goodness	60.50 [2]	49.27 [4]	100.91 [3]	97.56 [2]
Pride	15.36 [6]	70.48 [3]	17.86 [9]	93.32 [4]
Intelligence	27.27 [3]	81.90 [2]	36.04 [5–6]	96.26 [3]
Human rights	0.31 [16]	0.33 [16]	0.31 [19]	0.33 [19]
Willpower	2.51 [14]	0.00 [18–20]	2.51 [17]	0.00 [20]
Politeness	7.52 [8–9]	0.98 [14–15]	10.65 [12]	6.53 [17]
Love	84.95 [1]	239.17 [1]	105.92 [2]	318.46 [1]
Male dignity	0.00 [18–20]	0.00 [18–20]	0.00 [20]	2.28 [18]
Understanding	12.23 [7]	16.97 [8]	13.79 [10]	17.95 [13]
Rank	0.00 [18–20]	0.00 [18–20]	12.54 [11]	9.14 [16]
Dictionary coverage (% of all words)	0.70	1.00	1.30	1.90

Legend: reported figures (except for Dictionary coverage) were obtained by dividing the absolute frequency of a particular correlate of human dignity by the total number of words and multiplying the result by 10,000.

132 At that time, Ukraine was an integral part of the Russian empire, which shall be kept in mind in the following discussion.

Table 7.2 reports the relative frequencies of the same correlates of human dignity in the works of the two poets as in the face-to-face surveys.[133] The short version of the substation-based dictionary contains single equivalents of each correlate in Russian and Ukrainian, for example, *poriadochnost'* and *poriadnist'* for decency. The extended version includes synonym lists for each correlate, for instance, *poriadochn**, *blagorodn**, *dobroporyadochn**, and *chistoplotn** in Russian; *dobroporiadn**, *dobroches**, and *poriadn** in Ukrainian.[134]

In contrast to the survey, where the context was specified by the mere formulation of the question, in the analysis of the literary works, there was no a priori guarantee that a similar meaning was attached to the Russian and Ukrainian versions of the same word. A word can be used in several contexts and its scope may not be the same in different languages. In order to ensure the contextual compatibility of the Russian and Ukrainian versions of the dictionary based on substitution, the KWIC (key word in context) operation was used. Cases in which synonyms have divergent, incomparable meanings were singled out manually, which led to the further refinement of the search terms (this only happened with a few terms included in the extended version of the dictionary). All sentences containing the keywords were subsequently counted in an automated manner.

> 'To *honour*, to freedom, to brotherhood
> To the will of Ukraine' (Shevchenko).
> 'A prisoner of *honour* with no mercy,
> He foresaw his death to come' (Pushkin).

A note regarding human rights must be made. This concept, an invention of the second half of the 20th century, was not a part of the 19th-century discourse on human dignity either in the West or in

---

133 The analysis of observed and expected relative frequencies of the categories reported in Table 7.2 allows assessing whether differences in those frequencies reach the level of statistical significance. If one sets α at 0.05, most differences are statistically significant. The exceptions are Honesty, Courage and Human rights in the short version of the dictionary; Honesty, Understanding and Goodness (p=0.56) in its extended version.

134 * refers to a wild card, i.e. to any letter or a combination of letters.

the Russian empire. The search using a relevant combination of words (Russian and Ukrainian equivalents of 'human' NEAR 'right*') naturally produced less than perfect matches, for example, 'We decided... to go to Zhytomyr, to appear before the governor, to confess all our crimes hoping for God's mercy and for *human justice*'[135] (Shevchenko, emphasis added). In the 19th century, the concept of justice was arguably the closest match for human rights. Consequently, the relative frequencies of 'justice' seem to contain more relevant information under the circumstances.

That Pushkin and Shevchenko refer to love far more frequently than to the other correlates of human dignity comes as no surprise. After all, British romanticism had a major impact on both poets.[136] Our principal interest, however, lies in the area of honour and justice (as the closest substitute for human rights). Honour and politeness tied (ranking 8th-9th) in Shevchenko's works when the short dictionary based on substitution was used. The switch to the extended dictionary resulted in another tie, this time between honour and intelligence (ranking 5th-6th). The rank of honour in Pushkin's works is comparable—5th and 6th, respectively, even if the relevant absolute frequencies are much higher than in Shevchenko's case. The analysis of the relative importance of justice produces less consistent results: this word ranks 13th in Shevchenko's works when using the short dictionary and first when using the extended dictionary (the corresponding figures for Pushkin's works are 11th and 7th). The idea of justice—broadly defined—prevails in Shevchenko's works, whereas Pushkin clearly prioritises honour over justice.[137]

---

135 'Justice' in Russian (*pravo*sudie) and Ukrainian (*pravo*suddia) has 'right' (*pravo*) as a root word.

136 The relevant figure for Lord Byron's works is 285.33 (the case of a short dictionary based on substitution; calculations of the author).

137 The indication that the two poets have different social origins, nobility in the case of Pushkin and peasantry in the case of Shevchenko, does not invalidate the reported findings. Ukrainian culture historically survived in the lower social classes since the privileged classes in this country were mostly composed of representatives of the dominating nations (or the local nobles who adapted their cultures), Polish (in the 14–17th centuries) and Russian (in the 17–19th

To summarise, there is some continuity in the relative place occupied by honour, on one hand, in today's Russian and Ukrainian cultures, and, on the other hand, in the works of Pushkin and Shevchenko as poets representative of the 19th century Russian and Ukrainian cultures. However, judging by the relative frequencies, similar importance is placed on the idea of honour in Russia and Ukraine today, but not in the past. Pushkin referred to the idea of honour more often than Shevchenko did.

If the idea of human rights is translated as a particular expression of justice, then it has more support in the 19th century Ukrainian culture than in the Russian culture during the same period of time. Bearing in mind that human rights are also mentioned by the Ukrainian respondents more often than by the Russian respondents today, we see another continuous pattern. In the final account, both cultures have elements of honour cultures, although these elements tended to be stronger in the 19th century Russian culture. However, elements that are eventually compatible with the universalism of human rights have been stronger in the Ukrainian case, both now and in the past.

III.3 Is the perception of human dignity malleable?

The particular political, social and economic context has an impact on the perception of human dignity, as suggested by the comparative analysis of the number of the alternatives selected in today's Russia and Ukraine in the context of the military conflict between the two countries. Even if this impact cannot radically change long-term patterns, as shown by the comparative analysis of Russian and Ukrainian cultures now and in the 19th century, the issue of the malleability of honour and dignity cultures deserves a brief, separate discussion. Being the most up-to-date and the easiest to adjust,

---

centuries). In this respect, Mykhailo Hrushevsky wrote that Ukrainian cultural traditions managed to survive mostly 'from below, among ordinary people and the lower clergy' (1992b, p. 503; see also Subtelny, 2009, p. 223). In other words, Ukrainian culture was more closely connected to popular traditions in the 19th century than Russian culture.

the data retrieved from the Internet provide some insights in this regard.

The relative frequencies of the 20 words associated with human dignity change particularly rapidly in the Ukrainian- and Russian-language segments of the Internet. Pearson's r between these relative frequencies on February 3 and on March 23, 2016 was 0.25 for both these segments of the Internet, as opposed to 0.99 for the English-language segments of the Internet. This variability is a first indication of the high sensitivity of the perceptions of human dignity to the context of the military conflict.

Figure 7.3 'Relative frequencies of the 20 correlates of human dignity in the Russian-language, Ukrainian-language and English-language segments of the Internet, February 2016'

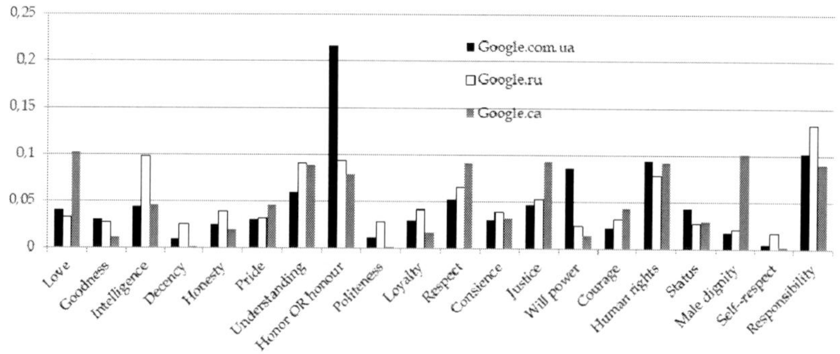

Legend: the number of the co-occurrences of each correlate with 'dignity' divided by the total frequency of 'dignity' in the corresponding segment.

The relative frequencies of mentions of honour appear high in both segments: 21.6% (1st rank) in the case of Ukraine and 9.4% (3rd rank) in the case of Russia. In the Ukrainian-language segment, honour refers to a clear outlier: no other correlate of dignity even comes close (Figure 7.3).[138] Two months later, honour became a top correlate of human dignity in the Russian-language Internet (28.2%,

138 Given the large size of the Google sample, standard errors of the population proportions tend to be small. It means that even small differences reported in Figure 7.3 are statistically significant, with no exception.

2nd rank), whereas its relative frequency in the Ukrainian-language segment of the Internet fell to 6.5% (5th rank).

One possible explanation refers to the current political context. The military conflict between Russia and Ukraine creates a breeding ground for the revival or strengthening of an honour culture. The Ukrainians may not be willing to turn the other cheek after being slapped on the face. The other eventual explanation is that the Internet users' opinions about correlates of human dignity diverge from the opinions of the other Russians and Ukrainians. The Internet penetration in Russia (70.5 Internet users per 100 people in 2014)[139] and especially in Ukraine (43.4) is lower than in the developed countries (91.6 in the UK, 87.1 in Canada, 86.2 in Germany). The latter considerations prompt an inquiry into the social predictors for the selection of honour and human rights in the course of the face-to-face interviews.

III.4 Predictors for the selection of human rights and honour as correlates of human dignity

The use of honour and human dignity as the dependent variables restricted the range of available options: both variables are nominal, or categorical (1 for 'selected' and 0 for 'not selected'). The binary static regression procedure served to identify the variables that are associated with the selection of either honour or human dignity by the respondent. In more technical terms, static regressions run separately for the Russian and Ukrainian face-to-face survey datasets produced a list of variables that have an impact on the odds[140] (chances) of associating human rights or honour with human dignity. The forward method was used with the probability of F to enter a new variable set at ≤ 0.05 and the probability of F to remove a variable—at ≤ 0.1.

139 The World Bank data retrieved from http://data.worldbank.org/indicator/IT.NET.USER.P2.

140 'Odds are obtained by dividing the number of times an outcome of interest *does* happen by the number of times when it *does not* happen' (Warner, 2013, p. 1013; emphasis added).

The long list of the predictor variables included the other correlates of human dignity (as suggested by the study of their co-occurrences) and a number of socio-economic and political indicators available in the datasets, namely, the respondent's age (at the ratio level of measurement in both datasets), gender (dummy for males in both datasets), level of education (separate dummies for secondary, for vocational, for higher education and for holders of a technical college degree, also in both datasets), marital status (separate dummies for singles, for married, for divorced and for people living in common-law relationships in the Russian dataset), occupation (separate dummies for workers, for students, for retired, for office workers, for self-employed individuals and for business owners in both datasets), household size (at the ratio level of measurement in the Russian dataset), self-reported wealth (separate dummies for the higher, upper-middle, middle/lower-middle and low income groups in both datasets), place of residence (separate dummies for the cities of various size in both datasets), region (separate dummies for the macro-regions in both datasets), nationality and language (dummies for Ukrainian in the Ukrainian dataset), voting intentions (dummy for those who intend to vote in the next presidential elections in the Russian dataset) and expectations as to the future socio-economic situation in the country (dummy for optimists, for realists and for pessimists in the Russian dataset). Some discrepancies between the survey designs in the two countries (because the question on correlates of human dignity was included in omnibus surveys) prevented the use of completely identical lists of predictor variables.

Table 7.3 'Results of binary statistic regressions to predict the odds of selecting human rights and honour as correlates of human dignity in Russia and Ukraine, Exp(B)'

	Russia, N=1,602		Ukraine, N=2,020	
	Human rights	Ho-nour	Human rights	Honour
Gender (Male)				0.737**
Education (trade school after grade 8–9)	[0.613*]		3.082**	
Education (trade school after grade 10–11)				1.661*
Education (Higher)				0.720**
Wealth (Higher)			0.477**	
Wealth (Middle and lower-middle)		0.698*		1.410**
Wealth (Lower)	[0.698*]			
Marital status (Common law marriage)		0.495*	n.a.	n.a.
Occupation (peasant)				1.479*
Occupation (Office)		0.667*		
Occupation (Self-employed)	0.254***			0.526**
City (Large, 500,000–1 billion)	0.643*	[0.736*]	X	
City (Mid-size, 100,001–499,999)	X		X	[0.717**]
City (Small, less than 100,000)	0.568***		0.397**	X
Area (Urban)	n.a.	n.a.	[0.710*]	
Region (South, Russia)	1.753**	0.585**	n.a.	n.a.
Region (Centre, Russia)		0.679*	n.a.	n.a.
Region (Urals, Russia)		X		
Region (Centre, Ukraine)	n.a.	n.a.	0.478***	X
Region (South, Ukraine)	n.a.	n.a.		X
Region (West, Ukraine)	n.a.	n.a.	0.326***	0.663**
Nationality (dual identity, Ukrainian and Russian, Ukraine)	n.a.	n.a.	0.382*	
Voter (Active)	0.567***		n.a.	n.a.
Expectations (Pessimist)	[0.496**]		n.a.	n.a
Expectations (Realist)	[0.616*]		n.a.	n.a
Expectations (Optimist)	X	2.211**	n.a.	n.a.
Decency (Selected)		0.427***		
Honesty (Selected)	1.652**	0.742*		[1.289*]
Conscience (Selected)		0.447***		0.633***

Self-respect (Selected)	0.523***		0.733**	0.378***
Justice (Selected)	0.685**		0.583***	0.627***
Respect (Selected)	0.633**		0.553***	0.687**
Courage (Selected)			X	
Loyalty (Selected)	[0.707*]			0.634***
Goodness (Selected)	0.717*			
Pride (Selected)		0.597***		0.520***
Intelligence (Selected)	0.717*	0.492***	0.674**	
Will power (Selected)		0.621**	0.609***	0.517***
Politeness (Selected)				0.601***
Male dignity (Selected)		0.652**	0.662**	0.751*
Understanding (Selected)			0.670**	
Rank (Selected)	0.364***			
Nagelkerke's R^2	0.170	0.258	0.202	0.282

Legend: results significant at a 0.05 level are marked by *, at a 0.01 level—by **, and at a 0.001 level—by ***. Variables that become significant after entering the socio-economic predictors or the other correlates of human dignity in the model are placed in square brackets []. Variables that become insignificant and, thus, are removed from the model after entering the socio-economic predictors or the other correlates of human dignity are marked by X. Variables not entered in the models are not shown. Reference categories are: female (for Gender), elementary education (for Education), 'No answer' (for Wealth), widowed (for Marital status), unemployed (for Occupation), village (City), the Volga federal district in Russia and the Eastern macro-region in Ukraine (for Region), 'No answer/Difficult to say' (for Voter and for Expectations).

Table 7.3 contains the results of four binary static regressions, two for human rights (in Russia and in Ukraine) and two for honour. The table reports changes in the odds, Exp(B), relevant to the comparison of the odds of a target event, namely, the selection of human rights or honour, across various groups or conditions (e.g., males versus females). The analysis was set up so that the coefficients in the binary logistic regression can be interpreted as information about the comparative odds of selecting human rights or honour for people who do *not* have a particular characteristic (e.g., some higher education) compared with people who *do* have it. This means that when Exp(B) exceeds 1.00, people with this characteristic are *less* likely to select human rights or honour. If the odds are less than 1.00, those who have this characteristic are *more* likely to select human rights or honour.

In the Russian case, the respondents associating human rights with human dignity tend to (i) be residents of the large cities (500,000–1,000,000 inhabitants) and small cities (fewer than 100,000 inhabitants), (ii) be self-employed or to own a business, (iii) likely or certainly cast their votes at the next presidential elections (i.e. be politically active), (iv) be pessimists who expect that hard times are still ahead or 'realists' who believe that hard times are now,[141] and (v) consider themselves as low-income people. People living in the southern part of Russia[142] are less likely to select human rights in their responses than Russians living in other parts of the country. The relevant odds are 1.753, i.e. they exceed 1.00. Human rights are often selected in Russia together with rank, self-respect, respect, justice, loyalty, goodness and intelligence (in this order). In contrast, the selection of human rights together with honesty appears unlikely. The impact of the other predictors turned out to be insignificant. The strength of the association between the predictors and the selection of human rights was weak-moderate with Nagelkerke's R^2=0.170 (this model explains 17% of the variance in the odds).

In the Ukrainian case, the chances of associating human rights with human dignity are higher among wealthy urban residents from the Western and Central regions.[143] Respect, justice, willpower, male dignity, understanding, intelligence and self-respect are likely to co-occur in the respondents' synonym lists (in this order).

People with different social profiles tend to select honour in both countries. In Russia, the odds of associating honour with human dignity for office workers are 0.667. Because these odds are less than 1.00, this tells us that office workers are more likely to select

141 Since 2015 Russia has been going through an economic crisis.

142 The regions of Rostov, Krasnodar, Volgograd, Astrakhan, Kalmykia, Stavropol, Adygea, Karachay-Cherkessia, Dagestan, Kabardino-Balkarskaya, Northern Ossetia-Alania, and Ingushetia. Chechnya was excluded from the survey.

143 The regions of Volyn, Ivano-Frankivsk, Lviv, Rivne, Ternopil, Khmelnitsky, Chernivtsi, Kyiv, Cherkasy, Chernihiv, Poltava, Sumy, Vinnitsa, Zhytomyr and Kirovohrad (Kropyvnytskyi).

honour in their responses than holders of other jobs. The respondents associating honour with human dignity tend to (i) live either in the central (it includes Moscow) or southern federal districts, (ii) work in offices, (iii) live with a common-law partner and (iv) consider themselves as people with middle and lower-middle income. Decency, conscience, intelligence, pride, willpower, male dignity, and honesty tend to co-occur in the respondent's synonym lists (in this order).

Some additional considerations must be kept in mind when interpreting the outcomes of the regression analysis of honour in Ukraine. Males with higher education and a lower-middle level of income living in the Western macro-region tend to associate honour with human dignity. The impact of the other variable, City (dummy for medium-size cities, 100,001–500,000 inhabitants) becomes significant after entering the other correlates of human dignity into the model. In terms of the elaboration paradigm (Babbie & Benaquisto, 2002, pp. 432–437), these two conditions are *specified* after controlling for the other correlates, i.e. they have an impact among those who choose particular correlates, namely, self-respect, willpower, pride, politeness, justice, conscience, loyalty, respect and male dignity (in this order). Honesty is unlikely to co-occur with honour in the respondents' answers. The impact of the choice of honesty becomes significant only after the socio-economic predictors are entered into the model. Honesty (in a negative manner) appears significant as a predictor of the selection of honour among males with some higher education living in the mid-size cities.

The profiles of the respondents, who associate human rights or honour with human dignity, can be summarised in the following manner. The supporters of a universalistic reading of human dignity tend to concentrate in urban areas of both countries. However, there is no evidence that would serve to associate them with representatives of the so-called 'urban creative class'. Self-employed individuals and business owners have more chances of selecting human rights in Russia, but only when they do *not* succeed in their economic endeavours (reporting a low level of income). Representatives of the urban creative class, such as office workers, lean instead toward selecting honour in Russia. The members of this group are also among the most active Internet users whose sensitivity to the issues of honour was highlighted previously. The profile of those who are likely to endorse honour in Russia have common features with the group of office workers whose representatives are sometimes pejoratively called 'office plankton' (a local equivalent for 'office drones') in this country. Similar conclusions can be drawn with respect to educated male urbanites in Ukraine.

These findings support a rather sceptical expectation as to the role that the 'new middle class' may eventually play in initiating and sustaining major social and political changes (Oleinik, 2012b; Oleinik, 2016b). The Revolution of Dignity in Ukraine was definitively not an example of a radical change initiated and carried out by the new middle class. Its relative success can be attributed to the broad representation of the various social groups among the protesters, from university students to peasants and the retired (Chapters 3 and 4).

Conclusion

In the final account, it appears that a black-and-white approach, i.e. whether a particular culture is an honour culture or not, does not capture all the nuances (shades of grey, to use the metaphor) of the perception of human dignity in Russian and Ukrainian cultures. Honour represents an important component of these two cultures, both historically and in the present. It would be a mistake, however, to believe that Ukrainians and especially Russians (because honour plays a relatively more central role in their culture) perceive human dignity through the prism of honour on its own.

The reported differences between the Russian and Ukrainian cultures may be perceived as marginal by some. For instance, one reviewer of an earlier version of this chapter indicated that the relative ranks of honour and human rights in both cases are remarkably similar, whereas the other believes that the text 'provides enough evidence to make a case for a wider than expected (by common sense) difference between Russia and Ukraine in regard to those key notions'. The picture is not clear cut. On one hand, the historical proximity of the two cultures requires one to pay close attention to 'marginal differences'. On the other hand, even small differences may be statistically significant, which is the case of the relative importance placed on human rights and certain other indicators. A study covering more diverse cases (cultures) is needed, in order to determine whether the list of associations with human dignity and their relative importance could be more radically different. Some preliminary data (Oleinik, 2016a) suggest that a larger-scale comparative study will be of help.

Honour culture can be better viewed as an ideal type. Max Weber (1949, p. 90) defines ideal types as analytical tools that assist the scholar in constructing hypotheses about reality, but do not necessarily describe it, especially in a direct manner. Both the Ukrainian and Russian cultures have some elements of honour culture, but they also include elements of other cultures. Merry's definition of cultures as heterogeneous constructs is relevant under the circumstances. She argues that 'cultures consist of repertoires of ideas and practices that are not homogeneous but continuously changing because of contradictions among them or because new ideas and institutions are adopted by members' (Merry, 2006, p. 11).

One of these new ideas and institutions refers to the concept of human rights in the circumstances of the cases under discussion. Human rights are far from being a key correlate of human dignity in Russia and Ukraine. At the same time, Ukrainian culture appears more compatible with a universalistic reading of human dignity that underpins the concept of human rights. This tendency may eventually be path dependent, as the content analysis of Shevchenko's works seems to indicate. The 2013–2014 Revolution of Dignity marked an important milestone in the movement from an honour culture to a culture based on more universalistic interpretations of human dignity. It must be acknowledged that the use of two reference points separated by some 180 years is clearly insufficient for testing the hypothesis of path dependence in a systematic manner. The content analysis of literary works that are representative of the Russian and Ukrainian cultures during the Soviet period will serve to bridge this gap at least partly.

The subsequent developments, namely the military aggression of neighbouring Russia, might eventually stop or even reverse this movement towards universalism in Ukraine. Path-dependence in the perception of human dignity does not rule out its malleability in rapidly and radically changing circumstances. One can hardly think of a better example of radical and rapid changes with a potential for impacting the perception of human dignity than Russia's annexation of Crimea and the military intervention in the regions of Luhansk and Donetsk. The analysis of the most up-to-date data—retrieved from the Internet—indicates that perceptions of human dignity are indeed malleable to a certain extent. The context of the ongoing military aggression represents a breeding ground for strengthening the emphasis on honour in both countries. This context constitutes a serious obstacle to the transition to a more universal interpretation. The transformation and opening up of Ukrainian culture will be neither smooth nor expedient under these circumstances. At war, arguments in favour of turning the other cheek after being slapped on the face will likely fall on deaf ears.

This study also has a practical implication. If cultures do indeed have a malleable character, then there is a need for monitoring changes in them on a regular basis. The more radical changes in the material and political environment of a culture, the shorter the periods of time between measurements should be. Such monitoring would, in addition, allow for more light to be shed on the issue of the eventual manipulation of Internet discussions (in Russia, a specifically created 'troll army' reportedly manipulates Internet discussions[144]). In the case of information available online, it can be done at little cost. But this study also shows that a valid and comprehensive analysis of a culture requires regular surveys and, in an ideal case scenario, in-depth interviews.

144 See, for instance, Walker, Shaun (2015, April 2). 'Salutin' Putin: inside a Russian troll house', *The Guardian*. Available from http://www.theguardian.com/world/2015/apr/02/putin-kremlin-inside-russian-troll-house.

Chapter 8
'Ukrainian economic thought at the crossroads'

Introduction

The 2013–2014 Maidan and the subsequent developments were characterised by the awakening of Ukrainians' national consciousness and the acceleration of the process of nation-state building (see the book's general Introduction, Chapters 3, 4, 6 and 10). This country is still defending its independence, including by military means. The military and geopolitical dimensions of the fight for independence tend to overshadow its intellectual dimension, however. An element of the sustainable (as opposed to fragile or failed) nation-state refers to a space for economic debates at the national level that may eventually contribute to the emergence of a distinctive economic thought. This chapter discusses the current state of intellectual debates in the area of economic sciences and argues that Ukrainian economists tend to contribute to scholarly discussions either in the West (in Western Europe and North America) or in the East (in Russia). As a result, an existing potential for economic debates at the national level that would be focused on the particular problems and challenges that Ukraine faces remains untapped. Ukrainian economists have not yet met the demand for the formulation of economic policies that are guided by national interests as opposed to the interests of external economic and political actors.

I. From an outside to inside focus in economic sciences

On the surface, academia in general, and scholars working in the area of economic sciences in particular, represent a large segment of the Ukrainian polity. More than 50,000 people are currently involved in research in this country (58,695 in 2014; 53,835 in 2015;

Derzhavna Sluzhba Statystyky Ukrainy, 2016d, pp. 42–43). A third of them have advanced academic degrees, *kandidat nauk* or *doktor nauk*.[145] For instance, in 2015, 7.7% of all researchers had a *doktor nauk* degree and 25.7% — a *kandidat nauk* degree. The relevant figures for Russia are comparable: the total number of researchers in Russia in 2015 was 379,411, of whom 7.4% held a *doktor nauk* degree and 22% — a *kandidat nauk* degree (Federal'naia Sluzhba Gosudarstvennoi Statistiki, 2017). 0.13% and 0.26% of the total population are involved in research in Ukraine and Russia respectably. Economists represent 3.9% (161) of the total number of *doktors nauk* and 3.5% (487) of the total number of *kandidats nauk* in Ukraine. In purely quantitative terms, Ukrainian economists form a community whose size is comparable with that in Canada, for instance. In 2011, 990 academics with advanced degrees in economics taught at Canadian universities (CAUT, 2014, p. 19).

The analysis of the publishing activity of Ukrainian researchers provides a better assessment of the situation in Ukrainian science. The well-known maxim in science — publish or perish, has had a particular translation for Ukrainian scientists in general and economists in particular: in order to survive in academia, one must publish either in Russian scholarly journals, or, even better, in Western European and North American scholarly journals. As a result, scientific life in Ukraine tends to be outward oriented. It comes as no surprise that studies of today's Ukrainian academic milieu are rare. How to study something that has not yet taken a well recognisable and particular shape?

The scientific community in Ukraine lives according to the rules and norms that are externally generated and imposed. These rules and norms are set either by people vested with political power (Osin, 2014) or simply 'imported' from abroad. Members of the ac-

145 Unlike in the system with a single advanced academic degree, PhD, two advanced academic degrees exist in Ukraine and some other post-Soviet countries, including Russia. The *doktor nauk* degree corresponds to *Habilitation* in the German system, whereas the *kandidat nauk* degree may be deemed as an equivalent to the PhD degree.

ademic community in Ukraine have not managed to elaborate, defend and enforce their own rules in a bottom up manner. In other words, the academics have not succeeded in finding internal sources of the institutional development in science. Douglass North (1990, p. 3) defines institutions as 'the rules of game' in a particular area of human activity, namely, science.

The demand for the autonomy of science at the national level is neither hypothetic nor abstract. The process of nation-state building requires an input from intellectuals and academics. Their advice and expertise help solve unique problems that the Ukrainian nation-state in the making faces. Existing solutions—they are discussed in textbooks and other scholarly sources—have to be adapted to the circumstances of a particular country. This general observation also applies to economic sciences. Georgy Kleiner (2016, p. 125; 2015, p. 116) argues that the need for a national economic thought is particularly high at the time of profound transformations and crises. Economic debates at the national level ideally lead to the development and implementation of a model for sustainable development of a country that represents the 'best fit' for its institutional environment.

The vulnerability of science to external influences is not unique to Ukraine. The autonomy of science cannot be taken for granted even in the most developed—judging by the level of research productivity and the size and scope of scientific output—countries. For instance, in the United States, science has been subject to attacks from business on several occasions, especially in the 19th and the early 20th centuries (Debouzy, 1992). Business people repeatedly attempted to impose their own rules of the game on scientists, which would have allowed transforming scientific organisations into profit-making enterprises like any other firm. Thorstein Veblen (1957, p. 62) lamented: 'the university is conceived as a business house dealing in merchantable knowledge. Placed under the governing hand of a captain of erudition, whose office it is to turn the means in hand to account in the largest feasible output'.

What makes the Ukrainian situation specific is the fact that in addition to the attempts of politicians (people vested with political power) and business people (people vested with economic power) to undermine the autonomy and integrity of scientific institutions, national institutions of science are weak compared with foreign institutions of science. The fact that Ukrainian scholars consider the publication of their contributions abroad as a first-best choice means that there is no 'game' at the national level, i.e. little or no interaction supported by national institutions of science. The situation in economic sciences is a case in point.

In the West, economics has some features of a paradigmatic science. Thomas Kuhn (1972, p. 88) defines scientific paradigm as 'the body of beliefs (one) could take for granted'. The body of beliefs that mainstream economists tend to take for granted includes 'stable preference, rational choice, and equilibrium structures' (Eggertsson, 1990, p. 5). For an emerging economy that is far from conditions of stability, these assumptions seem to be too restrictive. Several problems that the transitional economy confronts—in the midst of the military conflict and related trade wars—simply cannot be seen, let alone properly understood, through the lens of neoclassical economics. Attempts to remain within the range of beliefs that the other mainstream economists would share also explains the drift into predominantly applied research that avoids asking difficult theoretical questions.

In the East, economists have their own priorities regarding the topics that are important and publishable. The ideas of sovereignty and empire-building—political, but also economic—attract Russian social scientists' attention. For instance, eLibrary indexes 227 articles on the topic 'sovereign democracy' and 163 articles on the topic 'sovereign market'.[146] The issue of sovereignty certainly rings a bell for those interested in studying the process of nation-state building, but it must be first disentangled from the context of empire-building.

Several obstacles prevent Ukrainian economists from contributing to this discussion of sovereignty in Russia, however. First, the

---

146 The search was conducted on May 2, 2017. As indicated in the book's general Introduction, eLibrary (http://elibrary.ru/defaultx.asp) is the largest on-line depository and indexing service (RiNTs, Russian Index of Scientific Citation) of Russian-language scholarly publications.

on-going military conflict between Russia and Ukraine (Chapter 5) undermines incentives for any cooperation, including in science. Rational economic arguments hardly help when the issues of human dignity are at stake (see Chapter 7). Second, the Russian discussion focuses almost exclusively on the sovereignty of Russia itself. Russia aims to enhance its sovereignty at the expense of the sovereignty of the other countries, thus attempting to rebuild an empire, as the above-mentioned conflict confirms. Third, sovereignty represents only one form of nation-state building. In this regard, Michel Foucault differentiates between sovereignty, discipline and security as three alternative techniques that power holders may use in order to assert their control over a country. 'Sovereignty is exercised within the borders of a territory, discipline is exercised on the bodies of individuals, and security is exercised over a whole population' (Foucault, 2007, p. 11). In other words, the exclusive focus on sovereignty prevents social scientists from studying the entire range of techniques of power that underpin the process of nation-state building. The issues of territory (including the question of reshaping or protecting national borders) then, overshadow everything related to the control of human bodies and various processes.

The concept of security looks particularly promising for economic research. With its help, one can show, for instance, how to control individuals and their behaviour by shaping interactions on the market in a particular manner. Instead of explicitly allowing or prohibiting certain actions, it is possible to design interactions on the market in such a manner that they will bring outcomes desired by the power holders. The strategy of gate-keeping is a case in point: by controlling access to the market (or any other field of interactions) the power holders decide the ratio of buyers and sellers, which enables them to capture rents and to further enhance their power (Oleinik, 2015b; see also Section III of Chapter 5). The power elite in Russia were quick to realise the potential of gate-keeping and to seize its benefits. The builders of the Ukrainian nation-state may still need to learn how to use gate-keeping in the interests of this endeavour (see Chapter 9 for a discussion of potential positive effects of imposing temporary restrictions on the access to the national market). The concept of security also allows for finding strategies of resistance to the power that takes mostly unobservable and indirect forms.

This chapter provides some evidence to suggest that the sciences in Ukraine are still not embedded in national institutions and, consequently, Ukrainian scholars play the game whose rules they neither set nor influence. More specifically, the present chapter discusses the following research questions using economic sciences as an example. First, *what characterises current patterns in the publication activity of economists affiliated with research organisations in Ukraine*? Second, *how do these patterns relate to particular problems and challenges that Ukraine currently faces*?

II. Current state of economic sciences in Ukraine

This chapter uses bibliometric data about publications of scholars affiliated with Ukrainian scientific organisations in the West, in Russia, and in the national scholarly journals. As a source of information about publications of economists with a Ukrainian affiliation in Western Europe and North America, the Web of Science Core Collection (WoS), was chosen. The WoS is the most respected and authoritative source of information on publications in the most rigorously peer-reviewed periodicals in the world. More specifically, 35 journals in economics with the highest impact factor in 2014 were selected for the study. The search covered the period from 1991 through 2016.

eLibrary was used as a source of information about contributions of economists affiliated with Ukrainian research centres to the scholarly debates in the East, namely, in Russia. Compared with the WoS, eLibrary is far less selective: it includes most periodicals published in the Russian language. Ten economic journals with the highest citation index in this database were searched: *Voprosy Ekonomiki, Mirovaia ekonomika i mezhdunarodnye otnosheniia, Rossiiskii zhurnal menedzhmenta, Journal of Institutional Studies, Finansy,*

Problemy prognozirovaniia, Problemy teorii i praktiki upravleniia, Obshchestvo i ekonomika, Innovatsii and *Menedzhment v Rossii i za rubezhom*. The search covered the period from 2003 through 2015.[147]

Ukraine does not have a national database of scientific publications similar to eLibrary in Russia or Persée in France. Thus, contributions published in a single Ukrainian periodical, *Aktual'ni Problemy Ekonomiki* (Actual Problems of Economics), were analysed. This journal arguably has the highest international visibility (being indexed in the second largest Western database of scholarly publications, Scopus, and, for a short period of time—in 2008–2012, in the WoS),[148] but it is run by a Ukrainian research centre and publishes contributions mostly in Ukrainian (contributions in English and Russian are also accepted, yet they constitute a relatively small fraction of the published materials—13% of the shortlisted papers from this periodical). The 2011 impact factor was 0.039 (317th rank out of 321 in economics). The 2015 Scimagio Journal Rank was 0.124 and H-Index (the Hirsch index)—6.[149] Taking into consideration that *Actual Problems of Economics* is a monthly publication, the full dataset covered the period from 2008 through 2015, which produced a sample of 5,033 publications. Its subsets, however, were also used.

147 eLibrary was created in 1999 and it does not offer a comprehensive coverage for the early period of its existence.

148 More recently, another economic journal published in Ukraine was included in the WoS. *Ekonomichnyi Chasopys-XXI* (Economic Annals-XXI) has been indexed in the WoS since 2016. Its 2015 Scimago Journal Rank, 0.239, actually exceeds that of *Actual Problems of Economics* (http://www.scimagojr.com/journalsearch.php?q=21100310035&tip=sid&clean=0).

149 http://www.scimagojr.com/journalsearch.php?q=19700167903&tip=sid.

Table 8.1 'Number of scholarly publications included in the Web of Science Core Collection, selected countries, 1991–2016'

	Ukraine	Russia	Poland	Lithuania	Romania	Kazakhstan	Canada
Total, 1991–2016	149,636	840,150	502,206	43,615	174,838	13,143	1,721,835
Of those in past five years, 2012–2016	36,767	226,912	177,844	16,511	78,245	6,897	485,109
Share of publications in 2012–2016 in the Total	24.6%	27%	35.4%	37.9%	44.8%	52.5%	28.2%
Key disciplines, 1991–2016	Materials, physics condensed, physics applied	Physics applied, physics, physics condensed	Chemistry physical, materials, electrical engineering	Electrical engineering, materials, physics applied	Electrical engineering, materials, chemistry	Physics applied, chemistry, physics particles	Electrical engineering, biochemistry, neurosciences
Share of publications in the key disciplines, % of the Total	31.3%	16.8%	16.8%	19.9%	23.9%	15.1%	13.8%
Total in the area of economics, 1991–2016	1,652	4,028	4,048	1,846	7,372	371	21,110
% of Total 1991–2016	1.1%	0.5%	0.8%	4.2%	4.2%	2.8%	1.2%
Publications in the area of economics, 2012–2016	716	2,558	2,370	901	4,026	325	6,111

% of publications in 2012–2016	1.95%	1.1%	1.3%	5.5%	5.15%	4.7%	1.3%
Publications in the area of economics in 2012–2016 to the total number of publications in the area of economics, 1991–2016	43.3%	63.5%	58.5%	48.8%	54.6%	87.6%	28.9%

Source: Web of Science Core Collection.[150]

Legend: Materials refer to materials science multidisciplinary; Physics condensed – to physics of condensed matter; Physics – to physics multidisciplinary; Electrical engineering – to engineering electrical and electronic; Chemistry – to chemistry multidisciplinary; Physics particles – to quantum physics and Biochemistry – to biochemistry and molecular biology.

150 The search was conducted on May 1, 2017 using the country's name as a search term in the 'address' field, e.g. ADDRESS: (Ukraine).

The data about scholarly contributions of researchers affiliated with Ukrainian scientific organisations in the West (the WoS), in the East (eLibrary), and in their own country (*Actual Problems of Economics*) was analysed using methods of descriptive statistics and content analysis. 'Content analysis is a research technique for making replicable and valid inferences from texts (or other meaningful matter) to the contexts of their use' (Krippendorff, 2004, p. 18). In the circumstances, titles of the shortlisted contributions were content-analysed using the computer program QDA Miner with the module WordStat. The content analysis allowed for the identification of the most common words and their combinations, which, in turn, helped describe common themes in the publications.

Among the articles that scholars affiliated with Ukrainian universities and academic institutions published in scholarly journals indexed in the WoS, economic manuscripts represent a tiny fraction (Table 8.1). This pattern is common for the most post-socialist countries. They all inherited a heavy emphasis on physics, engineering and materials science—these disciplines were prioritised in the socialist system with its focus on the development of military technology and the productive forces. Nevertheless, the share of three core disciplines in the overall scientific output in Ukraine—a third (31.3%)—is significantly higher than in the other countries with a similar historical past. It suggests a more uneven development of research and a more marginalised position of the social sciences, including economics.

Economic sciences made some gains in the past five years (2012–2016), but they do not suffice for changing the overall pattern. Economists in Lithuania, Romania and Kazakhstan have been catching up more successfully. The progress in Kazakhstan in this area is particularly impressive: almost all (87.6%) publications in the area of economics were produced in this country recently, from 2012–2016. Like Ukraine, Kazakhstan is also going through the early stages of nation-state building. As with economists affiliated with research organisations in Ukraine, they actually underperform even compared to the other Ukrainian researchers: they represent 3.3–3.9% of all researchers with advanced academic degrees in this country, but produced 1.95% of publications indexed in the WoS in

2012–2016, i.e. two times less than predicted on the basis of the assumption of equal scientific productivity. Works of economists with a Ukrainian affiliation are not highly visible in eLibrary either.

The situation with publications in top economic journals appears to be even less promising. Scholars affiliated with Ukrainian scientific organisations published 77 articles in top 35 economic journals included in the WoS (in 1991–2015) and 114 articles in top 10 economic journals included in eLibrary (in 2003–2015). The distribution of these contributions by year of publication and periodical title shows that, on one hand, in 2011–2012 and 2014–2015 the number of studies indexed in the WoS actually exceeded the number of studies indexed in eLibrary (Figure 1). More time is needed to confirm if this fact reflects the sustainable re-orientation of Ukrainian economists from the East to the West.

Figure 8.1 'Number of scholarly articles authored by scholars affiliated with organisations in Ukraine published in top 35 economic journals included in the Web of Science Core Collection and in top ten economic journals indexed in eLibrary, 2003–2015'

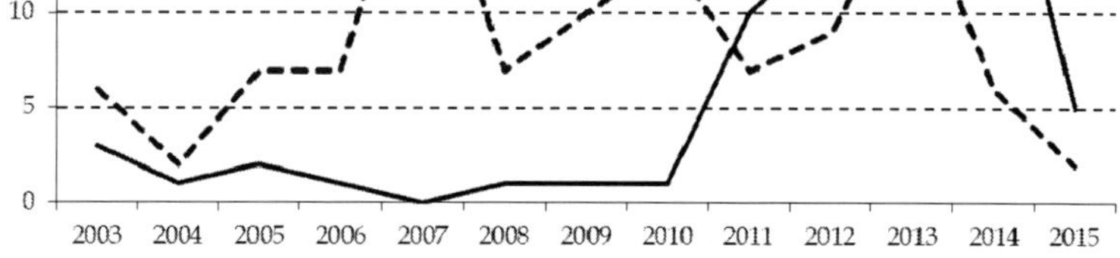

Source: Web of Science Core Collection and eLibrary.[151]

On the other hand, in both cases, publications tend to appear in only a few periodicals from the list of top journals. For instance, 93.5% of all articles written by authors with a Ukrainian affiliation

151 The search was conducted on 29.09.2015.

were published in a single periodical from the WoS list, *Value in Health.* 44% of all articles of scholars from Ukraine appeared in *Innovatsii,* a St. Petersburg based periodical included in eLibrary. These periodicals publish results of mainly applied research in rather narrow areas of economic knowledge (namely, pharma-economics and economics of innovation and technology). Furthermore, all contributions published in *Value of health* were authored by people affiliated with a single research centre, namely Lviv National Medical University, named after Danylo Halytsky. Thus, the visibility of Ukrainian economists abroad can be attributed to a particular culture, and research networks that progressively emerged in few selected places.

The content analysis of publication titles further confirms that the contributions to the WoS refer to the narrow area of pharma-economics. Results reported in Table 8.2 also suggest that priorities set in publications by authors with affiliations in Ukraine differ depending on where they publish their papers, in Russian language periodicals included in eLibrary, or in the national periodical *Actual Problems of Economics.* For instance, references to system approach and the operation of enterprises (i.e., the meso-level in economic analysis, as opposed to micro- and macro-economics) are more common in the contributions addressed to the Ukrainian readers.

Table 8.2 'Frequency of the most popular words in titles of publications authored by scholars affiliated with organisations in Ukraine, the Web of Science, eLibrary (2003–2015) and *Actual Problems of Economics* (2012–2015)'

Web of Science		**eLibrary**		**Actual Problems (in Ukrainian)**		**Actual Problems (in Russian)**	
Ukraine	57	*Ukrainy*	50	*Rozvytku*	61	*Razvitiia*	5
Analysis	26	*Innovatsionn**	21	*Ekonomichn**	44	*Analiz*	4
Cost	22	*Razvitiia*	20	*System**	32	*Aspekty*	4
Treatment	19	*Problemy*	15	*Ekonomiky*	25	*Upravleniia*	4
Pharmaeconomics	9	*Ekonomiki*	10	*Upravlinnia*	23	*Ekonomicheskikh*	4
COPD (chronic obstructive pulmonary diseases)	8	*Perspektivy*	9	*Formuvannia*	23	*Innovatsionnykh*	3
Costs	8	*Rossii*	7	*Pidpryiemstv**	20	*Menedzhmenta*	3
Evaluation	8	*Ekonomichesk**	11	*Analiz*	19	*Sistem*	3
Therapy	8	*Deiatel'nosti*	6	*Krain**	17	*Effectivnosti*	3
Patients	7	*Promyshlennosti*	5	*Innovatsi**	13		
Based	5	*SNG* (Commonwealth of Independent States)	5	*Ukrainy*	11		
Drugs	5	*Sostoianie*	5	*Umovakh*	10		
Effectiveness	5	*Formirovaniia*	5	*Diial'nosti*	9		
Formulary	5			*Politiky*	9		

Divergent emphases in the contributions made to the WoS, eLibrary and the Ukrainian audience are further illustrated by the most frequent clusters of words in publication titles (Figures 8.2–

8.4). In the case of eLibrary, one of the clusters contains the words 'industry' (*promyshlennosti* – *промышленности*), 'integrational' (*integratsionnykh* – *интеграционных*), 'Russia' (*России*) and 'Ukraine' (*Украины*). It can be interpreted as an indication that Russian-language publications of Ukrainian economists discuss (or rather discussed) the idea of a closer integration of the Ukrainian economy with the Russian economy; with specific emphasis on the industry. The expression 'industry of Ukraine' (*promyshlennost' Ukrainy* – *промышленность Украины*) is among the most common in this dataset, with the frequency of 4.

Figure 8.2 'Dendrogram reflecting co-occurrence of the most popular words in titles of articles authored by economists with a Ukrainian affiliation, eLibrary, fragment'

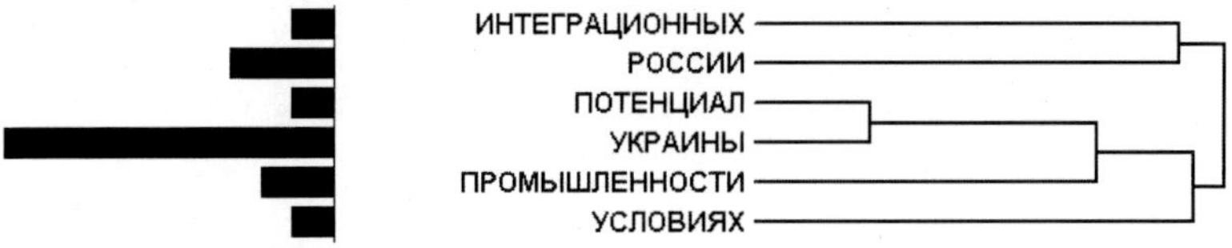

Legend: similarity index: Cosine theta.

In the case of the WoS, 'Ukraine', 'treatment' and 'cost' form a common cluster. This finding further confirms that the contributions made by Ukrainian economists to the English-language economic sciences have an applied and rather narrowly focused character.

Figure 8.3 'Dendrogram reflecting co-occurrence of the most popular words in titles of articles authored by economists with a Ukrainian affiliation, the WoS, fragment'

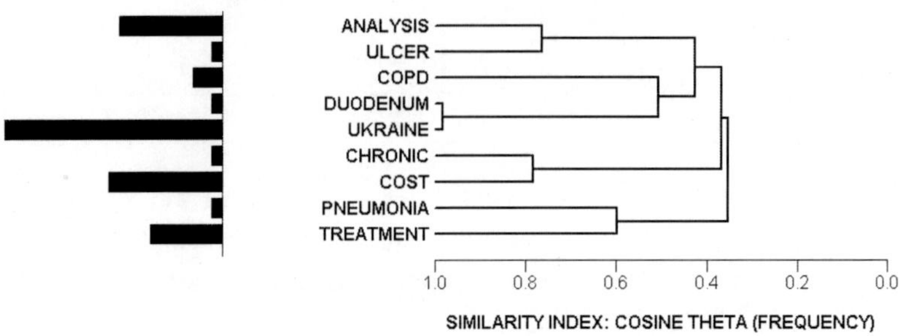

In the contributions to *Actual Problems of Economics* in 2012–2015, emphasis is made on 'governmental' (*derzhavnoi – державної*), 'policy' (*polityky – політики*) and 'instruments' (*instrumenty – інструменти*). When addressing the national audience, Ukrainian economists discuss government policies and tend to look at the economy through the lens of a system approach (the expression 'economic system' is one of the most common in this dataset with the frequency of 6). Those issues are of relatively little interest to the potential audience in the West or in the East. However, the building of the national market as an integral part of the nation-state (see Chapter 9) is impossible without addressing them.

Figure 8.4 'Dendrogram reflecting co-occurrence of the most popular words in titles of articles published in *Actual Problems of Economics*, fragment'

Legend: similarity index: Cosine theta.

III. Need for Ukrainian economists' greater contribution to nation-state building

Works of Ukrainian economists are highly visible neither in the West nor in the East. An explanation for this lack of visibility (not to speak about the impact of their works measured, inter alia, by the number of citations) refers to the differences in priorities at the international and national levels. Internationally, economists affiliated with Ukrainian research institutions found a rather narrow niche of purely applied research in very specific branches of economics. The search for concepts that would help better understand the process of nation-building in Ukraine does not have much chance to attract the attention of foreign readers unless this search is fuelled by healthy and active discussions at the national level. It is not enough to say that particular concepts or models are needed—they have to be proposed, criticised, eventually rejected, and subsequently improved, etc. There is currently no national economic debate in Ukraine, as the content analysis shows, on the economic theory and consequences of war (which is quite surprising, keeping in mind the annexation of Crimea and the ongoing military conflict in Eastern Ukraine occurred within this timeframe). Only one article was published on the related issues in 2016 in *Actual Problems of Economics*. There were few publications in *Actual Problems of Economics* discussing corruption, the other urgent problem that Ukraine faces. The list of omitted, forgotten or tabooed topics does not stop here.

The content analysis of the complete dataset of publications that appeared in *Actual Problems of Economics* in 2008–2016, i.e. after the 2008 financial crisis that particularly affected Ukraine—see subsection I.2 of Chapter 9, shows a more nuanced picture. Since *Actual Problems of Economics* publishes papers in several languages—Ukrainian, Russian and English, English versions of the publication titles were used at this stage, in order to increase the compatibility of the data.

A dictionary based on substitution was created for the purposes of content analysis. It includes eight codes: two codes referring to two major external markets for Ukraine, 'Europe' (the European Union) and 'Eurasia' (the Customs' Union); two codes describing the opposite orientations of the national economy, outward ('Openness') and inward ('Protectionism') and four codes created for key sectors of the Ukrainian economy, namely, 'Agriculture', 'Metal' (metallurgy, ferrous and non-ferrous), 'Processing industry' (machine-building) and 'Lumber' (timber industry; see Section III of Chapter 9). For instance, code 'Openness' includes words 'globali?at*', 'import', 'export', 'WTO' and expressions 'global_market*' and 'world_market*'.[152] Code 'Processing' includes words

152 * refers to any character or a combination of characters; ? refers to any character.

'machine-building' and 'processing' and so forth. After manually creating the theoretically informed dictionary, the content analysis was carried out in an automated regime: relevant codes were attached to the titles that contain the words and expressions included in this dictionary.

The analysis of the coding co-occurrences allows for the identification of several clusters (Figure 8.5). Agriculture emerges as Ukraine's 'hard currency'. Its products can be used in the trade with both the EU and the Customs' Union. Agriculture is also frequently mentioned together with open economy, as suggested by the connection between code 'Agriculture' and code 'Openness'. On the other hand, timber industry appears to be associated with both protectionist and free-trade policies, as will be discussed in greater detail in Section III of Chapter 9. The position of code 'Metal' indicates that the European market may be relatively more important for this industry than the market of the Customs' Union.

Figure 8.5 'Three-dimensional map of the coding co-occurrences, *Actual Problems of Economics*, 2008–2016'

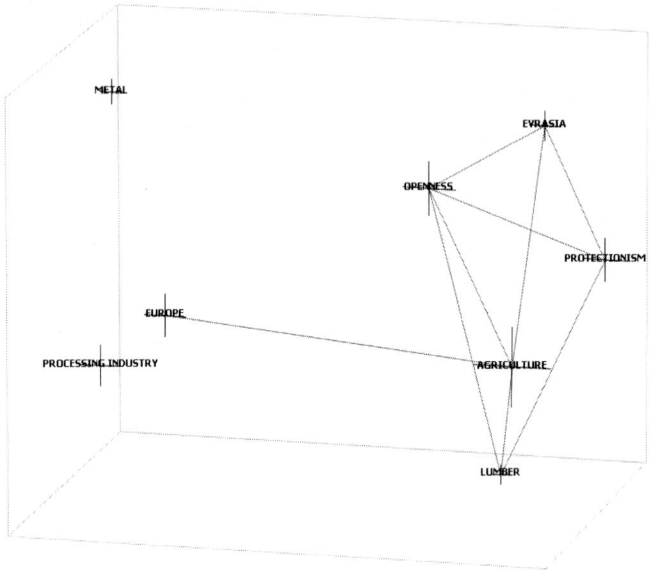

Legend: Stress = 0.155, pseudo R^2 = 0.963. This figure showing the coding co-occurrences in the window of 20 words (the average length of the publication title) was produced using WordStat v. 6.1.24. The size of the crosses reflects the relative frequencies of the codes, with 'Agriculture' coming first.

The emerging picture does not easily fit in standard textbook models. The search for a right combination of elements of protectionism and open economy is not an easy task but requires collective efforts of Ukrainian economists—their action in concert (see Chapter 6). In the present circumstances, Ukrainian economists have three options: (i) to accept rules of the game on the Western market for scholarly publications by deliberately omitting most issues relevant to the process of nation-state building; (ii) to accept rules of the game in the Russian academia by denouncing the idea of the Ukrainian nation-state and ignoring several important aspects of nation-state building and, (iii) to develop their own intellectual space for discussing economic aspects of nation-state building in the Ukrainian context, as well as in the other national contexts (see the general Introduction to this book, Chapters 3, 6 and 10). By choosing the third option, Ukrainian social scientists in general and economists in particular, would be able to intellectually contribute to the ongoing process of nation-state building in their country. A nation-state without its own intellectual life and debates is hardly possible.

The option of developing the space for Ukrainian economic debates does not exclude the publication of Ukrainian economists' works either in the West or in the East. The opposite is true: the existence of vivid and healthy intellectual debates at the national level would eventually attract the attention of foreign scholars and increase their willingness to learn more about these debates. After all, the issues of nation-state building could be of interest not only in the post-soviet countries, but also in Latin America, Africa, Middle East, and the Balkans, to list just a few macro-regions.

Conclusions

Practical steps toward creating a space for economic debates at the national level might potentially include the following. First, the creation of a national scientific database indexing publications in the leading Ukrainian scholarly journals will reduce information costs of searching relevant information. The experience of eLibrary suggests that such a database shall not be too inclusive, nevertheless. On the other hand, it is necessary to avoid considerations of personal and group loyalties when selecting periodical titles (and, eventually, monographs and dissertations) to be indexed in the database.

Second, there is a need for reforming the process of peer-review. Open intellectual debates are possible when the only criterion for participating in them refers to the merit of a contribution as opposed to the considerations of network membership, administrative resources, and so forth. The system of random selection of reviewers might eventually help minimise the impact of reviewers' personal and group biases (Oleinik, 2014). The other solution refers to open on-line review as a step preceding the formal publication.

Third, in the current conditions, research subventions and grants are scarce. The scarcity of research funds only increases the importance of transparency and fairness in their distribution. In order to minimise the impact of personal/group loyalties when awarding research grants, it is necessary to rely on open competition and the reformed process of peer-review, as outlined above (Oleinik, 2014, chapter 3; see also the general Conclusion of this book).

Fourth, truly free debates are impossible without the security of jobs in academia. The system of tenure (permanent employment after a 4–6 year trial period) represents an institutional precondition for academic freedom (Oleinik, 2014, chapter 4). The loss of tenure occurs either as a result of a serious infraction of the scholarly ethics or in the conditions of economic force majeure. Scientists in Ukraine, similarly to the other post-Soviet scientists, currently have no job security: their contracts can be terminated at any moment. Few dare to criticise the state of the Ukrainian economy and economic thought in these circumstances.

Fifth, concerted efforts are needed for popularising alternative solutions to the existing economic problems via the mechanism of Op-Ed commentaries written by economists for the general public. Members of the general public do not necessary have a good understanding of economic processes (populists of various sorts often capitalise on this ignorance). Based on the author's experience of publishing Op-Ed commentaries in the leading mass media of both Ukraine and Russia, the relative readership in the former case tends to be lower, all other conditions being equal. In other words, a popular demand for economic discussions is not 'natural', but needs to be created by conscious efforts, like anything else.

To summarise, the way to the West for Ukraine might well have its beginning in building the space of intellectual debates in general, and economic debates in particular, at the national level. Without the deep embeddedness of economic thought in national institutions of science, chances to succeed outside few narrow niches are minimal, if they exist at all.

Chapter 9
'The national market in the making'

Introduction

The recent economic development of Ukraine is by no means a success story. When the Soviet economy entered a period of stagnation in the 1970–1980s, the economic downturn took particularly manifest forms in Ukraine. The Ukrainian economy was, at that time, underperforming even by Soviet standards. For instance, Ukraine's national income—this indicator was preferred in the Soviet Union to Gross Domestic Product (GDP)—grew by 39% from 1970 to 1977, which is less than the Soviet average (+46%) and the corresponding figure for Russia (+47%; Tsentral'noe Statisticheskoe Upravlenie SSSR, 1978, p. 404). A similar situation was observed with the dynamics of industrial production (in Ukraine, the industry grew 95-fold between 1913 and 1977, whereas the Soviet average was 145-fold and the Russian industry grew 144-fold; Ibid., p. 126) and retail trade (its turnover increased by 921% between 1940 and 1977 in Ukraine and by 934% in the Soviet Union as a whole; Ibid., p. 451). Only Ukraine's agriculture fared relatively better, growing by 352% between 1913 and 1977 against 347% on average and 308% in Russia (Ibid., p. 205). The fact that Soviet statistics were not quite reliable and valid is of little relevance here since similar omissions and flaws supposedly characterised statistical figures for all the countries of the former Soviet Union.

After the fall of the Soviet Union, the shape of the Ukrainian economy only worsened—not only in relative, but also in absolute terms. In 2014, the Ukrainian economy was still smaller than in 1990. Using data from the State Statistics Service of Ukraine (SSSU), the country's GDP in 2014 can be estimated at 98.8% of the 1990 level.[153] GDP per capita is even further from the 1990 level.

153 Calculations of Alexander Valchyshen, the Head of Research and a Fixed Income Analyst at Investment Capital Ukraine LLC, using the SSSU data

'Ukraine's GDP per capita is still only 65% of what it was on the eve of the break-up of the Soviet Union. With 6,500 EUR at PPP, it corresponds to a mere 23% of the EU average, making Ukraine the second poorest country in Europe (after Moldova and followed by Kosovo)' (Adarov, Astrov, Havlik, Hunya, Landesmann & Podkaminer, 2015, p. 6). In other words, after 25 years of independence, the Ukrainian economy is still in worse shape than when it did not have an autonomous status.

The military conflict with Russia that began in 2014 (Chapter 5) caused an additional blow to the Ukrainian economy. In addition to the losses of infrastructure, the military confrontation undermined the trade between the two countries (Russia was Ukraine's key trade partner from 2009 to 2012). According to one estimate, 'the military conflict in Donbas reduced Ukraine's GDP by 2.5% [in 2014], including 1.9% due to the decline in the Donetsk and Luhansk regions and another 0.6% due to contagion effects' (Ibid., p. 14). Loans from the international financial institutions are partly alleviating the effect of the war, but the country is still expected to bear the full costs of confronting the military aggression. The payment of the price of the war is simply postponed to a later date and, thus, its economic effects will continue to be felt even after 'freezing' the conflict.[154]

As elsewhere in this book, the Russian case is used as a point of comparison in this chapter as well. In addition to being the parties of the ongoing military conflict, Ukraine and Russia have the largest economies of all the countries of the former Soviet Union. The GDP in both countries followed a somewhat similar path since 1991 (Figure 9.1), even if the Russian economy performed relatively better and now exceeds its 1990 level.

(https://eimg.pravda.com/files/4/8/4861068-state-budget.xlsx accessed March 21, 2017).

154 As of the time of writing, this outcome—a 'frozen' conflict of the type observed in Transnistria—seems to be the most likely.

Figure 9.1 'GDP growth (% to the previous year), Ukraine and Russia, 1991–2016'

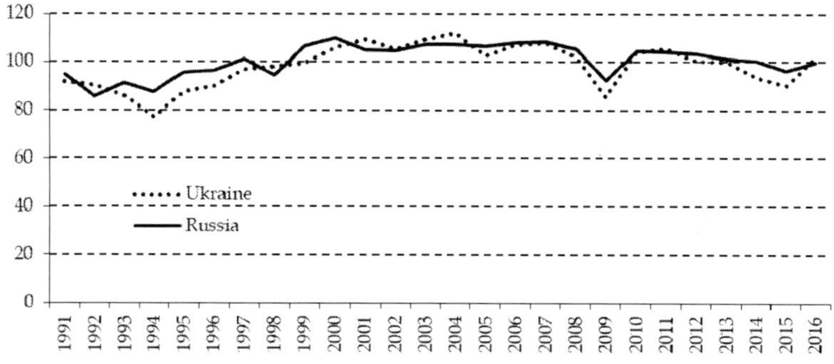

Source: World Bank, 2017.

Before the current crisis that affected both economies, the growth of the Russian economy has been propelled, on one hand, by oil and natural gas rents and, on the other hand, by domestic consumption. Clifford Gaddy and Barry Ickes (2005) note that oil and natural gas rents are correlated with Russia's GDP. The World Bank defines oil and natural gas rents as the difference between the value of crude oil and natural gas production at world prices and total costs of production (World Bank, 2017). In the 2000s, the share of oil and natural gas rents in Russia's GDP was between 10 and 15%. High oil and natural gas prices fuelled a boom in consumer spending, making domestic consumption a second source of economic growth in this country. By restricting and regulating access to two of the most dynamic sectors of the Russian economy—the oil and natural gas sector and the retail trade, the Russian power elite has been able to dominate businesses—national and foreign alike, by virtue of a constellation of interests in these markets (Oleinik, 2011a; Oleinik, 2015a; Oleinik, 2015b). In exchange for access to the markets and for the operation in the conditions of limited competition, businesses have been willing to contribute a part of the rents that they captured to group and individual endeavours of the Russian power elite.

What are the drivers of the Ukrainian economy? Ukraine does not possess significant oil and natural gas deposits. Consequently, oil and natural gas rents did not exceed 3% of this country's GDP, even when world prices of these commodities were high. There is also a substantial difference in the institutional environments in which the two economies operate. Russia restricted access to the national market and extracts administrative rents (rents captured by a gate-keeper) in addition to natural resources rents. 'Ukraine has a more open economy than Russia, and its trade orientation outside of the old Soviet Union is substantial' (Havrylyshyn, 2014, p. 180). This chapter discusses drivers—both existing and potential, of the Ukrainian economy. It is argued that *the strengthening of the national market may help transform the negative dynamics of Ukraine's economy*. Protectionist measures in this case have a temporary and forced character. Furthermore, the danger of the abuses of access control by the power elite has to be explicitly taken into account when adapting protectionist measures to the needs of nation-state building in Ukraine.

I. Externally driven economy

Ukraine has a long tradition of open economy. In Kievan Rus', international trade provided a major source of income for its rulers and population (see subsection 1.2.a in Chapter 1). Kievan Rus' emerged at the crossroads of trade routes, connecting, on one hand, Northern and Southern Europe ('from the Varangians to the Greeks' route) and, on the other hand, Eastern Europe to Asia. Kievan Rus' contributed to the international trade of furs, amber, honey, wax, grains and slaves (Hrushevsky, 1991, pp. 101, 258, 297; Subtelny, 2009, pp. 11, 22). More substantially, Kievan Rus' controlled these trade routes by performing the role of a gate-keeper of some kind. The Princes taxed goods transported through the territory of Kievan Rus' and offered protection and support to the traders willing to accept their conditions. As in the other early states, protection involved eliminating or neutralising the enemies of their clients (Tilly, 1985, p. 181). To offer protection, the Princes naturally needed armies, *druzhiny*, and regular military confrontations with the competing providers of similar services. In these circumstances, armed conflict was an integral part of negotiations of terms of trade agreements (Hedlund, 2005, p. 32), which echoes a more general observation made by Karl Polanyi (2001, p. 62) that 'external trade is, originally, more in the nature of adventure, exploration, hunting, piracy, and war than of barter'.

Modalities of transportation and trade routes have significantly changed since the 11th-12th centuries. Nevertheless, Ukraine still enjoys a central position in some transportation networks; for instance, in the network of pipelines connecting Russian oil and natural gas fields to the European customers. The network was built in the 1970s-1980s, when all key decisions were made in Moscow. The fall of the Soviet Union led to the emergence of several decision-makers on the post-Soviet space, namely, in Moscow and in Kyiv. Some actors in Ukraine attempted to use the situation of a bilateral monopoly (Russia has a monopoly over oil and natural gas fields whereas Ukraine—over the pipelines network) to their advantage, i.e. to capture a gate-keeper's rent (see Chapter 5 for a discussion of the organisation of this market). In the 1990s and the early 2000s they were rather successful. The Ukrainian government did not control the gate-keepers, allowing the significant accumulation of resources in private hands (the owners of various intermediaries from 'Itera' to 'RosUkrEnergo') and, thus, contributing to the spread of corruption in the country (Kuzio, 2012, p. 434) and to the conservation of energy inefficient businesses (Kuzmin, Shpak & Pyrog, 2016). The construction of pipelines bypassing Ukraine, the 'Blue Stream' and the 'Nord Stream', significantly weakened the bargaining position of the Ukrainian gate-keepers.

The gate-keepers in Ukraine never acted in concert, since they were private businesses connected with competing political groups. For instance, Dmytro Firtash, who controlled 'RosUkrEnergo', was a creation of President Leonid Kuchma. Oleksiy Ivchenko, one of the key figures in 'Itera', supported Ukrainian nationalists and President Viktor Yushchenko, whose relationships with the predecessor, President Kuchma, were complex to say the least (Kuzio, 2012, p. 434). It means, first, that the rents captured by the gate-keepers have been neither controlled by the government—let alone civil society organisations, nor fully used in the interests of nation-state building. Second, the gate-keepers did not really restrict access to the market in Ukraine or through its territory. Since the mid-1990s, when President Kuchma implemented 'shock therapy' policies, Ukraine has been one the most open economies in the world with the share of external trade (export and import combined) consistently exceeding the volume of its GDP (Figure 9.2). Kuchma's shock therapy is believed to be more radical and closer to the standards of neoliberalism than reforms carried out by the government of Boris Yeltsin and Yegor Gaidar in the early 1990s in Russia (Havrylyshyn, 2014, p. 175).

Figure 9.2 'Trade as % of GDP, Ukraine and Russia, 1991–2015'

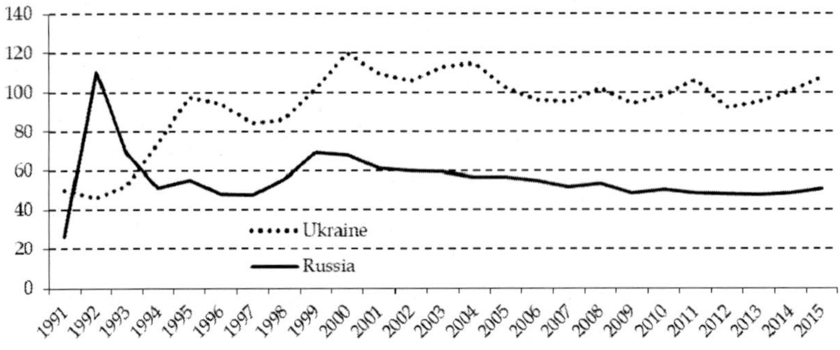

Source: World Bank, 2017.

Open economy has undeniable benefits, increasing productivity as a result of a deeper division of labour, and creating incentives to modernise. Thorstein Veblen considers the case of the German economy, which was relatively backward in the 19th century compared with the other European economies. He notes that 'it is apparently in commerce and the improvements in transportation that contact with the more advanced countries of the West first provoke movements of adjustment to the new state of things' (Veblen, 1939, p. 150). Today's Ukrainian economy also lags behind the developed economies and badly needs 'movements of adjustment'. At the same time, the high openness of the Ukrainian economy has also had three other consequences that undermine black-and-white thinking: the weakness of internal economic actors, the dependence of the situation in the Ukrainian economy on the situation in the world commodities markets, and its vulnerability to the use of the market as a weapon in a conflict situation.

I.1 External and internal actors of economic modernisation

The Ukrainian economy has been undergoing significant structural changes since this country declared independence in 1991. In 2001, the share of agriculture in the gross value added (GVA) was 16.1%; twelve years later—9.3%. The share of real estate and services for businesses increased from 6.9% to 12.1% of the GVA. The share of industry in the GVA decreased from 30.2% to 25.7% (Kuzmin et al., 2012). Such changes seem to be indicative of the transition toward a service-oriented, post-industrial economy. In Ukraine, however, the process of economic modernisation is completely externally driven. Internal actors, including the government and national businesses, have little say in this process, let alone control it.

Two forces determine parameters of economic modernisation in Ukraine: the international institutions, namely the International Monetary Fund (IMF), and the external markets—first of all, the commodities markets. The shock therapy in the mid-1990s was designed and carried out with the assistance of the IMF. The IMF, on more than one occasion, gave conditional loans to the Ukrainian government. As of the end of February 2017, the Ukrainian government served as a guarantor of IMF's loans totalling to 6.28 billion USD and as a direct recipient of IMF's loans totalling to 6.88 billion USD (Ministry of Finance of Ukraine, 2017). Taken together, IMF's loans amount to 18.35% of Ukraine's internal and external debt or 14.5% of the country's GDP in 2015 (90.615 billion USD; World Bank, 2017). IMF's loans are conditional: the applicant is expected, in exchange, to implement specific policies ranging from the 'Washington Consensus, as formulated by John Williamson (1990), focusing on three basic IMF requirements: a fully financed budget, a realistic exchange rate, and a recapitalisation of the banking system' (Åslund, 2009, p. 377) to more far-reaching demands for structural reform.

As stated in the introduction to this chapter, the Ukrainian economy has yet to reach its 1990 level. The next subsection contains some additional material, suggesting that policies inspired by the Washington consensus did not work quite as expected in the Ukrainian case. The reliance on external actors as the only drivers of economic modernisation may cause the weakness of the internal actors or even suppress them. Ukraine did produce quite a few business empires—all owned by so called 'oligarchs', but none of them appears to be willing and prepared to become an agens movens of economic modernisation and nation-state building.

Anders Åslund (2008, p. 157) rightly observes that compared to Russia, where 'the Russian state under Putin has defeated the oligarchs and re-imposed a strong (albeit highly corrupt) centralised political control', Ukraine 'is a competitive oligarchy, and accordingly a much more lively and open society'. The Ukrainian oligarchs compete for influence on the government. The problem is that under the currently existing arrangement, the government has a quite limited capacity for developing and implementing economic policies. It plays a mostly technical role in implementing blueprints prepared by the external actors or reacting to external shocks.

Furthermore, these oligarchs have opposing interests and views on the country's future. According to one account, an 'Eastern-Ukrainian oligarchy of Russian identity, who are interested in increasing exports and would like to achieve increasingly strong positions in the international markets... The other major economic interest group is more interested in the commercial, financial and food industry sector connected with international capital. As for their identity, they are Ukrainians who—contrary to the first group—mainly support growth in imports. Their natural allies are foreign producers exporting to the Ukraine, multinational companies and the population with purchasing power to consume' (Virág, 2012, p. 627).

Lastly, interests of the Ukrainian oligarchs tend to be highly circumstantial and changing in function of the situation in the external markets (Åslund, 2009, p. 384). No oligarchic group has a vested interest in modernising the Ukrainian economy as a whole and regardless of the global market dynamics. Internal economic actors did not emerge as leaders in nation-state building in either Russia or Ukraine. In the former case, they are suppressed by the all-mighty State. In the latter case, the oligarchs have more leeway but the overwhelming influence of the external actors on the country's economic policies simply makes their and the government's input in policy optional at best.

I.2 Dependence on the situation in the world commodities markets

The openness of Ukraine's economy made it vulnerable to the cycles in the global market dynamics. The economy either tends to unexpectedly overheat, as in the mid-2000s when the GDP's growth rates reached a two-digit level (112.1% in 2004), or suddenly collapse, as in the wake of the 2008 global financial crisis when Ukraine's GDP contracted deeper than in most other countries of the world (85.2% in 2009). These ups and downs are unpredictable since they remain outside the control of any particular actor, which complicates the matters even further (Adarov et al., 2015, p. 33; OECD, 2014, p. 32). Åslund (2001, p. 314) admits that no one had predicted the economic boom in Ukraine in the first half of the 2000s. A few years later, it became clear that a cycle in the global steel market has to be given most of the credit for this boom (Åslund, 2008, p. 374). The Ukrainian export that accounts for almost a half of the country's GDP closely follows the dynamics of the world prices for scrap metal and hot rolled steel (Dovbniak, 2009, p. 67), as Figure 9.3 confirms.

Figure 9.3 'Comparative dynamics of the value of Ukrainian exports, in hundred million USD, and hot rolled steel prices, in USD, 1996–2015'

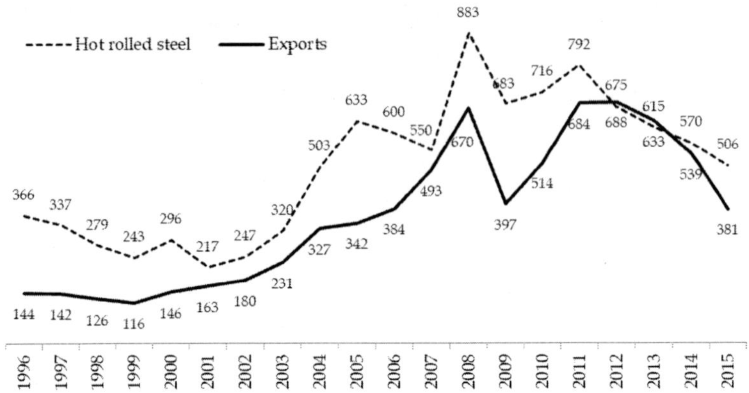

Source: Index Mundi (http://www.indexmundi.com/commodities/?commodity=cold-rolled-steel&months=300&commodity=hot-rolled-steel), the Economist Intelligence Unit (https://store.eiu.com/article.aspx?productid=960000296&articleid=1282943712) and the State Statistics Service of Ukraine.

It must be noted that Ukraine's economy depends specifically on the dynamics of the world commodity markets, i.e. the markets for products with minimal value added as opposed to processed products. The opening of the country's economy at the early stages of economic reforms, when national producers were still in the process of adapting to a new market environment, made them uncompetitive. The competitive sectors of the Ukrainian economy do not radically differ from those that Kievan Rus' had: agriculture (grains, honey) and basic processing of raw materials (furs and wax in the past, metals today). This specialisation represents a common feature of peripheral economies where 'with growing income, demand for imported machinery grows faster that the demand for exported primary materials' (Prebisch, 1959, p. 253). The structure of Ukraine's exports to, and imports from, the European Union is revealing. In 2016, Ukraine's exports to the EU were composed of base metals and articles thereof (22.1% of the total), vegetable products (16.1%), mineral products (12.8%) and machinery and appliances (11.5%). Ukraine imported from the EU mostly machinery and appliances (26.1%), then products of the chemical or allied industries (16.8%), transport equipment (10.7%) and plastic, rubber and articles thereof (7.1%; European Union, 2017).

I.3 Market as a weapon in a conflict situation

The openness of a country's economy may become a liability in the situation of an intensive conflict or a war of aggression like the one that has been waged against Ukraine by Russia since 2014. The existence of imbalances and asymmetries in the trade between parties in a conflict enables one or both of them to use economic levers in addition to purely military means. Before 2014, Ukraine's dependence on imports of natural gas from Russia reached a critical level: they covered up to a half of all needs of Ukrainian businesses and households in natural gas (Zhylyaeva, 2010, p. 57). Russia has a record of price discrimination, i.e. charging different prices in function of the customer's readiness to align with this country's policies (Chapter 5). Needless to say, the price that Ukraine had recently been charged exceeded the average. The painful cuts in the consumption of natural gas and the costly re-orientation to supplies from the European common market contributed to increasing the costs of the war for Ukraine.

In the context of the military confrontation, the openness of Ukraine's economy also had less direct but nevertheless sensitive implications. Before 2014, Eastern Ukraine and Western Ukraine were traditionally oriented to the different external markets, Russian and European correspondingly (Adarov et al., 2015, p. 66). The conflict with Russia contributed to the aggravation of regional divides along these lines: the economy of Left-bank Ukraine suffered from the collapse of the trade with Russia particularly severely (Chuzhykov, Fedirko & Chuzhykov, 2014, p. 31). In other words, the Ukrainian experience suggests that the orientation of regions to different trading partners in an open economy, coupled with the absence of policies of harmonisation at the regional level, has the potential to constitute an economic foundation of regional separatism.

II. The national market: a survival kit or an engine of development?

Between 2014–2016, the negative consequences of the openness of Ukraine's economy outweighed its positive effects. The world prices for hot rolled steel are in decline. The asymmetries that exist in the trade between Ukraine and Russia were used by the latter as an additional lever in the military confrontation. In response, Ukraine imposed restrictions on the trade with Russia, which in turn aggravated divides between the Western and Eastern regions of the country. In these circumstances, the national market, an institution that has been overlooked while opening the country's economy, plays the role of a safety net preventing its total collapse.

II.1 On the brink of a collapse

A series of the linear multiple regressions, method 'Forward' (with the probability of F for entry set at a 0.05 level and for removal at a 0.1 level), were run in order to assess the exact contribution of the national market to the country's economy and to compare this contribution with the effect of the other factors, namely, foreign trade and foreign direct investments (FDI). The regional-level data produced by the State Statistics Service of Ukraine inform this part of the analysis. Since the number of units of observation is relatively small,[155] the regional-level data in Ukraine must be used with caution. However, several precedents show that the analysis of the Ukrainian regional-level data can provide valuable insights (Chuzhykov et al., 2014; Grendash, 2012; Masliy, 2014; Nosova, 2013; OECD, 2014). The Gross Regional Product (GRP) is used as an outcome indicator (originally in billion Ukrainian hryvnas, UAH; Lg10 transformed). Previous studies (OECD, 2014, p. 31) suggest that

155 27 before the annexation of Crimea and the city of Sebastopol by Russia in 2014, 25 currently: 24 regions and the capital city.

among key contributors to economic growth in Ukraine are domestic demand, consumption, investments and net exports. For instance, domestic demand decreased by 26.4% in 2009, which was partly offset by an 11.6% increase in net exports.

In the present study, the contribution of the national market was operationalised through the following indicators: disposable income (originally in billion UAH; Lg10 transformed), average monthly salary (in UAH, Lg10 transformed in 2014), and retail trade turnover (originally in billion UAH; Lg10 transformed). The contribution of investments was operationalised through the financial results of enterprises before taxation (in billion UAH; Lg10 transformed in 2014), fixed capital investments (originally in billion UAH; Lg10 transformed) and foreign direct investments, FDI (originally in billion USD; Ln transformed), that of foreign trade—through total import of goods and total export of goods (originally in thousand USD; Ln transformed), export to import ratio (export coverage), import of goods from and export of goods to Germany and Russia (originally in thousand USD; Ln transformed), import of wood lumber and import of wooden furniture (originally in thousand USD; the latter was Lg10 transformed and the former—Ln transformed; the rationale for including these measures is provided in the next section). In addition, the impact of several other variables was controlled: accumulated total population, salary arrears (originally in billion UAH; Lg10 transformed), Internet penetration (% of the population who reported using the Internet past 12 months), and % of the total surface covered by forests.

Table 9.1 contains the results of the three regressions, for 2013, 2014 and 2015, showing the predictors whose contribution was statistically significant only. Two variables, disposable income and fixed capital investments, were removed from the models in order to address a collinearity problem. The case of disposable income is particularly relevant. This aggregate includes salaries and various transfers, with the exception of taxes and other mandatory payments. Disposable income, a proxy for the size of the national market, was highly correlated with the dependent variable, GRP (r=0.979 in 2013), and with several predictor variables. Leaving the excluded variables aside, the contribution of the national market (domestic consumption) outweighed the effect of the other predictors and controls. The impact of financial results of enterprises, a potential source of investment, was significant in 2013 only, before most businesses went into the red in 2014. Neither export nor import helped Ukrainian regions to cope with the economic crisis in 2013 and 2014. The contribution of export and FDI[156] became significant in 2015 only. Assessed separately, their impact did not exceed that of domestic consumption. The national market prevented a total collapse in the country's economy.

The national market plays the role of a life jacket in times of economic duress. Does it have the potential to become an engine of economic development? The short answer is no. In its present conditions, the national market can neither absorb the redundant output in some sectors, for instance, the machine-building output which used to be exported to the Russian market (Adarov et al., 2015, p. 47), nor increase domestic consumption without simultaneously creating inflationary pressures (OECD, 2014, p. 33). The national market has been relegated to the back stage of economic development for too long, practically since the start of economic reforms in the early 1990s. However, it could potentially perform the role of a driver of economic development, provided that the national market is first prepared for this role with the help of specifically designed and properly implemented economic policies.

156 FDI seem to substitute for the contribution of internal sources of investments, currently dried out.

Table 9.1 'Results of linear multiple regressions to predict the Gross Regional Product (Lg10 transformed) in Ukraine, 2013–2015'

	2013			**2014**			**2015**		
	Unstandardised B	**Std. error**	**Standardised Beta**	**Unstandardised B**	**Std. error**	**Standardised Beta**	**Unstandardised B**	**Std. error**	**Standardised Beta**
Retail trade turnover, Lg10 transformed	0.995***	0.071	0.804	0.933***	0.097	0.726	0.469***	0.087	0.400
Average monthly salary, UAH	0.000099*	0.000036	0.165	0.000134**	0.000035	0.294			
Enterprises' financial results before taxation, UAH billion	0.000009*	0.000003	0.093						
Total exports, Ln transformed							0.105***	0.024	0.356
Foreign Direct Investments, Ln transformed							0.066**	0.018	0.295
Constant	-0.103	0.239		-4.189***	0.894		0.795*	0.297	
R^2	0.977			0.951			0.966		
N	25			25			25		

Legend: results significant at a 0.05 level are marked by *, at a 0.01 level—by **, and at a 0.001 level—by ***.
Source: Derzhavna Sluzhba Statystyky Ukrainy, 2016a, Vol.1, p. 85; Vol. 2, pp. 15, 133, 374.

These policies have some roots in protectionism, but go beyond its old, and to a significant extent, discredited version. In the Ukrainian case, given the high degree of openness of the country's economy, and taking into account the lessons of implementing classical protectionist policies in some other countries, a new version of protectionism may be needed. On one hand, this new version aims to protect the national market, simultaneously maintaining and even increasing Ukraine's presence in the external markets, first of all in Europe and North America. On the other hand, the protectionist policies must be temporary. Since the very beginning, the task of re-opening Ukraine's economy in the progressive stages ought to be set. In other words, protectionism in Ukraine can work if it has a temporary character and is designed as a tool for making national producers more competitive in the external markets.

II.2 Goodwill to an asymmetrical solution

Raúl Prebisch and his fellow Latin American economists associated with the Programa Regional del Empleo para América Latina y el Caribe (PREALC), made the most recent attempt to formulate a comprehensive protectionist policy in the 1960s-1970s.[157] Namely, they promoted import substitution as a strategy for protecting the national market and for correcting disparities that exist between the less developed (peripheral) economies and the developed (central) economies. Prebisch (1959, p. 253) defined import substitution 'as an increase in the proportion of goods that is supplied from domestic sources' and considered it as 'the only way to correct the effects on peripheral growth of disparities in foreign trade elasticity'. The demand for imported machinery 'on the periphery' increases faster than the demand for commodities exported by the peripheral economies, which creates those disparities.

In the present situation, Ukraine has a peripheral economy: this country exports mainly commodities and goods with low value added and imports machinery and goods with high value added.

157 An earlier attempt made in the 17th and 18th centuries by the Mercantilists is thus excluded from consideration here.

Not surprisingly, some Ukrainian economists show interest in the issues of import substitution. For instance, Nataliya Yakymenko (2015, p. 156) from Kharkiv in Eastern Ukraine calls for meeting the country's domestic demand 'mainly through the development of national production, … using protectionist policies'. The process of import substitution was actually taking place in 2015, observes Myroslava Chekh with colleagues from Lviv in Western Ukraine (Chekh, Vasylytsya & Polovska, 2016, pp. 89–90), pointing out that the situation in some industries oriented to the national market, namely the textile industry and the food processing industry. Import substitution may be taking place indeed, but in a spontaneous, uncontrollable and, hence, unpredictable manner.

The other Ukrainian economists go even further, seeing in protectionist policies an element of national sovereignty understood as the government's capacity for formulating an independent economic policy guided by national interests (Melnik, 2015, p. 147). This argument echoes a definition of sovereignty in general, and economic sovereignty in particular, given by John Commons (1959, p. 384): 'sovereignty [is] the collective power of the concern laying down its working rules in the form of the common law, equity and administrative orders, for the purpose of better adjustment of men's transactions in a world of relative scarcity of resources'. Seen from this perspective, economic sovereignty constitutes an integral element of nation-state building. This process is still on-going in Ukraine (see the general Introduction to this book and Chapter 10), which provides an additional reason for being highly sensitive to the issues of this country's economic sovereignty. The national market represents an important element of a nation-state (Smith, 1991, p. 14).

In open economies, the governments have few levers for protecting or promoting particular industries. Governments in countries with the established, developed market economies do not necessarily need to intervene, since the national businesses can compete globally and consider an open economy to be their natural environment. In contrast, governments in countries with the less developed, peripheral market economies need to intervene and to protect the national market before their national businesses get prepared for global competition. The invisible hand of the market does not suffice in these circumstances and must be complemented by the visible hand of the government.

Protectionist policies were extremely popular from the late 1960s into the 1970s. The World Bank not only tolerated them but actually 'expressed considerable sympathy for the approach' (Bruton, 1998, p. 917). And this international organisation had a good reason for sympathising with protectionism since at that time it worked. Two factors help explain why protectionism started to subsequently fall out of fashion. The outward-oriented strategy of promoting export inspired by the experience of the Asian Tigers (Hong Kong, Singapore, South Korea and Taiwan) in the 1970s is one. National producers have no privilege at home. 'The basic notion is to keep the domestic economy open to foreign competition and foreign capital, and to ensure that exports are in no way penalised, if not specifically encouraged' (Ibid., p. 904). The awareness of the risks of rent-seeking by the governments that heavily rely on the visible hand is the other (Rose-Ackerman, 2004).

Counter-arguments can be developed with respect to both of these reasons. First, the outward-oriented strategy also fell out of fashion. It produced expected outcomes mainly in relatively small open economies (given the size of Ukraine's population, 42.6 million as of February 2017, this country has a potentially very large internal market). Similar to import substitution, the outward-oriented strategy does not create an environment conductive to learning. The latter strategy 'fails to appreciate that learning requires conditions that are essentially internal and dependent on the basic characteristics of the society' (Bruton, 1998, p. 903). Second, rent-seeking has more to do with the lack of an adequate response to a more general problem that exists in all economies, namely, 'who monitors the monitors' (Stiglitz, 1994, p. 78), than with import substitution as such.

Both problems with import substitution can potentially be alleviated by imposing temporal limits on protectionism and by reopening Ukraine's economy in the progressive stages, after building the national market and strengthening, with its help, national producers. In parallel with policies of import substitution, efforts to promote exportation have to be made. The promotion of export, especially to the European Union and North America, will create incentives for learning. Is such an asymmetrical situation—a partial openness of Ukraine's economy—defendable and practical? After all, the proposed strategy requires that the country temporarily protects its national market while still having a free access to the key prospective external markets.

Several arguments can be used in defense of the asymmetrical openness. Prebisch (1959, p. 264) offers one. He argues that 'protection has different meanings in the peripheral countries and in the industrial centers. In the former it is, up to a certain point, the instrument for correcting the effects of the disparity in income elasticity of demand for exports of primary commodities and for imports of industrial goods and does not hamper the rate of growth of world trade. In the industrial centers, by contrast, protection of primary production accentuates this disparity and tends to depress peripheral development and to decrease the rate of growth of world trade. The reduction or elimination of such protection at the centers has an implicit element of reciprocity'. As paradoxical as it may seem, in a reciprocal situation there are no duties in the centre, but duties and the other protectionist measures (tariffs, exchange rates, import licenses and so forth) may be simultaneously present in the periphery as a means to alleviate the disparities between the centre and the periphery.

The implementation of such arrangement requires the good will of the Western partners of Ukraine, both in a literal and figurative sense of this word. The acceptance of temporary asymmetrical economic relationships with Ukraine will give the West an opportunity for expressing its solidarity with this country, especially since no new 'Marshall plan' seems to be forthcoming, as of the time of this writing. Instead of (or in addition to) giving credits and providing technical assistance, both parties, Ukraine and the West, would potentially be better off in providing Ukrainian businesses with free access to the Western markets and by accepting Ukraine's protectionist policies during a transition period that may last from a few years to a decade or so. In terms of the costs for the West, both options may be comparable, but the acceptance of the asymmetric solution creates much more powerful incentives for learning.

In a literal sense, goodwill involves restrictions voluntarily taken by a party in a transaction. Commons (1959, p. 23) defines goodwill as a negative promise: a promise not to compete. He further adds that 'goodwill, being a social relation, implies reciprocity. It is the expectation of reciprocal beneficial transactions' (Ibid., p. 220). In the circumstances of the case, the West promises not to compete with Ukrainian businesses in the national market of this country during a certain period of time, in the expectation of reciprocal beneficial transactions in the future in the free markets.

In practical terms, the asymmetrical solution de facto currently exists. In the spring of 2015, the EU unilaterally abolished most trade barriers for imports from Ukraine, which particularly benefited agricultural products (Adarov et al., 2015, pp. 3, 10). The results of this unilateral abolition of trade barriers by the EU can be seen in Table 9.1: domestic consumption and exports emerged as two key drivers of Ukraine's economy in 2015. Nothing prevents the EU from taking a step further in formalising the existing arrangements and appreciating that Ukraine needs to temporarily shelter the national market from the European competition. During this transition period, the country will develop and implement 'an industrial policy for the restructuring/conversion of sectors that are not likely to withstand competitive pressures and/or the potential loss of traditional markets also needs to be devised as an inherent part of the long-run economic development strategy' (Ibid., p. 52).

A separate problem refers to the fact that the asymmetrical arrangement discussed in this section conflicts with requirements of the IMF Extended Fund Facility (EFF) package and obligations that Ukraine assumed as a member of the World Trade Organization (WTO) since 2009 (Ibid., p. 50). However, it is a question of negotiation and the Ukrainian government's capacity to persuade these international organisations that special circumstances exist in the case at hand. The absence of organised groups or political forces making the strengthening of the national market their top economic priority represents a far more serious problem. Ukrainian wooden furniture producers are an exception. They lobbied a law that can be considered to be a rare and rather successful example of protectionist policies in Ukraine.

III. Case of the timber industry: tensions between open economy and the national market

Before discussing some particularities of this law and its implementation, background information on the timber industry will help the reader to better understand the relevant context. Forests cover 17.6% of the Ukrainian lands: 10,633.1 Ha of 60,354.9 Ha (Derzhavna Sluzhba Statystyky Ukrainy, 2016b, p. 188). To compare: forest areas represent almost a half of Russia's territory. At the same time, forest rents extracted in Ukraine actually exceed those in Russia: 0.397% of GDP against 0.346% of GDP in 2015 correspondingly (World Bank, 2017). The World Bank defines forest rents as roundwood harvest times the product of average prices and a region-specific rental rate. Forests rents in Ukraine have significantly increased since 2011, currently reaching a historic high (Figure 9.4). This reflects the intensification of the exploitation of forests, a scarce resource in Ukraine. The exploitation of forests tends to be particularly high during the periods of low prices of the other important export commodity, steel: before 2002 and after 2011 (see Figure 9.3). In a sense, lumber substitutes steel in the Ukrainian exports and vice versa.

Figure 9.4 'Forest rents (% of GDP) in Ukraine and Russia, 1991–2015'

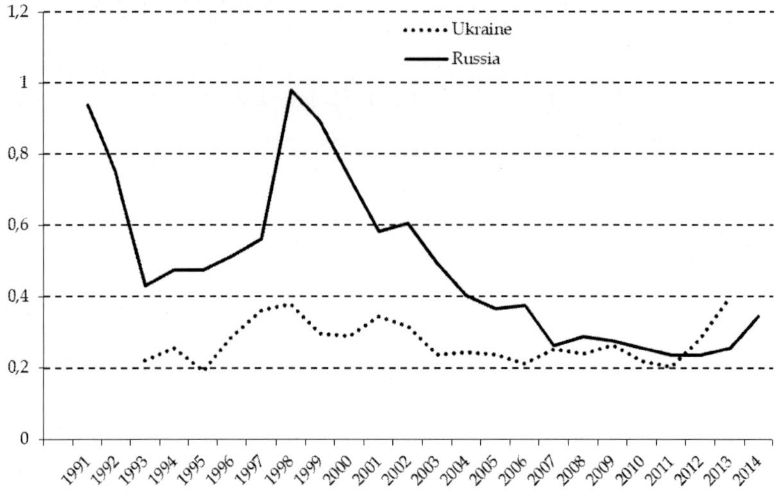

Source: World Bank, 2017.

The intensive exploitation of forest resources in a country in which they do not abound attracted policy-makers' attention well before the current crisis and the rise in forest rents that resulted from attempts to substitute lumber for the other export commodities. A first version of the Law of Ukraine 'On particularities of government regulation of businesses specializing in sale and export of wood lumber (*lisomaterialiv*)' was promulgated in September 2005 under President Viktor Yushchenko.[158] The most recent additions to the law were initiated by a group of MPs representing the entre political spectrum, from 'Samopomich' to 'Radikal'na Partiia Lyashka', from the West (5MPs from Lviv and one from Ivano-Frankivsk) as well as from the East (2MPs from Dnipro) and the Center (3MPs from Kyiv), in October 2015. They involve a 10-year ban on the export of lumber wood of all kinds except Pine effective

158 http://zakon2.rada.gov.ua/laws/show/2860-15.

November 1, 2015 and a similar ban on the export of Pine lumber effective January 1, 2017. No single vote against this ban was cast.[159]

The promulgation of the Law led to a series of controversies and public debates that have an international dimension: representatives of the EU actively contributed to them. Ecological concerns constitute the officially stated rationale for imposing the ban. Precious and rare wood, for instance, oak and the European beech, are particularly affected by the intensified lumber wood production. In addition to the large-scale legal lumber wood production, criminal logging abounds,[160] especially as other opportunities for making a living shrink in times of economic duress. Both of these problems seem to be exaggerated nonetheless. As a result of efforts aimed at forest restoration, Ukraine has even slightly increased (+0.7%) the surface of forest areas since its independence. According to various estimates, the extralegal logging amounts to 0.1 to 2.3% of the legal lumber wood production.[161]

An analysis of the structure of the Ukrainian trade with the EU suggests a more likely reason for imposing the ban. A key trend in the EU sawn hardwood trade in recent years has been increased dependence on imports of lower value product from Eastern Europe, notably Ukraine, Belarus, Russia, Bosnia and Serbia. In 2015 there were higher deliveries from the Ukraine (+37% to 350,000 cubic meters). This country exported more hardwood to the EU than Russia, Belarus and Serbia taken together (Global Wood Market

---

159 233 votes 'for', no abstentions, no vote 'against', 80 MPs did not take part in the voting, see http://w1.c1.rada.gov.ua/pls/zweb2/webproc4_1?pf3511=52828.

160 Article 246 of the Criminal Code of Ukraine criminalises logging without permit without imposing heavy penalties nevertheless.

161 The head of the State Forest Resources Agency of Ukraine estimates the volume of criminal logging at 24 thousand cubic meters in 2015, which represents approximately 0.1% of the legal logging (http://ukurier.gov.ua/uk/articles/hristina-yushkevich-shob-zupiniti-chornih-lisorubi/). A government sponsored study conducted with the help of GIS technologies in Zakarpattia, one of the most affected by criminal logging regions, suggests a higher figure: the total surface of areas of criminal logging is 2.3% of that of the legal logging (www.kmu.gov.ua/document/249450793/lis.pdf, see also an on-line map at http://texty.org.ua/d/deforestation/).

Info, 2016). The major importers of Ukrainian lumber are Romania, Slovakia, Poland and Austria (De Micco, 2015, p. 23), more specifically—furniture and home décor, namely, parquet, producers in these countries. A portion of their products is subsequently exported to Ukraine whose national producers cannot compete with their European counterparts. In other words, Ukraine exports a commodity—lumber wood, and imports a processed product with high value added—wooden furniture. The ban in these circumstances aims less to solve ecological problems than to temporarily protect the national market and Ukrainian producers of wooden furniture. The true objective of the ban cannot be officially acknowledged, since it clearly conflicts with Ukraine's obligations as a WTO member and a participant in the programs of economic integration with the EU. The Ukrainian government is simply not yet prepared to state and protect interests of national producers through the process of difficult negotiations with the international organisations.

Despite the government's lack of resolution and unwillingness to produce and implement a comprehensive set of policies to strengthen the national market, the ban on the export of lumber wood seems to be working, at least so far. The linear regression analysis of the region-level data, method 'Forward' (with the probability of F for entry set at a 0.05 level and for removal at a 0.1 level), shows that in 2013 and 2014 the logging was driven by the demands of export and import. In 2015, their impact became insignificant (Table 9.2). The dependent variable, the merchantable wood volume (originally in thousand cubic meters; Lg10 transformed), was predicted from a series of the independent variables, namely, forest area (% of the territory covered by forests), forest restoration (the area of new forests in Ha), lumber wood production (wood ripped or cut, divided into parts or peeled, 6mm plus thick, originally in thousand square meters; Lg10 transformed), total import of goods and total export of goods (originally in thousand USD; Ln transformed), export of wood (thousand USD), export of wooden furniture (thousand USD), import of wooden furniture (originally in thousand USD; Ln transformed) and total wooden furniture production (office, kitchen, living and dining room furniture, originally in units; Lg10 transformed).

The production of wood with low value added (lumber wood) had a positive and significant impact on the merchantable wood volume in 2013 and 2014 but not in 2015. The volume of total exports during the same period had a negative and significant impact, which may indicate that the lumber wood production tends to substitute the other commodities and products that Ukraine exports. The value of imports of furniture positively influenced the dependent variable in 2014 that immediately preceded the imposition of the ban. Ukraine produces and exports lumber wood at the same time it imports wooden furniture. This situation is typical for peripheral economies.

The 2015 pattern is different. The contribution of exports and lumber wood production became insignificant. At the same time, forest restoration positively contributed to the inter-regional variation in the merchantable wood volume. Does it mean that the ban helped make progress both in solving ecological problems and in protecting the national producers of furniture? The tentative answer is yes, but the 2016 data—not available at the time of writing[162]—are needed to further confirm this assumption.

162 The 2017 edition of the 'Regions of Ukraine' statistical yearbook is expected in December 2017.

Table 9.2 'Results of linear multiple regressions to predict the merchantable wood volume (Lg10 transformed) in Ukraine, 2013–2015'

	2013			2014			2015		
	Unstandardised B	**Std. error**	**Standardised Beta**	**Unstandardised B**	**Std. error**	**Standardised Beta**	**Unstandardised B**	**Std. error**	**Standardised Beta**
% of the total surface covered by forests	0.016**	0.005	0.431				0.015*	0.006	0.406
Total export, Ln transformed	-0.185**	0.053	-0.376	-0.297***	0.058	-0.546			
Lumber wood production, Lg10 transformed	0.376*	0.136	0.363	0.684***	0.088	0.728			
Imports of furniture, thousand USD				0.000006**	0.000002	0.381			
Forest restoration, Ha							0.000126**	0.000035	0.529
Constant	4.228***	0.805		5.618***	0.830		2.007***	0.109	
Adjusted R^2	0.744			0.807			0.696		
N	25			25			25		

Legend: results significant at a 0.05 level are marked by *, at a 0.01 level—by **, and at a 0.001 level—by ***.
Source: Derzhavna Sluzhba Statystyky Ukrainy, 2016a, Vol. 1, p. 261; Vol. 2, pp. 250, 319–320, 357–359, 426–594.

Conclusion

Ukraine currently lives in a period of economic duress. An unfavourable situation on the world commodities markets negatively affected the country's open economy. The national processing industries are unable to compete globally and even in the national market, as the case of furniture production suggests. More substantially, the country bears all the costs of the undeclared war waged by Russia. A part of the industrial, agricultural and transportation infrastructure has been either destroyed (in Donbas) or lost (in Crimea). The military expenditures have significantly increased—at the expense of investments and consumption. The military conflict that still remains without a solution in sight negatively influences expectations of businesses and households, which further undermines prospects of economic development. As Keynesian and heterodox economics predict, 'success in growth and macro stabilization have a common prerequisite, and that is a mood of optimism' (Kornai, 1997, p. 78).

In these circumstances, economic recovery will require massive public investment. 'Since the cash-stripped Ukrainian government will hardly be able to come up with adequate funds on its own, the EU could potentially play a crucial role here—ideally by designing a sort of "Marshall Plan" for Ukraine; similar plans have been advocated recently e.g. by George Soros and Dmytro Firtash' (Adarov et al., 2015, p. 21). No new Marshall plan seems to be forthcoming, however.

As a better alternative to credits and loans that simply postpone the payment of the costs caused by the current crisis, this chapter proposes the asymmetrical arrangement that involves a combination of temporary protectionism and the free access of Ukrainian producers to the Western markets. Being temporarily protected at home, Ukrainian producers will have more resources for competing globally. The unrestricted access to the Western market will provide them with powerful incentives to learn. In other words, Ukraine may need a combination of protectionism and the outward-oriented strategy.

At least three obstacles prevent Ukraine from moving in this direction. First, Ukraine has obligations to keep its economy open. Long and difficult negotiations will be needed to persuade the international organisations; first of all, the WTO and the EU, that this country's special circumstances require non-orthodox, exceptional measures. Goodwill of the international organisations will help accept the asymmetrical solution and enforce its implementation (so, for example, no unilateral extension of protectionist policies is possible).

Second, Ukrainian businesses and political parties prefer to wait and see if the current crisis may end as miraculously as the crisis in the 1990s instead of acting proactively and promoting at least a discussion of alternative economic policies for this country. Ukrainian furniture producers are an exception that confirms the rule. Without healthy economic debates (see Chapter 8) existing economic policies, neoliberal or protectionist, will not be adapted to the particularities of the economic and institutional environment in this country and, thus, will unlikely lead to the desired outcomes.

Third, protectionist policies create a risk of rent seeking and government representatives' opportunism in the other forms. Without solving the problem of incentives, not only for businesses but also for the government, any form of protectionism is doomed. 'Issues of incentives are at the core of economics: Some economists have gone so far to suggest that they are *the* economic problem' (Stiglitz, 1994, p. 47). The volunteer movement that emerged and was strengthened in Ukraine from 2013–2015 provides some ground for optimism in this respect. This movement is not satisfied with the role of a service provider, progressively assuming the function of an advocate and a watchdog controlling the government on a daily basis (see Chapter 10 for more detail). The civil society's control over the government potentially creates much needed incentives for its representatives and serves as a guarantee against the appropriation of benefits of the gate-keeping by them, as it has been occurring in Russia.

Chapter 10
'Volunteers: Actors of internal growth'

Introduction

The 2013–2014 Revolution of Dignity in Ukraine was driven by large scale grassroots mobilisation (Chapter 3). Russia's invasion in 2014, which immediately followed the fleeing of the then Ukrainian president Viktor Yanukovych, changed the overall dynamics of this mobilisation and the order of priorities of its participants. Russia's invasion in 2014 caught Ukraine by surprise. Expectations that Ukraine would be protected against potential invasion in the East by a taboo on 'intrafamilial violence' (strong ties that existed between the two countries in the past allowed some to describe them using the metaphor of a 'family' with Russia playing the role of an older brother) or by the Budapest Memorandum on Security Assurances of December 5, 1994 (Ukraine gave up nuclear weapons inherited from the Soviet Union in exchange for assurances of its territorial integrity given by Russia, the UK and the US) turned out to be false (Chapter 5). The country was clearly unprepared to defend itself either. Ukraine's armed forces were untrained and unfit for combat, undersupplied with almost everything (weaponry, clothing and even food), and switched sides at times (for instance, in Crimea). The police force often preferred to 'wait and see' instead of intervening and localising the threats of seizure of government buildings by the Russian military personnel under cover and pro-Russian militia. In these circumstances, many protesters and their supporters volunteered to protect the country against the invasion and to deal with its consequences, ranging from the growing number of internally displaced persons, to the influx of the wounded.

Ukraine of the early 2010s had some features of a fragile or even a failed state. 'A failed state is one that has few or no functioning state institutions that can confer identity and assure security to the population. In the process, the government loses its legitimacy, both nationally and internationally' (François & Sud, 2006, p. 142).

In 2013, Ukraine was found in the middle of the list of failed states (the 117th rank of 178; Fund of Peace, 2013). Despite this relatively comfortable overall standing (Russia, for instance, was ranked higher, i.e. was believed to have more features of a failed state), Ukraine's score for the legitimacy of the State (the lack thereof) was alarming: 7.8 of 10. Few considered the Ukrainian government to be effective. Even researchers sympathetic to this country admitted that post-Soviet Ukraine had a 'quasi modern state' at best (Harasymiw, 2002, p. 111). In other words, formal attributes of a state were present, but their contents raised serious concerns.

If Ukraine was able to stabilise the Eastern front in 2015, preventing further advances of the pro-Russian insurgents supported with ammunition, financial resources and personnel by Russia, this was to a significant extent a result of a surge in volunteerism and grass-root initiatives of the population of Ukraine. Volunteers fought alongside Ukrainian regular troops (Karagannis [2016] estimates the number of volunteer fighters at 10,000); organised supplies of ammunition, clothing, medications and food both to volunteer fighters and regular military personnel; helped forced migrants from Crimea and Eastern Ukraine to find a new place to live and to work; assisted the wounded in hospitals and in post-traumatic recovery; countered the Russian propaganda, and provided many other services that are normally expected to be supplied by the government. Without the active involvement of volunteers, the Ukrainian government in general—and the Ukrainian military in particular, would have found themselves in an even more difficult situation.

Not surprisingly, after 2013, civic organisations became one of the most trusted institutions in Ukraine. Surveys regularly conducted on representative samples by the Kyiv International Institute of Sociology (2012; 2015a) shows that in 2012 there were more respondents who did not trust civic organisations (29.4%) than those who trusted them (27.1%)[163]; in 2015, this ratio radically

163 In 2004 (the year of the 'Orange revolution'), this ratio was even more dramatic: 49.8% v. 12.5% (Stepanenko, 2006, p. 580).

changed (21% against 34.5% respectively). In 2016, volunteer initiatives were among three most trusted institutions in Ukraine, along with the Church and the military Table 10.1[164]).

Table 10.1 'To what extent do you trust the following socio-political institutions?, %'

	Completely distrust (1)	Rather distrust (2)	Difficult to say	Rather trust (3)	Completely trust (4)	Balance of trust and distrust (4+3–2–1)
Army	4.6	7.4	24.7	42.2	21.0	51.2
Your church	5.6	7.3	23.4	40.9	22.8	50.8
Volunteer initiatives helping internal forced migrants	3.9	6.4	34.0	42.8	12.9	45.4
Volunteer initiatives helping the Ukrainian army	5.3	8.1	31.3	40.6	14.7	41.9
Volunteer fighters' battalions	7.6	10.3	32.9	36.6	12.7	31.4
Local authorities	11.0	22.4	30.2	30.6	5.9	3.1
Ukrainian mass media	10.9	24.2	38.2	24.6	2.1	-8.4
Political parties	31.5	35.4	26.1	6.7	0.2	-60

Source: Kyiv International Institute of Sociology, 2016.

The volunteer movement is not a recent phenomenon in Ukraine. Civil society organisations (CSOs) have had a visible presence since the country's independence in 1991. According to various sources, the number of officially registered CSOs exceeded 60,000 in 2010

164 A high level of confidence in the military and the Church has been a consistent pattern in recent years—for instance, in 2007, these two institutions were also at the top of a similar list (Subtelny, 2009, p. 655).

(Palyvoda & Golota, 2010, p. 15) and 50,000[165] in the wake of the 2013–1014 Revolution of Dignity (OSCE, 2015, p. 4). However, active CSOs were significantly less numerous—4–6% of their total number (Palyvoda & Golota, 2010, p. 15). Active CSOs relied on paid-staff assisted by volunteers, who were recruited mainly among students (Ibid., p. 10). Before the most recent surge, volunteerism was to a significant extent externally promoted and driven (by foreign governments and international non-government organisations). The volunteer movement had neither a mass character nor enjoyed mass support. As a matter of fact, the word 'volunteerism' was imported from the Western discourse and weakly vernacularised in local settings.

Despite the most recent surge in volunteerism in Ukraine, its nature, scope and driving forces remain underexplored both by Ukrainian and international scholars. The Web of Science indexes 14 publications on this topic only; half of them appeared in 2015–2016.[166] This chapter aims to contribute to this literature in bridging the existing gap by enhancing our knowledge of the post-2013 volunteerism in Ukraine. In these circumstances, this study necessarily has an explorative character. It attempts to answer the research question as to *what are distinctive features of the volunteer movement in Ukraine*. It is argued that from 2014–2016, volunteer initiatives essentially emerged spontaneously and in a bottom-up manner. Initially, most of them had an informal character. These spontaneous, informal, loosely coordinated grass-root initiatives constitute a central element of Ukraine's emerging civil society. In addition, Ukrainian volunteers assume a leading role in the process of state- and nation-building either directly, by being appointed to the public service or getting elected to the Parliament, or indirectly, by supporting the project of the Ukrainian nation-state. Since the Ukrainian state was weak and fragile in 2013–2014, there was no other option but to start rebuilding it from the ground up.

165 The decrease may be attributed to a new Law on Civic Organisations entered in force on January 1, 2013 (Ghosh, 2014, p. 3).

166 The search was carried out on November 7, 2016 using TOPIC: (volunteer*) AND TOPIC: (Ukrain*) as key words.

This chapter is organised into four sections, not counting the introduction and conclusion. Section I offers a taxonomy of volunteerism and compares the Ukrainian case with the forms that volunteerism takes in other countries. It is suggested that the embeddedness of Ukraine's volunteer movement within the context of state- and nation-building constitutes its distinctive feature after 2013. In these circumstances, volunteers need to go beyond the role of a service provider. Sources of information and methods for processing it are described in Section II. This study uses both qualitative (in-depth interviews) and quantitative (a survey on a representative sample) data. Section III draws on the survey data, offering a social portrait of volunteers in today's Ukraine. It reports that the scope and scale of volunteerism tend to be comparable to those observed in North America. It also shows that there is a significant support for a project of building an independent nation-state in Ukraine among volunteers. The role of volunteers as social innovators is discussed in Section IV. This aspect of volunteerism is particularly valuable in the context of state- and nation-building.

I. Types and functions of volunteerism

I.1 Taxonomy of volunteerism

Definitions of volunteerism offered in the extant literature place emphasis on the lack of coercion and compensation in associated activities. The volunteer contributes time and resources out of good will and is free to cease at any time. Principal beneficiaries of volunteerism are individuals other than the volunteer, his or her family, social group or cause. 'Volunteerism is voluntary, deliberate service to others over time and without compensation' (Kilpatrick, 2007, p. 1016; see also International Labour Office, 2011, p. 13; Smith, 1997, p. 274). Some definitions also highlight an associational dimension of volunteerism that differentiates it from more individual, even solitary activities benefiting others. 'Most volunteer work takes place in connection with, or on behalf of, an organization, whose function is to define and support the role of the volunteer' (Wilson, 2003, p. 1466). Volunteer initiatives that take an organisational form exist along with the other CSOs, including those with paid-staff, which creates some confusion. All CSOs of a country constitute its non-profit sector, or the third sector that differ both from the state and the market (Salamon, Anheier & Associates, 1999, p. 5). Volunteerism refers to a segment of this larger non-profit sector, whose relative scope varies across countries and in time.

Because of their lack of self-interest, the behaviour of volunteers can hardly be explained in terms of rational choice. If people were to act only to maximise their pleasure, very few if anyone would volunteer. The example of volunteers, who risk not only their time and resources but also their lives, for example, volunteer fighters, illustrates this point particularly well (Karagannis, 2016, p. 149). Rational action (instrumentally rational, to use Max Weber's terms) involves considering 'the behavior of objects in the environment and of other human beings as "conditions" or "means" for the attainment of the actor's own rationally pursued and calculated ends' (Weber, 1968, p. 24). In contrast, the volunteer's choices do not derive from considerations of expediency. Instead, they are value-oriented (Smith, 1997, p. 285), which makes relevant the other ideal type of human behaviour outlined by Weber, namely, value-rational action. Ends in this case have some intrinsic value. Socioeconomics (Etzioni, 1988; Etzioni, 2002) develops various models of value-rational action and their empirical applications, including to studies of volunteerism.

The possible involvement of volunteers in social innovations also suggests that the concept of self-interested behaviour is of limited applicability to social and cultural entrepreneurship. In Schumpeterian tradition, entrepreneurs are key actors of social, economic and political changes. They search for new resources, organisational and institutional structures, as well as for new combinations of the existing ones (Schumpeter, 1983). Profit-seeking is believed to be a key motive of entrepreneurs. Entrepreneurs recognise 'some potential income that they could receive if only they could alter the institutional structure' (Davis & North, 1970, p. 133).

This motivation does not suffice to produce innovations if profits from them cannot be easily tapped, however.

A profit-seeker, for instance, is hardly interested in proposing and implementing an innovation whose beneficiaries constitute a large group with unclear and difficult to enforce boundaries (in other words, the innovation with features of a public good). Cultural innovations represent a case in point. The search for solutions that address unmet social needs of marginalised individuals involves costs but very little benefits to the innovator, even if the marginalised group has clear boundaries. A self-interested entrepreneur would be uninterested, whereas a social entrepreneur sees an opportunity in both situations. In contrast to the self-interested entrepreneur, the social entrepreneur 'embraces a blended value approach in which social [or cultural] outcomes are prioritised over financial ones' (Scheiber, 2016, p. 1696). Since they prioritise values over profit, volunteers are a good match for the role of social and cultural entrepreneurs. A study shows that the profile of social entrepreneurs usually includes volunteer experience (Ibid., p. 1704).

Flexibility of volunteer initiatives constitutes the other link connecting volunteerism with social and cultural entrepreneurship. Compared with other organisations, volunteer initiatives have a more versatile character. They easily emerge and disappear, which makes them 'ideal for social experimentation and innovation' (Smith, 1977, p. 277). The viability of an idea can be tested more rapidly and at less cost by first implementing it as a volunteer initiative. Important innovations that were subsequently adapted to the needs of business or government initially emerged as volunteer initiatives. Before becoming a cornerstone of the capitalist economy, the corporate form was originally invented through grass-root initiatives and used for supporting them. 'In the early period of American history, the corporate form was associated with semi-public activities (educational, religious, and semi-governmental activities) but with growing demand for large amounts of capital in transportation enterprises the advantages of this form of organisation led to its rapid adoption' (Davis & North, 1970, p. 142).

Volunteerism has various manifestations, and this term describes different, sometimes divergent phenomena. A taxonomy of volunteerism includes the following types: formal versus informal, grass-root versus paid-staff non-profit, service versus advocacy, active versus passive (checkbook), mandatory versus free, peacetime versus wartime, giving time versus giving money and making in-kind contributions (charity), volunteer initiatives in enabling versus constraining environments, and so forth. Volunteer initiatives that acquired a formal status (i.e. with state registration) prevail in the developed countries and serve as a model for the less developed countries promoted by means of programs of international assistance (Kamstra, Pelzer, Elbers & Ruben, 2016, p. 1032). If formally established and registered (non-government) organisations serve as a point of reference, then the count of all association memberships becomes a natural measure for the scale and scope of volunteerism. This indicator is actively used in comparative research (Curtis, Baer & Grabb, 2001; Kamstra et al., 2016), partly because relevant questions were included in several waves of the Word Values Survey project. Formal organisations may represent an important part of volunteer initiatives in some countries. The System of National Accounts 2008 allows obtaining quantitative estimates of the size and scope of this sector (Salamon, 2010).

However, by focusing exclusively on them, one omits initiatives with no state registration. The omission has particularly important consequences in the less developed countries with their strong traditions of extra-legality (De Soto, 2005). Extra-legal transactions do not involve references to the law, which limits the scope of the possible for the parties involved, but at the same time represent a unique opportunity for launching bottom-up initiatives when access to the law turns out to be complicated and associated with high costs.

David Smith (1997) discusses a related opposition between grass-root initiatives and paid-staff non-profit organisations. The former refers to spontaneous bottom-up volunteerism, whereas the latter—to volunteer activities organised in a 'top-down' manner and to a significant extent professionalised. 'By grassroots associations I mean locally based and basically autonomous, volunteer-run, non-profit groups that have an official membership of volunteers' (Smith, 1997, p. 269). He argues that grass-root initiatives (they range from delinquent gangs to self-help lay legal advocacy) still exist in the Western countries, but tend to be ignored in the statistics of volunteerism and in decision making within the 'official' voluntary sector composed of paid-staff non-profit organisations. The same author differentiates between volunteer initiatives as service providers (to people with special needs, for instance) and volunteers involved in advocacy and attempts to control the government by assuming the role of a watchdog. Politics constitutes a taboo for the volunteers as service providers. They complement the government in the areas where it cannot reach out to all representatives of the target groups. For volunteers involved in advocacy, politics represents a natural environment.

Various degrees of one's involvement in the work of volunteer associations lie at the origin of the difference between active and checkbook members. In contrast to active members, checkbook volunteers have limited involvement in volunteer initiatives. They 'claim membership in an organization but participate very little' (Painter & Paxton, 2014, p. 412; see also Curtis et al., 2001, p. 788). In the Western countries, namely in the US, studies indicate the existence of a trend toward increased checkbook membership in formal organisation at the expense of active membership. 'Moreover, the increase in checkbook memberships is smaller than the decline in active memberships' (Painter & Paxton, 2014, p. 421).

The term 'passive volunteer' may sound contradictory, but the underlying contradiction is not unique. Mandatory volunteerism involves some coercion, however soft it may be. In the US, 'some school districts have made community service a requirement of graduation… to promote civic virtues in adulthood' (Musick & Wilson, 2007, p. 464). Volunteer experience is expected and even required from students in some programs as a condition of their admission or graduation, for instance, in social work. Mandatory volunteerism does not necessarily provide a good service to those involved. 'Researchers found that "mandatory volunteerism" as a college requirement made some students *less* likely to freely volunteer in the future' (Kilpatrick, 2007, p. 1016).

Volunteerism at wartime has to be differentiated from volunteer initiatives at times of peace. Volunteer military service involves higher risks, including potential loss of life. Volunteer fighters contribute not only their time or resources, but also health or even life. Some countries, namely the US, actively relied on volunteer military service in the past. 'Voluntary service, most often performed in local militias, has historically been embraced as the system most consistent with Americans' concepts of liberty' (Neiberg, 2005, p. 187). In the case of Ukraine, volunteer fighters are singled out even by their name, *dobrovol'tsi,* whereas the vernacularised English term, *volontery*, applies to other volunteers.

A relevant divide refers to differences between those who contribute their time and efforts and those who contribute money or make in-kind contributions. In a sense, volunteer fighters, volunteers and donors can be placed on a continuum defined by the degree of involvement and sacrifice with volunteer fighters and donors located at its opposite ends. All three forms of volunteerism have common roots in the willingness to contribute to a common cause, but the intensity of its manifestation varies. The assumption that these three forms represent various facets of the same phenomenon is confirmed by the fact that individual money donations were consistently found to be associated with time contributed to nonprofit activity (Musick & Wilson, 2007, p. 134; Smith, 1997, p. 287; Wilson, 2003, p. 1467).

Highlighting the difference between volunteer initiatives in an enabling environment and volunteerism in a constraining environment helps one better understand particularities of the situation in, on one hand, the developed, mostly Western, countries, and, on the other hand, the less developed, mostly non-Western (Eurasian, Asian, African) countries. In the West, volunteerism is commonly considered as an element of an established political system, namely, democracy. Viewed from the neo-Tocquevillian perspective, voluntary organisations are building blocks of civil society. Civil society 'is populated by all sorts of formal and informal organisations like NGOs, associations based on kinship, social movements, community-based organisations, labour unions and professional associations' (Kamstra et al., 2016, p. 1028). Volunteer experience enables one to participate in politics in a more meaningful manner, which makes volunteer involvement 'a major engine of democratic participation' (Smith, 1997, p. 296). In other words, a democratic environment not only enables volunteer initiatives but also requires them. They 'go together', as Mark Musick and John Wilson (2007, p. 474) put it.

The existence of a stable, let alone democratic, environment cannot be taken for granted everywhere. What if volunteers act in a constraining environment: under conditions of political and/or economic instability, corruption and a weak or absent rule of law? The need for volunteer involvement may be particularly acute precisely in situations of conflict, lawlessness and insecurity. In these circumstances, associative membership provides an alternative source of social cohesion and stability, and helps citizens to defend themselves against corrupt governments. Both qualitative (Touraine, 1988, part V) and quantitative (Kamstra et al., 2016) studies show that low levels of economic development, democracy, political stability and rule of law are associated with high levels of associative membership. However, informal volunteer initiatives and active, even activist, forms of volunteerism may have better chances of survival in such environments.

I.2 Role of volunteer initiatives in state- and nation building

The previous discussion suggests that compared with volunteerism in a stable democratic environment, volunteer initiatives in emerging political systems take different forms (more informal and activist) and perform rather different functions (of a protective belt, of a watchdog and advocate against corrupt governments). Emerging political systems prevail in many parts of the world: Eurasia (countries of the Former Soviet Union except the Baltic States), Asia and Africa. They have an unstable and changing environment that constrains rather than enables volunteer initiatives, especially grassroot ones. In changing circumstances, the role of volunteers as potential social and cultural innovators becomes particularly important. In a sense, volunteers provide input in the construction of an emerging system. Depending on their input (or the lack thereof) the emerging system gets closer to or further from the Western model, i.e. the democratic nation-state. Alain Touraine (1988, pp. 130, 255–256) uses the term 'historical movements' to describe volunteer mobilisation in the emerging systems—they make history, literally.

The Western model of government, the democratic nation-state, is considered as a norm in geopolitics and international affairs (Badie, 1992). The non-Western countries are expected to sooner or later conform to this norm by building their own nation-states, preferably democratic. The process of building nation-states is neither well understood nor sufficiently operationalised into a set of policies that would be easy to implement in practice. Even its key components—state- and nation-building—are not studied enough (Virág, 2012, p. 622), not to speak of their combination. These gaps and omissions are particularly easy to spot when discussing the experience of non-Western countries in general and the situation of volunteers in these countries in particular.

State-building aims for consolidation of the state (Berger, 2006, p. 6). The next question then follows: what is the state? Following Gianfranco Poggi, Bohdan Harasymiw (2002, pp. 82–83) lists half a dozen distinctive features of the modern state (i.e., the Western model of the state), including territoriality, sovereignty, differentiation,[167] coercive control, bureaucracy, democratic legitimation, the rule of law, and nationhood, among several others. Nation, thus, is one of the constitutive elements of the state, which explains the use of the double name, nation-state. Taras Kuzio (1998, p. 136; see also Ibid., pp. 144, 162) further elaborates on this intersection of a nation

167 A non-modern State does not necessarily involve differentiation of functional subsystems. It represents an all-encompassing entity, as per definition of Thorstein Veblen (1939, p. 161): 'the State is a matter not easily expounded in English. It is neither the territorial area, nor the population, nor the body of citizens or subjects, nor the aggregate wealth or traffic, nor the public administration, nor the government, nor the crown, nor the sovereign; yet in some sense it is all these matters, or rather all these organs of the state. In some potent sense, the State is a personal entity, with rights and duties superior and anterior to those of the subjects, whether these latter be separately or collectively, in detail or in the aggregate or average. The citizen is a subject of the State'.

and a state: civil societies as a prerequisite for democratic legitimation of a state require 'national identities in order to function'.

In its turn, nation-building means 'the sum of policies designated to promote national integration' (Harasymiw, 2002, p. 204). Much like the modern state, the nation can be operationalised into a number of indicators. Anthony Smith (2004, pp. 16–17) includes in his list self-definition (how 'We', members of a nation, differ from 'Them', outsiders), shared myth and memory cultivation (Section II of Chapter 1 discusses this aspect in more detail), development of uniform public culture, territorialisation and legal standardisation. Territorialisation and public culture represent two areas in which the nation and the state tend to overlap. Both the nation and the state are embedded in a specific territory, a historic homeland, as a rule. As to the second overlapping area, on one hand, the feeling of national identity strengthens civil society. On the other hand, the existence of public culture with volunteerism as its integral element facilitates national integration and, thus, nation-building.

Smith also admits that the nation is a process (nation-building) rather than a finally achieved form. He outlines three routes of nation formation (Smith, 1991, pp. 9–12; Smith, 2002; Smith, 2004, pp. 21–22): West and North European, Eurasian (East European and Asian) and immigrant (North American and Australian). The North-West European route involves a lateral and civic mode of national mobilisation with aristocracy as a key player. The Eurasian route implies a more hierarchical and ethnic form of national mobilisation by efforts of nationally conscious intellectuals and religious figures. Pioneer settlers in overseas territories chose still the other, immigrant route. Compared with the North-West European route, the immigrant route has fewer aristocratic and bureaucratic elements. The thesis that nation-building can proceed via at least three different routes usefully contrasts with the assumption of the presumed universality of the Western model of state-building. The Eurasian route of nation-building seems to be relevant for discussing the case of Ukraine, an East European nation-state in the making.

When Ukraine's independence from the Soviet Union was proclaimed in 1991, Ukraine had neither a full-fledged statehood nor a well-defined nation. In Soviet times, key institutions of the state were concentrated in Moscow. Ukraine did not have its own state for extended periods of time prior to its inclusion in the Soviet Union either (see again Chapter 1 for more detail). As a result, Ukraine's elite had more in common with a sub-elite (Etzioni-Halevy, 1993, p. 95; see section IV of Chapter 6 for the relevant quote) rather than with a true power elite, the population of Ukraine in the circumstances. As for nationhood, there was consensus neither on the foundations of the Ukrainian nation, civic (as in the North-West European model) or ethnic (as in the Eurasian model), nor on a possible ethnic core of the nation, should the ethnic model of nationhood have prevailed. 'The issue in Ukraine was actually whether this ethnic core would be Ukrainian or some vague East Slavic or Ukrainian-Russian amalgam' (Subtelny, 2009, p. 606; see also Shulman, 2002; Wilson, 2002). In other words, not all Ukrainians self-defined by fully differentiating themselves from their Eastern neighbours, Russians. Kuzio's assertion (2012, p. 434) that 'domestic policies have never been pursued by any Ukrainian president from the perspective of Ukraine's national interests' comes as no surprise. National interests can hardly be stated without a well-defined nation.

State- and nation-building from scratch necessitated addressing two general issues. First, what is a right sequence of steps: nation-building first and then state-building or vice versa? Second, who can become agens movens of these processes? In the majority of neighbouring countries of Central and Eastern Europe (Russia represents a different case that necessitates a separate discussion), the birth of nations preceded the foundation of their states (Virág, 2012, pp. 629, 638–639). Their experience suggests that nation-building paves the way for state-building. During the first years of Ukraine's independence, however, members of its nascent power elite devoted principal efforts to state-building (Stepanenko, 2015). Compared with nation-building, state-building appeared to them to have a higher priority (keeping in mind that only the states are acknowledged as actors of international politics; Badie, 1992) and to be a manageable task. First Ukrainian 'President [Leonid] Kravchuk's insistence on the priority of state building as the preeminent political task during these first few years of independence made sense if he had in mind specifically these external, territorial aspects of the process' (Harasymiw, 2002, p. 98). Kuzio (1998, pp. 126–127) proposes a term reflecting the sequence of steps in post-Soviet Ukraine, state-nation. Kuchma, second President of Ukraine, proclaimed that state-building was completed by August 1996, with the adoption of the Constitution of this country.

The power elite of Ukraine cannot be said to fully control even state-building, however. Processes of state-building tend to be externally driven because of pressures to conform with international standards, i.e. the Western model of the modern state (Berger, 2006, p. 6). The International Monetary Fund, IMF, emerged as a key driver of state-building in the countries that started this process relatively late, including Ukraine. Relevant reforms, including administrative reforms, were launched under pressure and close guidance of the IMF. 'If it were not for pressure from the IMF, there would likely be no appreciable movement in the direction of modern state building' (Harasymiw, 2002, p. 165; see also Kuzio, 2015, p. 296). Global and international actors took care even of civil society, one of the central elements of the modern state, in this country. Until recently, Western donors funded most of the advocacy work in Ukraine and supported formal civil society organisations performing the other functions, e.g. providing services (Lutsevych, 2016). In 2010, 53% of funding for Ukrainian CSOs came through international donor support (Palyvoda & Golota, 2010, p. 10).

How successful was the externally driven process of state-building in Ukraine? On the face of it, state-building may well have been completed in the second half of the 1990s, indeed, when relevant formal institutions, including formal civil society organisations, were created. The circumstances surrounding Russia's military invasion begun in 2014 suggest that this success may be in appearance only. On one hand, it was preceded by large-scale and essentially non-organised (by formal civil society organisations) protests against the corrupt and ineffective Ukrainian government (Chapters 3 and 4). On the other hand, as mentioned in the introduction to this chapter, the country turned out to be completely unprepared for the invasion, having no functioning institutions—starting with the army, able to curb it.

Russia's military intervention, an external factor, sped up the process of nation-building in Ukraine, however. Smith (2004, p. 154) observes that warfare has been 'one of the most powerful factors in the creation of both nations and ethnic communities in every period of history'. According to Kuzio (1998, pp. 9–10), this observation also applies to the case of Western Ukraine, where military struggles with the neighbouring nations in the 17th-20th centuries, first of all Poland, contributed to strengthening Ukrainians' national consciousness and their self-perception as different from the Poles. Before Russia's intervention in 2014, no similar differentiation took place in Eastern Ukraine. Furthermore, this military intervention may have led an internal actor, nationalists, to assume a more active and responsible role in state- and nation-building. As a result, there is a chance that these processes in Ukraine may become internally as opposed to externally driven.

Nationalism as a potential driver of nation- and state-building is a controversial topic. Viewed in the perspective of the North-West European model of nation-state, nationalism has mostly negative connotations as something that undermines the civic nature of the nation. The Eurasian model of nation-state, as it was shown, does not involve a taboo on theorising and studying the link between nationalism, civil society and protests against a fragile or even failed state (Kuzio, 2014, p. 191). In these circumstances, a neutral, positive (as opposed to normative) definition of nationalism may be of help. Smith (2004, p. 183; see also Smith, 2002, p. 22) offers one: 'nationalism [is] an ideological movement for attaining and maintaining the autonomy, unity and identity of an existing or potential "nation"'. Smith further argues that one needs to acknowledge the existence of both positive and negative effects of nationalism. One of these positive effects, namely, nationalism, becoming a driver of collective mobilisation and inspiration to resist tyranny (Smith, 1991, p. 18), appears particularly relevant to the case of Ukraine.

Ukrainian nationalists, radical and moderate alike, actively participated in and formed a hard core of all mass protests that took place in post-Soviet Ukraine, namely, in the 'Ukraine without Kuchma' protests of 2000–2003, the subsequent Orange Revolution of 2004 and the 2013–2014 Revolution of Dignity (Kuzio, 2012, p. 433; Kuzio, 2014, p. 191; Shekhovtsov & Umland, 2014, p. 60). They were also quick to mobilise in response to Russia's military intervention. Ukrainian nationalism is usually associated with the Western part of this country. For instance, Russian propaganda uses the image of a Ukrainian volunteer fighter against the Red Army during and immediately after WWII from the West, *banderovets*, as a straw man representing Ukrainian nationalism. After 2013, unexpectedly to many, the nationalist movement emerged and strengthened in the Central and South-Eastern parts of the country. For example, the Azov battalion, one of the active players at the first stages of Russia's intervention, is often associated with a radical form of Ukrainian nationalism. However, this battalion is based in the East Ukrainian city of Mariupol and largely consists of local Russian speaking volunteer fighters (Karagannis, 2016, p. 143).

The centre of Ukrainian nationalism as a driver of nation-building may be moving from the West to the Centre and the East, which revives interest in discussions of possible locations—geographical, cultural and ethnic, of the 'middle ground' of this nation that was divided between the West and the East throughout most of its history (see the introduction to Chapter 1). 'One surprisingly likely middle-ground possibility is a slow Ukrainianisation[168] leading to a consolidation around Dnieper nationalism' (Wilson, 2002, p. 50). The initially slow Ukrainianisation of Central and Eastern Ukraine (with the river Dnieper as its central geographical and cultural symbol) was given a boost by the military confrontation with Russia, in conformity with Smith's theory regarding the role of warfare in nation-building. The search for the 'middle ground' that

168 This term refers to the use of Ukrainian language in everyday interactions and the transformation of Ukrainian culture into a major force of socialisation, secondary and then primary.

could become the foundation of the Ukrainian nation-state shall not be confused with discussions of Ukraine's geopolitical role either as a 'buffer' separating Europe from Russia or as a 'bridge' connecting them (see the general Introduction to this book). 'A buffer antagonises both Russia and Western Europe's supporters of good relations with Russia while a bridge places one Ukrainian foot inside Europe and another inside Eurasia, simultaneously displeasing both Moscow and Brussels' (Kuzio, 2012, p. 435). Furthermore, the metaphors of buffer and bridge simply distract attention from processes that are taking place within this country.

The intersection of volunteerism and the process of nation-state building in post-2013 Ukraine takes particularly manifest forms, which leads some scholars to express fears that the volunteers may go so far as to 'capture' the state in the making (Ghosh, 2014, pp. 11–12; Minakov, 2015; Stepanenko, 2015). As with any birth, the birth of a nation-state does not preclude some complications. To continue an apt metaphor of Lester Salamon and associates (1999, p. 33), if the period since the fall of Communism is termed the 'rebirth of civil society', 'this rebirth has not been without its delivery pains and the offspring, despite some remarkable energy, has hardly attained full maturity'. In Ukraine, the entire process may be especially painful given the fact that the birth of civil society happens simultaneously with the birth of a nation-state. This almost simultaneous 'double birth', as it were, provides one offspring, civil society, with additional degrees of freedom in shaping the other, the nation-state.

II. Data and methods

As with Chapters 3, 4 and 7, data from several sources inform the analysis of the post-2013 volunteerism in Ukraine. The format of a case study imposes no restriction in this respect. The first source is a series of qualitative in-depth interviews conducted with leaders of the volunteer movement in Ukraine. Twenty-two interviews were conducted in June 2016 in two regions of Ukraine, Kyiv (the national capital located in Central Ukraine) and Dnipro (a large industrial centre in the East). Each lasted from 1 to 2 hours. Of them,

14 interviews were conducted in Ukrainian, 7—in Russian and one—in both languages.[169] Respondents were recruited through purposeful sampling (the number of mentions of a particular volunteer initiative on the internet, including in the social networks, served as a criterion for inclusion[170]) with elements of the snowball method and the reliance on key informants (first participants shared with the author their contacts). The response rate was rather high, 46% (one should bear in mind that the author did not have any previous contacts in this milieu). The only group of volunteers who appeared to be unreachable is composed of volunteers who accepted appointments to the government as ministerial advisers or holders of other offices. This omission represents a limitation since a few former volunteer leaders recently entered the public service. The views and motivation of this particular group of volunteers remained unexplored as a result, which precluded the study of volunteers' direct (as opposed to indirect) involvement in nation- and state-building.

The interview guide contained questions on defining the meaning of volunteerism, power, democracy and trust; on personal experience of volunteerism before and after 2013; on characteristics of the interlocutor's volunteer initiative; on the perception of the state and foreign sponsors; and, of course, on the interlocutor's social, cultural and economic background.

---

169 This linguistic diversity excluded the application of the original method for assessing the reliability of the qualitative coding through the calculation of coefficients of correlations between matrixes of qualitative codes, matrixes of word co-occurrence and matrixes of codes attributed with the help of a dictionary based on substitution (see Footnote 64 on p. 156).

170 The lists of the post-2013 volunteer initiatives mentioned in a relevant article in the Ukrainian segment of Wikipedia (https://uk.wikipedia.org/wiki/%D0%A1%D0%BF%D0%B8%D1%81%D0%BE%D0%BA_%D0%B2%D0%BE%D0%BB%D0%BE%D0%BD%D1%82%D0%B5%D1%80%D1%96%D0%B2_%D1%80%D0%BE%D1%81%D1%96%D0%B9%D1%81%D1%8C%D0%BA%D0%BE-%D1%83%D0%BA%D1%80%D0%B0%D1%97%D0%BD%D1%81%D1%8C%D0%BA%D0%BE%D1%97_%D0%B2%D1%96%D0%B9%D0%BD%D0%B8_(2014%E2%80%92%D0%B4%D0%BE%D1%82%D0%B5%D0%BF%D0%B5%D1%80) accessed February 15, 2017) and by the Ministry of Information Policy of Ukraine (http://mip.gov.ua/content/volonterski--organizacii.html) were used to create a long list of potential interlocutors.

The second source is survey data. A set of questions on volunteerism were included in an omnibus survey conducted by the Kyiv International Institute of Sociology. The questions covered such issues as associational membership, the experience of active volunteerism, the amount of monetary contributions to volunteer initiatives and several dozens of the controls varying from the respondent's sex and gender to his or her political preferences and voting intentions. The data collection took place from 16 to 26 September 2016. A random stratified sample of the adult (>18 years) population covered all territories under control of the Ukrainian government at that time (thus excluding Crimea and some temporary occupied districts in Donbas) and included 2,040 respondents.

The use of such heterogeneous data makes triangulation possible in two forms: data triangulation and methodological triangulation (Perlesz & Lindsay, 2003). In the circumstances of the case, data triangulation involves mixing qualitative and quantitative data, whereas methodological triangulation—the application of qualitative and quantitative methods to the data analysis. The triangulation allowed for elaboration and complementarity (Brannen, 2005, p. 176). On one hand, the qualitative data helped design the instrument (questionnaire) for the survey research, and also helped interpret some patterns in the quantitative results (especially with respect to the intersection of volunteerism and nationalism). On the other hand, a precise estimate of the size and scope of Ukrainian volunteers' initiatives was obtained on the basis on the quantitative data. More specifically, the qualitative data was processed with the help of techniques of qualitative and quantitative content analysis, namely, manual coding and then axial coding, using QDA Miner v. 4.1.22. Axial coding is 'a process of relating the elements—[the codes]—to each other' (Scott & Garner, 2013, p. 95). The codebook contained key themes included in the interview guide, plus several themes that were identified in the process of coding (for instance, 'Facebook'—the uses of social networks by the volunteers, 'Social innovations'—new ideas and practices implemented by the volunteers, 'History'—references to the history of Ukraine, historical examples, 'Language'—the issues of using Ukrainian versus Russian language by the volunteers and some others), 26 codes in total (see Annex A).

The quantitative data was analysed using techniques of binary logistic regression, method 'Forward: conditional' (*F* values for the probability for stepwise Entry and Removal were 0.05 and 0.1 correspondingly) with the help of IBM SPSS Statistics v.24. Descriptive statistics was also used for the purposes of assessing the scope and scale of volunteerism in Ukraine.

The triangulation produced two types of outcomes, complementarity and elaboration (Brannen, 2005). Complementarity is observed when the qualitative and quantitative results diverge but together they generate insights. For instance, the qualitative and quantitative results shed light on different aspects of the volunteer movement: the former—on social innovations carried out by volunteers (Section IV), the latter—on predictors for the involvement into volunteering (Section III). Elaboration refers to the situation in which the qualitative data analysis exemplifies how the quantitative findings apply in particular cases. For instance, how volunteers of Ukraine managed to mobilise a significant amount of monetary and other resources is reported in Section III?

III. Portrait of Ukraine's volunteers

III.1 Scope and scale of volunteerism in today's Ukraine

In interviews, the interlocutors were invited to discuss meanings that they attribute to volunteerism. Several patterns emerged in their definitions of volunteerism.

III.1.a Volunteerism as a substitute for the weak state

First, they spontaneously reproduced several elements found in standard definitions, for instance, the lack of coercion and self-sacrifice:

> 'A volunteer... is a person who does something without any coercion and these things are most likely unrelated to his job. This person helps the others since he understands that if he doesn't help, no one else will help' (female, 25–39 y.o., Dnipro, interview in two languages).

The idea that volunteers are guided by the understanding that 'if not us then who?' was found in several other interviews (see also Karagannis, 2016, p. 147). The popularity of this principle perhaps can be explained by the particularities of the environment in which Ukraine's volunteer movement emerged. The fragile state offers little protection or support. The survey results allow for elaboration on this issue: only 1% of the population of Ukraine 'completely trust' the government, 14.2% 'rather trust' (75.6% either 'rather distrust' or 'completely distrust').[171] The level of generalised trust is also low, which undermines one's willingness to rely on other people. 18.5% of the general population believe that 'people can be trusted' (78.9% are of the opinion that 'one needs to be very careful in dealing with people').[172] Volunteers break this vicious cycle by taking risks and sacrificing narrowly defined individual interests. They begin by substituting the fragile state.

Second, the interlocutors highlight various degrees of self-sacrifice, from the highest in the case of volunteer fighters to the lowest in the case of supporters of volunteer initiatives who make monetary or in-kind contributions. 'Regular' volunteers are somewhere in between on this continuum:

> 'People give their time... Volunteers give the amount of time they can sacrifice at a particular moment. *Dobrovolets'* [volunteer fighter] gives all his time, gives himself entirely. After taking arms in his hands, he cannot excuse himself: "Sorry, today I can't, I need to go somewhere, see you in a week"' (male, 40–54 y.o., Kyiv, in Ukrainian).

---

171 The mean values of this indicator for the Wave 6 (2010–2014) World Values sample are 14.5%, 31.9%, 32.3% and 17.7% respectively (49 countries, N=88,852); see also subsection II.2 of the general Introduction to this book.

172 The mean value of this indicator for the Wave 6 (2010–2014) World Values sample is 24.2% (49 countries, N=88,852); see also subsection I.2 of the book's Conclusion.

'It's all about charity. Volunteerism is about charity. It's not about making money, it's about giving something. Some people give material things, the others—their time, a part of themselves. At times, the latter can be very difficult; you're almost exhausted, energetically' (female, 40–54 y.o., Dnipro, in Russian).

III.1.b Volunteerism as civic activism

Third, in addition to functions usually performed by volunteers in the West, the volunteer movement in Ukraine has a more pronounced civic (political) and national dimension. The interlocutors acknowledge that the mere term 'volunteerism' was initially (prior to 2013) imported from the Western countries. Volunteers were few and oriented mostly to providing services.

'I've first heard about volunteerism through an USAID program... The [foreign] volunteers came here, delivered lectures... I've learned from them that volunteerism is a selfless activity, it can be compared with a humanitarian mission. Word "volunteer" started to be actively used during the Euro [soccer cup] 2012. Volunteers performed the role of stewards who assisted in the organisation of various related events' (female, 25–39 y.o., Kyiv, in Ukrainian).

The state of volunteerism in Ukraine radically changed during the 2013–2014 Revolution of Dignity and the subsequent events. Volunteerism emerged as a mass phenomenon that is adapted to—vernacularised in—the local settings. The process of adaptation involved shifting emphasis from providing services to civic activism. Service provision has not disappeared from the volunteers' agenda (furthermore, the demand for their assistance significantly increased, namely, from the part of forced migrants, the military, the wounded, the veterans). In addition to providing services, however, leaders of the volunteer movement transformed into advocates of democracy and the nascent nation-state, a watchdog of the corrupt and still weak government.

'Volunteerism in Ukraine is rather specific... During [the 2013–2014] Maidan they were engaged in civic actions and supported the protesters: cooked meals for them, brought medications etc. And a still new form of volunteerism emerged with the start of the war, the Ukrainian-Russian or Russian-Ukrainian war' (female, 25–39 y.o., Kyiv, in Ukrainian).

> 'A volunteer is above all a citizen' (female, 24 y.o. and less, Kyiv, in Ukrainian).

> 'Volunteers are normal, conscious Ukrainians' (male, 40–54 y.o., Kyiv, in Ukrainian).

III.1.c Between informality and formality

The interlocutors' responses also shed light on reasons behind formalising (getting a state registration of) volunteer initiatives. A significant part of volunteer organisations that existed before 2013 had a formal status. These organisations often received support from foreign sponsors, government or non-government, which required their formal status for the purposes of accountability and taxation. In contrast, the vast majority of post-2013 volunteer initiatives came into existence without having any formal status. Their founders relied on family members, networks of friends and acquaintances or social networks. The Revolution of Dignity was not a Facebook revolution (Chapter 3), but Facebook started to play a key role in extending the social base of volunteerism. The question of whether to get a state registration became relevant at later stages in the evolution of post-2013 volunteer initiatives, when in addition to receiving money and in-kind contribution from the ordinary people, the volunteers started to interact with institutional sponsors—Ukrainian businesses, the government and/or foreign donors.

> 'Why did we get a state registration? Of course, we may well have skipped this, yet we wanted to get our initiative formalized and to get money on a banking account in a legal manner. To open a banking account, one needs to have a legal entity. We received money both on our [personal] credit cards and on our legal entity's account. If we didn't register, there would have been no significant change, perhaps we would have had less hassle, some things would have been easier' (male, 40–54 y.o., Kyiv, in Ukrainian).

> 'Initially we didn't have a [banking account]. [Our charitable] foundation emerged much later, when we had realised that we need to find additional sources of financial support. For instance, to receive some help from a legal entity, say, from a milk processing plant that was willing to supply some milk [to the military for free]' (male, 40–54 y.o., Kyiv, in Ukrainian).

The qualitative data indicate that post-2013 volunteerism tends to be informal, active (as opposed to checkbook) and to have a well pronounced civic and national dimension (as opposed to volunteerism as a service provider). The quantitative data allow for more nuances in this picture and assessing various degrees of the involvement of the population of Ukraine into volunteer activities. It also confirmed that Ukrainian volunteerism is connected to the building of a nation-state.

Previous studies showed that Ukrainian citizens' involvement into formal volunteer organisations tend to be rather modest. For example, the share of those volunteering for formal civil society organisations is estimated even after 2013 to be between 10 and 13% (Gatskova & Gatskov, 2016, p. 686; Lutsevych, 2016, p. 652). The previous discussion suggests, nevertheless, that the focus on membership in formal organisations may be misleading.

One of the questions included in the September 2016 survey was a standard indicator of association membership and participation. The respondents were offered 18 options (ranging from associations of stamp collectors to groups of election observers), including two alternatives specific to post-2013 volunteerism: participation in volunteer initiatives on behalf of forced migrants (internally displaced persons) and of the Ukrainian army (Annex B). Formal organisation membership and participation remain comparatively low and remarkably similar to those in the other post-Soviet country that did not have a recent surge in volunteerism, Russia: the average number of memberships was 0.411 (0.250 excluding post-2013 volunteer initiatives and 0.161 for post-2013 volunteer initiatives only). These figures would place Ukraine at the low end of the list of countries from the World Values Survey sample (Kamstra et al., 2016, p. 1035). In 1999–2004, few countries had lower relative numbers: Russia (0.375), Lithuania (0.236) and (Turkey 0.090). During the same period, Ukraine reportedly had a slightly higher average number (0.442).[173] It seems that in terms of formal association membership, Ukraine saw a slight decline in volunteerism during the

173 The 1999–2004 figure for Ukraine shall be taken with a grain of salt: the relevant data are not available on the World Values Survey website and the authors were not successful in identifying the pollster and the exact year of survey.

past 10–15 years. The decline takes a particularly manifest form as far as 'old', pre-2013 volunteer initiatives are concerned. Multidimensional scaling helps visualise how often the respondents declared to have simultaneous membership in particular associations (see Chapters 6 and 7 for more detail about this technique of correspondence analysis and its applications). Figure 10.1 shows that association memberships tend to form two clusters, pre-2013 organisations (the upper-right quadrant), post-2013 initiatives (the upper-left quadrant), whereas religious organisations are in a class of their own.

Figure 10.1 'Two-dimensional map of the co-occurrence of the membership in 18 organisations and initiatives'

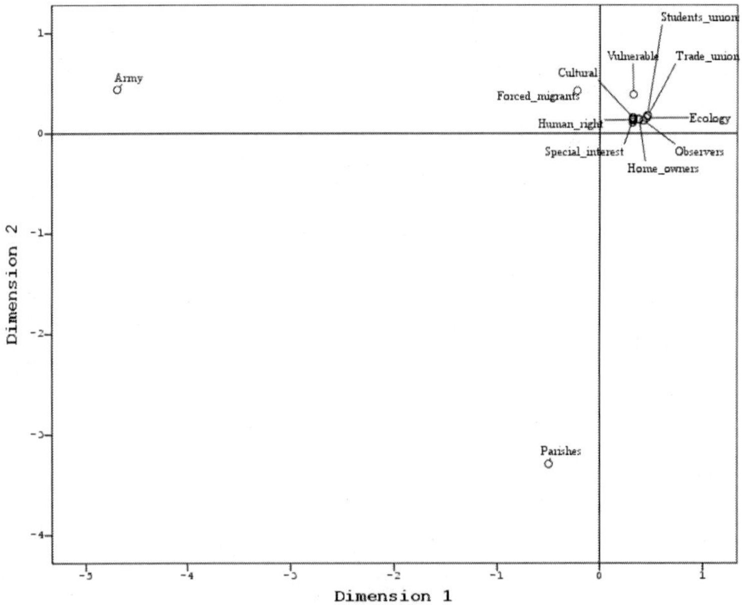

Legend: Stress = 0.00791, pseudo R^2 = 0.99742.

III.1.d Surge in volunteerism: a quantitative assessment

The picture radically changes if one ignores the issues of membership and focuses instead on time and resources spent on volunteering. Using this criterion, post-2013 Ukraine shall be included in the group of countries-leaders in the field of volunteer activities. The survey sample included 610 sponsors of volunteerism, or approximately 30% of the respondents. Multiplying this rate by the size of the permanent population aged 18 and over on January 1, 2016 (34,976,873; Derzhavna Sluzhba Statystyky Ukrainy, 2016e, p. 9), one can estimate that almost 10 million and a half of citizens of Ukraine donated money. Throughout the 12 months preceding the survey, sampled citizens of Ukraine contributed to volunteer initiatives 528,519.31 Ukrainians hryvnas (UAH), or 259.08 UAH (10.22 USD[174]) per respondent per year. Multiplying this figure by the number of adult inhabitants of Ukraine, one gets an estimate for the total amount of contributions to volunteer initiatives between September 2015 and September 2016, 357,491 million USD. Taking into consideration that Ukraine's GDP in 2015 was 90,615,000 million USD (World Bank, 2016), these voluntary contributions amount to 0.4% of the country's GDP. This figure is actually comparable to the total share of volunteers' contribution to the GDP of Canada, the country with one of the most developed associational sectors in the world (Curtis et al., 2001, p. 793). Donations to charities and associations represent from 0.44 to 0.49 of Canada's GDP between 1997 and 2012 (Emmett & Emmett, 2015, p. 24[175]). In the US, they amount to 0.25% of the GDP; in Norway—to 0.085% (Casey, 2016, p. 202).

In Ukraine, a comparable result has been achieved without a developed system of tax incentives (contributions to charities are generally tax exempted in the West). In addition to monetary contributions, both Ukrainians and Canadians also make contributions in kind. Comparative quantitative assessments of in-kind contributions pose a challenge, yet the relative amount of in-kind contributions in Ukraine may be higher than in Canada: in a poorer country (Ukraine), people simply have less money to donate to charities.

---

174 Using the mean exchange rate for 2016 as of October 31, 2016 (25.3482 UAH per 1 USD); data from http://www.exchangerates.org.uk/USD-UAH-exchange-rate-history.html, accessed October 31, 2016.

175 See also two source tables by Statistics Canada, CANSIM table 111-0002 (http://www5.statcan.gc.ca/cansim/a26?lang=eng&id=1110002) and CANSIM table 380-0064 (http://www5.statcan.gc.ca/cansim/a26?lang=eng&id=3800064), both accessed November 10, 2016.

> 'People still bring various things. All these items find a new home, at the end of the day. However, it's difficult to deal with things: you get a large volume of them, whereas you know specific requests and in order to meet them, you need to sort everything out' (male, 25–39 y.o., Kyiv, in Russian).

> 'An old man used to visit us once per week bringing 3 packs of cigarettes and 3 cans of canned meat products. He usually says: "Girls, everything will be fine". We reply: "For sure". He replies "Glory to Ukraine"[176] and walks away. We also had old ladies who wrote letters and brought knitted socks. [There was] a huge number of people like this' (female, 25–39 y.o., Dnipro, interview in two languages).

If making monetary and in-kind donation represents the least intensive form of involvement into volunteering, direct participation in volunteer initiatives requires a higher degree of one's involvement. The survey results show that approximately 7% of the respondents actually spent some time on volunteering during the 12 months that preceded the survey (approximately 2 million and a half of adult inhabitants of Ukraine). The volunteer rate in Canada, to continue the comparison, is sensibly higher: 47% (Statistics Canada, 2012, Table 2). The latter figure, however, reflects the forms of volunteering, namely mandatory and checkbook, that are virtually absent in Ukraine.

It is an established fact that the intensity of involvement in volunteerism is not the same across various groups of volunteers: there are always highly and weakly committed volunteers (Musick & Wilson, 2007, p. 28). At the same time, the intensity of volunteer participation turned out to be more significant in Ukraine. The survey sample included 142 active volunteers. In total, active volunteers spent on average 4,575 hours per month on volunteering, or 54,900 hours per year. Divided by Ukraine's adult permanent population, this figure gives approximately 5.8sec per head and per year. However, the mean time that active volunteers spent per year is much more significant, 387.62 hours (the median time is 120h). These figures are more than twice as large as the values of the corresponding indicators in Canada: the 2010 mean was 156h; the 2010

176 This is a standard greeting used by the Ukrainian nationalists. It must be noted, however, that the interview was conducted in the East.

median was 55h. In other words, more people are involved in volunteering in Canada than in Ukraine, but the intensity of their involvement is much higher in the case of the 'hard core' of Ukrainian volunteers.

Ukrainian volunteers appear to be more active and activist than their Western counterparts, which is in agreement with the previously mentioned finding that passive forms of volunteerism are common and on the rise in the West. Overall, the post-2013 volunteer movement has a mostly informal character. It is led by a relatively narrow number of highly committed and dedicated activists. Their initiatives benefit from the support, financial and in-kind, of a broader group of individual donors.

III.2 Predictors for the involvement into volunteering

Who are post-2013 volunteers in Ukraine? To answer this question, the impact on the involvement into volunteerism of a number of social, political and economic predictors was analysed. The dependent variable, the participation in volunteering, can be operationalised with the help of several questions included in the survey: How often did you work as a volunteer during the past 12 months (a nominal variable)?, How much time per month (in hours) on average did you spend on unpaid work in volunteer organisations and initiatives during the past 12 months (a scale variable)? and How much money in total (in UAH) did you give to charitable purposes during the past 12 months (a scale variable)? The distribution of answers to the two last questions turned out to be highly skewed and even various (log, ln, square root) transformations of the data did not allow for the achievement of a satisfactory result. In these circumstances, a safer, more conservative option was preferred: the first and the last variables were transformed into dummies ('1' for those who volunteered at least one time during the past 12 months and for those who gave at least some money to volunteer initiatives during the past 12 months, '0' for those who did not). The list of assumptions for binary logistic regression (Warner, 2013, p. 1008) is shorter than for multiple regression and these conditions are easier to meet. Namely, there is no requirement for normal distribution of the data. Furthermore, the dichotomous variables for assessing the involvement into volunteering were preferred for the sake of consistency with the results reported in the previous subsection.

The list of independent and control variables included more than 30 questions. Previous studies show that education level, age and gender may have an impact on one's involvement in volunteerism (Curtis et al., 2001, p. 795; Kamstra et al., 2016, p. 1037; Musick & Wilson, 2007; Painter & Paxton, 2014, pp. 413, 421). In addition to these controls, the impact of residence in particular areas (the West, the Centre, the South and the East of Ukraine; administrative regions; urban versus rural; cities of various sizes), language, occupation, self-assessed income and nationality was also assessed.

Compared with the controls, the choice of the independent variables derives from the assumption that volunteerism in Ukraine has an activist character and, consequently, a political dimension. Questions on the respondents' political and geopolitical orientations, generalised and institutional trust, values and memberships in various associations helped see how far Ukrainian volunteers are from the role of a simple service provider. Some of them necessitate brief comments. The Index of the efficiency of the Russian propaganda measures the respondent's susceptibility to take messages sent by the Russian media at face value: the more messages diffused by the country that is as of the time of writing at (undeclared) war with Ukraine, the higher the value of this variable (Kyiv International Institute of Sociology, 2015b). Associations with power give some clues as to the respondent's political values (see Chapter 6 for more detail). The inclusion of indicators from Hofstede's Power Distance Index (Hofstede, 1980, pp. 403–410), as well as the question on the preferred type of a political leader, has a similar rationale: how does the respondent perceive power, real and ideal (Chapter 6 offers more explanations on this issue)? Since most of the independent variables were originally nominal, they had to be dichotomised and transformed into dummy variables. In the final account, the impact of one scale (Index of the efficiency of Russian propaganda) and 190 plus dummy variables on the respondent's involvement into volunteerism was studied.

As mentioned previously, results of binary logistic regressions are somewhat hard to interpret. The variables that end up by being entered into regression have an impact on chances—odds—of the respondent to contribute either time or money to volunteer initiatives. Table 10.2 shows changes in the odds, Exp(B), of volunteering, for members of a group (e.g., voters against Ukraine's potential membership in NATO) compared with members of a relevant reference group (e.g., those who have no opinion on this issue or will not take part in such referendum). If Exp(B) exceeds 1.00, people with this characteristic are *less* likely to volunteer. If the odds are less than 1.00, those who have this characteristic are *more* likely to volunteer (more explanations are provided in Chapter 7). The independent and control variables entered in the model explain about 65% of the variation in odds-rates for active volunteers and about 74% of the variation in odds-rates for sponsors of volunteerism.

Table 10.2 'Results of binary statistic regressions to predict the odds of volunteering, Exp(B)'

Dependent variables	Worked as a volunteer			Contributed money		
	B	S.E.	Exp(B)	B	S.E.	Exp(B)
Voter of 'Demokratychnyi Al'ians' (1)				-3.341*	1.294	.035
Voter of 'UKROP' (1)				2.794**	0.939	16.343
Difficult to say for which party I would vote (1)				.796***	0.202	2.216
Voter of Dmytro Yarosh at the presidential elections (2)	-1.631**	0.589	0.196			
Voter against all at the presidential elections (2)				0.765*	0.346	2.149
Supporter of Ukraine's independent status (3)	-.779**	0.304	0.459			
Voter for the association with the Customs Union (3)				-0.966**	0.302	0.381
Voter against the association with the Customs Union (3)				-0.533*	0.228	0.587
Voter against NATO (3)				-0.419†	0.223	0.658
Index of the Efficiency of Russian propaganda	-0.024**	0.008	0.977	-0.017**	0.006	0.984
Power is associated with law (4)	-0.591*	0.308	0.554			
Power is associated with force (4)				-0.600**	0.195	0.549

Power is associated with politics (4)				-0.546*	0.213	0.579
Power is associated with control (4)				0.552*	0.272	1.736
Power is associated with might, *mogutnist'* (4)				0.839**	0.253	2.315
Power is associated with government (4)				0.528*	0.255	1.695
Desired boss: authoritarian type (5)				-1.172**	0.344	0.310
Gave money in response to calls on TV, the internet during past 5 years (6)	-0.698*	0.298	0.497	-3.326***	0.232	0.036
Worked as a volunteer during past 5 years (6)	-3.433***	0.488	0.032	1.988***	0.518	7.303
Gave clothes, food in response to calls on TV, the internet during past 5 years (6)				-0.999***	0.223	0.368
Gave blood during past 5 years (6)	-1.313***	0.405	0.269			
Participated in charity auctions during past 5 years (6)				-2.365***	0.387	0.094
Made significant financial contributions during past 5 years (6)				-4.651***	0.255	332.527
Made voluntary contributions in the other form during past 5 years (6)	-1.361**	0.503	0.256	-2.487***	0.366	46.134
Membership in cultural and architectural initiatives, fight against construction in protected area etc. (7)				2.633***	0.703	13.913
Membership in parents' associations at schools, kindergartens (7)				-1.809**	0.580	0.164
Membership in initiatives to help the army (7)	-1.385***	0.296	0.250	-1.523***	0.254	0.218
Other people can be trusted (8)	-0.695*	0.288	0.499			
State is to be rather distrusted (8)	-0.693**	0.266	0.500			
I'd prefer to live in a country with someone like Václav Havel as a president (8)				0.747*	0.352	2.110
I'd prefer to live in a country with someone like Bohdan Khmelnitsky as a president (8)	0.922*	0.387	2.513			

Volyn' (9)				1.854**	0.572	6.388
Dnipro (9)				-1.151***	0.308	0.316
Zhytomyr (9)				-1.540***	0.404	0.214
Ivano-Frankivsk (9)				1.105**	0.398	3.018
Lviv (9)				-1.248***	0.318	0.287
Rivne (9)				-1.237*	0.501	0.290
Ternopil (9)				-1.948***	0.464	0.142
Khmelnitsky (9)	-2.874***	0.643	0.056			
Lives in a village (10)	0.747*	0.326	2.110			
Age: 40–49 y.o. (11)				-0.611**	0.219	0.543
Education: complete secondary (8)	1.361*	0.631	3.899			
Education: higher (8)	-.705**	0.286	0.494			
Occupation: small business owner (12)	-1.227**	0.493	0.293			
Occupation: farmer, entrepreneur (12)				2.215***	0.629	9.163
Occupation: student (12)	-1.833***	0.521	0.160			
Occupation: in the military (12)				3.560**	1.116	35.149
Income: enough for buying food & clothes (8)	-.678**	0.271	0.507			
Worked as a volunteer during past 12 months (13)	-	-	-	0.846*	0.340	2.331
Contributed time to volunteer initiatives (13)	-2.918***	0.318	0.054	-2.515***	0.384	42.983
Made monetary contributions during past 12 months (13)	-1.209***	0.305	0.298	-	-	-
Constant	15.515***	1.857	5473242.498	10.771***	2.808	47624.447
Nagelkerke R^2	0.651			0.739		

Legend: levels of statistical significance: *** $p<0.001$, ** $p<0.01$, *$p<0.05$, † $p<0.1$. Reference categories: (1) No answer or a voter for the party with fewer than 15 potential votes; (2) No answer or for the candidate with fewer than 25 potential votes; (3) No answer/difficult to say or will not take part in the referendum; (4) Other associations with 'Power', no associations/difficult to say; (5) No answer or the question is not relevant (not employed); (6) no voluntary contributions/difficult to say; (7) No answer/difficult to say or did not participate in any initiative; (8) No answer/difficult to say; (9) Regions of Donetsk and Luhansk (parts of these regions under control of Ukraine); (10) Resident of a town, *selishche mis'kogo typu*; (11) 70 years and older; (12) No answer/difficult to say or the other job or unemployed; (13) Did contribute to volunteer initiatives. Variables removed: Dummy for voters of Yuri Boiko (from the Opposition Block known for his tolerant perception of Russia's role in Ukraine) was removed due to high collinearity between this dummy and the constant from the equation for predicting work in volunteer initiatives. The constant in binary logistic regression analysis can be interpreted as 'a logit score that is the same for all member of the sample (and that does not differ [across groups defined by this particular set of controls])' (Warner, 2013, p. 1016). If 'Voter of Boiko' correlates with the Constant, it means that his voters are close to the middle ground (the median respondent as defined by this particular set of the controls).

The impact of education on one's involvement in volunteerism in Ukraine is consistent with previous findings. Earlier studies showed that highly educated individuals exhibit the highest association membership rates in the West (Curtis et al., 2001, p. 795; Kamstra et al., 2016, p. 1037; Musick & Wilson, 2007, p. 119; Painter & Paxton, 2014, p. 421). In Ukraine, people with complete secondary education are less likely to volunteer. By contrast, people with higher education are more likely to be actively involved in volunteering. Gender does not have a significant impact, compared to, for instance, Canada (Musick & Wilson, 2007, p. 180). As to age, its influence appeared to be inconsistent. People in middle age tend to give more money to volunteer initiatives, which is consistent with previous findings (Kamstra et al., 2016, p. 1037; Musick & Wilson, 2007, p. 367; Painter & Paxton, 2014, p. 413). However, age has no impact on one's chances to be an active volunteer in Ukraine.

Geographical factors do not seem to have a clear and unambiguous influence on volunteering, contrary to the expectation that, taking into account relatively strong traditions of associational life in Western Ukraine (Subtelny, 2009, pp. 437–438[177]), volunteer initiatives would be concentrated in this part of the country. As a matter of fact, no 'big divide' between the East and the West seems to exist with respect to volunteerism. Survey results suggest the image of a mosaic rather than a clear-cut cleavage between the East and the West. The region of Khmelnitsky (in Western Ukraine) emerges as a stronghold of volunteerism. But active volunteers exist in urban areas (rural residents have higher odds to donate their time) of all parts of the country. As to sponsors of volunteerism, they tend

177 Orest Subtelny, namely, mentions that '"Rely on your own resources!" was the slogan of the activists in the "organic" sector of West Ukrainian society' between WWI and WWII. 'Samopomich' (Self-help), a today's political party created in Western Ukraine, positions itself as an heir of these traditions.

to concentrate in the regions of Dnipro, Zhytomyr, Lviv, Rivne and Ternopil—a mixture of Western and Eastern regions. Residents of the region of Ivano-Frankivsk, the other Western region, contribute less money, relatively speaking, to inhabitants of the regions of Donetsk and Luhansk. This finding is particularly noteworthy in light of the intersection of volunteerism and nation-state building: volunteerism seems to unite the nation instead of dividing it, as noted by some previously cited scholars.

Volunteers exhibit a high level of political consciousness: they have clear political preferences and these preferences lean towards democracy. For instance, voters of 'Demokratychnyi Al'ians' (Democratic Alliance), a democratic party, tend to contribute money to volunteering more actively than voters with no clear preferences. The other proof of volunteers' democratic orientation can be seen in their tendency to associate power with the law. They also tend to be rather sceptical about the state (those who believe that the state shall be rather distrusted have better chances to volunteer). At the same time, volunteerism involves a higher than average level of generalised trust, which is consistent with the previous findings (Musick & Wilson, 2007, p. 469). Those who believe that other people can be trusted have lower odds (i.e. higher chances) to volunteer.

The association between voting for Dmytro Yarosh, a nationalistically oriented potential presidential candidate (born notably in the region of Dnipro, i.e. in Eastern Ukraine) and active volunteering suggests that not only political, but also national consciousness may be at play. The assumption of the interconnection between volunteerism and the nation-state building is further supported by the fact that the respondents who prefer to see Ukraine as an independent country as opposed to its membership either in the European Union or in the Customs Union under aegis of Russia have more chances to be active volunteers. Interestingly enough, volunteers would not want to have someone like Bohdan Khmelnitsky as a political leader in Ukraine. Khmelnitsky's credentials as a promoter of Ukraine's nationhood were to some extent undermined by his backing of the project of Ukraine's association with Russia (Hrushevsky, 1996; see also Chapter 1). Geopolitical preferences of sponsors of volunteerism have a more ambivalent nature. Compared with those who have no opinion on this matter, potential voters for and against Ukraine's membership in the Customs Union have more chances to give money. The small yet positive impact of Russian propaganda needs explaining. The respondents who agree with at least some messages of Russian propagandists lean toward volunteering and sponsoring volunteerism. A closer look leads one to believe that this effect is mostly due to the perception of the US. Ukrainian volunteers seem to disapprove of the role played by both Russia and the US.

An activist character of volunteerism in Ukraine can be clearly seen in its connection with other association memberships and the participation in various forms of non-profit activities. Membership in post-2013 initiatives aiming to help the Ukrainian army increases one's likelihood of volunteering and to donate money. Membership in parents' councils reduces one's chances of donating money. The respondents who gave blood have lower odds (i.e. better chances) of volunteering. Participants in charity auctions have higher chances of donating money as well. As in the previous studies of volunteerism, individual money donations are associated with time spent on participating in volunteer initiatives.

Overall, the portrait of the post-2013 Ukrainian volunteer has heterogeneous elements. It would be more correct to speak of two portraits, one for the active volunteer who contributes his or her time, and the other for the sponsor of volunteer initiatives (unfortunately, the available data does not allow drawing a portrait of the third type of volunteers, volunteer fighters). The active volunteer tends to be politically and nationally conscious, which makes him or her an excellent candidate for a role in state- and nation-building. He or she has membership in multiple associations and the experience of participating in different volunteer initiatives. These characteristics are consistent with the assumption made on the basis of the literature review that volunteerism in post-2013 Ukraine involves a high level of commitment and has political (pro-democratic) and nationalist dimensions. Furthermore, volunteerism does not concentrate in Western Ukraine. Instead, volunteerism hot spots tend to be scattered across regions of Western, Central and

Eastern Ukraine, which may be indicative of the movement of the centre in state- and nation-building from the West to the other parts of Ukraine. The fact that the language spoken by the respondent did not affect one's chances for involvement in volunteerism further supports this finding.

The sponsor of volunteerism shares some characteristics with the active volunteer (membership in several associations, participation in various non-profit activities, and the experience of active volunteerism), but the others substantially differ. The sponsor has weaker and less consistent political and geopolitical preferences, which does not prevent his or her involvement in initiatives to help the Ukrainian army in curbing Russia's invasion. He or she seems to accept authoritarian leaders and to reject the democratic type of leader. Namely, the respondents whose preferred political leader is Václav Havel have higher odds of donating money.

IV. Social innovations made by Ukrainian volunteers

Volunteerism in Ukraine appears to be driven by highly committed activists, in contrast with a larger number of less active and dedicated individuals who constitute a core of volunteerism in the developed countries. The rich potential of these activists constitutes an important internal resource for state- and nation building. To make this argument more specific, the task of building a nation-state practically from scratch, i.e. from the bottom line of a fragile state that had in 2013 some elements of a failed state, calls for input from social and cultural innovations. Several institutions will have to be either re-invented de novo, or creatively adapted to the particularities of Ukrainian society. Some leaders of the volunteer movement appear to be prepared for this task.[178] They aim to initiate changes, to make innovations that would benefit the society as a whole.

---

178 Socio-economic profiles of several interlocutors quoted in this section may seem identical. It does not mean that only excerpts from interviews with few

> 'The key motivation here is to change something, to change the world around you, make this world a better place to live for you and for other people... Sometimes it is simple a desire to change, some people just like making changes... It's more about a mission to make positive changes. A question arises: what are positive changes, for whom they are positive? Everything depends on how what you're doing contributes to changing the system as a whole, to improving the operation of its particular segments' (female, 25-39 y.o., Kyiv, in Ukrainian).

> '[I want] to change, to change something. Umm [laugh] Now it's difficult to say what exactly [I want] to change. Why, for instance, do I all these things? Because I see that I can influence various processes, I see that some things are changing' (female, 40–54 y.o., Kyiv, in Ukrainian).

> 'We had a more principled position that we are self-sufficient in a sense and capable of... changing the country' (male, 40–54 y.o., Dnipro, in Ukrainian).

Some innovations initiated by leaders of the volunteer movement have an economic nature. Their benefits can be appropriated, which led some volunteers-innovators to become more conventional, profit driven entrepreneurs.

> 'There are civic leaders, whose former volunteer initiatives have progressively transformed into small business. It's not that bad. The fellows who at the very beginning produced combat boots (*bertsy*[179]) investing money from their pockets now have a small production facility. They don't get exorbitant profits. They cannot afford continue to invest their own money, however. They start to make some money. It's normal. It's how it should be' (female, 25-39 y.o., Kyiv, in Russian).

The other leaders of the volunteer movement consider a political career or a public servant career. A key related question is whether their efforts can achieve a critical mass or simply the existing system will change them at the end of the day.

> 'At one moment I realised that to solve the existing problems, volunteers' efforts do not suffice... We cannot keep substituting volunteer initiatives for the state. Either the system must be changed or the volunteer will change. Either volunteers will go to the public service and change it from within, or

---

leaders are actually cited. Since most leaders are in the same age groups (25–54 y.o.), their short descriptions look similar.

179 There was a significant shortage of combat boots, among other elements of military equipment, at the early stages of the military conflict.

they'd rather radically change what they have been doing so far' (female, 25–39 y.o., Kyiv, in Ukrainian).

'Some solutions were found as early as at the start of [Russia's invasion in] Donbas. We'd got some vision how things [related to forced migrants] should be done.—What do you mean by "vision"? How to organize their accommodation?—Yes. I recently visited Georgia during my holidays. I dropped by their Ministry responsible for assisting migrants. We had some 1.5h discussion with the staff. What they are doing now, we did in 2014. In other words, the organisation of work with forced migrants that we invented is similar to that used by this Ministry… It turned out that I can make contacts, do some GR work and I am quite happy with this discovery. I may now consider joining a political project or a government organisation, if our ideas are used for reforming relevant processes' (female, 25–39 y.o., Dnipro, interview in two languages).

Regardless of their subsequent evolution—towards innovations in the sphere of business or administrative reform, current and former leaders will be better off in maintaining connections with the volunteer movement as an 'incubator of innovations' and an almost endless source of ideas. Examples of three innovations born within the post-2013 volunteer movement illustrate its rich potential in this respect.

IV.1 Use of Facebook as a means to increase transparency

Many volunteer initiatives initially involved socially close participants—family members, friends, acquaintances. However, as they grow in size, the need to reach out to a larger number of active participants, and especially sponsors, becomes acute. On one hand, the resources of those who started an initiative were quickly depleting. On the other hand, the low level of generalised trust complicated the task of soliciting donations from personally unknown people. What were the guarantees that donations would not be simply appropriated or misused by those who had launched a call for monetary and/or in-kind contributions? Furthermore, most volunteer initiatives did not have a state registration at the very beginning, which excluded the use of banking accounts. Monetary contributions were accumulated on personal accounts of the volunteers who simply posted their credit card numbers in the social networks, first of all, Facebook.

The reliance on Facebook as a platform for communication and discussion suggested a solution: to post banking account statements, receipts, images or videos confirming what exactly was bought using the donated funds and who exactly received help. The solution emerged in a spontaneous manner. Textbooks on volunteerism do not contain it since they primarily target formal organisations that need to comply with at least some accounting requirements. Several volunteer initiatives started to post activity reports independently one from the other.

> 'If moneys are accumulated on [personal credit] cards and the amount of the donations keeps increasing all the time, we need to report how these donations are used, down to a last kopeck. As a result, the level of trust increases, which in turn leads to further increases in the amount of donations' (male, 40–54 y.o., Kyiv, in Ukrainian).

> 'It often happens that members of parliament collect donations and then these funds disappear. No one knows where they have gone. In our case, it never happens. We get [money], we buy [something], we take pictures [of it] and post or send them [to the sponsors]' (female, 24 y.o. and less, Kyiv, in Ukrainian).

> 'We had to gain trust. When a volunteer initiative is established, [its participants] create a Facebook account. Everything they receive on the [credit] card, they make public. We've got this amount of money; we spent it in such a way. Thank you very much, here are some pictures. In other words, a full activity report is expected.—Was this practice spontaneously invented or you imitated the practice used by the others?—Initially, when everything was bought for our own money, we didn't need to report to anyone. We just posted information about our visits [to a local battalion of volunteer fighters]. I was interested where the relatives of these guys are. We started to go there often, but I didn't know their families. Then I reckoned that perhaps the guys didn't want to tell their families where exactly they are stationed… I always believe than when I take someone else's money, I must give account of any related expenses. These are not my money, after all' (female, 40–54 y.o., Dnipro, in Russian).

IV.2 From social networks to social connections: on matchmaking

The other solution to the problem of trust and accountability refers to avoiding the need to accumulate money on the volunteers' account altogether. Instead, the volunteer may play the role of a matchmaker, i.e. someone who connects people in need of assistance with people who can offer such assistance. In a sense, volunteers spontaneously revived a traditional institute of *blatmeisters*, or contact makers (Ledeneva, 1999, p. 115) that existed in Ukraine in Soviet times. In the economy characterised by permanent shortages, individuals who knew how to find the right people with access to a good or service of interest, prospered. Volunteers as contact-makers do not seek profit, however. They also rely on modern technologies, such as social networks, as a tool for matchmaking, in addition to a more traditional way of facilitating contacts through the use of one's own connections (Facebook in addition to one's 'phonebook'). It is not by coincidence that the idea of a specialised matchmaking site for volunteers, www.volonter.org, was born in the milieu of volunteers (see below an excerpt from the interview with one of its creators).

> 'I helped... You know, if you know the system and people in the system. I have never been personally involved in buying or supplying anything. I simply gave contacts. Yes, I gave contacts' (female, 40–54 y.o., Kyiv, in Ukrainian).

> 'They did not ask the doctors for help, the wounded. They ask the volunteers instead. For instance, we come [to the hospital] and I hear: "X., I need an arm prosthesis". I look for relevant specialists. Or a something related to stomach. I take him to a specialist' (female, 24 y.o. and less, Kyiv, in Ukrainian).

> 'In the morning of November 30 [2013] we created a EuroMaidan SOS page and posted two messages. The first one: If you were wounded at Maidan, if your relatives got arrested, if you witnessed acts of violence [committed by the police]... call us and we'll provide some legal assistance free of charge. When we posted this message, we took risks since initially we didn't have any lawyer working for us... Then the second message was posted immediately: if you are a lawyer willing to provide legal assistance to the victims of the violence pro bono, call us. To our great surprise, it worked. Almost immediately we got calls, our messages were largely reposted, some media re-

published them. We started to work around the clock... Hundreds and hundreds people who were beaten, tortured, arrested, accused of criminal offenses, of administrative offenses came to see us. Relatives of the missing people called us, later we called relatives of the killed...' (female, 25–39 y.o., Kyiv, in Ukrainian).

'I created civic organisation "Center for the support of volunteerism—Voloner.org", there is a website with the same name. It will be host of a network of volunteer initiatives, a volunteer bourse of sorts... where activists or organisations present their initiatives... I've got this idea in 2014, when everyone was involved in volunteerism to some extent' (male, 25–39 y.o., Kyiv, in Ukrainian).

IV.3 Adaptation of some traditional social institutions for the purposes of volunteerism

In addition to the revival of the institution of matchmaking, volunteers adapted for their needs the other traditional institution, *zemliachestvo*. *Zemliachestvo* is a community of people born in the same region or locality. After moving to other places, members of *zemliachestvo* maintain contacts, organise community events and help each other. The institution of *zemliachestvo* tends to be particularly strong in traditional societies (among the post-Soviet countries, *zemliachestva* are active in Kazakhstan, see Oleinik, Yermekov & Kuatbekov, 2015, p. 189). Regions of Ukraine with a particularly strong sense of regional identity (for instance, some Western regions) have dense networks of *zemliachestva*. After 2013, social ties developed within these networks were used for the purposes of mobilisation of resources for volunteerism and also as a 'repository' of contacts that may eventually facilitate matchmaking. One interlocutor discusses the case of *zemliachestvo* of Volyn' (a Western region). The idea of how *zemliachestvo* works inspired the other to design a matchmaking website in a particular manner.

'After the Day of constitution I started to help my compatriot, X., who had been severely wounded [in the Eastern front]. His mom followed me begging to help: "We know, you can [help us]. Take us, as a volunteer. We don't ask anyone else since we heard that you know the best what can be done in the circumstances". To send him in a hospital abroad—it's difficult. One cannot simply take and send someone abroad. I said that they find a right person and I'll help them. All their family called me from Volyn'... And he [X.]

was sent to France, his leg was saved as a result of a series of unique surgeries' (female, 40–54 y.o., Kyiv, in Ukrainian).

'On our website, we have a map indicating regional origins of all the wounded, we used the idea of *zemliachetsvo* here. The map is subdivided by regions. It is clear that people from the region of Zhytomyr will be willing to provide help to the locals, people from Kyiv—to the wounded from this city etc.' (male, 25–39 y.o., Kyiv, in Ukrainian).

Conclusion

For scholars of volunteerism, the case of Ukraine is of certain interest. Volunteer initiatives initially tended to be foreign implants, as Ukrainian society did not have strong relevant traditions (except in a few regions, such as Galicia in Western Ukraine, where associational life was flourishing between WWI and WWII). Before 2013, they were financed and promoted foremost by foreign donors and did not have a truly mass support.

The situation changed after the 2013–2014 Revolution of Dignity and Russia's subsequent invasion. Volunteerism took a mass form and became one of the most trusted institutions in Ukraine. The scope and scale of post-2013 volunteerism is comparable to or even exceeds those in developed countries. This remarkable result was achieved as a result of a radical and rapid adaptation of volunteerism to local conditions. From an implanted institution, volunteerism has been transformed into a home-grown institution incorporating several elements of social institutions that existed in Ukraine's past—matchmaking, *zemliachestvo*, to cite just a few.

As a result of this transformation and vernacularisation, volunteerism in Ukraine has acquired a number of particular characteristics. Compared with the Western model that was replicated in Ukraine before 2013, the emerging Ukrainian model is less formal and formalised, more activist and has a strong political dimension. Much like their Western counterparts, volunteers in Ukraine provide services to those in need: the wounded, forced migrants, the veterans and so forth. At the same time, a volunteer in this country is more than just a service provider. He or she also has a potential to play an active role in state- and nation building. The volunteer is an advocate of democracy. Some scholars argue that democracy may be learned once relevant institutions are in place (Harasymiw, 2002, p. 10). In the Ukrainian case, this logic did not work quite well. To become operational, institutions of democracy have to be given a fresh start. And volunteers are prepared to have a say in this process, promoting and overseeing the implementation of the rules of a democratic game.

The volunteer is an advocate of the nascent Ukrainian nation as well. Volunteerism in this country seems to be connected to the nationalist movement, understood as an actor aiming to attain and maintain the autonomy, unity and identity of the Ukrainian nation in the making. Namely, they prioritise the project of maintaining Ukraine's independent status over proposals to join either the EU or the Customs Union. The fact that active volunteers are not concentrated in particular regions (e.g., in Western as opposed to Eastern Ukraine), the volunteer movement may well become a base for consolidation of the traditionally divided country—between the East and the West, between various regions (Shulman, 2006), between the Russian and Ukrainian speaking populations. Difficulties with using ethnicity (Harasymiw, 2002, pp. 213, 236), language or even borders (Kuzio, 1998, p. 100)—in a country involved into a protracted military conflict—for building the Ukrainian nation-state call for paying more attention to the volunteer movement combining both civic and nationalist elements.

Taking into consideration the significant potential for social innovation that volunteers in this country have, they may potentially support a larger project of making democracy work by vernacularising democratic institutions. Much like the volunteer movement in Ukraine, to be workable, the democratic nation-state in Ukraine needs to be adapted to national particularities and institutions. Vernacularised institutions of the democratic nation-state will necessary diverge from the blueprints and textbook examples. Furthermore, they can hardly be designed in advance. Instead, they will likely emerge as a result of multiple trials and errors, and numerous bottom-up initiatives, some of which will disappear whereas others will survive.

Annex A

Table 'Codebook and coding frequency'

Category	Code	Description	Count	% Codes	Cases	% Cases	Nb Words	% Words
concepts	Democracy	Definitions of democracy and associations with this term	29	1.9%	15	68.2%	2160	1.3%
concepts	Power	Definitions of power, associations with power	40	2.6%	22	100.0%	2704	1.6%
concepts	Trust	Definitions of trust, associations with trust	25	1.6%	19	86.4%	1811	1.1%
concepts	Volunteerism	Definitions of volunteerism	81	5.2%	22	100.0%	5950	3.5%
concepts	War	What the respondent thinks of the ongoing war, its consequences and prospects	128	8.3%	22	100.0%	9855	5.7%
government	Control	The idea of control: we need to control the government and its actions	43	2.8%	15	68.2%	3829	2.2%
government	Iron hand	The need for an 'iron hand' and rationale for it	14	0.9%	10	45.5%	1080	0.6%
government	Pressure	Situations in which the government is putting pressure on the volunteers. Why does it happen and in which forms	19	1.2%	12	54.5%	1999	1.2%
government	Registration	Issues of the state's registration: pros and cons	44	2.8%	20	90.9%	3331	1.9%

government	Substitution	Volunteers as performing functions that are normally carried out by the state	146	9.4%	22	100.0%	12790	7.4%
Maidan	2004	Perception of the Orange revolution	34	2.2%	18	81.8%	3164	1.8%
Maidan	2013	Perception and characterisation of the Revolution of Dignity	71	4.6%	19	86.4%	7115	4.1%
Maidan	Geopolitics	Geopolitical considerations, namely the issue of European integration or the association with Russia	51	3.3%	20	90.9%	3961	2.3%
Maidan	Language	Issues of language	22	1.4%	14	63.6%	1698	1.0%
volunteers	Amount	Estimations of the amount of resources at the volunteers' disposal. Dynamics of the contributions	49	3.2%	16	72.7%	3390	2.0%
volunteers	Background	Social profile and background of volunteers. Their socio-economic and political characteristics	130	8.4%	22	100.0%	10818	6.3%
volunteers	Facebook	The role of Facebook, its uses by the volunteers	101	6.5%	20	90.9%	8091	4.7%
volunteers	Foreign assistance	Forms in which assistance is actually provided and needed	79	5.1%	21	95.5%	7602	4.4%
volunteers	History	References to Ukraine's history	18	1.2%	6	27.3%	1105	0.6%
volunteers	Marginals	Previous marginal status of the volunteer because of his/her desire to change the system; the volunteer's unwillingness to accept rules of the game considered as unjust	21	1.4%	11	50.0%	1293	0.8%

volunteers	Power within	Power within volunteers' organisations and initiatives	33	2.1%	15	68.2%	2434	1.4%
volunteers	Pre-2013	NGOs and initiatives founded before the 2013 events	30	1.9%	16	72.7%	2989	1.7%
volunteers	Social innovations	Examples of social entrepreneurship: invention of a new practice or a successful adaptation of an existing one to the local conditions	65	4.2%	18	81.8%	6150	3.6%
volunteers	Starting point	How the respondent started volunteering, under which conditions	40	2.6%	19	86.4%	4566	2.6%
volunteers	Trust within	The role of trust in the operation of volunteers' initiatives	85	5.5%	21	95.5%	6959	4.0%
volunteers	Types	Types of volunteers (contributors, activists, those who started to work for the government...). Volunteers and *dobrovol'tsi* (volunteer fighters). Various degrees of the involvement. Various typologies, including using the criterion of one's closeness to the authorities	153	9.9%	22	100.0%	13840	8.0%

Annex B

Table **'Membership in which associations listed below did you have during the past 12 months (or in actions of which associations listed below did you take part during the past 12 months), a multiple response question'**

Association or initiative	Ukraine, 2016			Russia, 2014
	N	Percent of responses	Percent of cases	Percent of cases
1. Cultural and architectural initiatives, fight against construction in protected area, etc. (pre-2013)	24	1.0%	1.2%	1.5%
2. Associations of home and secondary home owners (pre-2013)	29	1.2%	1.4%	9%
3. Special interest groups: women, veterans, LGBT, car owners... (pre-2013)	12	0.5%	0.6%	1.4%
4. Human rights protection: legal aid, soldiers' mothers etc. (pre-2013)	6	0.3%	0.3%	2%
5. Professional associations, trade unions (pre-2013)	37	1.5%	1.8%	3.5%
6. School, university self-management, students' unions (pre-2013)	35	1.4%	1.7%	2.2%
7. National-patriotic movements (pre-2013)	18	0.8%	0.9%	1%
8. Control of electoral process (pre-2013)	37	1.6%	1.8%	2.4%
9. Local branches of political parties, youth parliaments, discussion clubs, caucuses (pre-2013)	11	0.5%	0.6%	1.6%
10. Parents associations at schools, kindergartens (pre-2013)	33	1.4%	1.6%	3.1%
11. Ethnic communities, diasporas, *zemliachestva* (pre-2013)	8	0.3%	0.4%	0.7%

12. Religious associations, parishes (pre-2013)	128	5.3%	6.3%	2.8%
13. Sport associations, tourist associations, hunters' associations, historical reconstruction, dog owners' associations etc. (pre-2013)	18	0.8%	0.9%	3.6%
14. Help to forced migrants (post-2013)	83	3.4%	4.0%	n.a.
15. Help to the army (post-2013)	245	10.2%	12.0%	n.a
16. Help to those in need (invalids, sick etc.) other than forced migrants and the army (pre-2013)	83	3.4%	4.1%	8.6%
17. Anti-corruption and other investigations (pre-2013)	10	0.4%	0.5%	1.2%
18. Ecological initiatives (pre-2013)	21	0.9%	1.0%	1.8%
In none of these	1,502	62.5%	73.6%	69.7%
Difficult to say	45	1.9%	2.2%	4.3%
No answer	20	0.8%	1.0%	0%
Total	2,405	100%	117.9%	120.4%

Legend: source of the data for Russia—a survey '2014-SP-52 Lithuania' carried out on a representative sample (N=1,504) between December 5 and December 18, 2014 by Levada-Center (it did not include alternatives 14 and 15). A higher membership rate in home owner associations can be partly explained by a higher pressure put by the Russian government on owners of apartments in multi-storey buildings. They are expected to bear an increasing burden of building maintenance and renovation costs. In other words, this type of membership has more mandatory elements in Russia than in Ukraine (also subsection I.2 of the book's Conclusion for further discussion).

Conclusion
'Guiding or helping hand? On the role of foreign assistance'

This book argues in favour of placing greater emphasis on the internal actors and processes in Ukraine when making sense of the situation in this country from 2013 on. If adapted by Western scholars, policy-makers and the public at large, what does such an approach involve in practical terms?

On one hand, the proposed take on the developments in Ukraine requires the understanding of particularities of the relatively early stages in nation-state building. This process has started in Ukraine relatively late—compared with the other countries of Western and even Eastern Europe. In a sense, Ukraine is currently at the same stage in nation-state building as the US in the mid-19th century where 'after the Declaration of Independence... most people still identified themselves not as Americans but as Virginians, New Yorkers or Rhode Islanders' (Turley, 2010, p. 45). In the Ukrainian case, regional identities also prevailed before the 2013–2014 Revolution of Dignity (Korostelina, 2014, p. 177; Wilson, 2002). Since no textbook or blueprint on how to build a nation-state exists, the actors involved have no other choice but to learn by doing. Finding a model of nation-state that would be a good fit for the institutional environment in Ukraine through trial and error does not exclude detours and dead ends down the road. Some tolerance toward potential mistakes of the nation-state builders is thus needed.

On the other hand, moving from an outside to inside focus does not exclude any external input altogether. The external input shall not suppress or substitute for the internal input nevertheless. Since there is no universal blueprint for building a nation-state, the teacher-pupil model seems hardly appropriate. A helping hand offered by the West will likely be more appreciated than a directing and guiding hand. The guiding hand limits the autonomy in decision making of those who are subject to it. The helping hand offers support without attempting to interfere with decision making. Programs of foreign assistance and aid shall be organised accordingly.

I. On an emerging concept of the Ukrainian nation

As argued in subsection I.2 of Chapter 10, nation-state building is impossible without nationalism in some form. The question, then, is which nationalism may constitute the foundation of the Ukrainian nation in the making. Anthony Smith (2002, pp. 8–9) opposes 'civic' and 'ethnic' models of nations. Nations of the former type prevail in Western Europe. They have at their origin a rational-legal association of individuals with a strong voluntarist component. Nations of the latter type are common in Eastern Europe and Asia. As their name suggests, genealogy and ethnicity play an important role. In other words, the civic model involves a great deal of individualism, whereas the ethnic model—of communitarianism.

As with any ideal type, civic and ethnic nations rarely exist in a pure form. Most existing (as opposed to imagined) nation-states represent a combination of their elements. Alain Touraine (1992, p. 312) expresses this idea in the following words: 'a conscious willingness to protect individuality and personal experience is a distinctive characteristic of the Subject. This does not exclude, however, the attachment to a community and its traditions'. The search for a right combination of individualism and communitarianism in a particular nation-state is neither automatic nor does it have a predetermined outcome. As a matter of fact, the Ukrainian nation will not take its final shape before several possible combinations are attempted in the circumstances at hand.

I.1 Nation forged by the shared experience of resistance

The Jewish experience of strengthening national consciousness through collective resistance to oppression represents a path in nation-state building that may be more likely in the case of Ukraine than some others. This assumption involves a paradox: relationships between Ukrainians and Jews were not always friendly and mutually beneficial in the past. When Ukraine was a part of the Polish-Lithuanian commonwealth in the 14th-17th centuries (see subsection I.2.d of Chapter 1), the Jews had a privileged status both in the cities, where they formed separate self-governing associations of trade and craftsmen, and in the countryside, where they had a monopoly on running taverns (*shinky* and *korchmy*) and often managed estates on behalf of the Polish absentee owners interacting with the Ukrainian peasants on a day-to-day basis (Gordon, 1983, p. 54–55). This led many Ukrainians to perceive the Jews as their enemy, if not arch-enemy. The mass uprising in the 17th century led by Bohdan Khmelnitsky[180] and later attempts to achieve Ukraine's autonomous status in 1917–1920 (see subsection I.2.g of Chapter 1) were accompanied by pogroms and mass killings of the Jews. According to some estimates, between 35,000 and 50,000 Jews were killed in pogroms in 1919–1920 alone (Subtelny, 2009, p. 363, see also Ibid., p. 128). How can one then argue that the experience of Jews provides valuable insights for making sense of Ukrainians' most recent attempts to build their nation-state?

Not having their own nation-state for most of their history, Jews were discriminated against in many places where they resided. They fled from the Holy Roman Empire of the 15th-16th centuries under pressure of Emperor Maximilian I—first to Poland and then to the territories of today's Ukraine (Hrushevsky, 1994, p. 255). They were murdered by the Nazis in Germany and the countries that they occupied in a highly systematic and 'rationalised' manner (Lozowick, 2002). The Jews learned that in order to protect themselves, they needed to work together in their efforts. This experience of oppression and especially Jews' collective resistance to oppression became a central element of their national identity. Their shared ethnicity greatly contributed to the Jews' group cohesion.

180 The historical novel *Taras Bulba* (1835) by Nikolai Gogol, a prominent writer of Ukrainian origin, contains several illustrations of prejudices that Ukrainians held against the Jews at that time. Works of Mykhailo Hrushevsky are not free of such prejudices either.

After all, Jews were targeted *because* of their ethnicity. However, not only ethnic Jews participated in their fight against oppression and extermination: namely, non-Jews on more than just one occasion helped the Jews to escape death in the Nazi concentration camps. Amy Allen (1999, p. 122) offers an interpretation of Hanna Arendt's thoughts in this respect: 'One does not need to "be" a Jew to resist in terms of a Jewish identity under attack'. Anyone who assisted the Jews in their actions in concert aiming to resist violence and oppression directly or indirectly contributed to their project of nation-building.

The Jewish experience is relevant to the ongoing process of building a Ukrainian nation-state in two senses. First, it shows how a community, including a nation, can be built without relying on exclusionary identity categories (ethnicity, gender and so forth). Allen (1999) uses the Jewish case as a model for proposing an idea of feminism that would be appealing not only to women. Anyone sympathetic to the fight against discrimination could join the ranks of feminists so defined. The experience of confronting the Russian aggression in Ukraine plays a similar role: one does not have to be an ethnic Ukrainian to say 'no' to violence. Anyone who says 'no' to violence directly or indirectly contributes to the success of the project of the Ukrainian nation-state, including ethnic Russians, Crimean Tatars, Jews, Georgians, Byelorussians and representatives of many other nationalities. The finding that the rejection of violence represents one of the distinctive features of the Ukrainian national culture (see Chapters 1 and 6) can be properly understood in light of the arguments above.

Second, the Jewish experience suggests that individual resistance to violence does not suffice. What makes a nation is the experience of collective resistance, the involvement in action in concert. Power understood in this book as human action in concert helps resist and limit violence. In addition to this, actions in concert allow for the creation of the infrastructure necessary for the functioning of a democratic state; namely, civil society and the public sphere. Civil society and the public space then can be perceived as products of such resistance in concert. 'Although power emerges out of individuals acting together, it also makes possible such collective action by providing the space within which such actions can be carried out' (Allen, 2002, p. 138). In other words, the experience of collective resistance constitutes an integral element of state-building too.

Seen from this perspective, the Ukrainian nation-state in the making has foundations that are neither purely ethnic nor purely civic. To paraphrase Arendt's understanding of her Jewishness, one does not need to be an ethnic Ukrainian to resist in terms of a Ukrainian identity under attack. The Ukrainians are united by their common experience of resistance to violence. The volunteer movement that emerged and was strengthened after 2013 probably serves as the best illustration (Chapter 10). This movement has a well pronounced nationalist dimension. At the same time, its ranks include not only ethnic Ukrainians. Some interviews that inform the analysis of the volunteer movement were conducted in Russian and with interlocutors who have Russian family names. Furthermore, the mass survey conducted in September 2016 (see Section II of Chapter 10 for its parameters) shows that among the self-identified Russians, the ratio of those who participate in volunteer initiatives targeting internally displaced persons is higher than among the self-identified Ukrainians (8%, N=113 and 3.8%, N=1,820 correspondingly). The ratio of volunteers who provide help to the Ukrainian army in two groups—the self-identified Ukrainians and respondents with a self-identified double identity, Ukrainian and Russian, is similar (12.6%, N=1820 and 10.5%, N=57 correspondingly).

A group of highly committed and patriotically oriented volunteers emerged as a driver of the 2013–2014 mass protests in Ukraine and the subsequent developments. Their capacity to act in concert has two dimensions: ethnic and civic. Connections with the nationalist movement illustrate the former (see Table 10.2 and relevant discussion in Chapter 10). 'Civic' associations with human dignity that the respondents have (law, human rights and so forth) and the record of involvement in a number of civic initiatives constitutes the latter. Prospects for the building of the Ukrainian nation-state will, to a significant extent, depend on whether this combination of civic and ethnic elements can be scaled up and replicated at the national level. Will representatives of the post-2013 volunteerism emerge as an agens movens of a larger-scale social—or, better, historical (see subsection I.2 of Chapter 10) movement and a new generation of Ukraine's power elite? The answer to this question is the key to the success or failure of the Ukrainian nation-state.

I.2 Scaling up the post-2013 volunteer experience

As of the time of writing this book, neither a negative nor a positive answer can be ruled out. The level of generalised trust has been declining in Ukraine since the first half of the 1990s (Figure 11.1; see also Section I of Chapter 2 and subsection III.1.a of Chapter 10). Neither the Revolution of Dignity nor the mobilisation against the Russian aggression has altered this negative trend. In fact, these events may instead have contributed to a recent aggravation of the situation: the mean value of this indicator for the Wave 6 (2010–2014) World Values sample is 24.2% (49 countries, N=88,852), the level of generalised trust in Russia is 30% and increasing, whereas in Ukraine it reached a historical low of 18.5% in 2016. Successful large scale action in concert requires a higher level of generalised trust.

Figure 11.1 'Generally speaking, would you say that most people can be trusted or that you need to be very careful in dealing with people?, % of those who believe that most people can be trusted, Ukraine and Russia, 1990–2016'

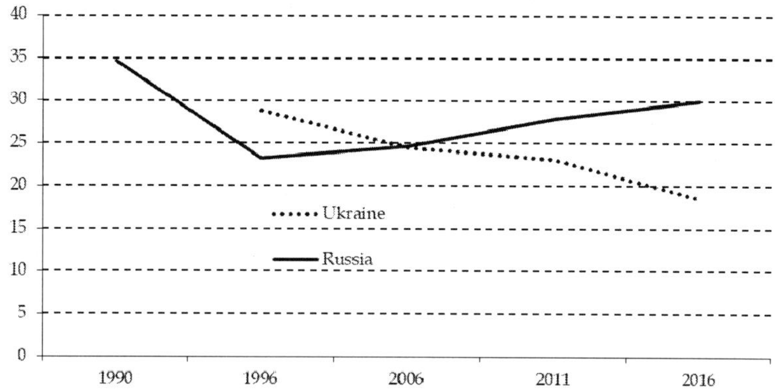

Source: World Values Survey Association, 2015; Levada Center, 2017, p. 21 and the Kyiv International Institute of Sociology. Sample sizes were N=2,811 in 1996, N=1,000 in 2006, N=1,500 and N=2,040 in Ukraine; N=1,961 in 1990, N=2,040 in 1996, N=2,033 in 2006, N=2,500 in 2011 and N=1,600 in 2016 in Russia.

The situation with homeowners associations (HOAs), illustrates difficulties with replicating the success of volunteer initiatives related to curbing the Russian aggression and with alleviating some of its consequences, namely, the flow of internally displaced persons (forced internal migrants), in the other spheres that also require volunteers' involvement. The provision of housing and public utilities (*zhitlovo-kommunal'ni poslugy*) in Ukraine lags behind international standards regardless of the choice of a specific point of comparison, the Western or the Russian one. For instance, Ukrainian households paid 0.6 UAH (0.023 USD) for 1 kw/h in December 2016, whereas households in Moscow, where tariffs tend to be higher than elsewhere in Russia—3.8 Russian Rubles (RUR, 0.059 USD). However, taking into consideration the difference in the level of GDP per capita in these countries, 2,115 USD against 9,057 USD in 2015 correspondingly (World Bank, 2017), Ukrainians spent a larger—1.65 times larger—share of their income on electricity.

One way to deal with these problems was through the creation of the HOA. The Law of Ukraine 'On homeowners associations' No. 2866-14 enacted in 2002 under President Leonid Kuchma[181] provides the legal framework for HOAs' operation. The legal acts define an HOA as a not-for-profit legal entity, created by co-owners for operation, management and maintenance of their indivisible and common property, i.e. the building and the adjacent territory (OECD, 2004). The HOA can sign contracts for the provision of housing and public utilities with service providers of their choice, as well as monitor and enforce them. Surveys show that the level of residents' satisfaction with the maintenance services tend to be higher in buildings with HOAs (Ibid.).

Despite the advantages of having a HOA and the government's attempts to promote their creation,[182] these associations remain rare in Ukraine. In September 2016, only 1.4% of Ukrainians participated in HOAs, whereas in Russia the corresponding figure was six times higher (9%; see Annex B to Chapter 10). In this light, official figures as to the number of HOAs in Ukraine shall be taken with a grain of salt. For instance, the State Statistics Service of Ukraine (SSSU), reports that there were 16,908 HOAs in 2013 and 25,754 HOAs in 2016. It means that 21.1% of all multi-storey buildings in the country (N=79,700) had HOAs in 2013 and about a third, 34.4% (N=74,900) in 2016 (Derzhavna Sluzhba Statystyky Ukrainy, 2016c).[183] Either the residents do not know about the existence of a HOA in their building; they do not make even a formal contribution to its operation, or the official statistics count HOAs that exist on

---

181 http://zakon2.rada.gov.ua/laws/show/2866-14 accessed April 03, 2017. Two other relevant documents are the Resolution of Cabinet of Ministers 'On realisation of the Law of Ukraine "On homeowners associations"' No. 1521 of 2002, and in the Order of the Ministry of Ukraine of Housing 'On approval of Typical statute of a homeowners association and Typical agreement among owners of residential units (apartments) and a manager' No. 141 of 2003.

182 By doing so, the government hopes to rid themselves of the responsibility for providing housing and public utilities.

183 The State Statistics Service of Ukraine does not collect data on the number of multi-storey buildings, the Ministry for Regional Development of Ukraine does.

paper only.[184] In any case, the need for bottom-up mobilisation and action in concert at the neighborhood level remain largely unmet.

A closer look at the social profile of members of HOAs included in the sample of the September 2016 survey (N=29, or 1.4% of the total number of respondents) suggests some clues as to why the self-organisation of homeowners remain problematic. Table 11.1 shows changes in the odds, Exp(B), of being a member of an HOA, for members of a group (e.g., people with higher education) compared with members of a relevant reference group (e.g., those who gave no answer or had difficulties with forming an opinion). Members of HOAs do not have clear political preferences—they support political leaders representing all the segments of the political spectrum, from nationalist (the Right Sector political party) to populist (the Block of Yulia Tymoshenko). They are likely involved in the other volunteer initiatives, as suggested by a positive value of Exp(B) for the group of the respondents who made no voluntary contribution during the past five years. Their track record includes traditional forms of volunteerism, such as membership in local branches of political parties or participation in parents' councils at schools. The involvement in the post-2013 volunteerism is manifestly absent.

Table 11.1 'Results of a binary statistic regression to predict the odds of being a member of a homeowner association in Ukraine, Exp(B)'

	B	Standard Error	Wald	Exp(B)
Voter of the Block of Yulia Tymoshenko	-3.667**	1.306	7.883	0.026
Voter of Gromadska Pozytsiia (Anatoliy Hrytsenko)	-4.496**	1.420	10.020	0.011
Voter of Samopomich	-4.047**	1.243	10.606	0.017
Voter of Right Sector	-6.772***	1.806	14.067	0.001

184 The fact that the number of credit unions in Ukraine reported by the SSSU largely exceeds the number of actual operating ones (1,091 against 577 in 2016) provides some support for the latter assumption, see subsection II.3 below for more detail.

Voter of Petro Poroshenko	-4.874***	1.261	14.936	0.008
Voter of Nadezhda Savchenko	-5.531***	1.402	15.571	0.004
Will not take part in the Presidential elections	-6.368***	1.329	22.972	0.002
Voter for the association with the European Union (EU)	-3.498***	0.905	14.944	0.030
The EU as a desirable geopolitical orientation for Ukraine	5.093***	1.133	20.204	162.946
Management is associated with power	-3.294***	0.745	19.549	0.037
Impunity is associated with power	-1.790**	0.613	8.522	0.167
No voluntary contributions during past 5 years	3.135**	1.046	8.975	22.977
Member of local branches of political parties, youth parliaments, discussion clubs, caucuses	-3.429*	1.371	6.258	0.032
Member of parents' councils at schools, kindergartens	-4.060***	0.895	20.557	0.017
Education: higher	-2.870***	0.808	12.619	0.057
Can afford some expensive items	3.397*	1.510	5.059	29.860
Ukrainian language	-2.673**	0.812	10.836	0.069
Constant	30.800***	6.724	20.984	23773033250000
Nagelkerke's R^2	0.651			

Source: survey of the Kyiv International Institute of Sociology carried out in September 2016 (N=2,040), see Section II of Chapter 10 for more detail.

Legend: Results significant at a 0.05 level are marked by *, at a 0.01 level—by **, and at a 0.001 level—by ***. Variables removed from the model due to a high collinearity: rural population, city dweller, human rights are associated with power. Reference groups are specified in the legend for Table 10.2 of Chapter 10.

The missing connection with the post-2013 volunteerism has to be taken into account when explaining the slow progress in the creation of HOAs in Ukraine. Volunteers involved in the post-2013 initiatives managed to overcome the problem of the low level of generalised trust by learning how to take risks and with the help of a series of institutional innovations (Section IV of Chapter 10). A similar approach is apparently necessary in the other spheres requiring volunteers' input and control, including the provision of housing and public utilities. In other words, there is a need for replicating and scaling up the model of the post-2013 volunteerism.

The ultimate target of this replication and scaling up consists in establishing a close link between the post-2013 volunteerism and Ukraine's power elite. Volunteers with the relevant experience are good candidates for being members of a new generation of political leaders and government officials (see also Section IV of Chapter 6). Without a radical change, Ukraine's power elite will hardly be able to build a sustainable nation-state and to move from the State as a model for the government to the commonwealth, i.e. to carry out two key missions mandated by the Revolution of Dignity and the subsequent developments. 'The main characteristic of government as a distinctive [from the State] political form is the absence of that force which fundamentally defines stateness. In contradiction to the State, what is decisive about government is not force but discussion, persuasion and negotiation with a view to reconciliation' (Stewart, 2001, p. 104).

Many members of the current power elite are simply too discredited to be up to these tasks. The introduction of the mandatory disclosure of all assets in possession of public office holders[185] was a shock to the Ukrainian public and the international observers: in this lower middle income country (as per World Bank's criteria) a significant part of its power elite, especially at the national level, emerged as millionaires (USD).[186] For instance, an inspection of assets in possession of 51 randomly selected Ukrainian MPs in 2015 (11.3% of their total number) shows that even after excluding real estate and less liquid assets (cars, boats, shares and equity, etc.), a

185 Their relevant declarations are included in the State Registry of Declarations of Persons Performing Functions of Government and Municipal Authorities. The National Agency on Corruption Prevention of Ukraine has the responsibility for maintaining this databank and for making its contents available to the public (at https://public.nazk.gov.ua/).

186 *Ukrain'ska Pravda*, a popular online political publication, offered an overview of the most outrageous declarations made by members of Ukraine's power elite at https://www.epravda.com.ua/publications/2016/10/31/609596/ (accessed April 03, 2017). Its title is self-explaining: 'Legends of the declarations'.

third of them—eighteen—have 1 million USD (or its equivalent in Euro or UAH) or more in cash or in bank accounts.[187] It must be remembered that these MPs were elected after the Revolution of Dignity and during the undeclared war waged by Russia.

II. On the role of foreign assistance and aid

In order to become the new power elite, participants in the post-2013 volunteer initiatives require assistance. A gardener's care is needed—not guidance, traditional teaching or direction, but assistance in their endeavours. Ukrainian intellectuals are expected to offer some (see Section IV of the general Introduction to this book). The foreign donors and sponsors can also contribute to the evolution of Ukrainian volunteers and to their becoming mature.

II.1 Vernacularising and de-politicising programs of assistance

Ukraine is by no means forgotten by foreign donors—governmental and non-governmental.[188] Orest Subtelny (2009) estimates that by 2002, US aid to Ukraine totalled 2.82 billion USD, making it—after Israel and Egypt, America's third-largest aid recipient (Subtelny, 2009).[189] The US may have been the largest donor of Ukraine

---

187 The mean value of liquid assets was 4.2 million (USD), median—591,000.

188 George Soros and the International Foundation 'Vidrodzhennia' (Renaissance) that he established are largest non-governmental donors of Ukraine (http://www.irf.ua/en/). This section, however, focuses on the role of foreign governments as donors of Ukraine.

189 The exact source of this figure is unknown. Data collected by the OECD Development Assistance Committee show that the amount of net aid flows from the US to Ukraine between 1992 and 2002 totalled to 1.86 billion USD (World Bank, 2017). The US Agency for International Development (USAID) reports amounts spent on economic and military assistance. According to this source, Ukraine received between 1990 and 2002 1.74 billion USD of economic assistance (in current USD) and 0.74 billion USD of military assistance, or 2.48 billion USD in total (USAID, 2017). It has to be noted that in the mid-1990s significant amounts of military assistance were provided to Ukraine in exchange of this country's agreement to give up its nuclear weapons. For instance, in 1994 only the country received 0.17 billion USD of military assistance.

in the past. In recent years, especially after 2013, the EU and Canada have significantly increased the amounts spent on assisting Ukraine (Figure 11.2). The data of the OECD Development Assistance Committee (DAC), suggest that the list of five biggest donors of Ukraine since the declaration of its independence includes the US, the EU, Germany, Canada and Japan. When assessing these figures, one has to bear in mind that in spite of significant volumes of US assistance in absolute terms, this country spent less on foreign aid than most other donors in relative terms, i.e. in terms of percentage of their GDP (Sachs, 2005, pp. 303–304).

Figure 11.2 'Net bilateral aid flows from selected OECD Development Assistance Committee donors to Ukraine (current USD), 1990–2014'

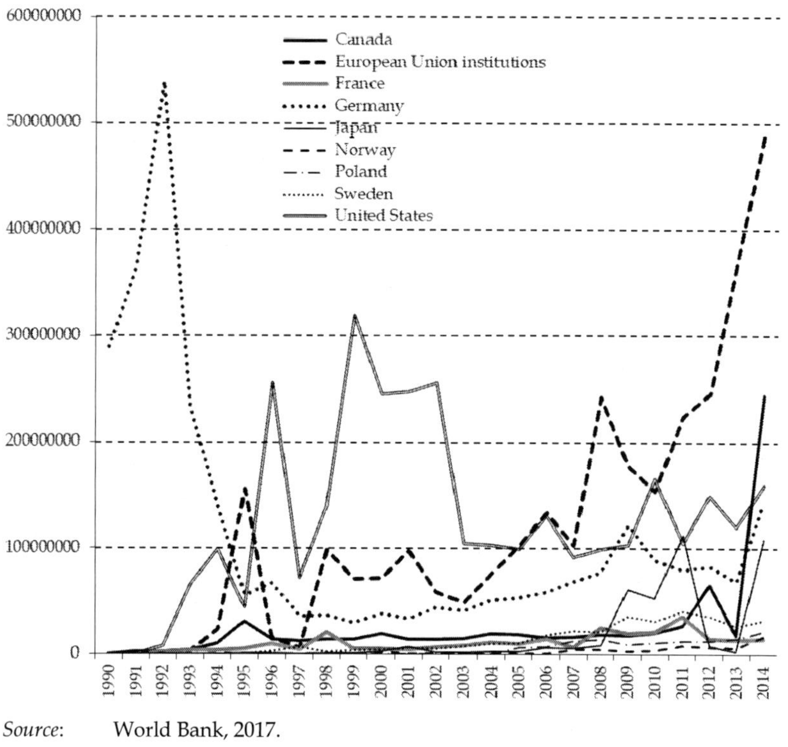

Source: World Bank, 2017.

II.1.a USAID programs

The US Agency for International Development (USAID), has a 60-year long record of providing development assistance. It was established by the Kennedy administration in November 1961 as part of its wider emphasis on foreign aid and national development, along with the Peace Corps, to coordinate and combine government foreign aid initiatives (Berger, 2006, p. 17). In Ukraine, the USAID has been supporting civil initiatives before the Revolution of Dignity, as well as since the post-2013 surge in volunteerism. The issues in foreign assistance in general and the USAID in particular emerged as one of the most prevalent themes in the interviews conducted with Ukrainian volunteers (see Section II of Chapter 10 for a description of the sample). It is the 8th most frequent theme out of 26 (Annex A to Chapter 10). Several leaders of the volunteer movement in this country first learned about volunteerism at events organised or sponsored by the USAID:

> 'I've first heard about volunteerism through an USAID program… The [foreign] volunteers came here, delivered lectures… —When did it happen?—I was at high school at that time, in the 1990s' (female, 25–39 y.o., Kyiv, in Ukrainian).[190]

> 'I must tell you that I like the USAID. I had first contacts with them back in 2007, when they [USAID] organised internships for young leaders from Ukraine in [the US Congress]. Five-year university students had internships in some congressional committees. I've got one of them and supervised her work. Eight years later, this kid [*dytyna*] works in the US Congress [as a liaison]. They also organise interesting seminars. I initially attended them. There are discussions, meetings with members of the Congress. It helps indeed make sense how [democracy] works' (female, 40–54 y.o., Kyiv, in Ukrainian).

It can hardly be denied that such an introduction to civic activism and volunteerism has beneficial effects. The 'teaching' of civic activism has several limits nevertheless. One of them refers to a belief that a general 'one size fits all approach' exists and can be replicated elsewhere. The lack of sensitivity to the local institutions, traditions and know-how may create difficulties for donors in aligning their

190 The rest of this quote is reproduced in subsection III.1.b of Chapter 10.

reform programmes to the great variety of country settings in which they operate (Kamstra, Pelzer, Elbers, & Ruben, 2016, p. 1026). The neglect of what is county- and culture-specific in civic activism probably did not have far-reaching consequences before 2013, taking into consideration its relative weakness and dependence on external sources of financial and organisational support. After the Revolution of Dignity, culture-specific aspects of civic activism have been taking more and more manifest forms (Chapters 3 and 10). In these circumstances, for instance, the ignorance of links between the post-2013 volunteerism and nation-state building may in fact become the suppressor of the potential for bottom-up mobilisation that exists in today's Ukraine.

II.1.b (Geo)political dimension

Foreign aid often has a geopolitical dimension, which represents its other limitation. The study of cycles in the US aid to Ukraine and Russia suggests that its amount and scope may be linked to political processes in these countries; namely, electoral cycles (Figure 11.3). The total amount of assistance administered by the USAID tends to increase before elections and in election years. It tends to decrease in non-election years. Since the fall of the Soviet Union in 1991, both Ukraine and Russia each held six presidential and seven parliamentary elections.[191] In the case of Ukraine, local peaks in the total amount of assistance fall on 1994 (a presidential and parliamentary elections year), 1999 (a presidential election year), 2002 (a parliamentary elections year) and 2010 (a presidential elections year).

---

191 Ukraine held presidential elections in 1991, 1994, 1999, 2004, 2010 and 2014; and parliamentary elections in 1994, 1998, 2002, 2006, 2007, 2012 and 2014. Russia held presidential elections in 1991, 1996, 2000, 2004, 2008 and 2012; and parliamentary elections in 1993, 1995, 1999, 2003, 2007, 2011 and 2016.

Figure 11.3 'Economic and military assistance provided to Ukraine and Russia through USAID programs, in constant 2005 USD'

Source: USAID, 2017.
Legend: U marks a year of presidential elections in Ukraine, u – a year of parliamentary elections in Ukraine, R – a year of presidential elections in Russia and r – a year of parliamentary elections in Russia.

Links between, on one hand, flows of foreign aid and, on the other hand, political processes in Ukraine are noticed by scholars studying post-Soviet transformations and by leaders of the volunteer movement in Ukraine. For instance, William DeMars (2015, pp. 240, 248) writes that 'Serbia in the year 2000 created the template for the strategic approach that other color revolutions later adapted... It is well documented that the governments of the US and several European countries provided foreign aid funding to the oppositions in Serbia and Ukraine'. More specifically, they provided training and technical assistance to 'Pora' (It's a high time)[192] and some other oppositional movements.

192 Not all 'Pora' leaders lived up to expectations. For instance, Vladyslav Kaskiv, after being elected as a MP in 2007 and the head of the State Agency for Investment and National Projects of Ukraine under President Yanukovych is currently accused of corruption and embezzlement.

> 'At that time [in the early 2000s] even I, then a student, realised that, for example, the "Pora" movement has external roots. Where exactly it was organised, I don't know—somewhere up there' (female, 25–39 y.o., Kyiv, in Ukrainian).[193]

> 'We were willing to change the political regime [in the 2000s]. At that time, in 2003–2004, after the rise of the "Ukraine without Kuchma" movement in general, there were many initiatives targeting the youth. Investments into the youth movements abounded, various trainings were conducted on non-violent resistance using the Serbian experience as an example' (female, 25–39 y.o., Kyiv, in Russian).

The Revolution of Dignity differs from the 2004 Orange Revolution in this respect since external forces and sponsors played a much more marginal role in its overall dynamics (see Chapter 3). The 2013–2014 mass protests and the subsequent mass resistance to the Russian aggression were driven from inside, not from outside. The fact that these events have had a weak if any impact on the amount of assistance provided to Ukraine by the US (Figures 11.2 and 11.3) indirectly confirms this observation.

As a result of these recent developments, the landscape of civil society in this country became very diverse and lively. Before 2013, most civil society organisations were established and funded with foreign assistance (USAID being one of its major sources), which impacted their agenda. The provision of services and the advocacy work were given priority. Compared with pre-2013 civil society organisations, post-2013 civic initiatives are established in a bottom-up manner and funded to a significant extent through voluntary donations of citizens and organisations (Chapter 10). They have an agenda more closely related to nation-state building, for instance, the protection of the country's territorial integrity and the help to internally displaced persons. What is even more important, post-2013 civic initiatives unite the war- and conflict-torn country rather than create new divisions, as some other institutions do, as discussed in subsection I.1 above.

In these circumstances, the geopolitical orientation of foreign assistance may interfere with the building of a nation-state in

193 This interviewee was active in the 'Pora' movement and thus offers an insider's take.

Ukraine and even suppress this internal process. By disembedding assistance from the geopolitical framework, i.e. by de-politicising foreign aid, the Western donors will avoid the risk of breaking the expectations of those in Ukraine and elsewhere who see them as supporters of an emerging viable and capable nation-state.

II.2 Supporting projects that demonstrated their viability

If international assistance is not guided by geopolitical considerations, what other factors could potentially determine its scope and orientation? Grassroots civil initiatives that demonstrated their viability represent one. Speaking metaphorically, foreign sponsors should feed the plants that grew in the local soil and thus are adapted to the local environment. David Smith (1997, pp. 296–297; see also Casey, 2016, p. 211) rightly points out that 'if the Third World manages to sustain development initiatives made by First and Second World governmental and non-profit organisations, this will be in large part because of the cumulative effects if indigenous [grassroots associations] in the Third World, not because of the Peace Corps or other First/Second World initiatives taken to the developing nations'. Instead of making bottom-up indigenous initiatives to compete with established NGOs and GONGOs for funds of international donors, these donors would do a better job by granting a privileged status to the former. Their representatives do not always excel in writing grant proposals and reports. This should not prevent them from accessing foreign aid, provided that they demonstrate their potential to make a contribution to the sustainable and internally driven development of Ukraine. In practical terms, foreign donors need to learn how to identify 'grant-eaters' among applicants to the programs that they administer and even how to discriminate against them.

II.2.a No food for grant-eaters

The expression 'grant-eater' cannot be found in the Oxford English dictionary. Google.com locates less than one thousand documents containing this word. At the same time, it can be frequently heard in discussions of relationships between foreign donors and the recipients of their aid in the post-Soviet countries. The Google search in Russian, Google.ru, produces more than 18,000 results.[194] A grant-eater makes a living by applying to various programs of foreign assistance. This individual has no genuine interest in achieving objectives declared by the sponsors. He or she simply developed good writing and communication skills (fluency in English or the other Western language being one of them). The grant-eater does not necessarily steal the money even if this happens too. The money simply goes to someone who will not use it for the intended purpose, leaving those who deserve support without any chance of getting it.

The larger the amount of foreign assistance, the higher the risk that there is a group of professional grant-eaters, all other conditions being equal. Ukraine is no exception. 'The catchword *granteaters* had quickly acquired a somewhat negative connotation for NGO activity in general' in this country, especially before the latest events (Stepanenko, 2006, p. 574). The expression 'grant-eater' was spontaneously mentioned in five interviews out of 22. The interview guide did not include specific questions on grant-eaters. The interviewees mentioned this issue when discussing foreign assistance in general and problems that exist with its delivery to the final recipients.

> 'I have no experience of working with NGOs that have staffers who specialise in applying to various grant programs only. They are called "grant-eaters" (*grantoidy*). They live a golden age now. Moneys are sent from abroad to help internal migrants and many other categories. And the "professionals" compete with the civil activists for these funds. I even know some well-respected organisations, American, whose representatives in Ukraine are involved in this "business". Yesterday an individual worked full-time in this organisation and today he suddenly emerges as a prominent civic leader and activist, proposes an idea [that will likely be supported by his former employer]. Tomorrow the individual indeed receives moneys from the or-

194 The search was carried out on April 05, 2017 using 'grant-eater' and *grantoed* as search terms correspondingly.

ganisation that yesterday employed him. But today he is nominally an independent figure and can formally apply to their programs' (male, 25–39 y.o., Kyiv, in Ukrainian).[195]

'It's a real problem. There are organisations that do something useful, but they are not good at writing grant proposals. We were in a similar situation—we simply didn't know all those [requirements]' (female, 25–39 y.o., Kyiv, in Ukrainian).

'Here is an example. It happened in November 2014, in the midst of battles [in the East]. Everyone is very tired and agitated. All the sudden, we—I mean the volunteers—receive an invitation to join a certain "First Volunteers' Association" group on the Facebook and to attend their first meeting in a 5-star hotel in Truskavets' [a resort in the Carpathians]. You're welcome. We had weeks of sleepless nights at that time. I even made a screenshot. R. [one of the most respectable representatives of the volunteer movement] responded very well, I beg your pardon: "You must be crazy"[196] and we all quitted this group. The meeting did not take place, actually. It seems that someone got a fatty grant… Later they contacted us again: "Don't you want to have a rest?" Volunteerism—is not about such things: wishful talks, 5-star hotels and wine and delis at the receptions. It's something completely different' (female, 25–39 y.o., Kyiv, in Ukrainian).

'It's possible to create an organisation that will be quite visible and successful in grant-making. There are way too many grant-eaters now.—How do you identify them? You also have grants, haven't you?—We select the tasks that are really needed, not just to produce a report and to please a sponsor. There are too many organisations that propose projects targeting internal migrants. Where are their results, do they have any? Organisations come and go, they organise trainings. They ask us: "We've got some funds. We need to find internal migrants now. Where can we find them?" I have a question here. How your project got funded, if you had never seen internal migrants with your eyes? They plan to conduct psychological trainings for internal migrants. I'm speechless… Groups of people with a good or long track-record in grant-making or those who are close to the sponsors [have better chances]. Corruption in this sphere also exists, you know. They get

195 To complete this description, it has to be added that this interviewee subsequently applied to a program administrated by the U.S. Embassy and, probably unexpectedly for him, received funds necessary to complete a project on which he had worked with his colleagues since 2014, an online platform for exchanging information about volunteers' initiatives (see Section IV of Chapter 10 for more detail).

196 The respondent actually quoted a stronger expression: 'You must have been overfucked' (*Vy iobnulis'*) and shared a copy of the relevant screenshot with the interviewer.

> fatty grants. I know one organisation that supposedly helped internal migrants to find jobs, to offer them psychological help. A woman (*tetia*) sits and teaches an internal migrant that he shouldn't chew a chewing gum at a job interview. The internal migrant left a Porsche sport car at home [in Donbas]. However, they have a very good track-record. All this is disgusting, simply disgusting. We are also considered by some as grant-eaters. But these are people who have never met us, have never seen what we actually do. They just overheard something. Somewhere, some people spread rumors. As a matter of fact, none of our grant proposals was successful. We simply can't write them, honestly. We don't have a staffer whose speciality is to write grants only. We all came from the street, so to speak' (female, 25–39 y.o., Dnipro, interview in two languages).

These opinions, however unpleasant they may be for some sponsors, suggest that criteria for identifying projects that merit their support probably need revising. For instance, nominations can be solicited: civil activists nominate their fellows who deserve the support the most. The task of identifying 'professional' grant applicants and changing selection criteria in such a manner that are discriminated against is even more urgent. A temporary ban on applications from former employees of grant-making organisations for grants administered by these organisations represents an immediate and relatively easy-to- implement remedy. They could be prevented from applying during a one-two year period after the end of their employment.

As a possibly more systemic solution, grant-making organisations could either launch separate programs targeting specifically civic 'start-ups' (with weaker formal requirements and the possibility for nominations from the other civil activists) or reduce the weight of 'track-record' as a criterion for assessing particular applications for funding, at least temporarily. Post-2013 civic initiatives, by definition, cannot compete with pre-2013 civil society organisations if they are judged solely or mainly on the basis of their track-record. In Ukraine, there is an increasing understanding that well established organisations, especially businesses and government bodies, should not be given priority in programs of foreign assistance anymore (Akulenko & Maistriuk, 2017). At a minimum, civic 'start-ups' should be able to compete with pre-2013 civic organisations, businesses and government bodies on equal footing. At maximum, a kind of 'affirmative action' may be needed to support civic initiatives that emerged between 2013–2015.

II.2.b Helping hand for grassroots initiatives

Negative discrimination against grant-eaters shall be complemented by positive discrimination against grassroots initiatives that show the most promise in solving problems that Ukrainian society faces. Instead of imposing criteria of importance and merit from outside, the sponsors will be well advised to look at existing grassroots initiatives and problems that they attempt to address. The sponsor then has discretion in identifying those problems that fall within its mandate. In other words, the long-list of problems that require intervention is identified in a bottom-up spontaneous manner, whereas their short-list results from the sponsor's discretionary decisions. This would limit the existing tendency to substitute the 'international' or even 'geopolitical' agenda of foreign donors for the 'national' agenda of local actors, especially those involved in post-2013 initiatives.

Hernando de Soto invited the governments and foreign sponsor to 'listen to the barking dogs' when dealing with problems that exist in developing and post-socialist countries. Before offering a solution to a problem, let alone implementing it, 'they will have to go out into the streets and roads and listen to the barking dogs' (De Soto, 2000, p. 179). The dogs bark when one crosses limits of a property regardless of whether this property is formally recognised or not. They know the real situation better than high profile lawyers or government officials or foreign experts. The dogs live on the ground. When offering this metaphor, De Soto had in mind the issue of identifying and legalising informal (extralegal) property. According to him, legal property shall have its source in extralegal—informally established and enforced—property rights.

This thinking can be generalised and applied to a broader set of problems. People who live on the ground know their problems better than anyone else and have solutions to offer. They simply need resources to try out these solutions and to identify those of them that really work. The sponsors' assistance is most appreciated at this stage. The volunteers interviewed for this book hold a high regard for the sponsors who listen to them and appreciate their experience and know-how.

> 'We also dealt with the Czech embassy [in Ukraine]. They offered us financial assistance since they knew our organisation. When working with a donor, we don't try to adjust our priorities to the sponsor's priorities. We have our own ideas and we search for a donor that has similar goals. The donor often, at least in our case, does not impose its conditions. Instead, the donor seeks advice as to how to achieve a desired result. Or, if the donor attempts to impose some conditions, we dissuade from doing so' (female, 25–39 y.o., Kyiv, in Russian).

> '[We worked with] the USAID, the UN Development Program, the "Vidrodzhennia" foundation.—Did you always apply to their programs or in some cases they invited you to work with them?—It is exactly what happened in the case of the USAID. They came and said: "Propose your ideas and we'll support them". It happened one year after we had started to work with the UN, they came next' (female, 25–39 y.o., Kyiv, in Ukrainian).

> 'They offer assistance, as a rule.—Please give more detail.—They come to visit us, we show what we do. We share our ideas and they propose that we join our efforts in realizing these ideas.—If I follow you correctly, they offer assistance in the realisation of your ideas?—That's how we worked with the USAID. They found that our ideas, our understanding of the situation is similar to theirs. And they offered us their financial support… We also work in a similar way with GIZ [Deutsche Gesellschaft für Internationale Zusammenarbeit]' (female, 25–39 y.o., Dnipro, interview in two languages).

Tasks relevant to nation-state building constitute the core of the long-list of problems to be addressed by Ukraine's nascent civil society. They include a wide range of problems from the protection of the country's territorial integrity to the provision of assistance to internally displaced persons. Foreign sponsors often consider anything related to the protection of the country's territorial integrity with suspicion. Indeed, using criteria prevalent in the Western societies, one's involvement in an armed conflict or support provided to military personnel has little to do with civil action, being instead associated with 'uncivil' action. Foreign grant-making organisations treat post-2013 civil initiatives accordingly, offering absolutely no support for those helping the Ukrainian army and, furthermore, tending to view such civil groups in a negative light.

> 'Our "Volunteers' Hundred" [a post-2013 civil imitative] had its own Facebook page with some 30 thousand subscribers... Subsequently, our original team split and moved in two divergent directions. The other girls, with strong connections to the international Jewish community, chose to focus more specifically on foreign grants. This excludes any association with the military issues, and also with politics. They realised [that] my position does not fit well with this. Thus, we separated. I said that I'd do things that I believe to be important. I help the guys [in the Ukrainian army] with some equipment—batteries, power generators, tools like axes. It is not ammunition anyway [seemingly tries to find an excuse for this involvement]' (female, 40–54 y.o., Kyiv, in Ukrainian).

Two considerations could be put forward in this respect. First, boundaries between 'civil' and 'uncivil' actions tend to be blurred at the early stages of nation-state building everywhere. The Civil War in the US is a case in point: legal, civil and 'uncivil' (i.e., military) arguments were equally important for the final determination of the shape of this nation (Turley, 2010). Furthermore, in contrast to the Civil War in the US, the current military conflict in Ukraine has a strong, if not decisive, external dimension. Is armed resistance to an externally driven aggression 'uncivil'? If it were not for volunteers' contribution to curbing Russia's aggression in 2013–2015, the country could simply have ceased to exist. In sum, it is problematic to apply criteria valid for a society at one stage in its development to a society that has not yet reached this stage and faces highly specific challenges.

Second, as noted previously, the experience of the post-2013 volunteerism contributes to the country's unity. Post-2013 civic initiatives aiming to protect the country's territorial integrity enjoy a high level of public trust across the country from the West to the East, except in the conflict zone (Table 10.1 in Chapter 10). Post-2013 civic initiatives helping internally displaced persons enjoy even more universal trust, in spite of their dealing with consequences of what may be perceived as 'uncivil' action. The quote reproduced above suggests that foreign sponsors support the latter but not the former because of their fear of being associated with any form of 'uncivility'. In other words, grant-making organisations exercise their discretion in short-listing some initiatives from the long-list rather than the others. This discretion, however legitimate it may be, should probably not extend to discriminating negatively against the initiatives left without their support by attaching, for instance, some negative labels to them. The task of finding a right balance here is difficult and requires an understanding of particularities of nation-state building in its early stages. At a minimum, foreign sponsors should not inadvertently create divisions in the volunteers movement, an otherwise highly unifying force. A combination of targeted support for some initiatives with tolerance towards the others[197] may be a reasonable solution.

II.3 Helping and letting the local actors do

The role of foreign donors in the building of a capable and viable nation-state in Ukraine can be summarised along the following lines. They help and let local actors grow and develop capacity for solving the existing numerous problems on their own, with no external input. At first glance, the proposed approach does not differ from the classical liberal principle of *laissez-faire*, i.e. let them do. There is a substantial difference, however. The principle of *laissez-faire* requires that actors are capable of autonomous operation. In the case of Ukraine, internal actors of socio-economic developments are still in the early stages of their development. The 2013–2014 Revolution of Dignity and the subsequent resistance to the external aggression created powerful incentives for their rapid development and simultaneously imposed a significant strain on their capacity to act. The volunteers worked around the clock at times, and this is not a figure of speech, as suggested by a quote below. Thus, before being able to do (*capable de faire*), they need to be assisted and empowered. In other words, the stage of empowerment must precede the stage of *laissez-faire* in the circumstances of the case.

> 'You know, during these two years, I've lived so many events that [their number] would be enough for several lives, it seems. It is as if I lived several lives. Now I want some tranquility. I've become calmer recently. I started to

---

197 Which does not extend to the toleration of war crimes and other violations of human rights, of course. Some members of volunteer fighters' battalions were accused of torturing the enemy fighters, for instance.

> sleep, I started to eat… I put 17kg on [laugh]' (female, 40–54 y.o., Kyiv, in Ukrainian).

Foreign donors empower the local actors—first of all, associated with the post-2013 volunteerism—by exercising transformative power over them. 'In a transformative use of power a dominant agent… exercises power over a subordinate agent for the latter's benefit. In doing so, the dominant agent's aim is not simply to act for the benefit of the subordinate agent; rather, the dominant agent attempts to exercise his power in such a way that the subordinate agent learns certain skills that undercut the power differential between her and the dominant agent' (Wartenberg, 1990, p. 184; see also Section I of Chapter 2 and Section II of Chapter 6). A key distinctive feature of transformative power is that 'it seeks its own elimination' (Ibid., pp. 192–193). Agnes Stewart (2001, p. 43) speaks of a paradox of emancipation in this context: 'the emancipation of the dominated can only be achieved by the intervention of an external agent, who must logically become another possible source of domination'.

Builders of a capable Ukrainian nation-state need the assistance of external agents. But, both logically and practically, the latter may become another source of domination. The chances of the transformation of assistance into domination are particularly high if geopolitical considerations guide foreign aid, overshadowing all the other rationales. A great deal of self-restraint is required from supporters of the building Ukraine from within. They are expected to contribute to the emergence of a truly independent Ukrainian nation-state as their peer, as opposed to a peripheral—let alone a puppet, state.

Chapter 9 showed what such an arrangement may look like in practice. Ukrainian producers are allowed to be temporarily sheltered from international competition in the national market, benefiting at the same time from the unrestricted access to the markets in the West. Instead of simply giving money to the Ukrainian government in the form of loans, technical assistance and investments into infrastructural projects (as, for instance, Jeffrey Sachs [2005] proposes), the Western partners can show their good will not to compete with Ukrainian producers in their home market before the latter emerge as empowered enough to compete with them in the global and national markets.

The same strategy of helping and letting the potential agens movens of nation-state building do can be applied in the other contexts too. Ukraine has one of the most problematic banking sectors in the world. Along with the commercial banks, it has a number of other financial institutions—financial companies, credit unions, pawnbrokers and so forth. Among various financial institutions, credit unions deserve particular attention. First, they have a potential for meeting the needs of agricultural producers in loans (Kyrychenko & Kudria, 2009). Agriculture remains one of the backbones of the Ukrainian economy, being a sector that can even now face global competition. Second, and more substantially, credit unions create an environment favourable to bottom up mobilisation and grassroots initiatives. As a matter of fact, the successful operation of credit unions requires them. It means that credit unions may potentially facilitate the spillover effects of the post-2013 volunteerism and to help scale up the relevant experience.

Similar to HOAs discussed previously, however, Ukrainian credit unions are in a deep crisis now. Their number as well as the number of their members has been declining (Figure 11.4). The cooperative movement is divided: three associations of credit unions exist at the national level (Volosovich & Krivosheeva, 2016). Some of these associations receive support from the foreign donors, including the USAID, whereas the others do not. These divisions prevent the cooperative movement from working on a common agenda and on its implementation.

In contrast to Ukrainian furniture producers (see Section III of Chapter 9), representatives of Ukrainian credit unions were not able to lobby the idea that credit unions—because of their associational nature and potential contribution to nation-state building—deserve a special status and separate treatment. The Law of Ukraine 'On credit unions' No. 2908-III was enacted in 2001 under President

Kuchma,[198] but under the current arrangement credit unions must meet the same financial criteria as the for-profit financial institutions and de facto compete with them (Yurkevych, 2009). Credit unions as non-profit organisations with a strong communitarian component need to be empowered before successfully competing with the other financial institutions, especially international banks. In other words, they shall be temporary sheltered from competition with the help of tax exemptions, for instance. In this scenario, there are chances that the post-2013 volunteerism would be able to revive the institution that has not lived up to expectations in Ukraine yet.

Figure 11.4 'Number of credit unions and their members in Ukraine, 2009–2016'

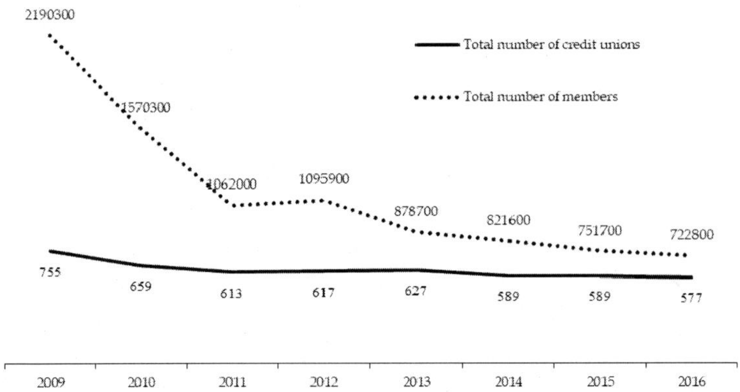

Source: Ukrainian Association of Credit Unions.[199]

To conclude, the two-stage solution—empowerment first, and freedom second—seems to be relevant for solving various problems that Ukraine is facing, being a latecomer in the process of nation-state building. Thus, it can potentially be applicable in the other institutional contexts; namely, in the countries that are at a similar stage in their development—former colonies, the countries of the

198 http://zakon3.rada.gov.ua/laws/show/2908-14/page2 accessed April 05, 2017.

199 http://vaks.org.ua/?menu=Financial_analyst# accessed June 26, 2017.

former Soviet Union and the former Yugoslavia (i.e. the countries that emerged after the dissolution of these two empires).

References

Adam, Frane (2008). Mapping social capital across Europe: Findings, trends and methodological shortcomings of cross-national surveys. *Social Science Information, 47*(2), 159–186.

Adarov, Amat, Astrov, Vasily, Havlik, Peter, Hunya, Gábor, Landesmann, Michael & Podkaminer, Leon (2015). *How to stabilise the economy of Ukraine: Background study*. The Vienna Institute for International Economic Studies. Retrieved from http://wiiw.ac.at/how-to-stabilise-the-economy-of-ukraine-dlp-3562.pdf.

Adorno, Theodor W., Frenkel-Brunswik, Else, Levinson, Daniel J., Sanford, R. Nevitt (in collaboration with Aron, Betty, Levinson, Maria Hertz & Morrow, William) (1950). *The authoritarian personality*. New York: Harper & Row.

Ailon, Galit (2006). What *B* would otherwise do: A critique of conceptualizations of 'power' in organizational theory. *Organization, 16*(6), 771–800.

Akulenko, Liubov & Maistiuk, Svitlana (2017, May 16). Chas grantozheriv dobigae kintsia [The time of grant-eaters is over]. *Ukrains'ka Pravda*. Retrieved from http://www.epravda.com.ua/publications/2017/05/16/624853/.

Alapuro, Risto (2005). Associations and contention in France and Finland: Constructing the society and describing the society. *Scandinavian Political Studies, 28*(4), 377–399.

Aleksandrova, Galina (2015). T. Shevchenko i O. Pushkin: punkty blyzhennya i linii rozmezhuvannya v literaturoznavstvi kintsia XIX—pochatku XX st. [T. Shevchenko and A. Pushkin: Common and divergent trends in Russian and Ukrainian literatures at the late 19th—early 20th centuries]. *Shevchenkoznavchi studii: zbirnyk naukovykh prats*, 18, 258–270.

Allen, Amy (1999). Solidarity after identity politics: Hannah Arendt and the power of feminist theory. *Philosophy and Social Criticism, 25*(1), 97–118.

Allen, Amy (2002). Power, subjectivity, and agency: Between Arendt and Foucault. *International Journal of Philosophical Studies, 10*(2), 131–149.

Appadurai, Arjun (1996). *Modernity at large: Cultural dimensions of globalization*. Minneapolis: University of Minnesota Press.

Appelbaum, Anne (2017). *Red Famine: Stalin's War on Ukraine*. Toronto: Signal.

Arendt, Hannah (1969). *On violence*. New York: Harcourt, Brace & World.

Arlacchi, Pino (1986). *Mafia et compagnies: L'éthique mafiosa et l'esprit du capitalisme*. Grenoble: Presses Universitaires de Grenoble.

Ashkanasy, Neal M. & O'Connor, Christine (1997). Value congruence in leader-member exchange. *The Journal of Social Psychology, 137*(5), 647–662.

Åslund, Anders (2001). Ukraine's return to economic growth. *Post-Soviet Geography and Economics, 42*(5), 313–328.

Åslund, Anders (2008). Reflections on Ukraine's current economic dilemma. *Eurasian Geography and Economics, 49*(2), 152–159.

Åslund, Anders (2009). Ukraine's financial crisis, 2009. *Eurasian Geography and Economics, 50*(4), 371–386.

Attia, Ashraf M., Aziz, Nergis, Friedman, Barry & Elhusseiny, Mahdy F. (2011). Commentary: The impact of social networking tools on political change in Egypt's 'Revolution 2.0'. *Electronic Commerce Research and Applications, 10*(4), 369–374.

Babbie, Earl & Benaquisto, Lucia (2002). *Fundamentals of social research*. (1st Cdn. ed.). Scarborough, ON: Thomson-Nelson.

Badie, Bertrand (1992). *L'Etat importé: Essai sur l'occidentialisation de l'ordre politique*, Paris: Fayard.

Badie, Bertrand (2000). *The imported state: The westernization of the political order*. (C. Royal, Trans.). Stanford, CA: Stanford University Press.

Beh, Eric J. & Lombardo, Rosaria (2014). *Correspondence analysis: Theory, practice and new strategies*. Chichester: John Wiley & Sons.

Beissinger, Mark R. (2007). Structure and example in modular political phenomena: The diffusion of bulldozer/rose/orange/tulip revolutions. *Perspectives on Politics, 5*(2), 259–276.

Beissinger, Mark R. (2011). Mechanisms of Maidan: The structure of contingency in the making of the Orange revolution. *Mobilization: An International Journal, 16*(1), 25–43.

Benda-Beckmann, Franz von (2002). Who's afraid of legal pluralism? *The Journal of Legal Pluralism and Unofficial Law, 34*(47), 37–82.

Benda-Beckmannn, Franz von & Benda-Beckmannn, Keebet von (2006). The dynamics of change and continuity in plural legal orders. *The Journal of Legal Pluralism and Unofficial Law, 38*(53–54), 1–44.

Benjamin, Gregg (2008). Translating human rights into Muslim vernaculars. *Comparative Sociology, 7*(4), 457–483.

Berger, Mark (2006), From nation-building to state-building: The geopolitics of development, the nation-state system and the changing global order. *Third World Quarterly, 27*(1), 5–25.

Berlin, Isaiah (1969). *Two concepts of liberty*. In Isaiah Berlin, *Four essays on liberty* (pp. 118–172). Oxford: Oxford University Press.

Berman, Jules J. (2013). *Principles of big data: Preparing, sharing, and analyzing complex information*. Waltham, MA: Morgan Kaufmann.

Bernard, Russell H. (2013). *Social research methods: Qualitative and quantitative approaches*. (2nd ed.). Thousand Oaks, CA: Sage.

Bernard, Russell H. & Ryan, Gery W. (2010). *Analyzing qualitative data: Systematic approaches*. Thousand Oaks, CA: Sage.

Beugelsdijk, Sjoerd, Maseland, Robbert & Van Hoorn, André (2015). Are scores on Hofstede's dimensions of national culture stable over time? A cohort analysis. *Global Strategy Journal, 5*(3), 223–240.

Biggs, Michael (2013). How repertoires evolve: The diffusion of suicide protest in the twentieth century. *Mobilization: An International Quarterly, 18*(4), 407–428.

Boltanski, Luc & Laurent Thévenot (1991). *De la justification: Les économies de la grandeur*. Paris: Gallimard.

Bourdieu, Pierre (1979 [1963]). *Algeria 1960*. Cambridge: Cambridge University Press and Paris: Editions de la MSH.

Bowman, James (2002). The lost sense of honour. *The Public Interest*, Fall, 32–49.

Bowman, James (2009). Decline of the honor culture. *Policy Review*, August & September, 27–39.

Brannen, Julia (2005). Mixing methods: The entry of qualitative and quantitative approaches into the research process. *International Journal of Social Research Methodology, 8*(3), 173–184.

Brennan, Andrew & Lo, Y.S. (2007). Two conceptions of dignity: Honour and self-determination. In Jeff Malpas & Norelle Lickiss (Eds.), *Perspectives on human dignity: A conversation* (pp. 43–58). Dordrecht: Springer.

Brice, William David & Jones, Wayne D. (2008). The cultural foundations of family business management: Evidence from Ukraine. *Eurasian Journal of Business and Economics, 1*(1), 3–23.

Brice, William David & Richardson, James (2009). Culture in family business: A two-country empirical investigation. *European Business Review, 21*(3), 246–262.

Brudny, Yitzhak M. & Finkel, Evgeny (2011). Why Ukraine is not Russia: Hegemonic national identity and democracy in Russia and Ukraine. *East European Politics and Societies, 25*(4), 813–833.

Bruton, Henry J. (1998). A reconsideration of import substitution. *Journal of Economic Literature, 36*(2), 903–936.

Bryman, Alan (2004 [2001]). *Social research methods.* (2nd ed.). Oxford: Oxford University Press.

Bryman, Alan & Bell, Edward (2016). *Social Research Methods.* (4th Cdn. ed.). Don Mills, ON: Oxford University Press.

Casey, John (2016). Comparing nonprofit sectors around the world: What do we know and how do we know it? *Journal of Nonprofit Education and Leadership, 6*(3), 187–223.

CAUT (Canadian Association of University Teachers) (2014). *CAUT Almanac of Post-Secondary Education in Canada 2013–2014.* Ottawa.

Cavazotte, Flavia, Hartman, Nathan S. & Bahiense, Erica (2014). Charismatic leadership, citizenship behaviors, and power distance orientation: Comparing Brazilian and U.S. Workers. *Cross-Cultural Research, 48*(1), 3–31.

Chabot, Sean & Duyvendak, Jan W. (2002). Globalization and transnational diffusion between social movements: Reconceptualizing the dissemination of the Gandhian repertoire and the 'coming out' routine. *Theory and Society, 31*(6), 697–740.

Chalmers, Don & Ryuichi, Ida (2007). On the international legal aspects of human dignity. In Jeff Malpas & Norelle Lickiss (Eds.), *Perspectives on human dignity: A conversation* (pp. 157–168). Dordrecht: Springer.

Chekh, Myroslava M., Vasylytsya, Oksana B. & Polovska, Vira T. (2016). Importzamishchennia ta zaluchennia inozemnykh investitsii v Ukrainu' [Import substitution and foreign directinvestment promotion in Ukraine]. *Actual Problems of Economics,* 4(178): 87–96.

Cho, Seong E. & Park, Han W. (2013). A qualitative analysis of cross-cultural new media research: SNS use in Asia and the West. *Quality & Quantity, 47*(4), 2319–2330.

Chuzhykov, Viktor, Fedirko, Oleksandr & Chuzhykov, Andrii (2014). Methodological background of post-Soviet regionalism: The case of Ukraine. *Baltic Journal of European Studies,* 4(1), 20–33.

Clément, Carine, Miryasova, Olga & Demidov, Andrei (2010). Ot obyvatelei k aktivistam: zarozhdayushchiesya sotsial'nye dvizheniya v sovremennoi Rossii [From passivity to activism: Nascent social movements in contemporary Russia]. Moscow: Tri kvadrata.

Coase, Ronald H. (1988 [1937]). The nature of the firm. In Ronald H. Coase, *The firm, the market and the law* (pp. 33–56). Chicago: The University of Chicago Press.

Cobbah, Josiah A.M. (1987). African values and the human rights debate: An African perspective. *Human Rights Quarterly, 9*(3), 309–331.

Coleman, James S. (1990). *Foundations of social theory.* Cambridge, MA: The Belknap Press of Harvard University Press.

Commons, John R. (1939 [1924]). *Legal foundations of capitalism*. New York: Macmillan.

Conduit, Edward (2001). Submissiveness and risk of heart disease. *Cross-Cultural Research, 35*(4), 347–369.

Contre le terrorisme, la plus grande manifestation jamais recensée en France (2015, January 01). *Le Monde*. Retrieved from http://www.lemonde.fr/societe/article/2015/01/11/la-france-dans-la-rue-pour-defendre-la-liberte_4553845_3224.html.

Correljé, Aad & Van der Linde, Coby (2006). Energy supply security and geopolitics: A European perspective. *Energy Policy, 34*(5), 532–543.

Coutin, Susan (1995). Ethnographies of violence: Law, dissidence and the state. *Law & Society Review, 29*(3), 517–539.

Crane, Andrew, Knights, David & Starkey, Ken (2008). The conditions of our freedom: Foucault, Organization, and Ethics. *Business Ethics Quarterly, 18*(3), 299–320.

Cummings, Sally N. & Ryabkov, Maxim (2008). Situating the 'Tulip Revolution'. *Central Asian Survey, 27*(3–4), 241–252.

Curato, Nicole (2014). Participation without deliberation: The crisis of Venezuelan democracy. *Democratic Theory, 1*(2), 113–121.

Curtis, James E., Baer, Douglas E., & Grabb, Edward G. (2001). Nations of joiners: Explaining voluntary association membership in democratic societies. *American Sociological Review, 66*(6), 783–805.

D'Anieri, Paul (2015 [2007]). *Understanding Ukrainian Politics: Power, Politics and Institutional Design*. London: Routledge.

Davis, Lance & North, Douglass C. (1970). Institutional change and American economic growth: A first step towards theory of institutional innovation. *Journal of Economic History, 30*(1), 131–149.

De Micco, Pasquale (2015, November). In-depth analysis. Ukraine's will to liberalise: Tested on many fronts. EU Policy Department, Directorate-General for External policies. Retrieved from http://www.europarl.europa.eu/RegData/etudes/IDAN/2015/549072/EXPO_IDA%282015%29549072_EN.pdf.

De Soto, Hernando (2000). *The mystery of capital: Why capitalism triumphs in the West and fails everywhere else*. New York: Basic Books.

De Soto, Hernando (2005 [1989]). *The other path: The economic answer to terrorism*. New York: Basic Books.

Dean, Mitchell (2009). Three conceptions of the relationship between power and liberty. In Stewart R. Clegg & Mark Haugaard (Eds.), *The SAGE handbook of power* (pp. 177–193). Thousand Oaks: Sage.

Debouzy, Marianne (1992). *Le capitalisme «sauvage» aux Etats-Unis: 1860–1900*. Paris: Seuil.

DeMars, William E. (2015). Follow the partners: Agency and explanation in the color revolutions. In William E. DeMars & Dennis Dijkzeul (Eds.), *The NGO Challenge for International Relations Theory* (pp. 237–261). London and New York: Routledge.

Derzhavna Sluzhba Statystyky Ukrainy (2016a). *Statystychnyi zbirnyk 'Regiony Ukrainy' 2016* [Statistical publication 'Regions of Ukraine in 2016']. 2 volumes. Kyiv.

Derzhavna Sluzhba Statystyky Ukrainy (2016b). *Statystychnyi shchorichnyk Ukrainy za 2015 rik* [2015 Statistical Yearbook of Ukraine], Kyiv.

Derzhavna Sluzhba Statystyky Ukrainy (2016c). Kil'kist' iurydychnykh osib za organizatsiinymy formamy [Number of juridical entities by organizational forms]. Retrieved from https://ukrstat.org/uk/edrpoy/ukr/EDRPU_2016/ks_opfg/arh_ks_opfg_16.htm.

Derzhavna Sluzhba Statystyky Ukrainy (2016d). *Naukova ta innovatsiina dial'nist' Ukrainy – 2015* [Research and innovations in Ukraine – 2015]. Kyiv.

Derzhavna Sluzhba Statystyky Ukrainy (2016e). *Rozpodil postiinogo naselennia Ukrainy za stattiu ta vikom* [Distribution of Ukraine's population by sex and age]. Kyiv. Retrieved from http://database.ukrcensus.gov.ua/PXWEB2007/ukr/publ_new1/2016/resident_2016.pdf.

Dickinson, Jennifer (2014). Prosymo maksymal'nyi perepost! Tactical and discursive uses of social media in Ukraine's Euromaidan. *Ab Imperio*, 3, 75–93.

Donnelly, Jack (1982). Human rights and human dignity: An analytic critique of non-Western conceptions of human rights. *The American Political Science Review*, *76*(2), 303–316.

Dovbniak, Taras F. (2009). Tsyklichnist' ukrainskoi ekonomiki v 2000–2008 rokakh [Ukrainian Economy Cycling in 2000–2008]. *Actual Problems of Economics*, *1*(91), 65–72.

Dowding, Keith (1996). *Power*. Minneapolis: MN: University of Minnesota Press.

Dowding, Keith (2014). Review of 'Market as a weapon: The socio-economic machinery of dominance in Russia'. *Contemporary Sociology: A Journal of Reviews*, *43*(4), 565–567.

Drul, Orest (2014, April 28). Kil'ka dumok pro gidnist' [Some thoughts on dignity]. *Zbruč*. Retrieved from http://zbruc.eu/node/21702.

Drydyk, Jay (2011). Responsible pluralism, capabilities, and human rights. *Journal of Human Development and Capabilities*, *12*(1), 39–61.

Dubovik, Anatoly (2016). The anarchist movement in Ukraine, 1980s-1990s. *Anarcho-Syndicalist Review*, 67, 25–33.

Dugin, Alexandr (2008). Proekt 'Imperiya' [The 'Empire' Project]. *Profil'*, 34.

Eckstein, Harry (1998a). Congruence theory explained. In Harry Eckstein, Frederic J. Fleron, Erik P. Hoffmann, & William M. Reisinger(with Ahl, Richard, Bova, Russell & Roeder, Philip G.), *Can democracy take root in post-Soviet Russia? Exploration in state-society relations* (pp. 3–33). Lanham, MA: Rowman & Littlefield Publishers.

Eckstein, Harry (1998b). Russia and the conditions of democracy. In Harry Eckstein, Frederic J. Fleron, Erik P. Hoffmann, & William M. Reisinger (with Ahl, Richard, Bova, Russell & Roeder, Philip G.), *Can democracy take root in post-Soviet Russia? Exploration in state-society relations* (pp. 349–381), Lanham, MA: Rowman & Littlefield Publishers.

Economist, the (2012, February 04). The value of friendship. 23–26.

Eggertsson, Thráinn (1990). *Economic behavior and institutions*. Cambridge: Cambridge University Press.

Emmett, Brian & Emmett, Geoffrey (2015). *Charities in Canada as an economic sector: Discussion paper*. Toronto: Imagine Canada. Retrieved from http://www.imaginecanada.ca/sites/default/files/imaginecanada_charities_in_canada_as_an_economic_sector_2015-06-22.pdf.

Erez, Miriam & Early, P. Christopher (1987). Comparative analysis of goal-setting strategies across cultures. *Journal of Applied Psychology, 72*(4), 658–665.

Ericson, Richard E. (2009). Eurasian natural gas pipelines: The political economy of network interdependence. *Eurasian Geography and Economics, 50*(1), 28–57.

Etzioni, Amitai (1988). *The moral dimension: Towards a new economics*. New York: Free Press.

Etzioni, Amitai (2003). Toward a new socio-economic paradigm. *Socio-Economic Review, 1*(1), 105–134.

Etzioni-Halevy, Eva (1993). *The Elite connection: Problems and potential of Western democracy*. Cambridge: Polity Press.

Eurogas (2011). *Statistical report 2011*. Brussels: Eurogas.

Eurogas (2012). *Statistical report 2012*. Brussels: Eurogas.

Eurogas (2013). *Statistical report 2013*. Brussels: Eurogas.

European Commission (2013). *EU Energy in Figures: Statistical Pocketbook 2013*. Luxemburg: Publications Office of the European Union.

European Union, Directorate General for Trade (2017). Trade in goods with Ukraine. Retrieved from http://trade.ec.europa.eu/doclib/docs/2006/september/tradoc_113459.pdf.

Fahmy, Shahira & Kim, Daekyung (2008). Picturing the Iraq war: Constructing the image of war in the British and US press. *International Communication Gazette, 70*(6), 443–462.

Federal'naia Sluzhba Gosudarstvennoi Statistiki (2011). Rossiya i strany Evropeiskogo Soyuza—2011 [Russia and EU member countries—2011]. Moscow. Retrieved from http://www.gks.ru/bgd/regl/B11_65/IssWWW.exe/Stg/14-07.htm.

Federal'naia Sluzhba Gosudarstvennoi Statistiki (2013). Rossiya i strany Evropeiskogo Soyuza—2013 [Russia and EU member countries—2013]. Moscow. Retrieved from http://www.gks.ru/bgd/regl/b13_65/Main.htm.

Federal'naia Sluzhba Gosudarstvennoi Statistiki (2017). Chislennost' issledovatelei po uchenym stepeniam. Retrieved from http://www.gks.ru/free_doc/new_site/business/nauka/nauka10.xls.

Fielding, Nigel (2010). Mixed methods research in the real world. *International Journal of Social Research Methodology, 13*(2), 127–138.

Fine, Saul (2013). A look at cross-cultural integrity testing in three banks. *Personnel Review, 42*(3), 266–280.

Finon, Dominique & Locatelli, Catherine (2008). Russian and European gas interdependence: Could contractual trade channel geopolitics? *Energy Policy, 36*(1), 423–442.

Flyvbjerg, Bent (2006). Five misunderstandings about case-study research. *Qualitative Inquiry, 12*(2), 219–245.

Foucault, Michel (1975). *Surveiller et punir: Naissance de la prison*. Paris: Gallimard.

Foucault, Michel (1976). *Histoire de la sexualité*. Volume 1: La volonté de savoir. Paris: Gallimard.

Foucault, Michel (1984a). *Histoire de la sexualité*. Volume 3: Le souci de soi. Paris: Gallimard.

Foucault, Michel (1984b). *Histoire de la sexualité*. Volume 2: L'usage des plaisirs. Paris: Gallimard.

Foucault, Michel (2007). *Security, territory, population. Lectures at the Collège de France, 1977–1978*. (G. Burchell, Trans.). Basingstoke and New York: Palgrave Macmillan.

Fournier, Anne (2010). Ukraine's Orange Revolution: Beyond Soviet political culture? In Paul D'Anieri (Ed.), *Orange Revolution and aftermath: Mobilization, apathy, and the state in Ukraine* (pp. 110–128). Baltimore: John Hopkins University Press.

François, Monika & Sud, Inder (2006). Promoting stability and development in fragile and failed states. *Development Policy Review, 24*(2), 141–160.

Freeman, Michael (2004). The problem of secularism in human rights theory. *Human Rights Quarterly, 26*(2), 375–400.

Friedman, Milton (1966). The methodology of positive economics. In Milton Friedman, *Essays in positive economics* (pp. 3–16). Chicago: The University of Chicago Press.

Fund of Peace, the (2013). The Failed States Index. Retrieved from http://library.fundforpeace.org/fsi13.

Gaddy, Clifford & Ickes, Barry (2005). Resource rents in the Russian economy. *Eurasian Geography and Economics, 46*(8), 563–567.

Gaidai, Tetiana (2007a). Rol' neformal'nikh institutsii v ekonomicheskoi transitologii [Role of informal institutions in the theory of transition]. *Nauchnye Trudy DonNTU: Seriia ekonomicheskaia, 31*(2), 75–80.

Gaidai, Tetiana (2007b). Institutsiina teoriia: doslidzhennia ekonomichnoi mental'nosti [Institutional theory and studies of economic mentality]. *Visnyk Kyivs'kogo natsional'nogo universytetu imeni Tarasa Shevchenka: Ekonomika*, 93, 4–7.

Gaidar, Egor T. (2006). *Gibel' imperii: uroki dlya sovremennoi Rossii* [Collapse of an empire: Lessons for modern Russia]. Moscow: ROSSPEN.

Gambetta, Diego (1991). 'In the beginning was the Word'... The symbols of the Mafia. *Archives Européennes de sociologie, 32*(1), 53–77.

Gambetta, Diego (1993). *The Sicilian Mafia: The business of private protection*. Cambridge, MA: Harvard University Press.

Gatskova, Kseniia & Gatskov, Maxim (2016). Third sector in Ukraine: Civic engagement before and after the 'Euromaidan'. *Voluntas, 27*(2), 673–694.

Gerschenkorn, Alexander (1992 [1952]). Economic backwardness in historical perspective. In Mark Granovetter & Richard Swedberg (Eds.), *The sociology of economic life* (pp. 111–130). Boulder: Westview Press.

Gintis, Herbert (2000). *Game theory evolving: A problem-centered introduction to modeling strategic interactions*. Princeton, NJ: Princeton University Press.

Givan, Rebecca K., Roberts, Kenneth M. & Soule, Sarah A. (2010). Introduction: The Dimensions of Diffusion. In Rebecca K. Givan, Kenneth M. Roberts, & Sarah A. Soule (Eds.), *The diffusion of social movements: Actors, mechanisms, and political effects* (pp. 1–15). Cambridge: Cambridge University Press.

Global Wood Market Info (2016, June 16). Rising EU imports of lower value Eastern European hardwood. Retrieved from https://www.globalwoodmarketsinfo.com/rising-eu-imports-of-lower-value-eastern-european-hardwood/.

Goethe, Johann W. (2005 [1809]). *Elective affinities*. (R.J. Hollingdale, Trans.). London: Penguin.

Göhler, Gerhard (2009). 'Power to' and 'power over'. In Stewart R. Clegg & Mark Haugaard (Eds.), *The SAGE handbook of power* (pp. 27–39). Thousand Oaks: Sage.

Gordon, Linda (1983). *Cossack rebellions: Social turmoil in the sixteenth-century Ukraine*. Albany, NY: State University of New York Press.

Green, Guy (2007). Human dignity and the law. In Jeff Malpas & Norelle Lickiss (Eds.), *Perspectives on human dignity: A conversation* (pp. 151–156). Dordrecht: Springer.

Gregory, Steven (1998), *Black corona: Race and the politics of place in an urban community*. Princeton Studies in Culture/Power/History. Princeton, N.J.: Princeton University Press. Retrieved from http://ehrafworldcultures.yale.edu/document?id=nk04-038.

Grendash, Taras (2012). Regional disparities in Ukraine. *Naukovy Pratsi Chornomors'kogo Derzhavnogo Universytetu imeni Petra Mogyly: Ekonomika, 177*(189), 116–120.

Grytsyak, Evgen (2013). Nenasyl'stvo zavzhdy peremagae [Non-violence always wins]. Available from http://texty.org.ua/pg/article/editorial/read/46215/Nenasylnyckyj_sprotyv_rozvalyv_SRSR_i_znyshhyv_GULAG.

Guérin, Daniel, Petry, François & Crête, Jean (2004). Tolerance, protest and democratic transition: Survey evidence from 13 post-communist countries. *European Journal of Political Research, 43*(3), 371–395.

Haller, Max (2002). Theory and method in the comparative study of values: Critique and alternative to Inglehart. *European Sociological Review, 18*(2), 139–158.

Harasymiw, Bohdan (2002). *Post-Communist Ukraine*. Edmonton and Toronto: Canadian Institute of Ukrainian Studies Press.

Harsanyi, John C. (1977). *Rational behavior and bargaining equilibrium in games and social situations*. Cambridge: Cambridge University Press.

Hashim, Mohsin S. (2010). Power-loss or power-transition? Assessing the limits of using the energy sector in reviving Russia's geopolitical stature. *Communist and Post-Communist Studies, 43*(3), 263–274.

Haugaard, Mark (2014). Power. In Michael Gibbons (Ed.), *The Encyclopedia of politicalthought*. (1st. ed.). John Wiley & Sons. DOI:10.1002/9781118474396.wbept0820.

Haugaard, Mark (2015). Concerted power over. *Constellations, 22*(1), 147–158.

Havrylyshyn, Oleh (2014). Ukraine: Greatest hopes, greatest disappointments. In Anders Åslund & Simeon Djankov (Eds.), *The great rebirth: Lessons from the victory of capitalism over communism* (pp. 165–184). Washington, DC: Peterson Institute for International Economics.

Hedlund, Stefan (2005). *Russian Path Dependence.* London and New York: Routledge.

Helkama, Klaus, Verkasalo, Markku, Myyry, Liisa, Silfver, Mia, Niit, Toomas, Manganelli, Anna-Maria, Andreeva, G.M., Stefanenko, T.G., Dubovskaya, E.M., Tikhomandritskaya, O.A. & Stetsenko, Anna (2012). Honour as a value in Finland, Estonia, Italy, Russia, and Switzerland. *Group Processes & Intergroup Relations, 16*(3), 279–297.

Heuer, Chelsea A., McClure, Kimberly J. & Puhl, Rebecca M. (2011). Obesity stigma in online news: A visual analysis. *Journal of Health Communication, 16*(9), 976–987.

Hiley, David (1987). Power and values in corporate life. *Journal of Business Ethics, 6*(5), 343–353.

Hodgson, Geoffrey M. & Jiang, Shuxia (2007). The economics of corruption and the corruption of economics: An institutionalist perspective. *Journal of Economic Issues, 41*(4), 1043–1061.

Hofheinz, Albrecht (2011). Nextopia? Beyond Revolution 2.0. *International Journal of Communication*, 5, 1417–1434.

Hofstede, Geert (1980). *Culture's consequences: International differences in work-related values.* Beverly Hills, CA: Sage.

Hofstede, Geert (1991). *Cultures and organizations: Software of the mind.* London: McGraw-Hill Book Company.

Hofstede, Geert (2006). What did GLOBE really measure? Researchers' minds versus respondents' minds. *Journal of International Business Studies, 37*(6), 882–896.

Hofstede, Geert & Bond, Michael H. (1984). Hosftede's culture dimensions: An independent validation using Rokeach's value survey. *Journal of cross-cultural psychology, 15*(4), 417–433.

Hofstede, Geert & McCrae, Robert R. (2004). Personality and culture revisited: Linking traits and dimensions to culture. *Cross-Cultural Research, 38*(1), 52–88.

Hofstede, Geert & Minkov, Michael (2013). VSM 2013 Values Survey Module 2013 manual. Retrieved from http://geerthofstede.com/research-and-vsm/vsm-2013/.

Hoskins, Bryony L. & Mascherini, Massimilano (2009). Measuring active citizenship through the development of a composite indicator. *Social Indicators Research, 90*(3), 459–488.

House, Robert, Javidan, Mansour, Hanges, Paul & Dorfman, Peter (2002). Understanding cultures and implicit leadership theories across the globe: an introduction to project GLOBE. *Journal of World Business, 37*(1), 3–10.

Howe, Richard H. (1978). Max Weber's elective affinities: Sociology within the bounds of pure reason. *American Journal of Sociology, 84*(2), 366–385.

Hrushevsky, Mykhailo (1956a). *Istoriia Ukrainy-Rusy* [History of Ukraine-Rus']. Volume 8, part 1: Vid Kurukivshchyny do Kumeishchyny (1626–1638) [From the agreement of Kurukovo to the defeat near Kumeiki (1626–1638)]. New York: Knigospilka.

Hrushevsky, Mykhailo (1956b). *Istoriia Ukrainy-Rusy* [History of Ukraine-Rus']. Volume 8, part 2: Pochatky Khmelnichchyny (1638–1648) [The start of Khmelnitsky's uprising (1638–1648)]. New York: Knigospilka.

Hrushevsky, Mykhailo (1956c). *Istoriia Ukrainy-Rusy* [History of Ukraine-Rus']. Volume 8, part 3: Khmelnichchyny v roztsviti (1648–1650) [The high point of Khmelnitsky's uprising (1648–1650)]. New York: Knigospilka.

Hrushevsky, Mykhailo (1958). *Istoriia Ukrainy-Rusy* [History of Ukraine-Rus']. Volume 10: Vid smerti Khmel'nitskogo go Gadiats'koi umovy [From Khmelnitsky's death to the Treaty of Hadiach], New York: Knigospilka.

Hrushevsky, Mykhailo (1991). *Istoriia Ukrainy-Rusy* [History of Ukraine-Rus']. Volume 1: Do pochatky XI vika [Before the start of the 11th century]. Kyiv: Naukova Dumka.

Hrushevsky, Mykhailo (1992a). *Istoriia Ukrainy-Rusy* [History of Ukraine-Rus']. Volume 2: XI-XIII vik [the 11th-13th century]. Kyiv: Naukova Dumka.

Hrushevsky, Mykhailo (1992b). *Istoriia Ukrainy-Rusy* [History of Ukraine-Rus']. Volume 3: Do roku 1340 [To year 1340]. Kyiv: Naukova Dumka.

Hrushevsky, Mykhailo (1993). *Istoriia Ukrainy-Rusy* [History of Ukraine-Rus']. Volume 4: XIV-XVI viky – vidnosyny politychni [XIV-XVI centuries – political aspects]. Kyiv: Naukova Dumka.

Hrushevsky, Mykhailo (1994). *Istoriia Ukrainy-Rusy* [History of Ukraine-Rus']. Volume 5: Suspil'no-politychnyi i tserkovnyi ustrii i vidnosyny v ukrain'sko-rus'kykh zemliakh XIV-XVII vikiv [Social, political and religious order in Ukrainian lands in the 14th-17th centuries]. Kyiv: Naukova Dumka.

Hrushevsky, Mykhailo (1995). *Istoriia Ukrainy-Rusy* [History of Ukraine-Rus']. Volume 6: Zhitie ekonomichne, kul'turne, natsional'ne XIV-XVIII vikiv [Economic, cultural and national life in the 14th-17th centuries]. Kyiv: Naukova Dumka.

Hrushevsky, Mykhailo (1996). *Istoriia Ukrainy-Rusy* [History of Ukraine-Rus']. Volume 9, part 1: Roky 1650–1654 [Years 1650–1654]. Kyiv: Naukova Dumka.

Hrushevsky, Mykhailo (1997). *Istoriia Ukrainy-Rusy* [History of Ukraine-Rus']. Volume 9, part 2: Roky 1654–1657 [Years 1654–1657]. Kyiv: Naukova Dumka.

Hrushevsky, Mykhailo (1999 [1909]). *History of Ukraine-Rus'*. Volume 7: The Cossack Age to 1625. (B. Strumiński, Trans.). Edited by Serhii Plokhy and Frank E. Sysyn. Edmonton and Toronto: Canadian Institute of Ukrainian Studies Press.

Ilko Kucheriv Democratic Initiatives Foundation (2014, February 03), Vid Maidanu-Taboru do Maidanu-Sichi: shcho zminylosya? [From Maidan-Tabir to Maidan-Sich: Common and diverse characteristics]. Retrieved from http://dif.org.ua/article/vid-maydanu-taboru-do-maydanu-sichi-shcho-zminilosya.

International Labour Office (2011). *Manual on the measurement of volunteer work*. Geneva.

Ivanickova, Mariana, Mihalcova, Bohuslava & Pruzinsky, Michal (2015). Intercultural differences in the Visegrad Group: The Hofstede model application. *Actual Problems of Economics, 6*(168), 284–292.

Jackson, Winston (2003). *Methods: Doing social research*. (3rd. ed.). Toronto: Prentice Hall.

Jansen, Thijs, Van Lier, Arie, Van Witteloostuijn, Arjen & von Ochssée, Tim Boon (2012). A modified Cournot model of the natural gas market in the European Union: Mixed-motives delegation in a politicized environment. *Energy Policy, 41*(1), 280–285.

Jen, Min H., Sund, Erik R., Johnston, Ron & Jones, Kelvyn (2010). Trustful societies, trustful individuals, and health: An analysis of self-rated health and social trust using the World Value Survey. *Health & Place, 16*(5), 1022–1029.

Jick, Todd D. (1979). Mixing qualitative and quantitative methods: Triangulation in action. *Administrative Science Quarterly, 24*(4), 602–611.

Johnson, Iryna (2005). Political trust in societies under transformation: A comparative analysis of Poland and Ukraine. *International Journal of Sociology, 35*(2), 63–84.

Kabasakal Arat, Zehra F. (2006). Forging a global culture of human rights: Origins and prospects of the International Bill of Rights. *Human Rights Quarterly, 28*(2), 416–437.

Kamir, Orit (2006). Honor and dignity in the Film *Unforgiven*: Implications for sociolegal theory. *Law & Society Review, 40*(1), 193–233.

Kamstra, Jelmer, Pelzer, Ben, Elbers, Willem & Ruben, Ruerd (2016). Constraining is enabling? Exploring the influence of national context on civil society strength. *Voluntas, 27*(3), 1023–1044.

Karagannis, Emmanuel (2016). Ukrainian volunteer fighters in the eastern front: Ideas, political-social norms and emotions as mobilization mechanisms. *Journal of Southeast European and Black Sea Studies, 16*(1), 139–153.

Kilpatrick, Shelley Dean (2007). Volunteerism. In Roy F. Baumeister & Kathleen D. Vohs (Eds.), *Encyclopedia of social psychology* (p. 1016). Thousand Oaks: Sage.

Kleiner, Georgy (2015). Ustoichivost' rossiiskoi ekonomiki v zerkale sistemnoi ekonomicheskoi teorii. Chast' I [Stability of Russian economy in the light of systems theory: Part I]. *Voprosy Ekonomiki*, 12, 107–123.

Kleiner, Georgy (2016). Ustoichivost' rossiiskoi ekonomiki v zerkale sistemnoi ekonomicheskoi teorii. Chast' II [Stability of Russian economy in the light of systems theory: Part II]. *Voprosy Ekonomiki*, 1, 117–138.

Klyuchevsky, Vasily (1956), *Sochineniia v 8 tomakh* [Works in 8 volumes]. Volume 1: Kurs Russkoi istorii. Chast' 1 [Course on Russian history. Part 1]. Moscow: Gosudarstvennoe izdatel'stvo politicheskoi literatury.

Klyuchevsky, Vasily (1957), *Sochineniia v 8 tomakh* [Works in 8 volumes]. Volume 2: Kurs Russkoi istorii. Chast' 2 [Course on Russian history. Part 2]. Moscow: Gosudarstvennoe izdatel'stvo politicheskoi literatury.

Kolářová, Marta (2004). Gender representation of the anti-globalization movement in the alternative media. *Czech Sociological Review, 40*(6), 851–868.

Kornai, János (1997). *Struggle and hope: Essays on stabilization and reform in a post-socialist economy*. Cheltenham, UK: Edward Elgar.

Korostelina, Karina V. (2014). *Constructing the narratives of identity and power: Self-imagination in a young Ukrainian nation*. Lanham, MA: Lexington.

Kostiuchenko, Tetiana (2012). Elite continuity in Ukraine: When networks matter (?). *Historical Social Research, 37*(2), 14–25.

Kostomarov, Nikolai (1861). Dve russkie narodnosti [Two Russian peoples]. *Osnova*, 3, 33–80.

Krawchenko, Bohdan (1983). Ethno-demographic trends in Ukraine in the 1970s. In Bohdan Krawchenko (Ed.), *Ukraine after Shelest* (pp. 101–119). Edmonton: Canadian Institute of Ukrainian Studies, University of Alberta.

Krippendorff, Klaus (2004). *Content analysis: An introduction to its methodology*. (2nd. ed.). Thousand Oaks, CA: Sage.

Kuhn, Thomas S. (1972 [1962]). Scientific paradigms. In Barry S. Barnes (Ed.), *Sociology of science: Selected readings* (pp. 80–104). Harmondsworth: Penguin Books.

Kujawski, Bernard & Abell, Peter (2011). Virtual communities? The middle east revolutions at the guardian forum: Comment is free. *The European Physical Journal B*, 83, 525–529.

Kuntz, Philipp & Thompson, Mark R. (2009). More than just the final straw: Stolen Elections as revolutionary triggers. *Comparative Politics, 41*(3), 253–272.

Kupatadze, Alexander (2008). Organized crime before and after the Tulip Revolution: The changing dynamics of upperworld-underworld networks. *Central Asian Survey, 27*(3), 279–299.

Kuzio, Taras (1998). *Ukraine: State and Nation Building*. London and New York: Routledge.

Kuzio, Taras (2012). Twenty years as an independent state: Ukraine's ten logical inconsistencies. *Communist and Post-Communist Studies, 45*(4–5), 429–438.

Kuzio, Taras (2014). Special Section: Re-evaluating democratic revolutions, nationalism and organized crime in Ukraine from a comparative perspective. *Communist and Post-Communist Studies, 47*(2), 191–193.

Kuzio, Taras (2015). *Ukraine: Democratization, corruption, and the new Russian imperialism*. Santa Barbara, CA: Praeger.

Kuzmin, Oleh, Shpak, Nestor & Pyrog, Olha (2016). Model of sustainable development of the national economy of Ukraine: Assessment of current state and prospects of development. *Econtechmod: An International Quarterly Journal, 5*(1), 43–50.

Kyiv International Institute of Sociology, the (2012). Dovira ukraintsiv do do sotsial'nykh institutsii [Trust of Ukrainians in social institutions]. Retrieved from http://www.kiis.com.ua/?lang=ukr&cat=reports&id=81.

Kyiv International Institute of Sociology, the (2015a), Dovira do sotsial'nykh institutsii ta grup [Trust in social institutions and groups]. Retrieved from http://kiis.com.ua/?lang=ukr&cat=reports&id=579&page=2.

Kyiv International Institute of Sociology, the (2015b). *Indeks rezul'tativnosti rossiiskoi propagandy* [Index of the efficiency of Russian propaganda]. Kyiv, mimeo.

Kyiv International Institute of Sociology, the (2016). Sotsial'no-politychni nastroi zhyteliv Ukrainy ta reiting pidtrymky partii i politichnykh lideriv [Social and political attitudes of the population of Ukraine and the level of support for political parties and political leaders]. Retrieved from http://kiis.com.ua/?lang=ukr&cat=reports&id=628.

Kyrychenko, Olexandr & Kudria, Ivan (2009). Kreditna bezpeka agrarnogo sektoru Ukrainy [Credit security of Ukraine's agriculture]. *Agrosvit*, 8, 23–26.

Lam, Simon S.K., Schaubroeck, John, & Aryee, Samuel (2002). Relationship between organizational justice and employee work outcomes: A cross-national study. *Journal of Organizational Behavior*, *23*(1), 1–18.

Ledeneva, Alena V. (1998). *Russia's economy of favours: Blat, networking and informal exchange*. Cambridge: Cambridge University Press.

Ledyaev, Valeri (1997). *Power: A conceptual analysis*. Commack, NY: Nova Science.

Ledyaev, Valeri (2008). Domination, power and authority in Russia: Basic characteristics and forms. *East European Politics*, *24*(1), 17–36.

Lee, Man Yee Karen (2011). Religion, human rights and the role of culture. *The International Journal of Human Rights*, *15*(6), 887–904.

Levada Center (2017). *Obshchestvennoe mnenie – 2016. Ezhegodnik* [2016 Yearbook of Public Opinion], Moscow. Retrieved from http://www.levada.ru/sbornik-obshhestvennoe-mnenie/obshhestvennoe-mnenie-2016/om-2016/.

Levada, Youri (1993). *Entre passé et l'avenir: L'homme soviétique ordinaire. Enquête*. (J. Tordjman & A. Berelowitch Trad.). Paris: Presses de la Fondation Nationale des Sciences Politiques.

Lewis, Milton (2007). A brief history of human dignity: Idea and application. In Jeff Malpas & Norelle Lickiss (Eds.), *Perspectives on human dignity: A conversation* (pp. 93–105). Dordrecht: Springer.

Lozowick, Yaacov (2002 [2000]). *Hitler's bureaucrats: The Nazi security police and the banality of evil*. London and New York: Continuum.

Luban, David (2005). Lawyers as upholders of human dignity (when they aren't busy assaulting it). *University of Illinois Law Review*, 2005, 815-845.

Lukes, Steven (2005). *Power: A radical view.* (2nd. ed.). Houndmills: Palgrave Macmillan.

Lutsevych, Orysia (2016). Civil society versus captured state: A winning strategy for sustainable change. *Development in Practice, 26*(5), 646–656.

Lyytikäinen, Laura (2014). *Performing political opposition in Russia: The case of the youth movement* Oborona. Helsinki: University of Helsinki Department of Social Research.

Ma, Agnes & Norwich, Brahm (2007). Triangulation and theoretical understanding. *International Journal of Social Research Methodology, 10*(3), 173–184.

Maddock, Rowland (1980). Energy and integration: The logic of interdependence in the Soviet Union and Eastern Europe. *Journal of Common Market Studies, 19*(1), 21–34.

Magosci, Paul Robert (2010 [1996]). *A history of Ukraine: The land and its peoples.* (2nd. ed.). Toronto: The University of Toronto Press.

Makarenko, Viktor P. (1998). *Russkaia vlast': teoretiko-sotsiologicheskie problemy* [Russian power: Theoretical and sociological aspects], Rostov-on-Don: Izdatel'stvo Severo-Kavkazskogo Nauchnogo Tsentra Vyshei Shkoly.

Maleki, Ammar & de Jong, Martin (2014). A proposal for clustering the dimensions of national culture. *Cross-Cultural Research, 48*(2), 107–143.

Mann, Michael (1986). *The sources of social power.* Volume 1: A history of power from the beginning to A.D. 1760. Cambridge: Cambridge University Press.

Manning, Clarence A. (1944). Schevchenko and Pushkin's 'To the Slanderers of Russia'. *Modern Language Notes, 59*(7), 495–497.

Marlyenko, Tatyana (2016). In the crosshairs of great powers: Linkage, leverage and conflict in Ukraine. In Karl Cordell & Stefan Wolff (Eds.), *The Routledge handbook of ethnic conflict* (2nd. ed.) (pp. 249–368). Milton Park: Routledge.

Marples, David R. (2007). *Heroes and villains: Creating national history in contemporary Ukraine.* Budapest: Central European University Press.

Marx, Karl (1889). *Capital: A critical analysis of capitalist production.* New York: Appleton & Co.

Mascherini, Massimilano, Vidoni, Daniele & Manca, Anna R. (2011). Exploring the determinants of civil participation in 14 European countries: One-size-fits none. *European Sociological Review, 27*(6), 790–807.

Masliy, Vadym V. (2014). Metody analizu teritorial'nogo rozpodilu priamykh inozemnykh investytsii v Ukraini' [Analysis methods of territorial distribution of foreign direct investments in Ukraine]. *Actual Problems of Economics, 7*(157), 454–462.

McAdam, Doug, Tarrow, Sidney & Tilly, Charles (2001). *Dynamics of contention*. Cambridge: Cambridge University Press.

McCormick, John P. (2001). Machiavellian democracy: Controlling elites with ferocious populism. *American Political Science Review, 95*(2), 297–313.

McFarland, Sam, Ageyev, Vladimir & Abalkina, Marina (1993). The authoritarian personality in the United States and the former Soviet Union: Comparative studies. In Willima F. Stone, Gerda Lederer, & Richard Christie (Eds.), *Strength and weakness: The authoritarian personality today* (pp. 199–225). New York: Springer-Verlag.

Mearsheimer, John (2014). Why the Ukraine crisis is the West's fault. *Foreign Affairs, 93*(5), 77–89.

Melnik, Tetiana, (2015). Zabezpechennia ekonomichnogo suverenitetu v umovakh vidkrytosti ekonomiky [The economic sovereignty support under the conditions of economy's openness]. *Marketing i menedzhment innovatsii*, 1, 147–157.

Menachem, Mautner (2008). From 'honor' to 'dignity': How should a liberal state treat non-liberal cultural groups? *Theoretical Inquiries in Law, 9*(2), 609–642.

Ménard, Claude (2005a). Theory of organizations: The diversity of arrangements in a developed market economy. In Anton Oleinik (Ed.), *The institutional economics of Russia's transformation* (pp. 88–111). Aldershot: Ashgate.

Ménard, Claude (2005b). Transaction cost economics: From the Coase theorem to empirical studies. In Anton Oleinik (Ed.), *The institutional economics of Russia's transformation* (pp. 45–64). Aldershot: Ashgate.

Merry, Sally Engle (1997). Legal pluralism and transnational culture: The Ka Ho'okolokolonui Kanaka Maoli Tribunal, Hawaii, 1993. In Richard A. Wilson (Ed.), *Human rights, culture & context: Anthropological perspectives* (pp. 28–48). London: Pluto.

Merry, Sally Engle (2006). *Human rights and gender violence: Translating international law into local justice*. Chicago and London: The University of Chicago Press.

Merton, Robert K. (1995). The Thomas theorem and the Matthew effect. *Social Forces, 74*(2), 379–424.

Meyer, John W. (2000). Globalization: Sources and effects on national states and societies. *International Sociology, 15*(2), 233–248.

Mickiewicz, Adam (1917 [1834]). *Pan Tadeusz or the Last Foray in Lithuania: A story of life among Polish gentlefolk in the years 1811 and 1812 in 12 books.* (G.R. Noyes, Trans.). London: J. M. Dent and Sons.

Mills, Wright Charles (1957). *The power elite.* New York: Oxford University Press.

Minakov, Mykhailo (2015, May). The third sector entering the first. Cooperation and competition of civil society, state and oligarchs after Euromaidan. *Paper presented at the conference 'Risks and Opportunities in the Civil Society – Public Institutions Relationship: Re-Assessing the EU and Global Policy Process'*, LUISS University, Rome.

Ministry of Finance of Ukraine (2017). Derzhavnyi ta garantovanyi derzhavoiu borg za stanom na 28.02.2017 [Sovereign and state guaranteed debt on February 28, 2017]. Retrieved from http://www.minfin.gov.ua/uploads/redactor/files/28.02.2017%20%D0%B1%D0%BE%D1%80%D0%B3.xlsm.

Moraski, Bryon & Giucanu, Magda (2013). European reactions to the 2008 Georgian–Russian War: Assessing the impact of gas dependence. *Studies in Comparative International Development, 48*(4), 432–456.

Morriss, Peter (2009). Power and liberalism. In Stewart R. Clegg & Mark Haugaard (Eds.), *The SAGE handbook of power* (pp. 54–69). Thousand Oaks: Sage.

Mulder, Niels (1996). *Inside Thai society: Interpretations of everyday life.* Amsterdam: The Pepin Press. Retrieved from http://ehrafworldcultures.yale.edu/document?id=ao07-060.

Muravieva, Olga V. (2013). Sopostavitel'nyi analiz metaforicheskikh kartin mira T.Shevchenka i A.Pushkina (na materiale russkoyazychnykh proizvedenii) [Comparative analysis of metaphors in the works of T. Shevchenko and A. Pushkin]. *Mova i kul'tura, 16*(1), 158–165.

Musick, Mark A. & Wilson, John (2007). *Volunteers: A social profile.* Bloomington, IN: Indiana University Press.

Nastych, Alla (2003). Elites and masses in the political process in Ukraine since 1991. *Perspectives on European Politics and Society, 4*(2), 299–330.

Neiberg, Michael (2005). Conscription and volunteerism. In Peter Karsten (Ed.), *Encyclopedia of war & American society* (pp. 187–189). Thousand Oaks: Sage.

Newman, Lawrence W. (2006). *Social research methods: Qualitative and quantitative approaches.* (6th. ed.). Boston, MA: Pearson.

Nikolayenko, Olena (2007). The revolt of the post-Soviet generation youth movements in Serbia, Georgia, and Ukraine. *Comparative Politics, 39*(2), 169–188.

Nikolenko, Olga (2011). Byron-Pushkin-Shevchenko (tipologii i transformatsii byronichnoyi poemy) [Byron-Pushkin-Shevchenko (types and transformations of Byronic poems)], *Filologichni nauky: Zbirnyk naukovykh prats'*, 9, 3–13.

North, Douglass C. (1981). *Structure and change in economic history*. New York: Norton.

North, Douglass C. (1990). *Institutions, institutional change and economic performance*. Cambridge: Cambridge University Press.

Nosova, Olga (2013). The innovation development in Ukraine: Problems and development perspectives. *International Journal of Innovation and Business Strategy*, 2, 1–13.

O'Connell, Rebecca (2013). The use of visual methods with children in a mixed methods study of family food practices. *International Journal of Social Research Methodology*, *16*(1), 31–46.

Obama, Barack H. (2009). Nobel Lecture: A just and lasting peace. *Nobelprize.org*. Retrieved from http://www.nobelprize.org/nobel_prizes/peace/laureates/2009/obama-lecture_en.html.

OECD (2014). OECD Territorial Reviews: Ukraine 2013. OECD Publishing.

Oleinik, Anton (2009). Inquiring into communication in science: Alternative approaches. *Science in Context*, *22*(4), 613–646.

Oleinik, Anton (2011a). *Market as a weapon: The socio-economic machinery of dominance in Russia*. New Brunswick and London: Transaction Publishers.

Oleinik, Anton (2011b). Mixing quantitative and qualitative content analysis: Triangulation at work. *Quality & Quantity*, *45*(4), 859–873.

Oleinik, Anton (2012a). Institutional exclusion as a destabilizing factor: The mass unrest of July 1, 2008 in Mongolia. *Central Asian Survey*, *31*(2), 153–174.

Oleinik, Anton (2012b). 'Office Plankton' as an asset resource of the existing political regime?' *Sociological research*, *51*(6), 10–22.

Oleinik, Anton (2014). *Knowledge and networking: On Communication in the Social Sciences*. New Brunswick, NJ and London: Transaction Publishers.

Oleinik, Anton (2015a). Benefits of entry control: the Russian case. *Post-Communist Economies*, *27*(2), 216–232.

Oleinik, Anton (2015b). *The invisible hand of power: An economic theory of gatekeeping*. London: Routledge.

Oleinik, Anton (2015c). On content analysis of images of mass protests: A case of data triangulation. *Quality and Quantity*, *49*(5), 2203–2220.

Oleinik, Anton (2015d). The language of power: A content analysis of presidential addresses in North America and the former Soviet Union, 1993–2012. *International Journal of the Sociology of Language*, 236, 181–204.

Oleinik, Anton (2016a). Introduction: Between universal and culture-specific interpretation of human dignity. *Comparative Sociology*, *15*(6), 625–638.

Oleinik, Anton (2016b). Corruption on the road: A case study of Russian traffic police. *IATSS Research*, *40*(1), 19–25.

Oleinik, Anton, Popova, Irina, Kirdina, Svetlana & Shatalova, Tatiana (2014). On the choice of measures of reliability and validity in the content-analysis of texts. *Quality and Quantity*, *48*(5), 2703–2718.

Oleinik, Anton, Yermekov, Momysh & Kuatbekov, Zharas (2015). Power distance, sub-ethnic groups and teams of civil servants: Overlooked factors of administrative reform in Kazakhstan? *Public Policy and Administration*, *30*(2), 182–205.

Olson, Mancur (1993). Dictatorship, democracy, and development. *American Political Science Review*, *87*(3), 567–576.

Onwuegbuzie, Anthony J. & Leech, Nancy L. (2005). On becoming a pragmatic researcher: The importance of combining quantitative and qualitative research methodologies. *International Journal of Social Research Methodology*, *8*(5), 375–387.

Open Europe (2014, April 16). Divided we stand: Where do EU states stand on further sanctions on Russia? Retrieved from http://archive.openeurope.org.uk/Article/Page/en/LIVE?id=19876&page=FlashAnalysis.

Opp, Karl-Dieter (2011). The production of historical 'facts': How the wrong number of participants in the Leipzig Monday Demonstration on October 9, 1989 became a convention. *Jahrbücher für Nationalökonomie und Statistik*, *231*(5–6), 598–607.

Organization for Security and Co-operation in Europe (OSCE) (2015). Civil society and the crisis in Ukraine, special monitoring mission in Ukraine. Retrieved from http://www.osce.org/ukraine-smm/141046.

Osin, Vadim (2014). Akademiia i politicheskii rezhim: neopatrimonial'naia nauka v Ukraine (i Moldove) [Academy and the political regime: Neopatrimonial science in Ukraine (and Moldova)]. *Ab Imperio*, 3, 295–360.

Osipian, Ararat L. (2010). Corrupt organizational hierarchies in the former Soviet Bloc. *Transition Studies Review*, *17*(4), 822–836.

Ostrom, Elinor (1998). A behavioral approach to the rational choice theory of collective action. *American Political Science Review, 92*(1), 1–22.

Ozel, Bulent & Park, Han W. (2012). Online image content analysis of political figures: An exploratory study. *Quality & Quantity, 46*(4), 1013–1024.

Painter II, Matthew A. & Paxton, Pamela (2014). Checkbooks in the heartland: Change over time in voluntary association membership. *Sociological Forum, 29*(2), 408–428.

Palyvoda, Lyubov & Golota, Sophia (2010). *Civil society organizations in Ukraine: The state and dynamics (2002–2010)*. Kyiv: Publishing house 'Kupol'.

Patriarch Kirill (2011). Address at the grand opening of the third Assembly of the Russian world. *Russian Politics & Law, 49*(1), 57–64.

Pearce, David W., Ed. (1992 [1981]). *Macmillan dictionary of modern economics*. (4th. ed.). London: Macmillan.

Perlesz, Amaryll & Lindsay, Jo (2003). Methodological triangulation in researching families: Making sense of dissonant data. *International Journal of Social Research Methodology, 6*(1), 25–40.

Persson, Matts (2014, April 16). The EU remains a long way off agreeing tougher sanctions on Russia. *The Telegraph's blogs*.

Pilipenko, Ganna (2013). Vplyv cultury na spivvidnoshenniia derzhavnoi ta rynkovoi koordinatsii v Ukraini [Cultural impact on the ratio of public and market coordination in Ukraine]. *Naukovyi Visnyk Natsional'nogo Girnychogo Universytetu*, 3, 118–125.

Pipes, Richard (1974). *Russia under the Old Regime*. London: Weidenfeld and Nicolson.

Pipes, Richard (1999). *Property and freedom*. New York: Alfred A. Knopf.

Pivovarov, Yuri S. (2006). *Russkaia politicheskaia traditsiia i sovremennost'* [Russian political tradition and current situation]. Moscow: INION RAN.

Pleyers, Geoffrey & Glasius, Marlies (2013). La résonance des «mouvements des places»: connexions, émotions, valeurs. *Socio*, 2, 59–80.

Plokhy, Serhii (2010). Poltava: The battle that never ends. *Harvard Ukrainian Studies, 31*(1–4), xii-xxv.

Plokhy, Serhii (2015). *The gates of Europe: A history of Ukraine*. New York: Basic Books.

Pohorila, Natalia (2008). Basis for regime legitimacy: Study of attitudes toward privatization in Ukraine. In Anton Oleinik (Ed.), *Reforming the state without changing the model of power? On administrative reform in post-Socialist countries* (pp. 191–214). London: Routledge.

Polanyi, Karl (2001 [1944]). *The great transformation: The political and economic origins of our time*. Boston: Beacon Press.

Pratchett, Lawrence (2004). Local autonomy, local democracy and the 'new localism'. *Political Studies, 52*(2), 358–375.

Prebisch, Raúl (1959). Commercial policy in the underdeveloped countries. *The American Economic Review, 49*(2), 251–273.

Prosser, Jon & Schwartz, Dona (2005). Photographs within the Sociological Research Process. In Jon Prosser (Ed.), *Image-based research: A sourcebook for qualitative researchers* (pp. 115–130). London: Falmer.

Raskov, Danila (2014). Izbiratel'noe srodstvo' ekonomiki i religii: traktovka M. Vebera [Elective affinity of economy and society: a reading of M. Weber]. *Khristianskoe chtenie* [Christian reading], 1, 115–133.

Razumkov Centre (2013). Yakym integtatsiinym napryamom mae ity Ukraina? [What is the right format of association for Ukraine?]. Retrieved from http://old.razumkov.org.ua/ukr/poll.php?poll_id=865.

Razumkov Centre (2017). Sotsial'no-politychna sytuatsiia v Ukraini [Social and political situation in Ukraine]. Retrieved from http://razumkov.org.ua/uploads/socio/2017_Press_reliz_4_company.pdf.

Reid, Anna (2015 [1997]). *Borderland: A journey through the history of Ukraine*. New York: Basic Books.

Reisinger, William M. (1998). Survey research and authority patterns in contemporary Russia. In Harry Eckstein, Frederic J. Fleron, Erik P. Hoffmann, & William M. Reisinger (with Ahl, Richard, Bova, Russell & Roeder, Philip G.), *Can democracy take root in post-Soviet Russia? Exploration in state-society Rerations* (pp. 163–173). Lanham, MA: Rowman & Littlefield Publishers.

Reporters Without Borders (2014). 2013 World Press Freedom Index: Dashed hopes after spring. Retrieved from https://rsf.org/en/news/2013-world-press-freedom-index-dashed-hopes-after-spring.

Reyfman, Irina (1995). The emergence of the duel in Russia: Corporal punishment and the honour code. *The Russian Review, 54*(1), 26–43.

RIA Novosti (2011, December 24). Inzhener-geodezist podschital uchastnikov mitinga na prospekte Sakharova [Specialist in geodesy calculated the number of protesters at Sakharov Avenue]. Retrieved from http://www.ria.ru/society/20111224/525177803.html.

Riley, Stephen (2010). Human dignity: Comparative and conceptual debates. *International Journal of Law in Context, 6*(2), 117–138.

Rinne, Tiffany, Steel, G. Daniel & Fairweather, John (2012). Hofstede and Shane revisited: The role of power distance and individualism in national-level innovation success. *Cross-Cultural Research, 46*(2), 91–108.

Risen, James & Poitras Laura (2014, May 31). N.S.A. collecting millions of faces from web images. *The New York Times*. Retrieved from https://www.nytimes.com/2014/06/01/us/nsa-collecting-millions-of-faces-from-web-images.html.

Rodriguez, Philippe-André (2015). Human dignity as an essentially contested concept. *Cambridge Review of International Affairs, 28*(4), 743–756.

Rokeach, Milton (1969). The role of values in public opinion research. *The Public Opinion Quarterly, 32*(4), 547–559.

Rose, Gillian (2012). *Visual methodologies: An introduction to researching visual materials*. (3rd. ed.). Thousand Oaks: Sage.

Rose, Richard (1995). La liberté, valeur fondamentale. *Revue Internationale des Sciences Sociales*, 145, 519–536.

Rose-Ackerman, Susan (2004). Governance and corruption. In Bjorn Lomborg (Ed.), *Global crises, global solutions* (pp. 301–344). Cambridge: Cambridge University Press.

Rousseau, Jean-Jacques (1844). *Œuvres complètes avec des notes historiques*. Volume 1: Les confessions. Discours. Politique. Paris: Furne et Cie.

Sachs, Jeffrey (2005). *The end of poverty: Economic possibilities of our time*. New York: The Penguin Press.

Said, Abdul Aziz (1979). Precept and practice of human rights in Islam. *Universal Human Rights, 1*(1), 63–79.

Sakwa, Richard (2014). *Frontline Ukraine: Crisis in the borderlands*. London and New York: I.B. Tauris.

Salamon, Lester M. (2010). Putting the civil society sector on the economic map of the world. *Annals of Public and Cooperative Economics, 81*(2), 167–210.

Salamon, Lester M., Anheier, Helmut K. & Associates (1999). Civil Society in Comparative Perspective. In Lester M. Salamon, Helmut K. Anheier, Regina List, Stefan Toepler, S. Wojciech Sokolowski & Associates, *Global civil society: Dimensions of the nonprofit sector* (pp.3–39). Baltimore, MD: Johns Hopkins Center for Civil Society Studies.

Samelson, Franz (1993). The authoritarian character from Berlin to Berkeley and beyond: The odyssey of a problem. In Willima F. Stone, Gerda Lederer, & Richard Christie (Eds.), *Strength and weakness: The authoritarian personality today* (pp. 22–43). New York: Springer-Verlag.

Scheiber, Laura (2016). How social entrepreneurs in the third sector learn from life experiences. *Voluntas, 27*(4), 1694–1717.

Schelling, Thomas S. (1960). *The strategy of conflict*. Cambridge, MA: Harvard University Press.

Schmidt-Felzmann, Anke (2011). EU Member States' energy relations with Russia: Conflicting approaches to securing natural gas supplies. *Geopolitics, 16*(3), 574–599.

Schumpeter, Joseph A. (1983 [1934]). *The theory of economic development: An inquiry into profits, capital, credit, interest and the business cycle*. New Brunswick: Transaction Publishers.

Scott, Greg & Garner, Roberta (2013). *Doing qualitative research: Designs, methods, and techniques*. Boston: Pearson.

Scott, John (2001). *Power*. Cambridge: Polity Press.

Senderov, Valery A. (2015), Ot 'vseslavianskoi federatsii' k 'russkomu miru' [From the Pan-Slavic Federation to the Russian World]. *Voprosy filosofii*, 3, 137–145.

Sharp, Gene (2012 [1993]). *From dictatorship to democracy: A conceptual framework for liberation*. London: Serpent's Tail.

Shchedrovitskii, Petr (2000). Russkii mir i transnatsional'noe russkoe [The Russian world and the trans-national Russian]. *Russkii Zhurnal*. Retrieved from http://old.russ.ru/politics/meta/20000302_schedr.html.

Shekhovtsov, Anton & Umland, Andreas (2014). Ukraine's radical right. *Journal of Democracy, 25*(3), 58–63.

Shkirda, Alexandre (2004 [1982]). *Nestor Makhno: Anarchy's Cossack. The struggle for free Soviets in the Ukraine 1917–1921*. Edinburgh: AK Press.

Shulga, Mykola & Boyko, Nataliya (1999). A sociological portrait of the Government of Ukraine. *International Journal of Sociology, 29*(3), 76–96.

Shulman, Stephen (2006). Cultural comparisons and their consequences for nationhood in Ukraine. *Communist and Post-Communist Studies, 39*(2), 247–263.

Shultziner, Doron (2007). Human dignity: Functions and meanings. In Jeff Malpas & Norelle Lickiss (Eds.), *Perspectives on human dignity: A conversation* (pp. 73–92). Dordrecht: Springer.

Simmel, Georg (1978 [1907]). *The philosophy of money*. (T. Bottomore & D. Frisby, Trans.). London: Routledge & Kegan Paul.

Simon, Herbert A. (1951). A formal theory of the employment relationship. *Econometrica, 19*(3), 293–305.

Simon, Herbert A. (1953). Notes on the observation and measurement of political power. *The Journal of Politics, 15*(4), 500–516.

Smith, Anthony D. (1991). *National identity*. London: Penguin Books.

Smith, Anthony D. (2002). When is a nation? *Geopolitics, 7*(2), 5–32.

Smith, Anthony D. (2004). *The antiquity of nations*. Cambridge: Polity.

Smith, David Horton (1997). Grassroots associations are important: Some theory and a review of the impact literature. *Nonprofit and Voluntary Sector Quarterly, 26*(3), 296–306.

Statistics Canada (2012). *Canadian Social Trends,* 93 (Summer). Retrieved from http://www.statcan.gc.ca/pub/11-008-x/2012001/t/11638/tbl02-eng.htm.

Stebelsky, Ihor (2014). *Placing Ukraine on the map: Stepan Rudnytsky's nation-building geography*. Kingston, ON: Kashtan Press.

Stepanenko, Victor (2006). Civil society in post-Soviet Ukraine: Civic ethos in the framework of corrupted sociality? *East European Politics and Societies, 20*(4), 571–597.

Stepanenko, Viktor (2015). Konfiguratsii panuvannia ta sprotuvy v konteksti institutsional'nykh osoblyvostei rozvutky gromadians'kogo suspil'stva v Ukraini [Modalities of power and resistance in the context of institutional particularities of the development of civil society in Ukraine], In Ministry of Science and Education of Ukraine et al., *Derzhava ta global'ni sotsial'ni zminy* [The State and global social changes] (pp. 88–92). Conference proceedings Kyiv.

Stevenson, Nick (2014). Human(e) rights and the cosmopolitan imagination: Questions of human dignity and cultural identity. *Cultural Sociology, 8*(2), 180–196.

Stewart, Agnus (2001). *Theories of power and domination: The politics of empowerment in late modernity*, London: Sage.

Stiglitz, Joseph E. (1994). *Whither socialism*? Cambridge, MA: The MIT Press.

Subtelny, Orest (2009 [1988]). *Ukraine: A history*. (4th. ed.). Toronto: University of Toronto Press.

Suliak, Sergei (2012). Moldaviia i Russkii mir: vozmozhno li vozvrashchenie? [Moldova and the Russian world: Is the return possible?]. *Rusin, 3*(29): 5–32.

Suslov, Mikhail (2012). Geographical metanarratives in Russia and the European East: Contemporary pan-Slavism. *Eurasian Geography and Economics, 53*(5), 575–595.

Swedberg, Richard (2003). *Principles of economic sociology*. Princeton and Oxford: Princeton University Press.

Szabó, Máté (1996). Repertoire of contention in post-communist protest cultures: An East European comparative survey. *Social Research, 63*(4), 1155–1182.

Tairova-Yakovleva, Tatiana (2011). *Ivan Mazepa i Rossiiskaia imperiia: istoria 'predatel'stva'* [Ivan Mazepa and the Russian Empire: A history of a 'betrayal']. Moscow: Tsentrpoligraf.

Tarrow, Sidney (1993). Modular collective action and the rise of the social movement: Why the French Revolution was not enough. *Politics & Society, 21*(1), 69–90.

Tarrow, Sidney (2011 [1994]). *Power in movement social movements and contentious politics.* (3rd. ed.). Cambridge: Cambridge University Press.

Tarrow, Sidney & McAdam, Doug (2005). Scale shift in transnational contention. In Donatella Della Porta & Sidney Tarrow (Eds.), *Transnational protest and global activism* (pp. 121–147). Lanham, MD: Rowman & Littlefield.

Taylor, Adam (2013, December 9), Why Ukraine isn't 'The Ukraine', and why that matters now. *Business Insider.* Retrieved from http://www.businessinsider.com/why-ukraine-isnt-the-ukraine-and-why-that-matters-now-2013-12.

Temirkulov, Azamat (2008). Informal actors and institutions in mobilization: The periphery in the 'Tulip Revolution'. *Central Asian Survey, 27*(3), 317–335.

Teschke, Benno (2011). Geopolitics. In Bertrand Badie, Dirk Berg-Schlosser & Leonardo Morlino (Eds.), *International encyclopedia of political science* (pp. 970–972). Thousand Oaks, CA: Sage.

Thompson, Beverly Y. (2007). The global justice movement's use of 'jail solidarity' as a response to police repression and arrest: An ethnographic study. *Qualitative Inquiry, 13*(1), 141–159.

Tilly, Charles (1977). Getting it together in Burgundy, 1675–1975. *Theory and Society, 4*(4), 479–504.

Tilly, Charles (1978). *From mobilization to revolution.* Reading, MA: Addison-Wesley.

Tilly, Charles (1985). War making and state making as organized crime. In Peter B. Evans, Dietrich Rueschemeyer, & Theda Skopol (Eds.), *Bringing the state back in* (pp. 169–191). Cambridge: Cambridge University Press.

Tilly, Charles (1995). Contentious repertoires in Great Britain, 1758–1834. In Mark Traugott (Ed.), *Repertoires and cycles of collective action* (pp. 15–42). Durham: Duke University Press.

Tilly, Charles (2002). Violence, terror and politics as Usual. *Boston Review, 27*(3–4). Retrieved from http://bostonreview.net/archives/BR27.3/tilly.html.

Tilly, Charles (2009). Power and democracy. In Stewart R. Clegg & Mark Haugaard (Eds.), *The SAGE handbook of power* (pp. 70–88). Thousand Oaks: Sage.

Timokhin, Oleksandr (2009). Intersub'ektivny vymir liberalizmy: do fenomenologii braterstva [An inter-subjective dimension of liberalism: Toward phenomenology of fraternity]. *Filosofs'ka Dumka* [Philosophical Thought], 1, 96–108.

Touraine, Alain (1988). *La parole et le sang: Politique et société en Amérique Latine*, Paris: Odile Jacob.

Touraine, Alain (1992). *Critique de la modernité*. Paris: Fayard.

Touraine, Alain (1994). *Qu'est-ce que la démocratie?* Paris: Fayard.

Touraine, Alain, Dubet, François, Wievorka, Michel, & Strzelecki, Jan (1982). *Solidarité*. Paris: Fayard.

Traugott, Mark (1993). Barricades as Repertoire: Continuities and Discontinuities in the History of French Contention. *Social Science History*, 17(2), 309–323.

Traugott, Mark (1995). Recurrent patterns of collective action. In Mark Traugott (Ed.), *Repertoires and cycles of collective action* (pp. 1–14). Durham: Duke University Press.

Tsentral'noe Statisticheskoe Upravlenie SSSR (1978). *Narodnoe khoziaistvo SSSR v 1977 godu* [Public economy in the Soviet Union in 1977]. Moscow: Statistika.

Tsygankov, Andrei P. (2012). *Russia and the West from Alexander to Putin: Honour in international relations*. Cambridge: Cambridge University Press.

Turley, Jonathan (2010). Uncivil action. *America's Civil War, 23*(5), 44–51.

Tzjaven, Sun, (2015). Taras Shevchenko i Aleksandr Pushkin: Tvorcheskii dialog dvukh geniev [Taras Shevchenko and Aleksandr Pushkin: The art dialog between two geniuses]. *Aktual'ni problemy gumanitarnykh nauk: movoznavstvo, literaturoznavstvo*, 12, 232–236.

Ukraine: An illustrated tour guide (2012), Kyiv: Presa Ukrainy.

Ukrains'ka Pravda (2014, January 22). Klychko: Zavtra—poperedzhuval'nyi straik [Klychko: Tomorrow—a preliminary strike]. *Ukrains'ka Pravda*. Retrieved from http://www.pravda.com.ua/news/2014/01/22/7010816/.

USAID (U.S. Agency for International Development) (2017). U.S. foreign aid by country. Retrieved from https://explorer.usaid.gov/cd/UKR.

Van Aelst, Peter & Walgrave, Stefaan (2001). Who is that (wo)man in the street? From the normalisation of protest to the normalisation of the protester. *European Journal of Political Research, 39*(4), 461–486.

Van Laer, Jeroen & Van Aelst, Peter (2010). Internet and social movement action repertoires. *Information, Communication & Society, 13*(8), 1146–1171.

Veblen, Thorstein (1934 [1899]). *The theory of the leisure class: An economic study of institutions*. New York: The Modern Library.

Veblen, Thorstein (1939 [1915]). *Imperial Germany and industrial revolution*. New York: The Viking Press.

Veblen, Thorstein (1957 [1918]). *The higher learning in America: A memorandum on the conduct of universities by business men*. New York: Sagamore Press.

Virág, Attila (2012). The cultural and geopolitical dimensions of nation-building in the Ukraine. *Society and Economy, 34*(4), 619–641.

Volosovich, Svetlana & Krivosheeva, Victoria (2016). Samoregulyuvannia rynku kredytnykh poslug fizychnym osobam [Self-regulation of the credit services market for individuals]. *Economic Annals-XXI, 158*(3-4(2)), 79–82.

Waardenburg, Jacques (2002). *Religionsgeschichtliche Versuche und Vorarbeiten: Islam: Historical, social, and political perspectives*. Berlin: Walter de Gruyter.

Wada, Takeshi (2012). Modularity and transferability of repertoires of contention. *Social Problems, 59*(4), 544–571.

Walgrave, Stefaan, Bennett, W. L., Van Laer, Jeroen, & Breunig, Christian (2011). Multiple engagements and network bridging in contentious politics: Digital media use of protest participants. *Mobilization: An International Journal, 16*(3), 325–349.

Walgrave, Stefaan & Verhulst, Joris (2011). Selection and response bias in protest surveys. *Mobilization: An International Journal, 16*(2), 203–222.

Walzer, Michael (1983). *Spheres of justice: A defense of pluralism and equality*. New York: Basic Books.

Warner, Rebecca M. (2008). *Applied statistics: From bivariate through multivariate techniques*. Thousand Oaks: Sage.

Warner, Rebecca M. (2013). *Applied statistics: From bivariate through multivariate techniques*. (2nd. ed.). Thousand Oaks: Sage.

Wartenberg, Thomas E. (1990). *The forms of power: From domination to transformation*, Philadelphia, PH: Temple University Press.

Weber, Max (1949 [1904]). 'Objectivity' in social science and social policy. In Max Weber, *The methodology of the social sciences* (Edward A. Shils & Henry A. Finch, Eds. and Trans.) (pp. 49–112). Glencoe, IL: Free Press.

Weber, Max (1968 [1922]). *Economy and society: An outline of interpretative sociology*. (Roth Guenther & Claus Wittich, Eds.). New York: Bedminster Press.

Wieviorka, Michel & Dubet, François (1996). Touraine and the method of sociological intervention. In Jon Clark & Marco Diani (Eds.), *Alain Touraine* (pp. 55–76). London: Falmer.

Williamson, Oliver E. (1991). Comparative economic organization: The analysis of discrete structural alternatives. *Administrative Science Quarterly, 36*(2), 269–296.

Wilson, Andrew (2002). Elements of a theory of Ukrainian ethno-national identities. *Nations and Nationalism, 8*(1), 31–54.

Wilson, Andrew (2005). *Virtual politics: Faking democracy in the post-Soviet world*. New Haven, CT: Yale University Press.

Wilson, Andrew (2014). *Ukraine crisis: What it means for the West*. Hew Haven, CT and London: Yale University Press.

Wilson, John (2003). Volunteerism. In Karen Christensen & David Levinson (Eds.), *Encyclopedia of community: From the village to the virtual world* (pp. 1466–1470). Thousand Oaks: Sage.

Wilson, Richard A. (Ed.) (1997). *Human rights, culture & context: Anthropological perspectives*. London: Pluto.

World Bank (2016). Open data: Ukraine. Retrieved from http://data.worldbank.org/country/ukraine?view=chart.

World Bank (2017). Open Data. Retrieved from http://data.worldbank.org/.

World Values Survey Association (2009). World Values Survey 1981–2008 Official Aggregate v.20090901. Retrieved from www.worldvaluessurvey.org.

World Values Survey Association (2015). World Values Survey 1981–2014 Longitudinal aggregate v.20150418. Retrieved from www.worldvaluessurvey.org.

Wrong, Dennis H. (1980). *Power: Its forms, bases and uses*. New York: Harper Colophon Books.

Yakymenko, Nataliya V. (2015). Mechanism of strategic import substitution in Ukraine's economy. *Actual Problems of Economics, 10*(172), 154–159.

Yavornitsky, Dmitry (1990 [1892]). *Istoriia zaporiz'skykh kozakiv, u 3 tomakh* [History of Zaporozhian Cossacks in 3 volumes]. Volume 1. Lviv: Svit.

Yavornitsky, Dmitry (1991 [1895]). *Istoriia zaporiz'skykh kozakiv, u 3 tomakh* [History of Zaporozhian Cossacks in 3 volumes]. Volume 2. Lviv: Svit.

Yavornitsky, Dmitry (1992 [1897]). *Istoriia zaporiz'skykh kozakiv, u 3 tomakh* [History of Zaporozhian Cossacks in 3 volumes]. Volume 3. Lviv: Svit.

Yurkevych, Oksana (2009). Kredytni kompanii: cutnist', pravovi zasady ta mechanizm funktsionuvannia [Credit companies: The essence, legal basis and mechanism of functioning]. *Actual Problems of Economics,* 12, 175–181.

Zhylyaeva, Nadia M. (2010). Perspektyvy pidvyshchennia konkurentospomozhnosti ekonomiky Ukrainy: galuzevi i regional'ni priorytety [Prospects of competitiveness increase for Ukrainian economy: Sectoral and regional priorities]. *Actual Problems of Economics,* 4(106), 51–59.

Index

E

F

G

M

N

O

P

R

S

T

U

V

W

Y

Z

SOVIET AND POST-SOVIET POLITICS AND SOCIETY

Edited by Dr. Andreas Umland

ISSN 1614-3515

1 *Андреас Умланд (ред.)*
Воплощение Европейской конвенции по правам человека в России
Философские, юридические и эмпирические исследования
ISBN 3-89821-387-0

2 *Christian Wipperfürth*
Russland – ein vertrauenswürdiger Partner?
Grundlagen, Hintergründe und Praxis gegenwärtiger russischer Außenpolitik
Mit einem Vorwort von Heinz Timmermann
ISBN 3-89821-401-X

3 *Manja Hussner*
Die Übernahme internationalen Rechts in die russische und deutsche Rechtsordnung
Eine vergleichende Analyse zur Völkerrechtsfreundlichkeit der Verfassungen der Russländischen Föderation und der Bundesrepublik Deutschland
Mit einem Vorwort von Rainer Arnold
ISBN 3-89821-438-9

4 *Matthew Tejada*
Bulgaria's Democratic Consolidation and the Kozloduy Nuclear Power Plant (KNPP)
The Unattainability of Closure
With a foreword by Richard J. Crampton
ISBN 3-89821-439-7

5 *Марк Григорьевич Меерович*
Квадратные метры, определяющие сознание
Государственная жилищная политика в СССР. 1921 – 1941 гг
ISBN 3-89821-474-5

6 *Andrei P. Tsygankov, Pavel A.Tsygankov (Eds.)*
New Directions in Russian International Studies
ISBN 3-89821-422-2

7 *Марк Григорьевич Меерович*
Как власть народ к труду приучала
Жилище в СССР – средство управления людьми. 1917 – 1941 гг.
С предисловием Елены Осокиной
ISBN 3-89821-495-8

8 *David J. Galbreath*
Nation-Building and Minority Politics in Post-Socialist States
Interests, Influence and Identities in Estonia and Latvia
With a foreword by David J. Smith
ISBN 3-89821-467-2

9 *Алексей Юрьевич Безугольный*
Народы Кавказа в Вооруженных силах СССР в годы Великой Отечественной войны 1941-1945 гг.
С предисловием Николая Бугая
ISBN 3-89821-475-3

10 *Вячеслав Лихачев и Владимир Прибыловский (ред.)*
Русское Национальное Единство, 1990-2000. В 2-х томах
ISBN 3-89821-523-7

11 *Николай Бугай (ред.)*
Народы стран Балтии в условиях сталинизма (1940-е – 1950-е годы)
Документированная история
ISBN 3-89821-525-3

12 *Ingmar Bredies (Hrsg.)*
Zur Anatomie der Orange Revolution in der Ukraine
Wechsel des Elitenregimes oder Triumph des Parlamentarismus?
ISBN 3-89821-524-5

13 *Anastasia V. Mitrofanova*
The Politicization of Russian Orthodoxy
Actors and Ideas
With a foreword by William C. Gay
ISBN 3-89821-481-8

14 *Nathan D. Larson*
Alexander Solzhenitsyn and the Russo-Jewish Question
ISBN 3-89821-483-4

15 *Guido Houben*
Kulturpolitik und Ethnizität
Staatliche Kunstförderung im Russland der neunziger Jahre
Mit einem Vorwort von Gert Weisskirchen
ISBN 3-89821-542-3

16 *Leonid Luks*
Der russische „Sonderweg"?
Aufsätze zur neuesten Geschichte Russlands im europäischen Kontext
ISBN 3-89821-496-6

17 *Евгений Мороз*
История «Мёртвой воды» – от страшной сказки к большой политике
Политическое неоязычество в постсоветской России
ISBN 3-89821-551-2

18 *Александр Верховский и Галина Кожевникова (ред.)*
Этническая и религиозная интолерантность в российских СМИ
Результаты мониторинга 2001-2004 гг.
ISBN 3-89821-569-5

19 *Christian Ganzer*
Sowjetisches Erbe und ukrainische Nation
Das Museum der Geschichte des Zaporoger Kosakentums auf der Insel Chortycja
Mit einem Vorwort von Frank Golczewski
ISBN 3-89821-504-0

20 *Эльза-Баир Гучинова*
Помнить нельзя забыть
Антропология депортационной травмы калмыков
С предисловием Кэролайн Хамфри
ISBN 3-89821-506-7

21 *Юлия Лидерман*
Мотивы «проверки» и «испытания» в постсоветской культуре
Советское прошлое в российском кинематографе 1990-х годов
С предисловием Евгения Марголита
ISBN 3-89821-511-3

22 *Tanya Lokshina, Ray Thomas, Mary Mayer (Eds.)*
The Imposition of a Fake Political Settlement in the Northern Caucasus
The 2003 Chechen Presidential Election
ISBN 3-89821-436-2

23 *Timothy McCajor Hall, Rosie Read (Eds.)*
Changes in the Heart of Europe
Recent Ethnographies of Czechs, Slovaks, Roma, and Sorbs
With an afterword by Zdeněk Salzmann
ISBN 3-89821-606-3

24 *Christian Autengruber*
Die politischen Parteien in Bulgarien und Rumänien
Eine vergleichende Analyse seit Beginn der 90er Jahre
Mit einem Vorwort von Dorothée de Nève
ISBN 3-89821-476-1

25 *Annette Freyberg-Inan with Radu Cristescu*
The Ghosts in Our Classrooms, or: John Dewey Meets Ceauşescu
The Promise and the Failures of Civic Education in Romania
ISBN 3-89821-416-8

26 *John B. Dunlop*
The 2002 Dubrovka and 2004 Beslan Hostage Crises
A Critique of Russian Counter-Terrorism
With a foreword by Donald N. Jensen
ISBN 3-89821-608-X

27 *Peter Koller*
Das touristische Potenzial von Kam''janec'–Podil's'kyj
Eine fremdenverkehrsgeographische Untersuchung der Zukunftsperspektiven und Maßnahmenplanung zur Destinationsentwicklung des „ukrainischen Rothenburg"
Mit einem Vorwort von Kristiane Klemm
ISBN 3-89821-640-3

28 *Françoise Daucé, Elisabeth Sieca-Kozlowski (Eds.)*
Dedovshchina in the Post-Soviet Military
Hazing of Russian Army Conscripts in a Comparative Perspective
With a foreword by Dale Herspring
ISBN 3-89821-616-0

29 *Florian Strasser*
Zivilgesellschaftliche Einflüsse auf die Orange Revolution
Die gewaltlose Massenbewegung und die ukrainische Wahlkrise 2004
Mit einem Vorwort von Egbert Jahn
ISBN 3-89821-648-9

30 *Rebecca S. Katz*
The Georgian Regime Crisis of 2003-2004
A Case Study in Post-Soviet Media Representation of Politics, Crime and Corruption
ISBN 3-89821-413-3

31 *Vladimir Kantor*
Willkür oder Freiheit
Beiträge zur russischen Geschichtsphilosophie
Ediert von Dagmar Herrmann sowie mit einem Vorwort versehen von Leonid Luks
ISBN 3-89821-589-X

32 *Laura A. Victoir*
The Russian Land Estate Today
A Case Study of Cultural Politics in Post-Soviet Russia
With a foreword by Priscilla Roosevelt
ISBN 3-89821-426-5

33 *Ivan Katchanovski*
Cleft Countries
Regional Political Divisions and Cultures in Post-Soviet Ukraine and Moldova
With a foreword by Francis Fukuyama
ISBN 3-89821-558-X

34 *Florian Mühlfried*
Postsowjetische Feiern
Das Georgische Bankett im Wandel
Mit einem Vorwort von Kevin Tuite
ISBN 3-89821-601-2

35 *Roger Griffin, Werner Loh, Andreas Umland (Eds.)*
Fascism Past and Present, West and East
An International Debate on Concepts and Cases in the Comparative Study of the Extreme Right
With an afterword by Walter Laqueur
ISBN 3-89821-674-8

36 *Sebastian Schlegel*
Der „Weiße Archipel"
Sowjetische Atomstädte 1945-1991
Mit einem Geleitwort von Thomas Bohn
ISBN 3-89821-679-9

37 *Vyacheslav Likhachev*
Political Anti-Semitism in Post-Soviet Russia
Actors and Ideas in 1991-2003
Edited and translated from Russian by Eugene Veklerov
ISBN 3-89821-529-6

38 *Josette Baer (Ed.)*
Preparing Liberty in Central Europe
Political Texts from the Spring of Nations 1848 to the Spring of Prague 1968
With a foreword by Zdeněk V. David
ISBN 3-89821-546-6

39 *Михаил Лукьянов*
Российский консерватизм и реформа, 1907-1914
С предисловием Марка Д. Стейнберга
ISBN 3-89821-503-2

40 *Nicola Melloni*
Market Without Economy
The 1998 Russian Financial Crisis
With a foreword by Eiji Furukawa
ISBN 3-89821-407-9

41 *Dmitrij Chmelnizki*
Die Architektur Stalins
Bd. 1: Studien zu Ideologie und Stil
Bd. 2: Bilddokumentation
Mit einem Vorwort von Bruno Flierl
ISBN 3-89821-515-6

42 *Katja Yafimava*
Post-Soviet Russian-Belarussian Relationships
The Role of Gas Transit Pipelines
With a foreword by Jonathan P. Stern
ISBN 3-89821-655-1

43 *Boris Chavkin*
Verflechtungen der deutschen und russischen Zeitgeschichte
Aufsätze und Archivfunde zu den Beziehungen Deutschlands und der Sowjetunion von 1917 bis 1991
Ediert von Markus Edlinger sowie mit einem Vorwort versehen von Leonid Luks
ISBN 3-89821-756-6

44 *Anastasija Grynenko in Zusammenarbeit mit Claudia Dathe*
Die Terminologie des Gerichtswesens der Ukraine und Deutschlands im Vergleich
Eine übersetzungswissenschaftliche Analyse juristischer Fachbegriffe im Deutschen, Ukrainischen und Russischen
Mit einem Vorwort von Ulrich Hartmann
ISBN 3-89821-691-8

45 *Anton Burkov*
The Impact of the European Convention on Human Rights on Russian Law
Legislation and Application in 1996-2006
With a foreword by Françoise Hampson
ISBN 978-3-89821-639-5

46 *Stina Torjesen, Indra Overland (Eds.)*
International Election Observers in Post-Soviet Azerbaijan
Geopolitical Pawns or Agents of Change?
ISBN 978-3-89821-743-9

47 *Taras Kuzio*
Ukraine – Crimea – Russia
Triangle of Conflict
ISBN 978-3-89821-761-3

48 *Claudia Šabić*
"Ich erinnere mich nicht, aber L'viv!"
Zur Funktion kultureller Faktoren für die Institutionalisierung und Entwicklung einer ukrainischen Region
Mit einem Vorwort von Melanie Tatur
ISBN 978-3-89821-752-1

49 *Marlies Bilz*
Tatarstan in der Transformation
Nationaler Diskurs und Politische Praxis 1988-1994
Mit einem Vorwort von Frank Golczewski
ISBN 978-3-89821-722-4

50 *Марлен Ларюэль (ред.)*
Современные интерпретации русского национализма
ISBN 978-3-89821-795-8

51 *Sonja Schüler*
Die ethnische Dimension der Armut
Roma im postsozialistischen Rumänien
Mit einem Vorwort von Anton Sterbling
ISBN 978-3-89821-776-7

52 *Галина Кожевникова*
Радикальный национализм в России и противодействие ему
Сборник докладов Центра «Сова» за 2004-2007 гг.
С предисловием Александра Верховского
ISBN 978-3-89821-721-7

53 *Галина Кожевникова и Владимир Прибыловский*
Российская власть в биографиях I
Высшие должностные лица РФ в 2004 г.
ISBN 978-3-89821-796-5

54 *Галина Кожевникова и Владимир Прибыловский*
Российская власть в биографиях II
Члены Правительства РФ в 2004 г.
ISBN 978-3-89821-797-2

55 *Галина Кожевникова и Владимир Прибыловский*
Российская власть в биографиях III
Руководители федеральных служб и агентств РФ в 2004 г.
ISBN 978-3-89821-798-9

56 *Ileana Petroniu*
Privatisierung in Transformationsökonomien
Determinanten der Restrukturierungs-Bereitschaft am Beispiel Polens, Rumäniens und der Ukraine
Mit einem Vorwort von Rainer W. Schäfer
ISBN 978-3-89821-790-3

57 *Christian Wipperfürth*
Russland und seine GUS-Nachbarn
Hintergründe, aktuelle Entwicklungen und Konflikte in einer ressourcenreichen Region
ISBN 978-3-89821-801-6

58 *Togzhan Kassenova*
From Antagonism to Partnership
The Uneasy Path of the U.S.-Russian Cooperative Threat Reduction
With a foreword by Christoph Bluth
ISBN 978-3-89821-707-1

59 *Alexander Höllwerth*
Das sakrale eurasische Imperium des Aleksandr Dugin
Eine Diskursanalyse zum postsowjetischen russischen Rechtsextremismus
Mit einem Vorwort von Dirk Uffelmann
ISBN 978-3-89821-813-9

60 *Олег Рябов*
«Россия-Матушка»
Национализм, гендер и война в России XX века
С предисловием Елены Гощило
ISBN 978-3-89821-487-2

61 *Ivan Maistrenko*
Borot'bism
A Chapter in the History of the Ukrainian Revolution
With a new introduction by Chris Ford
Translated by George S. N. Luckyj with the assistance of Ivan L. Rudnytsky
ISBN 978-3-89821-697-5

62 *Maryna Romanets*
Anamorphosic Texts and Reconfigured Visions
Improvised Traditions in Contemporary Ukrainian and Irish Literature
ISBN 978-3-89821-576-3

63 *Paul D'Anieri and Taras Kuzio (Eds.)*
Aspects of the Orange Revolution I
Democratization and Elections in Post-Communist Ukraine
ISBN 978-3-89821-698-2

64 *Bohdan Harasymiw in collaboration with Oleh S. Ilnytzkyj (Eds.)*
Aspects of the Orange Revolution II
Information and Manipulation Strategies in the 2004 Ukrainian Presidential Elections
ISBN 978-3-89821-699-9

65 *Ingmar Bredies, Andreas Umland and Valentin Yakushik (Eds.)*
Aspects of the Orange Revolution III
The Context and Dynamics of the 2004 Ukrainian Presidential Elections
ISBN 978-3-89821-803-0

66 *Ingmar Bredies, Andreas Umland and Valentin Yakushik (Eds.)*
Aspects of the Orange Revolution IV
Foreign Assistance and Civic Action in the 2004 Ukrainian Presidential Elections
ISBN 978-3-89821-808-5

67 *Ingmar Bredies, Andreas Umland and Valentin Yakushik (Eds.)*
Aspects of the Orange Revolution V
Institutional Observation Reports on the 2004 Ukrainian Presidential Elections
ISBN 978-3-89821-809-2

68 *Taras Kuzio (Ed.)*
Aspects of the Orange Revolution VI
Post-Communist Democratic Revolutions in Comparative Perspective
ISBN 978-3-89821-820-7

69 *Tim Bohse*
Autoritarismus statt Selbstverwaltung
Die Transformation der kommunalen Politik in der Stadt Kaliningrad 1990-2005
Mit einem Geleitwort von Stefan Troebst
ISBN 978-3-89821-782-8

70 *David Rupp*
Die Rußländische Föderation und die russischsprachige Minderheit in Lettland
Eine Fallstudie zur Anwaltspolitik Moskaus gegenüber den russophonen Minderheiten im „Nahen Ausland“ von 1991 bis 2002
Mit einem Vorwort von Helmut Wagner
ISBN 978-3-89821-778-1

71 *Taras Kuzio*
Theoretical and Comparative Perspectives on Nationalism
New Directions in Cross-Cultural and Post-Communist Studies
With a foreword by Paul Robert Magocsi
ISBN 978-3-89821-815-3

72 *Christine Teichmann*
Die Hochschultransformation im heutigen Osteuropa
Kontinuität und Wandel bei der Entwicklung des postkommunistischen Universitätswesens
Mit einem Vorwort von Oskar Anweiler
ISBN 978-3-89821-842-9

73 *Julia Kusznir*
Der politische Einfluss von Wirtschaftseliten in russischen Regionen
Eine Analyse am Beispiel der Erdöl- und Erdgasindustrie, 1992-2005
Mit einem Vorwort von Wolfgang Eichwede
ISBN 978-3-89821-821-4

74 *Alena Vysotskaya*
Russland, Belarus und die EU-Osterweiterung
Zur Minderheitenfrage und zum Problem der Freizügigkeit des Personenverkehrs
Mit einem Vorwort von Katlijn Malfliet
ISBN 978-3-89821-822-1

75 *Heiko Pleines (Hrsg.)*
Corporate Governance in post-sozialistischen Volkswirtschaften
ISBN 978-3-89821-766-8

76 *Stefan Ihrig*
Wer sind die Moldawier?
Rumänismus versus Moldowanismus in Historiographie und Schulbüchern der Republik Moldova, 1991-2006
Mit einem Vorwort von Holm Sundhaussen
ISBN 978-3-89821-466-7

77 *Galina Kozhevnikova in collaboration with Alexander Verkhovsky and Eugene Veklerov*
Ultra-Nationalism and Hate Crimes in Contemporary Russia
The 2004-2006 Annual Reports of Moscow's SOVA Center
With a foreword by Stephen D. Shenfield
ISBN 978-3-89821-868-9

78 *Florian Küchler*
The Role of the European Union in Moldova's Transnistria Conflict
With a foreword by Christopher Hill
ISBN 978-3-89821-850-4

79 *Bernd Rechel*
The Long Way Back to Europe
Minority Protection in Bulgaria
With a foreword by Richard Crampton
ISBN 978-3-89821-863-4

80 *Peter W. Rodgers*
Nation, Region and History in Post-Communist Transitions
Identity Politics in Ukraine, 1991-2006
With a foreword by Vera Tolz
ISBN 978-3-89821-903-7

81 *Stephanie Solywoda*
The Life and Work of Semen L. Frank
A Study of Russian Religious Philosophy
With a foreword by Philip Walters
ISBN 978-3-89821-457-5

82 *Vera Sokolova*
Cultural Politics of Ethnicity
Discourses on Roma in Communist Czechoslovakia
ISBN 978-3-89821-864-1

83 *Natalya Shevchik Ketenci*
Kazakhstani Enterprises in Transition
The Role of Historical Regional Development in Kazakhstan's Post-Soviet Economic Transformation
ISBN 978-3-89821-831-3

84 *Martin Malek, Anna Schor-Tschudnowskaja (Hrsg.)*
Europa im Tschetschenienkrieg
Zwischen politischer Ohnmacht und Gleichgültigkeit
Mit einem Vorwort von Lipchan Basajewa
ISBN 978-3-89821-676-0

85 *Stefan Meister*
Das postsowjetische Universitätswesen zwischen nationalem und internationalem Wandel
Die Entwicklung der regionalen Hochschule in Russland als Gradmesser der Systemtransformation
Mit einem Vorwort von Joan DeBardeleben
ISBN 978-3-89821-891-7

86 *Konstantin Sheiko in collaboration with Stephen Brown*
Nationalist Imaginings of the Russian Past
Anatolii Fomenko and the Rise of Alternative History in Post-Communist Russia
With a foreword by Donald Ostrowski
ISBN 978-3-89821-915-0

87 *Sabine Jenni*
Wie stark ist das „Einige Russland"?
Zur Parteibindung der Eliten und zum Wahlerfolg der Machtpartei im Dezember 2007
Mit einem Vorwort von Klaus Armingeon
ISBN 978-3-89821-961-7

88 *Thomas Borén*
Meeting-Places of Transformation
Urban Identity, Spatial Representations and Local Politics in Post-Soviet St Petersburg
ISBN 978-3-89821-739-2

89 *Aygul Ashirova*
Stalinismus und Stalin-Kult in Zentralasien
Turkmenistan 1924-1953
Mit einem Vorwort von Leonid Luks
ISBN 978-3-89821-987-7

90 *Leonid Luks*
Freiheit oder imperiale Größe?
Essays zu einem russischen Dilemma
ISBN 978-3-8382-0011-8

91 *Christopher Gilley*
The 'Change of Signposts' in the Ukrainian Emigration
A Contribution to the History of Sovietophilism in the 1920s
With a foreword by Frank Golczewski
ISBN 978-3-89821-965-5

92 *Philipp Casula, Jeronim Perovic (Eds.)*
Identities and Politics During the Putin Presidency
The Discursive Foundations of Russia's Stability
With a foreword by Heiko Haumann
ISBN 978-3-8382-0015-6

93 *Marcel Viëtor*
Europa und die Frage nach seinen Grenzen im Osten
Zur Konstruktion ‚europäischer Identität' in Geschichte und Gegenwart
Mit einem Vorwort von Albrecht Lehmann
ISBN 978-3-8382-0045-3

94 *Ben Hellman, Andrei Rogachevskii*
Filming the Unfilmable
Casper Wrede's 'One Day in the Life of Ivan Denisovich'
Second, Revised and Expanded Edition
ISBN 978-3-8382-0044-6

95 *Eva Fuchslocher*
Vaterland, Sprache, Glaube
Orthodoxie und Nationenbildung am Beispiel Georgiens
Mit einem Vorwort von Christina von Braun
ISBN 978-3-89821-884-9

96 *Vladimir Kantor*
Das Westlertum und der Weg Russlands
Zur Entwicklung der russischen Literatur und Philosophie
Ediert von Dagmar Herrmann
Mit einem Beitrag von Nikolaus Lobkowicz
ISBN 978-3-8382-0102-3

97 *Kamran Musayev*
Die postsowjetische Transformation im Baltikum und Südkaukasus
Eine vergleichende Untersuchung der politischen Entwicklung Lettlands und Aserbaidschans 1985-2009
Mit einem Vorwort von Leonid Luks
Ediert von Sandro Henschel
ISBN 978-3-8382-0103-0

98 *Tatiana Zhurzhenko*
Borderlands into Bordered Lands
Geopolitics of Identity in Post-Soviet Ukraine
With a foreword by Dieter Segert
ISBN 978-3-8382-0042-2

99 *Кирилл Галушко, Лидия Смола (ред.)*
Пределы падения – варианты украинского будущего
Аналитико-прогностические исследования
ISBN 978-3-8382-0148-1

100 *Michael Minkenberg (ed.)*
Historical Legacies and the Radical Right in Post-Cold War Central and Eastern Europe
With an afterword by Sabrina P. Ramet
ISBN 978-3-8382-0124-5

101 *David-Emil Wickström*
Rocking St. Petersburg
Transcultural Flows and Identity Politics in the St. Petersburg Popular Music Scene
With a foreword by Yngvar B. Steinholt
Second, Revised and Expanded Edition
ISBN 978-3-8382-0100-9

102 *Eva Zabka*
Eine neue „Zeit der Wirren"?
Der spät- und postsowjetische Systemwandel 1985-2000 im Spiegel russischer gesellschaftspolitischer Diskurse
Mit einem Vorwort von Margareta Mommsen
ISBN 978-3-8382-0161-0

103 *Ulrike Ziemer*
Ethnic Belonging, Gender and Cultural Practices
Youth Identitites in Contemporary Russia
With a foreword by Anoop Nayak
ISBN 978-3-8382-0152-8

104 *Ksenia Chepikova*
'Einiges Russland' - eine zweite KPdSU?
Aspekte der Identitätskonstruktion einer postsowjetischen „Partei der Macht"
Mit einem Vorwort von Torsten Oppelland
ISBN 978-3-8382-0311-9

105 *Леонид Люкс*
Западничество или евразийство? Демократия или идеократия?
Сборник статей об исторических дилеммах России
С предисловием Владимира Кантора
ISBN 978-3-8382-0211-2

106 *Anna Dost*
Das russische Verfassungsrecht auf dem Weg zum Föderalismus und zurück
Zum Konflikt von Rechtsnormen und -wirklichkeit in der Russländischen Föderation von 1991 bis 2009
Mit einem Vorwort von Alexander Blankenagel
ISBN 978-3-8382-0292-1

107 *Philipp Herzog*
Sozialistische Völkerfreundschaft, nationaler Widerstand oder harmloser Zeitvertreib?
Zur politischen Funktion der Volkskunst im sowjetischen Estland
Mit einem Vorwort von Andreas Kappeler
ISBN 978-3-8382-0216-7

108 *Marlène Laruelle (ed.)*
Russian Nationalism, Foreign Policy, and Identity Debates in Putin's Russia
New Ideological Patterns after the Orange Revolution
ISBN 978-3-8382-0325-6

109 *Michail Logvinov*
Russlands Kampf gegen den internationalen Terrorismus
Eine kritische Bestandsaufnahme des Bekämpfungsansatzes
Mit einem Geleitwort von Hans-Henning Schröder und einem Vorwort von Eckhard Jesse
ISBN 978-3-8382-0329-4

110 *John B. Dunlop*
The Moscow Bombings of September 1999
Examinations of Russian Terrorist Attacks at the Onset of Vladimir Putin's Rule
Second, Revised and Expanded Edition
ISBN 978-3-8382-0388-1

111 *Андрей А. Ковалёв*
Свидетельство из-за кулис российской политики I
Можно ли делать добро из зла? (Воспоминания и размышления о последних советских и первых послесоветских годах)
With a foreword by Peter Reddaway
ISBN 978-3-8382-0302-7

112 *Андрей А. Ковалёв*
Свидетельство из-за кулис российской политики II
Угроза для себя и окружающих (Наблюдения и предостережения относительно происходящего после 2000 г.)
ISBN 978-3-8382-0303-4

113 *Bernd Kappenberg*
Zeichen setzen für Europa
Der Gebrauch europäischer lateinischer Sonderzeichen in der deutschen Öffentlichkeit
Mit einem Vorwort von Peter Schlobinski
ISBN 978-3-89821-749-1

114 *Ivo Mijnssen*
The Quest for an Ideal Youth in Putin's Russia I
Back to Our Future! History, Modernity, and Patriotism according to *Nashi,* 2005-2013
With a foreword by Jeronim Perović
Second, Revised and Expanded Edition
ISBN 978-3-8382-0368-3

115 *Jussi Lassila*
The Quest for an Ideal Youth in Putin's Russia II
The Search for Distinctive Conformism in the Political Communication of *Nashi,* 2005-2009
With a foreword by Kirill Postoutenko
Second, Revised and Expanded Edition
ISBN 978-3-8382-0415-4

116 *Valerio Trabandt*
Neue Nachbarn, gute Nachbarschaft?
Die EU als internationaler Akteur am Beispiel ihrer Demokratieförderung in Belarus und der Ukraine 2004-2009
Mit einem Vorwort von Jutta Joachim
ISBN 978-3-8382-0437-6

117 *Fabian Pfeiffer*
Estlands Außen- und Sicherheitspolitik I
Der estnische Atlantizismus nach der wiedererlangten Unabhängigkeit 1991-2004
Mit einem Vorwort von Helmut Hubel
ISBN 978-3-8382-0127-6

118 *Jana Podßuweit*
Estlands Außen- und Sicherheitspolitik II
Handlungsoptionen eines Kleinstaates im Rahmen seiner EU-Mitgliedschaft (2004-2008)
Mit einem Vorwort von Helmut Hubel
ISBN 978-3-8382-0440-6

119 *Karin Pointner*
Estlands Außen- und Sicherheitspolitik III
Eine gedächtnispolitische Analyse estnischer Entwicklungskooperation 2006-2010
Mit einem Vorwort von Karin Liebhart
ISBN 978-3-8382-0435-2

120 *Ruslana Vovk*
Die Offenheit der ukrainischen Verfassung für das Völkerrecht und die europäische Integration
Mit einem Vorwort von Alexander Blankenagel
ISBN 978-3-8382-0481-9

121 *Mykhaylo Banakh*
Die Relevanz der Zivilgesellschaft bei den postkommunistischen Transformationsprozessen in mittel- und osteuropäischen Ländern
Das Beispiel der spät- und postsowjetischen Ukraine 1986-2009
Mit einem Vorwort von Gerhard Simon
ISBN 978-3-8382-0499-4

122 *Michael Moser*
Language Policy and the Discourse on Languages in Ukraine under President Viktor Yanukovych (25 February 2010–28 October 2012)
ISBN 978-3-8382-0497-0 (Paperback edition)
ISBN 978-3-8382-0507-6 (Hardcover edition)

123 *Nicole Krome*
Russischer Netzwerkkapitalismus
Restrukturierungsprozesse in der Russischen Föderation am Beispiel des Luftfahrtunternehmens "Aviastar"
Mit einem Vorwort von Petra Stykow
ISBN 978-3-8382-0534-2

124 *David R. Marples*
'Our Glorious Past'
Lukashenka's Belarus and the Great Patriotic War
ISBN 978-3-8382-0574-8 (Paperback edition)
ISBN 978-3-8382-0675-2 (Hardcover edition)

125 *Ulf Walther*
Russlands "neuer Adel"
Die Macht des Geheimdienstes von Gorbatschow bis Putin
Mit einem Vorwort von Hans-Georg Wieck
ISBN 978-3-8382-0584-7

126 *Simon Geissbühler (Hrsg.)*
Kiew – Revolution 3.0
Der Euromaidan 2013/14 und die Zukunftsperspektiven der Ukraine
ISBN 978-3-8382-0581-6 (Paperback edition)
ISBN 978-3-8382-0681-3 (Hardcover edition)

127 *Andrey Makarychev*
Russia and the EU in a Multipolar World
Discourses, Identities, Norms
With a foreword by Klaus Segbers
ISBN 978-3-8382-0629-5

128 *Roland Scharff*
Kasachstan als postsowjetischer Wohlfahrtsstaat
Die Transformation des sozialen Schutzsystems
Mit einem Vorwort von Joachim Ahrens
ISBN 978-3-8382-0622-6

129 *Katja Grupp*
Bild Lücke Deutschland
Kaliningrader Studierende sprechen über Deutschland
Mit einem Vorwort von Martin Schulz
ISBN 978-3-8382-0552-6

130 *Konstantin Sheiko, Stephen Brown*
History as Therapy
Alternative History and Nationalist Imaginings in Russia, 1991-2014
ISBN 978-3-8382-0665-3

131 *Elisa Kriza*
Alexander Solzhenitsyn: Cold War Icon, Gulag Author, Russian Nationalist?
A Study of the Western Reception of his Literary Writings, Historical Interpretations, and Political Ideas
With a foreword by Andrei Rogatchevski
ISBN 978-3-8382-0589-2 (Paperback edition)
ISBN 978-3-8382-0690-5 (Hardcover edition)

132 *Serghei Golunov*
The Elephant in the Room
Corruption and Cheating in Russian Universities
ISBN 978-3-8382-0570-0

133 *Manja Hussner, Rainer Arnold (Hgg.)*
Verfassungsgerichtsbarkeit in Zentralasien I
Sammlung von Verfassungstexten
ISBN 978-3-8382-0595-3

134 *Nikolay Mitrokhin*
Die "Russische Partei"
Die Bewegung der russischen Nationalisten in der UdSSR 1953-1985
Aus dem Russischen übertragen von einem Übersetzerteam unter der Leitung von Larisa Schippel
ISBN 978-3-8382-0024-8

135 *Manja Hussner, Rainer Arnold (Hgg.)*
Verfassungsgerichtsbarkeit in Zentralasien II
Sammlung von Verfassungstexten
ISBN 978-3-8382-0597-7

136 *Manfred Zeller*
Das sowjetische Fieber
Fußballfans im poststalinistischen Vielvölkerreich
Mit einem Vorwort von Nikolaus Katzer
ISBN 978-3-8382-0757-5

137 *Kristin Schreiter*
Stellung und Entwicklungspotential zivilgesellschaftlicher Gruppen in Russland
Menschenrechtsorganisationen im Vergleich
ISBN 978-3-8382-0673-8

138 *David R. Marples, Frederick V. Mills (eds.)*
Ukraine's Euromaidan
Analyses of a Civil Revolution
ISBN 978-3-8382-0660-8

139 *Bernd Kappenberg*
Setting Signs for Europe
Why Diacritics Matter for European Integration
With a foreword by Peter Schlobinski
ISBN 978-3-8382-0663-9

140 *René Lenz*
Internationalisierung, Kooperation und Transfer
Externe bildungspolitische Akteure in der Russischen Föderation
Mit einem Vorwort von Frank Ettrich
ISBN 978-3-8382-0751-3

141 *Juri Plusnin, Yana Zausaeva, Natalia Zhidkevich, Artemy Pozanenko*
Wandering Workers
Mores, Behavior, Way of Life, and Political Status of Domestic Russian Labor Migrants
Translated by Julia Kazantseva
ISBN 978-3-8382-0653-0

142 *David J. Smith (eds.)*
Latvia – A Work in Progress?
100 Years of State- and Nation-Building
ISBN 978-3-8382-0648-6

143 Инна Чувычкина (ред.)
Экспортные нефте- и газопроводы на постсоветском пространстве
Анализ трубопроводной политики в свете теории международных отношений
ISBN 978-3-8382-0822-0

144 *Johann Zajaczkowski*
Russland – eine pragmatische Großmacht?
Eine rollentheoretische Untersuchung russischer Außenpolitik am Beispiel der Zusammenarbeit mit den USA nach 9/11 und des Georgienkrieges von 2008
Mit einem Vorwort von Siegfried Schieder
ISBN 978-3-8382-0837-4

145 *Boris Popivanov*
Changing Images of the Left in Bulgaria
The Challenge of Post-Communism in the Early 21st Century
ISBN 978-3-8382-0667-7

146 *Lenka Krátká*
A History of the Czechoslovak Ocean Shipping Company 1948-1989
How a Small, Landlocked Country Ran Maritime Business During the Cold War
ISBN 978-3-8382-0666-0

147 *Alexander Sergunin*
Explaining Russian Foreign Policy Behavior
Theory and Practice
ISBN 978-3-8382-0752-0

148 *Darya Malyutina*
Migrant Friendships in a Super-Diverse City
Russian-Speakers and their Social Relationships in London in the 21st Century
With a foreword by Claire Dwyer
ISBN 978-3-8382-0652-3

149 *Alexander Sergunin, Valery Konyshev*
Russia in the Arctic
Hard or Soft Power?
ISBN 978-3-8382-0753-7

150 *John J. Maresca*
Helsinki Revisited
A Key U.S. Negotiator's Memoirs on the Development of the CSCE into the OSCE
With a foreword by Hafiz Pashayev
ISBN 978-3-8382-0852-7

151 *Jardar Østbø*
The New Third Rome
Readings of a Russian Nationalist Myth
With a foreword by Pål Kolstø
ISBN 978-3-8382-0870-1

152 *Simon Kordonsky*
Socio-Economic Foundations of the Russian Post-Soviet Regime
The Resource-Based Economy and Estate-Based Social Structure of Contemporary Russia
With a foreword by Svetlana Barsukova
ISBN 978-3-8382-0775-9

153 *Duncan Leitch*
Assisting Reform in Post-Communist Ukraine 2000–2012
The Illusions of Donors and the Disillusion of Beneficiaries
With a foreword by Kataryna Wolczuk
ISBN 978-3-8382-0844-2

154 *Abel Polese*
Limits of a Post-Soviet State
How Informality Replaces, Renegotiates, and Reshapes Governance in Contemporary Ukraine
With a foreword by Colin Williams
ISBN 978-3-8382-0845-9

155 *Mikhail Suslov (ed.)*
Digital Orthodoxy in the Post-Soviet World
The Russian Orthodox Church and Web 2.0
With a foreword by Father Cyril Hovorun
ISBN 978-3-8382-0871-8

156 *Leonid Luks*
Zwei „Sonderwege“? Russisch-deutsche Parallelen und Kontraste (1917-2014)
Vergleichende Essays
ISBN 978-3-8382-0823-7

157 *Vladimir V. Karacharovskiy, Ovsey I. Shkaratan, Gordey A. Yastrebov*
Towards a New Russian Work Culture
Can Western Companies and Expatriates Change Russian Society?
With a foreword by Elena N. Danilova
Translated by Julia Kazantseva
ISBN 978-3-8382-0902-9

158 *Edmund Griffiths*
Aleksandr Prokhanov and Post-Soviet Esotericism
ISBN 978-3-8382-0903-6

159 *Timm Beichelt, Susann Worschech (eds.)*
Transnational Ukraine?
Networks and Ties that Influence(d) Contemporary Ukraine
ISBN 978-3-8382-0944-9

160 *Mieste Hotopp-Riecke*
Die Tataren der Krim zwischen Assimilation und Selbstbehauptung
Der Aufbau des krimtatarischen Bildungswesens nach Deportation und Heimkehr (1990-2005)
Mit einem Vorwort von Swetlana Czerwonnaja
ISBN 978-3-89821-940-2

161 *Olga Bertelsen (ed.)*
Revolution and War in Contemporary Ukraine
The Challenge of Change
ISBN 978-3-8382-1016-2

162 *Natalya Ryabinska*
Ukraine's Post-Communist Mass Media
Between Capture and Commercialization
With a foreword by Marta Dyczok
ISBN 978-3-8382-1011-7

163 *Alexandra Cotofana, James M. Nyce (eds.)*
Religion and Magic in Socialist and Post-Socialist Contexts I
Historic and Ethnographic Case Studies of Orthodoxy, Heterodoxy, and Alternative Spirituality
With a foreword by Patrick L. Michelson
ISBN 978-3-8382-0989-0

164 *Nozima Akhrarkhodjaeva*
The Instrumentalisation of Mass Media in Electoral Authoritarian Regimes
Evidence from Russia's Presidential Election Campaigns of 2000 and 2008
ISBN 978-3-8382-1013-1

165 *Yulia Krasheninnikova*
Informal Healthcare in Contemporary Russia
Sociographic Essays on the Post-Soviet Infrastructure for Alternative Healing Practices
ISBN 978-3-8382-0970-8

166 *Peter Kaiser*
Das Schachbrett der Macht
Die Handlungsspielräume eines sowjetischen Funktionärs unter Stalin am Beispiel des Generalsekretärs des Komsomol Aleksandr Kosarev (1929-1938)
Mit einem Vorwort von Dietmar Neutatz
ISBN 978-3-8382-1052-0

167 *Oksana Kim*
The Effects and Implications of Kazakhstan's Adoption of International Financial Reporting Standards
A Resource Dependence Perspective
With a foreword by Svetlana Vlady
ISBN 978-3-8382-0987-6

168 *Anna Sanina*
Patriotic Education in Contemporary Russia
Sociological Studies in the Making of the Post-Soviet Citizen
With a foreword by Anna Oldfield
ISBN 978-3-8382-0993-7

169 *Rudolf Wolters*
Spezialist in Sibirien
Faksimile der 1933 erschienenen ersten Ausgabe
Mit einem Vorwort von Dmitrij Chmelnizki
ISBN 978-3-8382-0515-1

170 *Michal Vít, Magdalena M. Baran (eds.)*
Transregional versus National Perspectives on Contemporary Central European History
Studies on the Building of Nation-States and Their Cooperation in the 20th and 21st Century
With a foreword by Petr Vágner
ISBN 978-3-8382-1015-5

171 *Philip Gamaghelyan*
Conflict Resolution Beyond the International Relations Paradigm
Evolving Designs as a Transformative Practice in Nagorno-Karabakh and Syria
With a foreword by Susan Allen
ISBN 978-3-8382-1057-5

172 *Maria Shagina*
Joining a Prestigious Club
Cooperation with Europarties and Its Impact on Party Development in Georgia, Moldova, and Ukraine 2004–2015
With a foreword by Kataryna Wolczuk
ISBN 978-3-8382-1084-1

173 *Alexandra Cotofana, James M. Nyce (eds.)*
Religion and Magic in Socialist and Post-Socialist Contexts II
Baltic, Eastern European, and Post-USSR Case Studies
ISBN 978-3-8382-0990-6

174 *Barbara Kunz*
Kind Words, Cruise Missiles, and Everything in Between
The Use of Power Resources in U.S. Policies towards Poland, Ukraine, and Belarus 1989–2008
With a foreword by William Hill
ISBN 978-3-8382-1065-0

175 *Eduard Klein*
Bildungskorruption in Russland und der Ukraine
Eine komparative Analyse der Performanz staatlicher Antikorruptionsmaßnahmen im Hochschulsektor am Beispiel universitärer Aufnahmeprüfungen
Mit einem Vorwort von Heiko Pleines
ISBN 978-3-8382-0995-1

177 *Anton Oleinik*
Building Ukraine from Within
A Sociological, Institutional, and Economic Analysis of a Nation-State in the Making
ISBN 978-3-8382-1150-3

178 *Peter Rollberg,*
Marlene Laruelle (eds.)
Mass Media in the Post-Soviet World
Market Forces, State Actors, and Political Manipulation in the Informational Environment after Communism
ISBN 978-3-8382-1116-9

***ibidem*-Verlag**

Melchiorstr. 15

D-70439 Stuttgart

info@ibidem-verlag.de

www.ibidem-verlag.de
www.ibidem.eu
www.edition-noema.de
www.autorenbetreuung.de